M000287951

Violence at Sea

Violence at Sea

PIRACY IN THE AGE OF GLOBAL TERRORISM

Edited by **Peter Lehr**

Routledge
Taylor & Francis Group
New York London

Routledge is an imprint of the
Taylor & Francis Group, an informa business

Routledge
Taylor & Francis Group
270 Madison Avenue
New York, NY 10016

Routledge
Taylor & Francis Group
2 Park Square
Milton Park, Abingdon
Oxon OX14 4RN

Routledge is an imprint of Taylor & Francis Group, an Informa business

Printed in the United States of America on acid-free paper
10 9 8 7 6 5 4 3 2 1

International Standard Book Number-10: 0-415-95320-0 (Hardcover)
International Standard Book Number-13: 978-0-415-95320-7 (Hardcover)

Library of Congress Cataloging-in-Publication Data

Violence at sea : piracy in the age of global terrorism / editor, Peter Lehr.
p. cm.
Includes bibliographical references and index.
ISBN 0-415-95320-0 (hardback)
1. Pirates. 2. Hijacking of ships. 3. Terrorism. I. Lehr, Peter.

G535.V56 2006
364.16'4--dc22 2006016261

Visit the Taylor & Francis Web site at
http://www.taylorandfrancis.com

and the Routledge Web site at
http://www.routledge-ny.com

Contents

Introduction

PETER LEHR

The New "Pirate Wind"

Virtually all oceans of the world have had a long history of maritime piracy, from the early days of seafaring in small, coast-hugging vessels all through the age of oared and sailed ships up to the heydays of imperialism, when British, French, Dutch, and U.S. frigates gave battle to pirate vessels along the East African coast, in the Sulu Sea, or in the Caribbean. With the advent of steamships, which usually outran and massively outgunned any pirate ship around, maritime piracy finally met its fate at some date in the nineteenth century when the last pirate ship had been sunk — or so it seemed. The pirates infesting the Northern African coast of the Mediterranean had finally been defeated by the U.S. Navy in the Algerian War of 1815; the whole Indian Ocean had been turned into a British lake, courtesy of the Royal Navy; the Caribbean became a backwater of diverse colonial powers; and the waters of the Asia-Pacific, including the South China Sea, were being heavily patrolled by warships of several Western and Japanese fleets. In the twentieth century, nobody was talking about acts of piracy any longer. Although some opportunistic forms of piracy still existed as an on-again, off-again form of maritime crime, it was the East–West conflict which monopolized security discussions, pushing everything else to the sidelines. But now, roughly fifteen years after the end of the Cold War, the demise of the Soviet Union as the so-called evil empire, and the inauguration of a new world order of peace (which, of course, died still in its infancy), we have to grudgingly accept that maritime piracy is back with a vengeance: since the middle of the 1980s, the numbers of pirate attacks and their victims keep on rising, and — all the new security mechanisms hastily installed under the impact of 9/11 notwithstanding — there is no end in sight.

Why did piracy have such a successful comeback, and where exactly do acts of piracy take place? First, it should be pointed out again that piracy was never completely gone — it continued to exist, albeit on a low, sporadic, and opportunistic level, in some backwaters of the world's oceans. For example, old Malayan fishermen still revel in stories about their pre-Second World War raids on non-Western (mostly Chinese) vessels. And in Caribbean waters, attacks on private yachts can also be traced back several decades into the first two decades of the twentieth century. These opportunistic attacks form the background to an early international attempt to come to grips with the menace: the League of Nations, formed after the First World War, chose piracy as one of the first offences to be codified. But the full force of the new "pirate wind" came in the mid-1980s, following a global sea change: After the end of the Cold War and the demise of the Soviet Union and the Eastern bloc, most parts of the world shifted their focus from security relations to trade relations. The trend towards globalization and liberalization brought about a tremendous increase in international business and trade, especially so in sea trade, since the bulk of all goods transported goes by ship. It is only human that licit forms of international business and trade are accompanied by their illicit twin, which basically means various forms of business crime including organized crime and, whether in an opportunistic or an organized fashion in close cooperation with organized crime syndicates, maritime piracy. Therefore, from a global, macro-level perspective, this new wave of maritime piracy can be explained tentatively by two push-and-pull factors:

Globalization and liberalization brought about a vast increase in international trade at sea; and when more goods — and more of high value — are transported by sea, there are more (potential) targets for criminal activities.

Parallel to that, the end of the Cold War and the demise of the USSR as the second superpower brought about a general withdrawal of warships, especially so in the Asia-Pacific and the Indian Ocean. A lower interest in maritime affairs and a lower number of warships on patrol means lower security for licit forms of trade and higher security for illicit activities.

For a considerable period of time, the reemerging phenomenon of piracy was largely ignored — especially by ship owners. In many cases, ship owners explicitly ordered their ship masters not to report on pirate attacks — neither officially nor unofficially — for fear of rising Property and Indemnity (P&I) premiums on the one hand and lengthy official investigations on the other, during which the respective ship would have to remain in harbor, thus losing money for the owner — roughly US$25,000 per day. From the ship owners' perspective, piracy-related losses simply appeared to be negligible transaction costs, amounting to less than one percent of the total income generated by maritime trade, while measures to "harden" their ships would have been (and still are) rather expensive. Of course, from a crew's perspective, the costs were not so negligible: their lives and their property were (and still are) at stake. For them, pirate attacks were and are far from anonymous transaction costs — they get very personal. It is not surprising, therefore, that professional shipping associations like the British National Union of Marine, Aviation and Shipping Transport Officers (NUMAST) or the Baltic and International Maritime Council (BIMCO) were among the first to put piracy on the international agenda.

The Location of the Threat

Now piracy may well be an international and global phenomenon, impinging on the security of maritime traffic in African, Indian, Asian, and American waters. But the weekly and annual piracy reports from the International Maritime Bureau (IMB) indicate that nearly 50 percent of such acts are being committed in an area which is known under the name "Maritime Asia" — a maritime region stretching from the Red Sea, the Persian Gulf, the Arabian Sea, and the Bay of Bengal through the Strait of Malacca all the way to the South China Sea and even the East China Sea. Since this maritime region, formerly known as the Maritime Silk Road, is home of some of the world's busiest Sea Lines of Communication (SLOC), this sorry fact could again be explained from a global perspective by pointing at the huge traffic there. The Strait of Malacca, for example, is even dubbed "the iron highway" because of its very dense traffic: roughly 30 percent of world trade is passing through the Strait, two thirds of the world's supply of liquefied natural gas and about 50 percent of the world's crude oil. And, again, we could state that more traffic simply means more potential targets.

In the first part of the book, giving us an idea about the location of the threat, Peter Lehr and Hendrick Lehmann, Vijay Sakhuja, and Gerard Ong-Webb show us that on a regional level, many other factors contribute to the reemergence of piracy. In the case of the northern part of the Indian Ocean (the Arabian Sea and the Bay of Bengal), the reemergence of piracy is at least partially of a political nature, as Lehr and Lehmann, and Vijay Sakhuja point out in their articles. On the rims of the Arabian Sea, we find trouble spots like Somalia, a failed state and a new pirates' paradise; we find the current hot spot for all kinds of maritime crime, including piracy in the Persian Gulf; and last but not least, we find a "Cold War at Sea" still going on between the navies of India and Pakistan which greatly hampers attempts to establish meaningful measures for governance at sea. In the Bay of Bengal, we are faced with piratical attacks by the Sea Tigers, the naval arm of the LTTE, who prowl the waters of the Palk Strait between Sri Lanka and India. The frequent pirate attacks along the coast of Bangladesh are the exception to this rule, since they are more related to autochthonous forms of organized crime: they are directed not so much against modern merchant vessels, but rather against traditional sailing crafts to be found in this country's vast river systems. From the Bay of Bengal, we sail into the waters of Southeast Asia next. In his chapter on the Strait of Malacca and the South China Sea, Gerard Ong-Webb shows how factors such as busy SLOCs, topography, low levels of governance at sea, endemic corruption, and the presence of organized criminal groups are turning this part of "Maritime Asia" into the most piracy-prone region of the world. Here, too, it seems that politics (or rather, ideologies) start to appear as a factor which has to be taken into consideration. Taken together, all the factors described by Lehr and Lehmann, Sakhuja, and

Ong-Webb present modern day maritime pirates — both opportunistic and organized — with an attractive window of opportunity.

The Nature of the Threat: Tactics, Capabilities, and Groups

The second part of the book will show us how modern-day pirates make use of this window of opportunity. In the first chapter of this part, the author Rupert Herbert-Burns introduces us to the tactical methodologies of contemporary piracy from low-level assault or armed robberies against ships (LLAR) to medium-level armed assault and robbery (MLAAR), and major criminal hijack (MCHJ), the most serious form of piracy. He also examines the advent and impact of hostage taking and ransom demands by pirates in African and Asian waters. The following two case studies by Rommel Banlaoi and Jeffrey Chen deal with the actors themselves: who is playing a role in this deadly piracy game? So far, there is no figure of international fame like Captain Blackbeard was in his time. The modern-day business of piracy tends to be committed on a rather anonymous basis by different groups. Some operators, however, are discernible, either by occupation (organized crime syndicates) or by name (ASG, GAM). Obviously, as seen in Gerard Ong-Webb's chapter, modern-day piracy is not only about personal gain any more. It could soon turn into either "political piracy" — that is, piracy to finance a guerilla or terrorist movement — or even into "maritime terrorism." Thus, both Banlaoi and Chen examine whether there is a nexus between maritime terrorism and piracy in Asian waters, and on what level it could be found — if such a nexus exists in the first place.

Banlaoi and Chen provide us with detailed insights into the worlds of the Abu Sayyaf Group (ASG) and the Free Aceh Movement (Gerakan Aceh Merdeka, GAM). Both groups do have an ideological/political agenda, and both groups reportedly embark on acts of piracy, probably merely seeking an additional source of income for their land-based insurgencies. Is this still piracy committed for private gain, or is this already maritime terrorism committed for political aims, or is it something in between? The authors answer this question by analyzing the fine line between piracy and terrorism. Specifically, they address the double role that ASG and GAM members play both as pirates and as terrorists in the Philippine waters (ASG) and the Strait of Malacca (GAM); the use of piracy to fund terrorist operations; and the potential to transform their knowledge into tools for maritime terrorism.

Responses: International Law, Politics, and Tactics

The third part of the book focuses on reactions to piracy, from a global level all the way down to the tactical sphere. Many observers, including this editor, tend to be rather skeptical when it comes to commenting on the successes of various antipiracy measures so far. This is not to argue that nothing has been done to curb maritime piracy — quite the contrary, as several of our authors argue: even before 9/11, quite an impressive array of unilateral, bilateral, and multilateral measures in different parts of the world against piracy as well as against other forms of maritime-related crimes has been developed, and, sometimes, even put into force. However, this impressive list of measures notwithstanding, piracy still is rampant in many of the world's oceans for various reasons.

Martin Murphy, Chris Rahman, and J. N. Mak shed some more light on the difficulties of combating maritime piracy, on the successes and on the failures so far. The reference point for all attempts to tackle piracy on a multilateral level is, of course, the United Nations' Law of the Sea Convention (usually abbreviated UNCLOS or LoSC). Martin Murphy starts with a critical assessment of piracy and UNCLOS: is international law congruent in assisting governments as they try to mitigate piracy in regional waters? For example, the United Nations' definition of piracy does not really facilitate the fight against piracy, since it restricts acts of piracy to the high seas — exactly where they usually do not happen. Chris Rahman then turns our attention to multilateral approaches to combat piracy, focusing on Southeast Asian waters and ASEAN. He focuses on the question of whether such initiatives are effective or rather a pipedream. The editor's own research, unfortunately, points in the latter direction — he remembers just how deep-seated mutual suspicions and distrust still are among certain ASEAN member states or between India and Australia. Chris Rahman, being more knowledgeable than the editor in this respect, provides us with a much more detailed answer, and not only in the negative.

So far, we have been "attacking" the pirates on water only. But even pirates have bases on land, usually in remote villages on remote islands, where the stark poverty provides both a convenient recruitment base and an enabling environment with a low level of law and order, for example. Their fences, however, are to be found in the cities. So are their business contacts, their banks, their connections to crime syndicates, and their spotters in the ports. In his highly interesting case study on the Malaysian fishing community of Hutan Melintang, J. N. Mak provocatively raises the topic of confronting pirates on land, with a focus on the socioeconomic impulses for piracy: is there an argument for addressing factors such as poverty and unemployment in coastal communities so as to lessen incentives for fishing communities to embark on acts of piracy? Malaysia had a comparable poverty-eradication program in the 1970s already, with some success. Why not try the same approach in other countries?

Admittedly, for the ships' crews who are the potential victims of piracy, such discussions are not that relevant. They put their lives in jeopardy whenever they sail into piracy-prone waters. They cannot afford to wait until new security measures have been put in place effectively. They want the problem solved right now. The question that remains to be discussed, therefore, concerns tactical approaches to confronting pirates preying on merchant vessels: how effective or useful are Western warships as tools in the fight not only against worldwide terrorism but also against piracy; and what role could private security firms play in this regard? One remembers that some private security firms offer former Gurkha soldiers as maritime security guards, while others go even further, offering armed and armored vessels to escort ships with high-value cargoes through dangerous waters such as the Strait of Malacca. Bob Snoddon, a former member of the Royal Navy, critically examines existing approaches and their shortcomings.

This book concludes with a glimpse into the near future. Interestingly, the fight against piracy got a major boost only after 9/11. Given that transport by air was attacked on 9/11; and transport by rail, on 11 March 2004, in Madrid — transport by ship could be next. And the potential victims of such an act of "new" piracy would no longer be nameless Filipino or Pakistani crewmembers, they would be "us" — which is why piracy, in its new avatar as maritime terrorism, is finally being seen as a serious threat to maritime security. After 9/11, several new measures for security at sea came into force, geared for fighting maritime terrorism, however, not piracy. In his article concluding the book, Sam Bateman starts by reexamining some likely and other more or less unlikely threats against ships and ports as well as against the container transportation chain in general. He then analyzes international and national responses to these threats, such as the ISPS code, the Container Security Initiative (CSI), and the Customs-Trade Partnership Against Terrorism (C-TPAT). Are they adequately calibrated for, or effective in, mitigating attacks on merchant vessels at sea or at anchor? And, more generally, what impact do all these new security measures have on piracy (if any)? In his conclusion, Bateman pleads for a more balanced, sober threat assessment as a first step in countering the threat. "Beating up" the threat by peddling the usual "doomsday-scenarios" only allows some interest groups to exploit the situation.

If the new security measures are successfully implemented, the maritime world will hopefully soon be a much safer place. Acts of maritime terrorism might be averted; acts of piracy, greatly reduced — and, by extension, other forms of maritime crime like smuggling and illegal emigration might be curbed as well. And the life of the ordinary Filipino, Pakistani, or Kiribati crew member would be that much easier.

1

Somalia — Pirates' New Paradise

PETER LEHR AND HENDRICK LEHMANN

In the early morning hours of Saturday, 5 November 2005, the cruise liner *Seabourn Spirit* found itself under attack by pirates rapidly approaching in two small speedboats. The — ultimately unsuccessful — brazen attack took place roughly 100 sea miles off the southern coast of Somalia. It was witnessed by dozens of Western passengers, rudely woken up by rocket-propelled grenades (RPGs) and salvoes from assault rifles. The global media coverage of the event drove home to an international audience that this attack was only the most spectacular one of a series of acts of piracy, targeting local, regional, and international shipping — including UN ships carrying food-for-aid for the war-torn country. Between March and November 2005, no less than 32 vessels had become victims of attacks in coastal waters of Somalia.[1] This article intends to shed some light on the new wave of piracy emanating from the coasts of this unfortunate country, which started in early 2005 after a lull of two years.

First, we shall examine some recent pirate attacks, both to illustrate the magnitude of the problem and to give an impression of the patterns of piratical attacks in or near Somalian waters. In the very special case of Somalia — a so-called *failed state* par excellence — it is also important to provide the reader with a general background before dealing with maritime piracy and maritime terrorism. The second part of the chapter will thus deal with questions such as the following. What exactly happened in this country to qualify for this category? Does the whole of Somalia fall into the failed state category or are there exceptions? And how likely is it in the foreseeable future that a Somalian government — either the current *Transitional Federal Government* (TFG) or a successor — will succeed in establishing a modicum of law and order in that state? The third part of the chapter will then deal with the pirates themselves. Who are they? Are they foreign mercenaries of the global al-Qaeda network, using Somalia's coasts as a training ground for future acts of maritime terrorism, as some experts claim? Or are they locals — either fisher folk, former navy members, members of today's militias, or a mixture of all these elements? The fourth and last part will sketch out some recommendations for the future. The basic assumptions for the recommendation will be that a) the

Somalian Transitional Federal Government will fail to establish its authority over the country's plethora of militias, and b) that for this reason, the "war" against piracy — and possibly maritime terrorism — emanating from Somali waters will have to be fought by an extraregional force.

Somalia as a Pirates' Paradise: Recent Examples

Somalia, situated at the famous Horn of Africa, has one of the longest coastlines in Africa: from the border to Djibouti near the Bab el-Mandeb in the Gulf of Aden to the border, to Kenya at the East African coast, the Somali coast stretches for roughly 3,300 kilometers. From a geostrategic perspective, Somalia's northeastern part along the Gulf of Aden to the Cape Guardafui — the very Horn of Africa — is ideally placed to control and possibly interdict shipping coming from or going to the Red Sea: it juts out like a dagger into the Arabian Sea, thus forming the distinctive Gulf of Aden. The much longer Banaadir Coast along Somalia's Arabian Sea side is somewhat less important, but still, the sea lines of communication (SLOCs) — connecting the Red Sea to East Africa and to South Africa run parallel to this particular coast — and it is there that most acts of piracy happen. During November and December 2005, no less than seven ships and their crews were believed held hostage in Somalian waters: four near the central Eyl district at Puntland's East African coast and three in the southern Lower Jubba region in the area of Kismaayo/Chisimayu.[2]

The MV Semlow Hijack

MV *Semlow*, an 58-meter cargo ship, is one of four ships of the Kenyan-based Motaku Shipping Agency. On 27 June 2005, the day of the attack, it was under charter by the UN World Food Program to bring food aid to the Somalian victims of the Boxing Day tsunami of December 2004, carrying 850 tons of rice donated by Germany and Japan. In the early evening hours of that day, it was attacked "some 55 km [about 30 sea miles] from the Somali coast" by a gang of 15 to 20 men in "three fiberglass speedboats with powerful outboard motors," armed with pistols, AK-47 assault rifles, and rocket-propelled grenades (RPGs).[3] The pirates fired at the ship to force it to stop, and boarded it. They stole US$8,500 from the captain's safe, looted the crew members' valuables, took the captain and his nine-men crew hostage, and then forced the frightened crew to sail to a destination located at Somalia's central coast, roughly 100 sea miles northeast of Mogadishu. There, the captain was ordered to phone the owner of the MV *Semlow*, Inayet Kudrati, to inform him that he had to pay a ransom of US$500,000 — an exorbitant amount of money for the rather small shipping company. While diplomats from Kenya, Sri Lanka (the captain of the MV *Semlow* is a Sri Lankan), Tanzania, and the UN tried to negotiate with the pirates, the crew members were kept prisoner on board of the ship. The crew witnessed the hijacking of the Egyptian cement carrier *Ibn Batuta* in late September, and they were then made to sail their ship, accompanied by the newly "acquired" Ibn Batuta, to another destination, about 200 sea miles from Mogadishu. Finally in late September, a ransom of US$135,000 was paid — probably by the UN World Food Program, although the UN denies this — and on 3 October, both ships could sail on. Fortunately, despite some tense situations, none of the crew members was injured or otherwise harmed during the ordeal.

The MV *Semlow* was not the only WFP-chartered ship being hijacked while carrying food-for-aid for Somalia: on 12 October, the MV *Miltzow* was attacked and hijacked by a gang of pirates in the Somali port of Merka while offloading its cargo of 850 tons of food aid. Again, the UN's WFP immediately moved to condemn the action: "It is scandalous that a small number of profiteers would once again hijack humanitarian food supplies destined for fellow Somalis."[4] Fortunately, the ship and its crew were released only two days later, probably after ransom had been paid, and probably also as a result of the intense international pressure. Just as in the cases of the *Semlow* and the *Ibn Batuta*, nobody was harmed. But it is somewhat ironic — at least from the actors' viewpoint — that a second ship of the Motaku Shipping Agency, MV *Torgelov*, was hijacked on 8 October near the port of el-Maan shortly after its sister ship MV *Semlow* had been released. Even more ironically, the MV *Torgelov* was carrying food, oil, and other supplies for the *Semlow* and was meant to replenish her at the port of el-Maan before returning home to Mombasa. This incident illustrates the special danger of piracy for local shipping which simply cannot avoid Somalia's troubled waters. The negotiations for ransom for the crew and the cargo of that vessel were still going on in late November when this chapter was finalized.

Some of the observations made by the *Semlow's* captain, Sellathurai Mahalingam, as quoted by *Time Asia*, are quite interesting. First, the captain reported that at one time a male Somali came on board with a message stating "the Somali Navy has captured your vessel."[5] Of course, this could simply be an example of the pirates' hyperbole and self-aggrandizement, but it raises some questions about the fate of the erstwhile Somali Navy, its facilities, and its sailors. Second, the captain and his chief engineer were brought 30 miles inland to meet the pirate bosses. As Captain Mahalingam dryly remarked, "At that stage I realized that all the coastal villages were involved."[6] We will deal with both topics in detail a little later. Here, suffice it to say that the magnitude of Somalia's pirate problem now seems to be comparable with that in Southeast Asian waters: in both regions, we are basically confronted by a flourishing organized maritime crime or a veritable "piracy industry," as compared with mere "maritime mugging" elsewhere.

The Seabourn Spirit Attack

Seabourn Cruises' *Seabourn Spirit* was rated as the world's best small cruise ship by Condé Nast in early 2005.[7] With an overall length of roughly 440 feet, it can accommodate 208 passengers, served by a crew of 150.[8] Several voyages can be booked, amongst them a 16-day voyage from Alexandria/Egypt to Mombasa/Kenya via the Red Sea, the Gulf of Aden, and the East African Banaadir Coast of Somalia.[9] The cruise ship came under attack on the 13th day of its voyage at around 5:30 a.m. local time on Saturday, 5 November 2005, roughly 100 sea miles off the Banaadir Coast. As in the case of the MV *Semlow* attack described above, the attack was put forward by a gang of pirates on board of two 25-foot fiberglass boats, and as in the case of the *Semlow*, the pirates attempted to stop the vessel with a barrage of RPGs and AK-47 rounds. This time, however, their attack was unsuccessful, thanks to determined counteractions by the crew: while the captain and his crew on the bridge first tried to ram and capsize one of the boats to prevent the pirates from boarding and then increased speed to outrun them, other crew members under the command of the ship's security officer successfully deployed a sonic weapon to frighten the attackers off. This Long Range Acoustic Device (LRAD) was developed after the attack on the USS *Cole* in October 2000 as a nonlethal weapon to keep small boats from approaching U.S. warships.[10] None of the passengers was harmed during the action, but one crew member suffered minor injuries from shrapnel. One of the RPGs actually penetrated the hull, damaging a stateroom, while one other RPG was reported to have bounced off the stern. Further minor damages were caused by the pirates' gun fire. For security reasons, the ship proceeded to Port Victoria/Seychelles for some repairs instead of going to Mombasa/Kenya as originally planned. From there, the cruise liner sailed on to Singapore right on schedule.[11]

Apart from the highly publicized *Seabourn Spirit* attack, at least two other vessels came under attack during the same weekend, but without making major headlines. On Sunday, 6 November, the day after the *Seabourn* attack, a cargo ship came under attack in the very same waters, and just as in the former attack, the cargo ship was fired on with RPGs and assault rifles, and it also succeeded in outmaneuvering and outrunning the pirates. The hijacking of a Thai merchant ship, carrying sugar from Brazil to Yemen, on Monday, 7 November, northeast off Mogadishu, being the third pirate attack in an eventful long weekend, also failed to make headlines comparable to the *Seabourn Spirit* attack. Even the Thai newspaper reporting it seemed to be interested in this run-of-the-mill hijacking for ransom only because it happened so close to the cruise liner attack. An attempted mutiny of a Thai merchant ship's Somali crew earlier this year — conducted with the intent to take over the ship and to sail it into Somalian waters — was also brought to the attention of the public for the first time on this occasion.[12] It seems that not only the Western public is notoriously disinterested in crimes committed on the "lawless sea" — at least as long as they are not as spectacular as the *Seabourn Spirit* attack.

The Case of the Taiwanese Trawlers

Quite an interesting case in point is the hijacking of three Taiwanese-owned trawlers in August 2005. On 15 August, these trawlers were taken over by pirates while fishing in Somalia's exclusive economic zone (EEZ). The trawlers were made to sail to an island some 30 sea miles south of Kismaayo, where the 48 crew members of Taiwanese, Chinese, Indonesian, and Vietnamese origin have been held hostage ever since. The pirates reportedly belong to the Marehen clan of Juba Valley from the south of Somalia. What is of interest in this case is the self-description of the pirates and their rationale behind the hijacking and the ransom demands — US$5,000 for each of the crew members: first, the pirate gang declared themselves to be the National Volunteer Coast Guard of Somalia; second, they explained that the National Volunteer Coast Guard had "impounded" the trawlers for illegal fishing in Somali waters; and third, that they had imposed a fine of US$5,000 on each of the crew members for the act of poaching in Somali waters. At first glance, this may sound ridiculous, but illegal fishing by foreign fishing fleets in Somali waters is a problem indeed, as we shall elaborate on later in this article.

Here, suffice it to say that such acts of piracy usually happen below the radar screen of the international (shipping) community, which means there is no comparable pressure on the pirates as in the *Semlow* and *Seabourn Spirit* cases, which again means negotiations for ransom can be quite protracted. And that again means that the life of crew members could be in danger in such cases, since, sooner or later, pirates may run out of patience and resort to killing them just to make a point.

Reactions So Far

The muted reactions even in the media of states directly affected by such cases of piracy are a good indicator of overall reactions so far in regard to this new upsurge of high-seas piracy off Somalia's coasts: nothing much has been done apart from the issuing of warnings by several sources and appeals for help from the transitional government of Somalia and some neighboring states, usually directed at the UN's International Maritime Organization (IMO) or at the Security Council itself.

For example, the U.S. Department of State issued a new piracy warning on Friday, 18 November, in which U.S. citizens in general and shippers in particular were advised to avoid the Port of Mogadishu and to stay at least 200 sea miles off the Somali coasts. Shippers transiting the Horn of Africa and transiting the Gulf of Aden were also strongly advised to travel in convoys and to maintain good communications contact at all times.[13] The State Department's piracy warning mirrored warnings issued by the International Maritime Bureau (IMB). In its daily piracy warnings, the IMB had advised ships to keep a distance of at least 150 sea miles from the Somali coast well before the *Seabourn Spirit* attack, but for several reasons, these warnings largely went unheeded. Now the IMB classifies the Somali coast as the most dangerous piracy hot spot in the Indian Ocean, and also advises international shipping to stay at least 200 sea miles off the coast.

These warnings virtually turn Somalian waters into a maritime "no-go" zone. If the UK's National Union of Marine, Aviation and Shipping Transport (NUMAST) has its way, the coastal waters of the hapless state may even be declared a war zone, with all the legal consequences, including skyrocketing insurance rates. Unfortunately, as the acting director-general of the Kenya Maritime Authority, Captain Frederick Wahutu, stated, "sea vessels will always ply in these waters because commercial interests override the dangers."[14] Indeed, giving Somalian waters a wide berth may be an option for international long-distance trade, but definitely not for local fishing vessels or for the tramp ships serving the smaller ports around the shores of the Arabian Sea — ships like the *Semlow* and the *Ibn Batuta*.

It is thus not very surprising that spokespersons of regional governments regularly demand that the Transitional Federal Government of Somalia set up a navy, coast guard, or maritime police force to patrol its coastal waters. Given the current state of affairs, this is wishful thinking: the Somalian government in exile around President Yusuf and Prime Minister Ali Mohamed Geedi does not even dare to move to its own capital city, Mogadishu, for fear of its own security. How, then, could it even start to think of setting up a maritime security agency at this stage? Instead, and more realistically, Somalian Prime Minister Geedi appealed to neighboring countries to send naval vessels to impose a modicum of law and order in the country's waters.[15] However, the neighboring countries he was appealing to are in not much of a position to come to Somalia's rescue. Ethiopia, apart from being landlocked is sliding deeper and deeper into domestic problems after its flawed parliamentary elections; Eritrea is preparing for a new border war with Ethiopia; and Kenya, already overstretched anyway in attempts to stabilize its northern neighbor, simply does not have enough patrol crafts to monitor Somalia's waters, even though Kenyan sources agree that Somalian piracy poses a serious problem for its own shipping: during the last 15 years, at least 188 Kenyan crew members have been held hostage in various piracy-related cases of kidnapping for ransom, and seven cargo ships and several fishing vessels have been captured.[16] So, while Geedi is hoping for help from his neighbors, his neighbors are looking for help from an international force, maybe in the shape of a U.S. or NATO naval task force.

The regional states are also finding ready support from national and international tourism and shipping organizations. On the national Kenyan level, tourism bodies such as the Kenya Association of Hotel Keepers and Caterers fear the impact on their own tourism industry, especially after the *Seabourn Spirit*'s planned port visit in Mombasa was cancelled for security reasons immediately after the attack. The cruise liner business fears for its image of providing a safe and fun vacation, and, indeed, there are indicators that potential cruise line passengers are already thinking twice about possible destinations: "We like to go to more exotic places, but with the world situation the way it is with terrorists, we said, let's stay within the United States — let's go to Hawaii."[17] And, finally, organizations such as the already mentioned NUMAST fear for the security of commercial shipping in general. Together, these organizations form a powerful lobbying group at the UN's International Maritime Organization (IMO), demanding nothing less than international action in the shape of intensified patrolling or an embargo against Somalia's exports, the latter to prevent militias involved in acts of piracy from having the financial means necessary to buy weapons and boats. It is a well-known fact that diverse Somalian militias finance themselves through activities such as illegal logging for charcoal and illegal fishing, but it is doubtful whether an embargo would help curb acts of piracy. Rather, it could provide an incentive for "more of the same" in regard to maritime crime. It even can be argued that the recent invoking of a defunct UN Security Council Resolution, the Resolution 733 of 1992 (Implementing an Arms Embargo on Somalia), denies the transitional government the means to successfully impose law and order on the country.[18] Seen from this perspective, the arms embargo seems to be counterproductive. It is to be expected, therefore, that the problem of piracy will have to be dealt with by way of continuous patrolling and monitoring activities, conducted by third parties. In the view of some of the organizations mentioned, the logical candidate for this job would be NATO's Combined Task Force 150, which is currently present in the Horn of Africa area as part of Operation Enduring Freedom, albeit with a focus on the Gulf of Aden.

The International Maritime Organization (IMO) reacted with a resolution on "Piracy and Armed Robbery Against Ships in Waters off the Coast of Somalia." The IMO Assembly's 24th session agreed that this resolution has to be brought to the attention of the United Nations Security Council. The Assembly also requested the IMO secretary-general to continue monitoring the situation, to report to the IMO Council on developments, and to establish and maintain cooperation with the United Nations Monitoring Group on Somalia. Additionally, the resolution calls upon the Transitional Federal Government of Somalia to bring the resolution to the attention of the interim parliament, the Transitional Federal Assembly. In accordance with the request, the assembly is to initiate appropriate and suitable actions to prevent and suppress acts of piracy and armed robbery against ships originating from Somali territory. The TFG should bring the resolution to the attention of all other parties concerned in Somalia and seek from them the immediate termination of all acts of piracy and armed robbery against ships sailing in waters off the coast of Somalia. As we shall see later on, this part of the resolution bore some surprising fruit.

Background: Somalia as a "Failed State"

Somalia has a population of just a little less than 10 million people, 85 percent of whom are Somali, the remaining 15 percent mostly Bantu. Somalis are still mostly nomadic pastoralists, divided along clan lines. The origins of modern-day Somalia can be traced back to an Arab sultanate, founded in the seventh century by Yemenite immigrants from the famous Quraish tribe. During the 15th and the 16th centuries, most of Somalia's coastal towns formed part of the Portuguese *Estado da India.* After this period, two waves of British and Italian colonialism washed over the country before it became independent on 1 July 1960, after a merger of British Somaliland and Italian Somaliland — the latter being under UN trusteeship. The official name of the country was *Somali Republic.* Somalia's first constitution, adopted after a nationwide referendum in June 1961, was based on democratic Western European models and provided for a parliamentary system of government. Not surprisingly given the pastoralist background mentioned above, the new republic's political parties were based on clan loyalties rather than political platforms. A rift between pro-Arab pan-Somali militants fighting for a national unification with the Somali-inhabited territories in Ethiopia and Kenya, notably the Ogaden, and Somali modernists focusing on economic and sociopolitical developments within the country, further aggravated the complicated and protracted nation-building.

On 21 October 1969, after roughly seven years of party-based parliamentary politics, Major General Muhammad Siad Barre seized power in a bloodless coup, backed by Somalia's army and police forces. Barre more or less successfully governed the clan-based country for eleven years and three months. During the first "scientific socialist" phase, his government was supported and equipped by the USSR. When the USSR chose to back its other East African socialist client, Ethiopia under Mengistu, in the 1977 Ogaden Conflict, Barre threw out his Soviet military advisers. To replace them, he invited in U.S. forces, granting them access to the Somali bases in 1980, thus turning Somalia into a Western client. His political gamble paid off in 1982, when the United States provided him with arms and ammunition to assist Somali troops in defending Somalian territory against renewed Ethiopian attacks. On the domestic front, he proved to be much less successful: from the very beginning, Barre's government was faced with insurgencies in Somalia itself. His ham-handed attempts to come to grips with these domestic challenges — for instance, he sent the Somali National Air Force to bomb cities in Somalia's Northwest — resulted in a rapid economic and political decline. Even worse, until December 1990, Somalia's armed forces, Barre's original power base, had dissolved into armed groups largely based on clan identities, loyal to former commanders who also happened to be tribal chiefs.[19] In January 1991, his authoritarian government finally collapsed. None of the contending anti-Barre forces, however, succeeded in filling in the resulting power vacuum and in establishing a government. Instead, Somalia became embroiled in factional fighting along clan lines, governmental institutions ceased to function, the armed forces gave way to clan-based militias, and warlordism spread. In most parts of the country, this state of anarchy still prevails. In two parts of the country, however, a modicum of law and order has been reintroduced so far: Somaliland and Puntland.

Forces of Separatism: Somaliland and Puntland

The northern clans of Somalia were the first to make the best out of a bad situation: only four months after the downfall of the Barre government, in May 1991, they declared an independent *Republic of Somaliland.* Somaliland is situated at Somalia's Gulf of Aden coast, sharing borders with Djibouti in the Northwest, Ethiopia in the West, and Puntland in the Northeast. Somaliland includes the administrative regions of Awdal, Woqooyi Galbeed, Togdheer, Sanaag, and Sool. The town of Hargeisa is the capital. So far, Somaliland has not been recognized by any other government, but in spite of this, its government, based on one dominant ruling clan and financed by American military assistance programs, has maintained a stable existence.

The administrative regions in Somaliland's Northeast — Bari, Nugaal, and northern Mudug — followed suit only in 1998, seven years later. Unlike the clans of Somaliland, the clans controlling these regions did not go for full independence. Instead, they declared an autonomous state as part of the Somali Republic under the name of Puntland with the explicit aim of reestablishing law and order and establishing a legitimate, representative government. Since 2002, however, Puntland has experienced the reemergence of civil strife. In addition, Puntland disputes its borders with neighboring Somaliland. This border dispute has already resulted in some clashes between the two contesting armed forces.

Forces of Peace: The UN Intervention

The civil war following the anti-Barre putsch resulted in a humanitarian disaster: in roughly two years, about 300,000 people died of starvation. To alleviate the widespread famine, especially in the South, the United Nations embarked on a humanitarian relief effort under the name of Operation Restore Hope in December 1992. Various Western forces were part of that mission, among them German *Bundeswehr* forces in one of their first missions "out of area." For reasons which need not be repeated here, some UN forces became embroiled in the civil war itself. One of the ill-fated attempts to hunt down some of the most notorious clan leaders involved the downing of two U.S. helicopters during the hunt for clan leader and former general Muhammad Farah Aidid in Mogadishu in October 1993. The killing of 18 U.S. soldiers in this incident and the widely televised dragging of some of their corpses through the streets of the city led to an ignominious withdrawal of the U.S. forces in March 1994. The United Nations Operation in Somalia (UNOSOM-II) was consequently downsized and formally ended by 31 March 1995.[20] Several peace agreements between the major players in Somalia, the Somali National Alliance (SNA) and the Somali Salvation Alliance (SSA), were brokered by the UN, and two successive governments in exile could be established, first the Transitional National Government and then, after its downfall, the current Transitional Federal Government.

The Transitional Federal Government

The declaration of a Transnational Federal Government (TFG) in October 2004 in Mombasa/Kenya was widely hailed as a final breakthrough and the beginning of the end of the protracted civil war in Somalia. But as the International Crisis Group dryly commented in one of their reports, "in the world of Somali politics, unfortunately, no news is ever purely good news and the progress of the peace process has been largely downhill since then."[21] One of the problems is that, obviously, both President Yusuf and Prime Minister Geedi seem to be quite reluctant to relocate their government to their own capital, Mogadishu. In their July 2005 report, ICG states that "[the] people of Mogadishu and their leaders have been working overtime to calm fears via a broad-based initiative to remove militias and their heavy weapons from the city, dismantle roadblocks and prepare former government buildings for TFG use. Instead of welcoming these efforts, Yusuf and his allies have dismissed them as window dressing, issued scathing attacks on the leaders, including the speaker of parliament, and seized on every setback or violent incident as proof the government should be based elsewhere […] Even more disturbing is the possibility Yusuf's supporters may have been involved in orchestrating some of the violence."[22]

A case in point is the assassination of BBC producer Kate Peyton on 9 February 2005. She was shot while preparing to cover a Transitional Federal Parliament visit to Mogadishu sounding out the possibility of a relocation of government. Her killer was identified by eyewitnesses as a certain Mohamed Salaad Tafey, a Somali national born in Ethiopia who is said to have links with Ethiopian intelligence services. These somewhat shady links offer an alternative explanation to the official one, which blames jihadi groups for the event: the attack may have been "organised by supporters of the Yusuf faction […] in order to scuttle the parliamentary delegation's mission."[23] In very much the same vein, the faction of president Yusuf attempted to paint an "accidental discharge of a grenade"[24] by one of Prime Minister Ali Mohamed Geedi's body guards at a rally in Mogadishu on 4 May 2005 as a terrorist attack.

So far, only one faction of the Transitional Federal Government moved to the capital. This faction consists of politicians hailing from clans hostile to the president's and the prime minister's respective clans, but with strong links to clans dominating the capital. Based on a similar "clan links" rationale, the factions of Yusuf and Geedi have chosen the town of Jahwhar, some miles northeast of Mogadishu, as its provisional seat of government. All in all, the TFG's reluctance to move to its own capital does not augur well for Somalia's political future. For the foreseeable future, Somalia remains a failed state trapped in a state of perennial civil war.

Somali Piracy — Analyzing the Problem

To successfully conduct acts of piracy with a fair chance of getting away with them depends on something which is usually called an "enabling environment." Along the Strait of Malacca and the South China Sea, such an enabling environment exists courtesy of geographical facts: the coasts of these waters frequently feature mangrove swamps, and the waters themselves are virtually littered with islands and islets — both of which provide convenient hiding places for ambushes and for shelter in the rather unlikely case of being spotted by maritime law-enforcement vessels. In the case of Somalia, its coasts may well run parallel to important sea lines of communications, thus being of eminent geostrategic value, but unlike maritime Southeast Asia, it does not have too many islets providing shelter for pirates lying in waiting. Here, the enabling environment is formed by the failed state itself: the absence of a central authority willing and capable to uphold law and order, the dissolution of such law-enforcement agencies into clan-based militia, and squabbling warlords provide an excellent environment for the spread of illegal activities, among them organized crime and terrorism. At the seaside, organized crime and, probably in the future, terrorism, acquire a distinctive maritime flavor: activities such as illegal fishing or smuggling along the coasts of the Arabian Sea happen even in the best of times, and in difficult times, it may just be a small step from these activities toward maritime organized crime/piracy or toward maritime terrorism. So let us turn to the shores of Somalia to take a look at the post-putsch developments there.

The Fate of Somalia's Navy

In the years before the putsch, protection of Somali waters, including its EEZ, was the task of the navy, founded in 1965 with the help of Soviet military advisers. The Somali navy had its bases at Berbera in the Gulf of Aden (today part of breakaway Somaliland), Mogadishu at the Banaadir-Coast, and Kismaayo/Chisimayu in the south near the border to Kenya, and it also operated a radar site up at Merca (also Banaadir-Coast, near Mogadishu) to monitor the movement of ships. As deemed to be appropriate for a small coastal navy, its inventory consisted of Soviet-origin inshore patrol forces, including two Soviet *Osa-II* missile-armed fast attack craft with SSN-2A Styx missiles, four Soviet *Mol* PFT torpedo-armed fast attack craft, and several patrol craft of the Soviet *Poluchat* type. The biggest vessel of the Somali navy was a Soviet *Polnocny*-class LST capable of carrying 5 tanks and 120 soldiers. Since the maintenance of all of the Somali army, air force, and navy weapon systems had been in the hands of Soviet military personnel, most of the more sophisticated weapons soon fell into disrepair and were reported as unserviceable soon after the Soviets left in 1977. The navy's vessels were bound to share this fate in the years after the Soviet withdrawal, except maybe for one patrol craft procured from the United States. Thus, in regard to their naval weapon systems, the Somali navy was definitely not operational from 1991 onward.[25]

The fate of the navy's seagoing personnel is unknown, but it is likely that they returned to their previous professions in the civil maritime sector. It would be tempting and not too improbable to argue that some of them joined their own clan-based militia, bringing with them their naval know-how, but to call them the core of the present-day pirates would definitely be too conjectural. As long as we cannot interview some of Somalia's pirates, we have to leave this interesting question open.

Piracy: Continuation of Maritime Protection by Other Means?

To explain why a sea-lane that only a decade ago was relatively untroubled has suddenly become one of the world's most risky waterways for shipping lines, we must turn to more established facts. For many Somalis, especially marine experts and coastal dwellers, the current problem of piracy began when foreign fishing boats started invading the country's fishing grounds after the fall of the Somali government in early 1991. Since the various rebel groups failed to fill in the vacuum and instead turned on each other, an opportunity arose for foreign vessels to poach in the country's territorial waters and to fish for diverse species in its exclusive economic zone. Somali fishermen witnessed an increase in the number of foreign boats fishing illegally off the coast of southern Somalia.[26] These foreign boats come from a variety of countries such as Belize (French or Spanish-owned purse seiners operating under a flag of convenience to avoid EU regulations); France (purse seiners targeting tuna); Honduras (EU purse seiners targeting tuna under a flag of convenience); Japan (longliners under license to Somaliland); Kenya (Mombasa-based trawlers); Korea (longliners targeting swordfish seasonally); Pakistan; Saudi Arabia; Spain (purse seiners targeting tuna); Sri Lanka (trawlers, plus longliners targeting shark under license to Somaliland and based at Berbera); Taiwan (longliners targeting swordfish seasonally); and Yemen (trawlers financed by a seafood importer in Bari, Italy).[27]

The Dutch nongovernmental organization Ocean Training and Promotion (OTP)[28] has collected information suggesting that between 1991 and 1999 more than 200 foreign vessels had been engaged in illegal fishing along the

Somali coastline. In one case in January 1998, a Taiwanese fishing fleet was apprehended in Somali waters carrying "licenses of dubious legality, written on ex-Somali government letterhead and signed by a warlord in Mogadishu claiming to represent the previous Barre government, and providing fishing access rights to demarcated areas of the Somali zone."[29] Since illegal licensing is a lucrative business for various coast-based warlords, and illegal fishing an even more lucrative business for foreign trawlers, worth approximately US$300 million per year,[30] it is to be expected that stamping out this practice will be a challenge for any new government in Mogadishu.

While some Somali warlords and several foreign fishing fleets obviously have prospered through this arrangement for more than a decade now, Somali fisher communities found themselves more and more on the losing end, for at least three reasons:

- Foreign trawlers ventured ever closer to the beaches, thus depriving even Somali inshore fishing vessels of their catch.
- Reports indicate that the foreign trawlers use universally prohibited fishing equipment, including nets with very small mesh sizes and sophisticated underwater lighting systems, thus turning the Somali seabed into a wasteland.
- Reports indicate that there is a certain level of violence when it comes to dealing with Somali fishing vessels: equipment of Somali fishermen is frequently destroyed by foreign trawlers, and some small Somali fishing boats have even been rammed by larger foreign vessels.

The ongoing encroachment of foreign trawlers on the exclusive economic zone of Somalia in flagrant violation of international law did not go unnoticed by the UN. The Office of the United Nations Resident & Humanitarian Coordinator for Somalia sees the lack of protection by maritime law-enforcement agencies as the main cause for illegal, unreported, and unregulated (IUU) fishing activities by foreign vessels. These illegal fishing activities conducted by foreigners divert much-needed resources away from Somalia's coastal population, whose livelihood could otherwise improve considerably. The lack of EEZ monitoring and patrolling also encourages human trafficking, often with fatal consequences for those who seek to leave Somalia for a better life elsewhere. In a recent press release, the UN resident therefore argues that to improve the situation, it is indispensable to establish an organization mandated to safeguard the Somali coastline until the Somali authorities are able to undertake such functions by themselves.[31]

Establishing such an organization, which also could deal with the problem of piracy, will take some time. In the meantime, however, and with no central authority to protect them, the local fishing community has turned to what they would call self-defense. In 2002, for example, there were reports of Somali inshore fishing boats being involved in armed clashes with unidentified foreign trawlers. The Somali fishermen reportedly engaged these illegal fishing boats equipped with equally illegal licenses with assault rifles and rocket-propelled grenades.[32] Some of the foreign trawlers retaliated in kind, also using firearms or, in some cases, high-pressure hoses in order to capsize their smaller Somali competition. The above-mentioned hijacking of three Taiwanese trawlers in August 2005 can be seen as part of this Somalian "self-defense": as mentioned above, the trawlers were "impounded" by a self-declared Somali Volunteer National Coast Guard for illegal fishing, and the ransom of US$5,000 for each of the 48 crew members was declared to be a "fine" for this criminal act. The frustration of local young fishermen provides one answer to the "who done it" question regarding piracy: seeing their waters being exploited by technically more advanced foreign high-sea trawlers forced them to start looking elsewhere for their livelihood. The second answer can be found in the bitter fisheries conflict itself: learning their deadly trade struggling for their own economic survival against powerful, aggressive, and technically more sophisticated foreign competition, some Somali fishermen gradually turned from fighting against encroaching foreign fishing vessels to preying on commercial shipping in what they perceive to be their waters. Equipped with speedboats and an array of light weapons such as assault rifles and RPGs, the young fishermen quickly realized that commercial cargo ships were much easier targets than foreign trawlers similarly equipped with assault rifles and RPGs.[33]

One question remains unanswered so far. While the two answers given above can explain the phenomenon of Somali piracy in general, they cannot explain why we have witnessed such an alarming upsurge from early 2005 onward. There are two possible — and not necessarily mutually exclusive — ways to answer this question: a "natural" one and a political one. The first answer is straightforward: the upsurge in piracy in early 2005 is a result of the Boxing Day tsunami of 26 December 2004. While Western media reports focused on Aceh, Indonesia, as the most affected region by far and, quite understandably, on the Thai tourist resorts Phuket, Phi Phi Island, Krabi, and Khao Lak, where many Western tourists perished, other regions affected by the tsunami remained largely uncovered. Somalia is one of these regions. Here, an estimated 40,000 to 50,000 people got killed, whole coastal villages were devastated, and much of the fishing gear was destroyed. Preying on vessels sailing through Somali waters near the coast would be a logical way out of misery, since waiting for the nonexistent government to step in would be equal to starving to death.

However, some observers offer a second, much more interesting answer for the 2005 rise in piracy. For them, the upsurge can be explained by a power struggle between the Yusuf and Geedi factions of the Transitional Federal Government and the hostile Mogadishu faction of the TFG on the other. For example, a Jane's report linked the upsurge to an attempt by President Yusuf to "curtail the flow of weapons to his opponents" by introducing "a blockade on the overland transit of Yemeni weapons to Mogadishu from Boosaaso, the Puntland port controlled by his clan."[34] Yusuf's embargo is said to have resulted in an 85 percent price hike in the arms bazaars of Mogadishu, meaning that the Mogadishu faction is in need of some additional income. The authors of this report do admit that, so far, there is only "circumstantial evidence linking the Mogadishu faction to pirate attacks," but they see the evidence strengthened by clan connections: the coastal clans controlling the region from which piracy emanates and the clans controlling the region of Mogadishu have close links and are united in their opposition to the Yusuf faction of the TFG.[35] As compelling as this explanation may sound, it is not completely satisfactory: given the near complete control over the coastal regions these clans enjoy, why do they not smuggle in cheap weapons by themselves, instead of using the spoils of piracy to acquire them on the already grossly overpriced Mogadishu arms bazaar? But, as we stated above, the reason behind the rise in piracy may very well be a mixture of both elements, natural and political, in a kind of push-and-pull combination.

Maritime Piracy or Maritime Terrorism?

While most of the pirate attacks off the coasts of Somalia went rather unnoticed outside of the shipping industry and a small circle of maritime specialists, the attack on the *Seabourn Spirit* was widely publicized and commented on. The Australian foreign minister, Anthony Downer, for example, did not rule out the possibility that the attack was not just an act of piracy but rather meant to be an act of maritime terrorism. Proponents of the "maritime terrorism school of thought" pointed at some interesting facts to support their theory: first, the attack was put forward by no more than a dozen operators in two small fiberglass boats. In their view, this number simply is insufficient to hijack a cruise liner with several hundred people on board: the Somali militants would never have been able to physically control both passengers and crew. Second, the militants never even made an attempt to disable the ship's propulsion and steering, and to board the ship; instead, they fired RPGs and hosed the ship with salvoes from their AK-47 assault rifles, probably with the intention of seriously damaging the ship, maybe even setting it afire. The ultimate fate of the hapless *Achille Lauro* or the successful terrorist attack on the *Super Ferry 14* in February 2004 in the Bay of Manila may have played a role in such a scenario: both ships burned fiercely and finally sunk.[36]

This attempt to second-guess the attackers is based on the assumption that the whole attack was thoroughly planned and thought through from the beginning to the end. It is much easier to assume that the attackers had learnt from previous attacks that (a) it is quite easy to stop a ship with a volley of RPGs and some machine gun fire, and (b) the frightened and unarmed crew does not offer any resistance. It is fair to assume that militants involved in the risky business of high-seas piracy so far away from the shores, and very probably having some previous experience in bullying Somali villagers, are not that easily daunted by the sheer number of more or less defenseless passengers and crew members. The *Achille Lauro* hijack in 1985 proves that the likelihood of such a hijack being successful should not be discounted: 450 crew members and 97 passengers of the 631-foot-long cruise ship were taken hostage by just four terrorists.[37] The *Seabourn Spirit* is certainly more luxurious than the *Achille Lauro* but much smaller: it is only 439 feet long, has a crew of 150, and can accommodate 208 passengers.[38] For determined and experienced pirates, this is hardly "mission impossible." The difference between these two attacks, then, would have been that the *Achille Lauro* hijackers were interested in political ends, while the Somali pirates were interested in private ends: either robbing the passengers and making an escape or robbing them and taking some of them hostage for ransom. Hijacking the whole ship would probably have been too risky for them. But then again, this is just another attempt to second-guess the attackers.

In all probability, the rationale behind the brazen attack was much more prosaic, as Jayant Abhyankar, deputy director of the International Maritime Bureau (IMB), argued. The pirates attacked at night, and maybe all they saw was the silhouette of a large ship without realizing they were up against a cruise ship with quite a lot of people on board.[39] And he is definitely right when he further states that so far there is no hard evidence for a correlation between maritime terrorism and piracy, and both still remain "two different phenomenon altogether" indeed.[40] As long as we cannot question or interview the attackers, we can only guess at their rationale for the attack, and that seems to be purely commercial and not terrorist. So let us turn to the facts that we actually know or that we can at least deduce from the recent attacks.

Somali Piracy: (Preliminary) Findings

First, it is undeniable that Somali pirates are getting more and more sophisticated. In previous years, they mainly preyed on local fishing inshore vessels not far off the coast, attacking them and robbing their crew rather at "knife-point" than gun-point. The returns of these small-scale ventures which could be called maritime muggings obviously have been invested into more sophisticated equipment, that is, automatic weapons including RPGs, satellite phones, navigation gear, and fast fiberglass boats nicknamed Volvos because of their high-powered outboard engines. Investing in this high-tech equipment brought with it higher mobility and more lethality, thus enabling the pirates to gradually widen their range of possible targets from small and slow inshore fishing vessels to larger offshore trawlers and finally to international shipping in even more distant waters off the coast of Somalia: the *Seabourn Spirit* attack took place roughly 100 sea miles off the coast, and the International Maritime Bureau now recommends to international shipping to stay at least 250 sea miles off the Somali coast to be reasonably safe from attack.

Second, given the fact that the pirates now strike quite far away from the coast, it is very likely that they operate from a "mother ship." By contrast, it is highly unlikely that the pirates venture out 100 sea miles on board of two relatively small 25-foot power boats: loitering in Somali waters for hours and waiting for new prey is easier done on board of a larger vessel, such as a small freighter or a larger dhow — both types being rather ubiquitous and thus innocuous in the Arabian Sea — than confined to small boats with low free-board. Of course, for attacks against vessels further inshore such as the MV *Semlow* and the *Ibn Batuta*, the pirates do not need a mother ship, but further out, it would greatly facilitate operations. The IMB confirmed the existence of such a mother ship shortly after the attack on the cruise ship. Some Kenyan sources report that there may be two or three mother ships plying the waters around Somalia, and a U.S. warship recently even intercepted a vessel which could have been used in such a role. But so far, the mother ship everybody is looking for remains a mystery, although it has reportedly been spotted three times since late July 2005: it is known that this ship launches the speed boats involved in the recent attacks, but the name of the ship, its owner, nationality, and identity of its crew are still unknown.[41]

Third, although we do not yet know how many pirate gangs are currently operating in Somali waters, it is obvious that given their highly sophisticated modus operandi, we have to deal with organized piracy, not with mere acts of ad-hoc piracy occasionally being committed by impoverished fisher folk. Small-time maritime muggers would simply rob the crew of vessels at anchor or at the most inshore near the coast and make off with their loot. The breed of Somali pirates, however, hijacks whole ships for ransom, which implies they have a network of land-based connections and protection, reportedly reaching as far as to the Mogadishu faction of the Transitional Federal Government. One should remember Captain Mahalingam's trip to meet the pirates' bosses in a village 30 miles away from the coast. Although it is probably unfair to claim that all the coastal villages are involved, as the captain stated, at least not in the sense of "actively involved," it seems that some of the coastal clans have formed their own militias which have turned to the sea. In all probability, these militias are a result of the Somali fisher communities' self-defense against encroaching foreign trawlers. Such fisher folk do have experience in maritime matters, some of them may even have been in the navy, and — as the examples of maritime Asia shows — they are closely-knit enough to offer at least "passive" support in the sense of "actively turning a blind eye." And, as we can see, if they choose to "go active," they make for formidable pirates.

Conclusion: How Do We Tackle the Problem?

As we pointed out above, the Transitional Federal Government of Somalia seems unable to establish its authority in Somalia. The TFG is not even willing to move to its own capital for security reasons. As long as this important first step has not been taken, it is highly unlikely that the government in exile will succeed in establishing law-enforcement agencies in Somalia, such as a police force for upholding law and order on its territory or a maritime agency responsible for maritime law and order. We will not see a Somali navy or coastguard or maritime police patrolling Somali waters in years to come. Unfortunately, Somalia's immediate neighbors sharing the sea lines of communication with it — Kenya in the South, Eritrea and Djibouti in the North, and Yemen on the other side of the Gulf of Aden — cannot do much to redress this situation by simply extending their own EEZ patrols into adjacent Somali waters. All these states simply do not have enough patrol crafts for such a venture: currently, the navies of Eritrea and Yemen both possess roughly a dozen patrol crafts, while the navy of Kenya can only deploy six missile crafts and two patrol vessels. These forces are hardly sufficient for patrolling their own EEZ. Since neither the fledgling transitional government of Somalia nor the other East African regional states will be able to provide effective measures to curb piracy in the foreseeable future, we have to look for other solutions.

The Combined Task Force 150

Several counterpiracy specialists have already suggested that the NATO naval forces at the Horn of Africa, the Combined Task Force 150, should expand operations. This force includes ships and planes from the navies of the United States, the United Kingdom, Canada, France, Germany, and Pakistan. Being part of Operation Enduring Freedom, its task is to patrol the Gulf of Aden and the adjacent waters of the Horn of Africa to suppress acts of terrorism — not only attacks as such, but also the smuggling of weapons and ammunition and people. In theory at least, the CTF 150's area of operation includes the whole Horn of Africa region, defined as "the total airspace and land areas out to the high-water mark of Kenya, Somalia, Ethiopia, Sudan, Eritrea, Djibouti and Yemen."[42] In practice, however, the task force concentrates on the Gulf of Aden area. Combating maritime crime in general or maritime piracy in particular is nothing the task force is focusing on. A reduction of piracy in the Gulf of Aden can thus be seen rather as a side-effect of the sustained patrolling of these waters, probably forcing Somali pirates to prey on the Banaadir Coast of Somalia, which is not regularly affected by patrolling activities.

Unfortunately, spokespersons for this task force have reacted quite lukewarmly to such ideas. They see their job first of all in curbing international terrorism as part of the global war on terrorism. Anything else would (a) stretch their mandate too far and (b) overburden their available assets even more. Monitoring Somali waters on a continuous basis is, therefore, out of question. There are only some exceptions to this rule: as mentioned above, a U.S. Navy ship rescued a Thai merchant ship from being hijacked after a mutiny, and, in mid-November 2005, the German frigate *Lübeck* escorted the German cruise ship MS *Deutschland* on its way through the Gulf of Aden.[43]

Even more recently, in January 2006, the USS *Winston S. Churchill* intercepted and seized a suspicious vessel (a dhow) after firing two warning shots 54 miles off the coast of Somalia.[44] But in general, "simple" criminal acts such as piracy are not their problem. The experience of maritime piracy elsewhere shows that piracy in itself simply is not sexy enough to merit an international naval law-and-order enforcement effort. To get the Task Force really interested, one should try to sell piracy off the coast of Somalia as training runs by potential maritime terrorists of al-Qaeda. As we remember, the attack on the *Seabourn Spirit* was actually claimed to be a terror attack.

As of the time of this writing, there are basically three Islamist groupings active in Somalia. The oldest one is al-Itihaad al-Islaami, a group which had its heydays in the 1990s when it could field a militia numbering roughly 1,000 fighters. After some ill-fated terror attacks in Ethiopia, the group was formally disbanded in 1997, but a core group around some of its leaders is still active. A second group, and probably the most vicious one at the moment, is a loose network of Jihadists based and active in Mogadishu. This network is said to have contacts with al-Qaeda. Al-Qaeda itself forms the third Islamist group to be found in Somalia, but it is the smallest of the three groups by far. All in all, the Islamist movements seem to be in a minority position, and reports stating that Somalia is an important base for al-Qaeda are definitely on the alarmist side. Overstating the threat emanating from a Somalia-based al-Qaeda makes eminent sense for the transitional government, though, since an al-Qaeda presence is always a very good excuse to garner additional funding from foreign donor states. However, apart from the mere presence of some al-Qaeda operators in the country, there is no evidence — not even the most circumstantial — connecting them to planned or attempted acts of maritime terrorism. So this ill-disguised attempt to get foreign naval forces (both the U.S. Navy and NATO forces at the Horn of Africa) interested in the current state of maritime lawlessness off the shores of Somalia will not work anytime soon. Other solutions are needed.

Private-Sector Solutions: Outsourcing as a Quick Fix

So, instead of a joint task force tackling the problem, individual or private solutions seem to be preferable or at least operable at the moment. For example, there is currently a French private security firm active in Somali waters, whose list of services include specialized antipiracy and maritime counter-terrorism operations. This company offers close protection and escorts for ships traveling through these waters, they provide negotiators in the case of a ship and its crew being hijacked, and — as our source maintained — they even offer to "reacquire" hijacked ships from their new possessors by certain "other" measures, that is, by hijacking them back. Of course, such activities cannot possibly eradicate the problem since they rather treat the symptoms but not the disease itself. But these rather clandestine activities are overshadowed by another public-sector security firm, which — if everything goes according to plan — could have an impact on piracy in Somali waters.

In November, in quite a surprising move, the TFG awarded a US$50 million two-year private contract to the U.S. company Topcat Marine Security to help fight piracy off the Somalia coast. Under the deal, the company will supply all the necessary equipment and training to create a new Somali coastguard and other special forces tasked with monitoring the coastline.[45] The firm, which is confident that it will succeed in eradicating piracy very quickly, will also go for the mother ship from which the pirates are said to operate.[46] Given the fact that there are no functioning government institutions in Somalia — no police, no navy, no coast guard, no infrastructure, but instead a plethora of militias under the command of various clan lords — this is quite a tall order. The easiest part may be ferreting out and capturing the mother ship, since this could be accomplished from an offshore base in the form of a Topcat mother ship — in a way of speaking, this would be a fight between Somali pirates on the one side and privateers with a government-in-exile letter of marque on the other. Setting up naval bases for the new government coast guard, building up the infrastructure, training the newly hired coast guard officers, and maintaining the coast guard's Topcat-delivered equipment, however, requires a firm footing on Somali coastal territory. Thus, this part of the deal can only be accomplished if the transitional government would be able to provide Topcat with a reasonably safe working environment, that is, ports at least not in the hand of hostile clans probably living off the spoils of piracy and waterborne smuggling themselves. Since the TFG is not even confident enough to move to its own capital Mogadishu for fear of its security, this outsourcing of maritime law-and-order responsibilities may look good on paper, but implementing it may turn out to be quite another story.

But even if we consider for a moment that Topcat will succeed in establishing such bases to conduct antipiracy patrols from there, lessons from the history of piracy show that such maritime policing efforts only address part of the problem. As long as little or no governance in large parts of Somalia persists, and as long as there are no viable alternative economic opportunities for the coastal communities, piracy and other forms of maritime crime will continue. The Strait of Malacca and the piracy emanating from the coasts of Sumatra are a case in point.[47] In the long run at least, the only viable solution to eradicate the problem is to reestablish law and order in Somalia at large, setting up a reasonably strong government, including all the usual trappings of a working political system, and then tackling the question of socioeconomic development of Somalia in cooperation with international donors. But that is, admittedly, an even taller order. So let us wish Topcat well, and in the meantime, let us continue to give Somalia's coastline a wide berth — or let us be prepared to pay ransom if we get caught anyway.

Notes

1. *The Sunday Herald* (Glasgow), 11 November 2005.
2. Hassan Barise: "Somalia — where pirates roam free," *BBC News Africa*, 11/11/05 (http://news.bbc.co.uk/go/pr/fr/-/2/hi/africa/4424264.stm).
3. Simon Robinson/Xan Rice: "In Peril on the Sea. The waters off Somalia are infested with pirates — and things are getting worse," *Time Asia*, Monday, 7 November 2005, Vol. 166, No. 20.
4. Rob Hauser, WFP country director for Somalia, as quoted by IRIN News.org: "Somalia: TFG seeks help to police coastline as pirates strike again," http://www.irinnews.org/report.asp?ReportID=49530&SelectRegion=Horn_of_Africa (accessed 12/20/05).
5. Simon Robinson/Xan Rice: "In Peril on the Sea … ."
6. As quoted by Robinson/Rice: "In Peril on the Sea … ."
7. See the results of their 2005 poll at http://www.concierge.com/bestof/cruisepoll/smallships (accessed 11/16/05).
8. Data from the fact sheet at the website of Seabourn Cruises, "Seabourn Spirit ship facts." See their website at http://www.seabourncruiseweb.com/fleet/spirit.html (accessed 11/15/05).
9. Data from http://www.ivoya.com/luxury_cruises/seabourn/spirit/cruises_2005/calendar.htm (accessed 11/16/05).
10. For more information on LRAD, see http://www.defense-update.com/products/l/LRAD.htm (accessed 11/18/05).
11. See for example the reporting of the incident in *Scotland on Sunday*: "Pirates attack luxury cruise ship," 6 November 2005.
12. "Thai merchant ship with 23 crewmembers hijacked," *The Nation* (Bangkok), 11 November 2005. The ship and its Thai crew was rescued by a US Navy warship that happened to be nearby.
13. See the U.S. Department of State's travel warning for East Africa, 18 November 2005, at http://travel.state.gov/ (accessed 11/23/05).
14. As quoted in Patrick Beja: "Where Kenyans are at risk as warlords take charge," *The Standard* (Nairobi), Friday, 14 October 2005 (http://www.eastandard.net/print/news.php?articleid=30502; accessed 11/23/05).
15. Matthew Lee: "Dire piracy warnings for Somali coast," *Mail & Guardian Online* (Johannesburg), 23 November 2005.
16. Patrick Beja: "Where Kenyans are at risk as warlords take charge," *The Standard* (Nairobi), Friday, 14 October 2005 (see online at http://www.eastandard.net/print/news.php?articleid=30502; accessed 11/23/05).
17. A cruise passenger's opinion, quoted in Gina Mangieri: "Hawaii preferred for cruising after piracy elsewhere," *Khon2 — Hawaii's News Channel*, 6 November 2005.
18. So the opinion of Ali A. Jama, SomaliaWatch.Org, in "Protecting International Maritime Industry That Use the Coastal Somali Waters," *AllPuntland.Com*, Saturday, 12 November 2005. http://www.allpuntland.com/news1/eng/news_item.asp?NewsID=1890 (accessed 12/02/05).
19. For more on Somalia's history, see for example http://www.historyofnations.net/africa/somalia.html (accessed 11/28/05).
20. See http://www.un.org/Depts/DPKO/Missions/unosom2.htm (accessed 11/28/05) for more information on UNOSOM I and II.
21. International Crisis Group: "Somalia: Continuation of War By Other Means?" *Africa Report No. 88*, 21 December 2004, p. 1.
22. International Crisis Group: "Counter-Terrorism in Somalia: Losing Hearts and Minds? *Africa Report No. 95*, 11 July 2005, p. 14.
23. Ibid.
24. International Crisis Group, "Counter-Terrorism … ," p. 15.
25. Data taken from IISS: *The Military Balance 1989–1990*, London: Brassey's Autumn 1989, p. 113.
26. BBC World News, January 2, 2000. http://news.bbc.co.uk/1/hi/world/africa/583781.stm (accessed 11/28/05).
27. Scott Coffen-Smout: "Pirates, Warlords and Rogue Fishing Vessels in Somalia's Unruly Seas," http://www.chebucto.ns.ca/~ar120/somalia.html (accessed 12/02/05).

28. One of OTP's aims is "to support needy Somali communities in fisheries development (Infrastructures, capacity building and marine resources conservation)." www.somalicivilsociety.org/partners/partner_oceantp.php (accessed 11/25/05).
29. Scott Coffen-Smout.
30. This is the current UN estimate. See "Illegal fishing off Somalia nets $300m a year," *Mail & Guardian Online*, 01 September 2005. http://www.mg.co.za/articlePage.aspx?articleid=249733&area=/breaking_news/breaking_news—africa/ (accessed 12/02/05).
31. Office of the United Nations Resident & Humanitarian Coordinator for Somalia, Press Release, September 1, 2005.
32. BBC World News, June 14, 2002. http://news.bbc.co.uk/1/hi/world/africa/2045372.stm (accessed 11/25/05).
33. See Abdulkadir Khalif: "How Illegal Fishing Feeds Somali Piracy," *The East African* (Nairobi), November 15, 2005. Available online by *Somaliland Times* at http://www.somalilandtimes.net/200/08.shtml (accessed 12/02/05).
34. "Piracy and Politics in Somalia," *Jane's Terrorism & Security Monitor*, November 16, 2005.
35. Ibid.
36. In the case of the *Achille Lauro*, the fire leading to its sinking — coincidentally off the coast of Somalia — on Friday, 2 December 1994, was caused by accident.
37. The bulk of the 748 passengers had left the ship for an overland trip at Alexandria. For details, see for example Bohn, Michael K.: *The Achille Lauro Hijacking. Lessons in the Politics and Prejudice of Terrorism*. Washington, DC: Brassey's 2004.
38. Data from the fact sheet at the website of Seabourn Cruises, "Seabourn Spirit ship facts." See at http://www.seabourncruiseweb.com/fleet/spirit.html (accessed 11/15/05). Actually, at the time of the attack, there were 161 crew members and 151 passengers aboard.
39. See his interview "Indian waters are fairly safe" from 16 November 2005, at http://in.rediff.com (accessed 11/17/05).
40. Ibid.
41. Andrew Mwangura, Kenyan Seafarers' Association, in a Reuters interview. See Daniel Wallis: "Pirates attack more ships off Somalia: Official," *Reuters/Yahoo News*, Friday, 11 November 2005.
42. Major General John F. Sattler, USMC: "Joint Task Force Horn of Africa Briefing," Friday, 10 January 2003 (http://www.defenselink.mil/transcripts/2003/t01102003_t0110hoa.html; accessed 12/10/05).
43. Presse und Informationsstelle Marine, Djibouti: "Fregatte Lübeck trifft Kreuzfahrtschiff MS Deutschland im Golf von Aden," 19 November 2005 (http://www.marine.de/01DB070000000001/vwContentByKey/W26JCELR184INFODE; accessed 11/25/05).
44. Krane, Jim: "U.S. Navy Seizes Pirate Ship Off Somalia," *Associated Press*, 01/22/2006.
45. BBC World News. http://news.bbc.co.uk/2/hi/africa/4471536.stm. (Accessed 11/25/2005).
46. Ibid.
47. The question of how to eradicate piracy is taken up by J. N. Mak in a later chapter of this book.

2
Sea Piracy in South Asia

VIJAY SAKHUJA

This chapter attempts to examine the phenomenon of sea piracy in South Asian waters. In particular, it examines sea piracy–related incidents in Bangladesh, India, and Sri Lanka. Given that the pirates are the enemies of all (*hostis humani generis*) and need to be brought to book, the chapter highlights the lacuna in the legal system to prosecute the perpetrators of piracy. The chapter also looks at the South Asian maritime-force infrastructure to counter sea piracy. Finally, by way of a case study of the Liberation Tigers of Tamil Eelam (LTTE), the paper argues that there is a link between piracy and terrorism.

Geographical Settings

South Asian waters are home to important Sea Lines of Communication (SLOCs) and maritime choke points. A large volume of international long-haul maritime cargo from the Persian Gulf, Africa, and Europe transits through this sea space. This sea-borne trade, primarily oil, affects virtually every aspect of the daily lives of most people of the world. The shipping lane that passes through the Arabian Sea and the Bay of Bengal and enters the strategic choke point of South East Asia has great geostrategic importance to the United States, China, Japan, Korea, Taiwan, and the South East Asian countries. Given these conditions, the South Asian waters are booming with maritime activity, and both economic and security interests concentrate there.

By its very location, South Asia lies between the Strait of Hormuz and the Strait of Malacca. The primary cargo through the Strait of Hormuz is oil/gas. The Strait of Hormuz is fairly deep; vessels of 160,000 dead-weight tonnage can pass through the waterway, and nearly 15.5 million barrels of oil flow through it daily.[1] From the Persian Gulf, the sea-lane transits through the Arabian Sea, almost hugging the Indian coast toward the Strait of Malacca. The Strait of Malacca is the world's busiest sea-lane with over 200 vessels transiting through it every day. Each day, about 10.3 million barrels of oil are carried through this strait.[2] Virtually all ships destined for East Asia carrying Liquefied Natural Gas (LNG) and Liquefied Petrol Gas (LPG) pass through the Malacca Strait, and the issue of safety is likely to grow in importance as East and South East Asia's energy imports grow. It is estimated that the number of tankers transiting through this sea-lane will increase to 59 per day in 2010 from 45 in 2000. Similarly, the LPG tanker traffic is expected to increase to seven per day in 2010 from five in 2000 and the daily LNG tanker traffic is expected to rise to twelve per day from eight in 2000.[3]

Both these choke points have the potential to become major flash points. There are alternatives to the Strait of Malacca but there are no other routes to transport the Persian Gulf oil other than through pipelines over land, which have their own vulnerabilities. These two choke points can thus be called the end terminals of the sea-lane transiting through the South Asian waters.

If one traces the SLOC from the Persian Gulf, much of the mercantile traffic transits through the Arabian Sea before ships turn northeast into the Bay of Bengal south of Dundra Head in Sri Lanka. This SLOC then passes close to the Indian islands of Andaman and Nicobar before entering the Malacca Strait. Thus, mercantile traffic transiting through the Strait of Hormuz and the Strait of Malacca passes through the South Asian maritime space, which means that any unforeseen contingency or development in the Malacca Strait has security implications for the region.

South Asian Piracy

The International Maritime Organisation (IMO), through their Maritime Safety Committee Circular MSC/Circ 622 of 22 June 1993,[4] has classified sea piracy into three broad categories:

a. Low-Level Assault or Armed Robbery. This is generally carried out from the vicinity of land from small, high-speed craft by groups of petty thieves armed with machetes, clubs, and occasionally low-velocity weapons such as pistols and shotguns.
b. Medium-Level Armed Assault and Robbery. This is carried out by people who are better organized and more heavily involved than those in the low-level category.
c. Major Criminal Hijacks. This involves extreme violence. In some cases, the cargo is discharged or transferred to another ship. In other cases, the ship is renamed, restaffed, or sold by the pirates. Crew members are sometimes left adrift or killed.

These are broad guidelines to facilitate understanding of the phenomenon. However, each piracy-prone area has its own characteristics, intensity, frequency, lethality, and modus operandi. Besides, geography, social, political, and domestic economic considerations contribute to the nature of piracy. According to Prabhakaran Paleri, sea piracy has many variants such as Asian piracy, Southeast Asian piracy, West African piracy, South American piracy, and so on. Apart from that, there is also marine mugging, cargo hijacking, and vessel hijacking.[5]

Piracy in Indian ports essentially involves petty theft and the boarding of vessels both within and outside port area. From one reported incident in 1993 to thirty-five in 2000, the figure has dropped to fifteen in 2004.[6] In 2004, there were eleven incidents involving boarding vessels and four cases of attempted boarding. With five incidents, Chennai [formerly Madras, ed.] in South India has the dubious distinction of witnessing the highest number of boardings during the last four years.[7] But at the same time, the Indian maritime forces have earned the unique distinction of apprehending a pirate vessel, bringing to the fore the commitment of India to fight sea piracy.

The investigations by the Indian Coast Guard reveal that

> there were cases of fishermen boarding vessels at anchorage for petty considerations from the ships with the connivance of the crew, and the ships thereafter reporting the incidents to the Piracy Reporting Center as acts of theft. These cases were reported by the coast guard to the concerned shipping company which was expected to take action against the crew involved.[8]

According to a review of the nature of piracy in Indian waters, the Indian brand of piracy appears to be nonviolent and not an organized activity. However, the IMB does cite several Indian ports like Chennai and Kandla as piracy prone.[9] It has been argued that piracy in Indian waters is of a low level and fairly well contained by the coast guard with active cooperation from the shipping community, the harbor police, and the Directorate General of Shipping. The piracy in Indian waters "is more a social issue than one of organized crime in India."[10]

According to the *International Chamber of Commerce Annual Report on Piracy at Sea, 2003*, Bangladesh ranked second in terms of attacks on ships. But the IMB has been singularly appreciative of the Bangladeshi efforts to curb piracy in their waters, witnessing a sharp decline from 58 incidents in 2003 to 17 in 2004.[11]

An analysis of incidents over the last eight years in Bangladesh shows that at least 75 percent of the incidents were carried out in harbor/port areas. Piracy is rampant in its seaports and has hit trade since mariners/ships are reluctant to use the ports of Chittagong and Mongla. This has forced foreign shipping companies to impose additional fees for discharging cargo in these ports, resulting in higher costs for export and import of goods. These ports are vulnerable and insecure for visiting ships. The Bangladesh authorities are conscious of this tarnished image of their ports but have not made any significant progress in containing this problem.

> Some of the most serious pirate attacks have taken place in the territorial waters of Bangladesh. In one incident pirates attacked and killed 14 fishermen; the trawler carrying fish worth US$50,000 was hijacked. The survivors reported that the pirates were carrying automatic weap-

ons and ordered the crew to jump overboard.[12] In another incident, pirates attacked a fishing vessel off the coast of Pattakhali and threw 13 crew members overboard.[13] In June 1998, MV *Britoil 4*, a Singapore-flagged vessel, was attacked in Chittagong port and one crewmember killed.[14] In 2004, Bangladesh police found the bodies of 16 fishermen in the ice chamber of their boat F.B *Kausara*. Fish and fishing equipment had been stolen from the boat, and the pirates had locked the men into the fish-storage ice chamber, where they died of severe cold and suffocation.[15]

Bangladesh shares a riverine border with India. This makes transborder piracy easier. The hostages are often sent away with instructions to the families of others to arrange for ransom. The money-for-prisoners swap usually takes place on the Indian side at Canning, Dakghat, or Jharkahali. Bangladesh ratified the 1988 UNCLOS III, but has yet to ratify the 1988 Rome Convention aimed at curbing piracy and armed robbery at sea. Till recently, Bangladesh had no agreement with India, its maritime neighbor, on antipiracy patrols. It has now been agreed that India and Bangladesh will explore the possibility of conducting joint exercises between their two navies in the near future.[16]

Although waters off Sri Lanka have generally remained free from piracy, the northeastern waters have witnessed frequent acts of piracy. LTTE rebel forces are reported to hijack ships and boats of all sizes, and kidnapping and killing of crew members is a common practice. There is also evidence of hijacked vessels in the LTTE fleet. According to Gunaratna, some Southeast Asian intelligence agencies believe that the LTTE has hijacked foreign vessels, but the affected governments have failed to present conclusive evidence implicating the LTTE. Since the LTTE has demonstrated quite regularly its mastery of phantom shipping — changing the ship's name and appearance — it is likely that it is also engaged in maritime crime even outside Sri Lankan waters.[17]

For instance, MV *Sik Yang*, a 2,818-ton Malaysian-flag cargo ship, was reported missing. The ship sailed from Tuticorin, India on 25 May 1999 with a cargo of bagged salt and was due on 31 May at the Malaysian port of Malacca. The fate of the ship's crew of 15 is unknown. The vessel was apparently hijacked by the LTTE, probably to be used as a phantom vessel. A report of 30 June 1999 confirmed that the vessel had been hijacked by the LTTE.[18]

In another incident, a merchant vessel, the MV *Cordiality*, was captured, and five Chinese crewmembers were allegedly killed by the LTTE near the port of Trincomalee.[19] In August 1998, a Belize-flagged general cargo vessel, the MV *Princess Kash,* was hijacked by LTTE rebels.[20] While on its way to Mullaitivu, an LTTE stronghold, the Sri Lankan Air Force bombed the vessel to prevent the ship's cargo from falling into the hands of the LTTE. The status of the 22 crew members is still not known.

Other vessels hijacked by the LTTE are the *Irish Mona* (August 1995), *Princess Wave* (August 1996), *Athena* (May 1997), *Misen* (July 1997), *Morong Bong* (July 1997), and the *Cordiality* (Sept 1997).

Legal Aspects of Piracy

The subject of piracy is dealt with in Articles 100–107 of the 1982 *United Nations Law of the Sea Convention*. The definition of piracy under the 1982 Convention (Article 101) is very narrow. It states that piracy consists of any of the following acts:

- Any illegal acts of violence or detention, or any act of depredation, committed for private ends by crew or the passengers of any ship or private aircraft, and directed:
- On the high seas, against another ship or aircraft, or against persons or property on board such ship or aircraft;
- Any act of inciting or of intentionally facilitating an act described in subparagraph (a) or (b).

Article 100 of the 1982 Convention provides for all states to "cooperate to the fullest possible extent in the repression of piracy on the high seas or in any place outside the jurisdiction of any state." Warships and other vessels and aircraft on government service (Article 99) have a right to visit foreign vessels suspected of involvement in piracy, the slave trade, or unauthorized broadcasting. Provision is also made in the 1982 Convention for seizure by foreign vessels (Article 107); retention or loss of nationality (Article 104); jurisdiction of state seizing a vessel (Article 105); and liability for unjust seizure (Article 106).

The Indian Navy enjoys a unique regulation contained in the Navy Act 1957. This Act was passed by the Indian parliament and includes the term "pirate" in Section 3, Chapter I in the definition of *enemy*: "enemy includes all armed rebels, armed mutineers, armed rioters and pirates and any person in arms against whom it is the duty of any person to act." Further, Section 34 states, "If the Commanding Officer of a naval vessel fails to pursue the enemy, whom it is his duty to pursue, then the punishment prescribed for him may range from imprisonment extending up to 7 years or if such act is committed to assist the enemy, he may even be punished with death."

The Regulations for the Navy (REGS, IN) Part I derived from the Navy Act 1957 clearly states:

> If any armed vessel, not having commission as a warship from a recognised government, whether de facto or de jure, should commit piratical acts and outrages against the vessels or goods of India's citizens or of the subjects of any other foreign power in amity with India, and if cred-

> ible information should be received thereof, such armed vessel shall be seized and detained by any of Indian naval ships falling in with her, and sent to the nearest Indian port where there is a court of competent jurisdiction for the trial of offences committed on the high seas, together with the necessary witnesses to prove the act or acts and with her master and crew in safe custody, in order that they may be dealt with according to law.

The above regulations provide clear guidelines to Indian naval vessels while dealing with acts of piracy. The Indian maritime forces observe strict rules of engagement in accordance with international laws, treaties, and conventions. These broadly dictate guidelines for procedures to be followed when investigating suspected ships:[21]

a. The visit and search is to be done with tact and consideration.
b. True character is to be established by first examining papers, and if there is a doubt the crew may be questioned and cargo examined.
c. If the vessel flees or does not cooperate, it may be pursued and brought to by force, if necessary. A graduated increase in force is to be used till the vessel surrenders. Initial warnings are to be given on the radio, and if there is no response, gun shots may be fired across the bows of the ship. The next phase involves firing into the ship to cripple the vessel by aiming at the steering position. All efforts must be made to prevent loss of life.
d. The Commanding Officer is the best judge at the scene of action to decide the quantum of force to be applied. When in doubt, he is to consult his superiors, keeping in mind the situation.

The Coast Guard Act, 1994, governs the Bangladesh Coast Guard (BCG).[22] According to the Act, the BCG is required to perform several functions such as:

a. Protection of the national interests in the maritime zones of Bangladesh
b. Prevention of the illegal entering or leaving of Bangladesh through the maritime zones of Bangladesh
c. Enforcement of any warrant or any other order of any court or other authority in respect of any ship which has entered the territorial waters of Bangladesh or of any person on board such ship
d. Ensure the security of persons working in the maritime zones of Bangladesh
e. Prevention of the handing over and smuggling of drugs
f. Patrolling in the maritime zones of Bangladesh
g. Rendering assistance to the appropriate authorities for the security of the sea ports

h. Suppression of destructive and terrorist activities occurring in the maritime zones of Bangladesh, and rendering assistance in this behalf to other authorities

The Act does not mention sea piracy or armed robbery in seaports. It only refers to "suppression of destructive and terrorist activities occurring in the maritime zones of Bangladesh," which makes it vague to combat sea piracy or for that matter armed robbery onboard ships.

As far as Sri Lanka is concerned, it enacted The Piracy Act, No.9 of 2001 and was notified in the Gazette of the Democratic Socialist Republic of Sri Lanka on 10 August 2001.[23] It provides for suppression of piracy in Sri Lankan waters and for matters connected therewith or incidental thereto. Piracy is termed as an offence under Part II, Section 3:

> Any person who dishonestly takes or appropriates any ship, by means of theft, force, intimidation, deception, fraud or by other similar means, shall be guilty of the offence of piracy and shall on conviction be punished subject to the provisions of Sections 8, 9, and 10 of this Act with imprisonment of either description for a term not less than five years and not exceeding ten years and shall also be liable to a fine not less than one million rupees and not exceeding ten million rupees or of an amount equal to the value of the ship in respect of which the offence is committed whichever is the greater.[24]

The Case of MV *Alondra Rainbow*

The standoff between the hijacked MV *Alondra Rainbow*, a 7,000-ton Panama-registered vessel belonging to Japanese owners, and an Indian warship in November 1999, and its final capture, is regarded as a great success for the maritime community countering sea piracy. The vessel was en route from Kuala Tanjung, Indonesia, to Milke in Japan.[25] The Piracy Reporting Center of the International Maritime Bureau had announced through a worldwide broadcast that pirates had captured the vessel. According to the Center, the crew of the vessel were found safe in Thailand and the vessel was expected to turn up in an Indian port to discharge cargo. What followed was a drama on the high seas leading to the arrest of pirates who came up for trial in Mumbai.

The incident highlighted the cooperation and coordination among governments, international agencies, and mariners at sea. Some of the important aspects of the operation carried out by the Indian maritime forces against MV *Alondra Rainbow* were:

a. Worldwide alert by the Piracy Reporting Center, Kuala Lumpur, and NAVAREA VIII
b. Prompt sighting report by MV *al Shuhadaa*, a merchant vessel operating in the west coast of India

c. Quick response by Indian maritime security forces
d. The importance of maritime air surveillance capability to shadow and track the vessel
e. Use of firepower to counter determined hijackers
f. Importance of special forces to board vessels and apprehend culprits
g. Close cooperation between navy and coast guard
h. Close coordination between the PRC, Kuala Lumpur, and Indian MRCCs[26]

The Indian authorities received accolades for capturing the pirates and the ship, and the International Maritime Bureau noted:

> This problem is not one which can be solved by law enforcement alone or by industry alone. It needs cooperation and further to this, it needs the will of governments to act against this heinous crime, … It was fantastic to see the Indian authorities act under the auspices of international law to intercept the ship.[27]

By February 2003, the Mumbai Sessions Court accepted the charges and the 15 pirates were given an imprisonment of seven years and a fine. The director of the International Maritime Bureau noted:

> We are delighted that India took the difficult decision to assume jurisdiction and are very pleased with the outcome, … It has been a long hard road for them to get to this day, but hopefully this conviction will deter other pirates. I hope this case serves as a warning that the world will no longer tolerate this crime and that those who engage in it can expect tough justice when they are caught.[28]

Notwithstanding this accomplishment, the success of prosecuting the pirates remains suspect. On 18 April 2005, the Mumbai High court overruled the Sessions Court ruling and acquitted all the accused. The case highlighted the fact that notwithstanding these legal instruments and tools, the success of prosecuting pirates is poor.

According to Commodore RS Vasan, "the failure of the concerned agencies to make a case and prove it in the High Court raises many questions and points to some of the possible systemic/organizational failures which led to the acquittal of the criminals."[29] Vasan also notes that "the failure of the prosecution was also largely due to the unwillingness of the Japanese Master of the vessel to identify the culprits for reasons best known to him. However, it has been indicated that after the trauma both the Japanese crew members (the master and the engineer) were not going to sea again and even feared reprisals should they identify the culprits in a Court of Law."[30]

Some Success Stories

While the Alondra Rainbow incident can be termed as a legal debacle for the maritime community, there have been successes, too. Interestingly, on 18 February 2003, a Chinese court in the city of Shantou handed out jail sentences to ten pirates of Indonesian origin for hijacking a Thailand-registered oil tanker, the *Siam Xanxai*, in June 1999 while it was in Malaysian waters, and for sailing the hijacked ship into Chinese waters.[31] The sentences include jail terms ranging from ten to fifteen years and a fine up to US$3,600. The court announced that the pirates initially stole two high-speed hovercrafts before hijacking the ship. They boarded the *Siam Xanxai*, then repainted and renamed the vessel and locked up the 17 Thai sailors before taking the hijacked ship to ports in the Philippines and Taiwan and finally into southern China. The pirates had falsified the ship's documents and even changed the ship's port of registration to Singapore. The vessel, along with its cargo of 1,900 tons of diesel fuel worth around US$1 million, had earlier been returned to its Thai owners.

China also put on trial 38 people involved in maritime crime including those involved in slaying 23 crew members of MV *Cheng Sheng*.[32] The crew was handcuffed, blindfolded, beaten to death and their bodies thrown overboard. Reportedly, the pirates posed as officers of the Chinese antismuggling police and operated in a gang. The Intermediate People's Court, in the southern province of Guangdong, charged the gang with crimes including murder, robbery, and possession of weapons, drugs, and explosives. The *Beijing Morning Post*, a state run publication, noted that it was China's biggest case of robbery and murder in 50 years of Communist rule.

Regional Response to Sea Piracy

There are no bilateral or multilateral agreements among regional countries to challenge sea piracy. But regional countries are conscious of the menace, and the issue is often discussed during bilateral interaction. Since 1995, the Indian Navy has hosted several navies from South Asia and South East Asia as part of "Milan," [Hindi for "meeting", ed.] a biannual gathering of warships. The issue of sea piracy is discussed during seminars and official discussions. More recently the Indian Navy hosted the International Fleet Review (IFR), the first of its kind since independence.[33] Addressing the gathering of naval ships from 23 countries, the Indian prime minister noted:

> The Indian Navy plays a crucial role in India's co-operation with other countries, especially those that share maritime borders. Active co-operation between navies is a must in [these] times of sea piracy, gunrunning and drug menace, which are all part of international terrorism ... by institutionalized arrangements we can actually say that we have built bridges of friendship" which happened to be the theme of the fleet review.[34]

However, India has been actively participating in counterpiracy operations. In a strategic move to safeguard its sea-lanes of communications, the U.S. government has entered into a bilateral cooperative arrangement with the Indian government to protect its merchant fleet against attacks from pirates in the Malacca Strait. The INS *Sharda* assumed responsibility from the USS *Cowpens* for escorting U.S. commercial ships carrying "high value" goods that transit the Straits.[35] According to the bilateral arrangement, U.S. naval ships patrolled the seas in Southeast Asia while the Indian Navy concentrated in the Bay of Bengal and the Indian Ocean. It has also agreed to hold joint operations that would include search-and-rescue exercises to assist ships in distress in the Indian Ocean region, to ensure safety in and security of the sea-lanes, and to undertake antipiracy surveillance and maintain general order. Similarly, India and Japan undertook an antipiracy exercise in November 2000.

Regional Maritime Forces

India

The Indian Navy and the Coast Guard are responsible for maintaining maritime order in the Indian EEZ. They are equipped with surface ships and maritime aircraft to undertake patrolling and surveillance of the sea areas. The naval forces also include special helicopters for deployment of quick-reaction forces, marine commandos, diving teams, and damage-control units. The Indian Coast Guard has grown over the years and plays a dominant role in policing Indian waters with patrol vessels, interceptor boats, and aircraft. In addition, marine customs and police forces play an important role in handling criminal acts in and off Indian ports.

The maritime forces are based at various naval and coast guard stations and ports along the east and the west coasts of India. Substantial forces are also deployed in the Andaman and Nicobar Islands and the Lakshadweep group of islands. The control of naval forces is exercised by the Naval Headquarters through the Flag Officers Commanding-in-Chief based at Mumbai [formerly Bombay, ed.], Kochi, and Vishakhapatnam. Similarly, the Coast Guard Headquarters at New Delhi exercises control over coast guard forces through Commander, Coast Guard Region based at Mumbai, Chennai, and Port Blair. Additionally, Maritime Operation Centers (MOC) and Maritime Regional Coordination Centers (MRCC) are located at Mumbai, Kochi, Vishakhapatnam, and Port Blair. These agencies maintain a constant communication network with maritime forces and also with maritime centers located in neighboring countries, including the Piracy Reporting Center at Kuala Lumpur. India is also the coordinator of NAVAREA VIII for broadcasting weather reports, safety messages, and other information relating to the safety of mariners at sea.

Pakistan

The Maritime Safety Agency (MSA), along with the Pakistan Navy, is responsible for maintaining order in the Pakistani waters. The MSA was established in 1987 as a paramilitary force and is responsible for protecting unauthorized exploitation of Pakistan's EEZ and enforcing national and international maritime laws in Pakistan's waters.

The MSA has limited material resources, and its force structure is largely built around some former Pakistan Navy ships that have been transferred to the MSA. MSS *Nazim* (formerly PNS *Tughril*, an old decommissioned U.S. Navy destroyer) is the frontline vessel. There are also four Offshore Patrol Vessels (OPV), two old Fast Patrol Boats (FPB), and two Britten-Norman Maritime "Defender" aircraft. The human resources are very limited and are composed of a battalion each of two/three officers and twenty men. These units are based at Gwadar and Pasni.

Pakistan also has a coast guard. The force includes in its inventory two helicopters, two hovercrafts, and more than a dozen fast patrol crafts. The primary purpose of this agency is to check smuggling along the coast, and its operations are limited to the territorial waters. Pakistan is the coordinator of NAVAREA IX.

Sri Lanka

Unlike India and Pakistan, which have paramilitary maritime forces, in Sri Lanka it is the Sri Lanka Navy (SLN) which has the responsibility of carrying out policing roles in the country's maritime areas. Besides fighting the LTTE in Sri Lanka's northeastern waters, the navy undertakes deep-sea surveillance and monitors illegal activities at sea. The SLN force structure is centered around two Offshore Patrol Vessels, a large number of fast attack craft, and a variety of aircraft. But most of the time, the SLN is engaged in countering the LTTE, which also possesses a credible naval force to challenge the SLN.

Bangladesh

The Bangladesh Coast Guard has been in existence for more than a decade now. It began its operational activities with two patrol crafts borrowed from the Bangladesh Navy. It has been tasked to safeguard Chittagong and Mongla ports that serve about 90 percent of Bangladesh's trade. The Coast Guard plays a key role in the surveillance of the seacoast of Bangladesh. It undertakes surveillance and patrolling of the EEZ by curbing illegal activities including smuggling and piracy, and by ensuring the maritime security of personnel, vessels, and installations.

Links Between Piracy and Terrorism: The Case of the LTTE

According to Brian Jenkins, an expert on terrorism and security, it is incorrect to conclude that an increase in piracy will result in an increase in the terrorist threat. He also notes that there is no indication that terrorists and pirates are operating in close cooperation. Their aims are different.[36] Similarly, Captain Mat Taib Yasin, a former Royal Malaysian Navy officer, and Senior Fellow at the Maritime Institute of Malaysia (MIMA), opines that "[the] pirate wants to enjoy his loot. The terrorist wants to destroy the enemy, get political mileage — and he's prepared to die."[37]

Analysts and strategists have been studying the phenomenon of sea piracy and terrorism, but they have different understandings of the two phenomena. There are clear distinctions in the final purpose of these activities. The terrorists seek attention for their cause, inflicting as much harm and damage as possible to achieve their political objectives, whereas the pirates simply seek economic gains.

This distinction seems to be eroding in the context of the LTTE, which has engaged in both activities. For instance, a ship with a cargo of 32,000 mortar shells from Zimbabwe Defence Industries (ZDI) left the Mozambican port of Beira on 23 May 1997, supposedly en route to Colombo, Sri Lanka. The consignment belonged to the Sri Lankan government. The ship did not reach its destination. ZDI assumed that the Sri Lankan government had sent a ship to collect the munitions, but the company alleged that the consignment was loaded onto a ship called the *Limassol,* one of the LTTE freighters.[38]

In some cases, the LTTE has not been so successful. A case in point is the ship that anchored off Cochin port in South India in 1993. The vessel was carrying a consignment of AK-47 rifles from a Russian company for the Ministry of Defence (MOD) of the Government of India.[39] The Captain had informed the port authorities of the cargo and the consignee. The MOD denied having ordered any such consignment. Enquiries revealed that a person who had visited the company's headquarters in Moscow posing as a senior official of the MOD with forged identity papers had ordered the consignment. He had the payment for the consignment made by a bank remittance from New York. Nobody claimed the consignment and it was confiscated. The Indian authorities strongly suspected LTTE had ordered the consignment, and its plans to effect a mid-sea transfer from the ship to one of its own smaller vessels had failed.

The LTTE have engaged in "wolf packs" using speed boats to carry out attacks against Sri Lankan naval vessels. The speedboats are powered by Johnson 200/Yamaha engines that are able to generate a top speed of over 35 knots and are manned by two-person Black Tiger suicide crew. Besides the 122 mm artillery shells that are stuck to the gunwale of the boat, other explosives are also carried. Another feature of these boats is that the front of the boat is fitted with spikes that fasten the boat to its target once they have collided. It is believed that these boats are armor plated and the design and construction is indigenous to the LTTE. Members of the Tamil population are by tradition expert boat builders, and the LTTE have used speedboats as suicide weapons in the past. The Sri Lankan navy has lost more than a dozen ships on account of these attacks.

Concluding Remarks

It is evident that piracy-related incidents in Asian waters are limited to petty theft and the boarding of vessels both within and outside port area. Overall, in 2004, the Indian subcontinent witnessed 32 attacks as against 87 incidents reported in 2003. Given that the piracy-related incidents in South Asia are declining in Bangladesh and Indian ports, and that no piracy-related incidents are reported in waters off Sri Lanka, Pakistan, and Maldives, this is indeed a welcome development.

However, there are no bilateral and regional agreements to offer a framework within which cooperation can be achieved among the South Asian countries. Assistance should also be made available to states that require help to update their laws and regulations in this context. The penalties and punishments must be seen as a deterrent to any attempted attacks. Acts of piracy, hijacking, and other maritime violence should be considered crimes under international law and thus demand a concerted effort at the international level with effective support from coastal states' administrators and law-enforcement agencies.

Notes

1. See "Worries Grow Over Tankers' Vulnerability to Attack" at http://www.planetark.org. According to Tatsuo Masuda, President of the Asia Pacific Energy Research Centre, the Strait of Hormuz in the Middle East and Strait of Malacca in South East Asia, are heavily used by tankers.
2. Ibid.
3. Ibid.
4. International Maritime Organization, "Piracy and Armed Robbery Against Ships, Recommendations to Governments for Combating Piracy and Armed Robbery against Ships," *Maritime Safety Committee Circular MSC/Circ 622* (London), 22 June 1993.
5. Prabhakaran Paleri, *Role of the Coast Guard in the Maritime Security of India* (New Delhi: Knowledge World, 2004), pp. 137–38.
6. ICC International Maritime Bureau, *Piracy and Armed Robbery Against Ships, Report for the Period January 1–December 31*, 2004, p. 4.
7. Ibid.
8. Prabhakaran Paleri, pp. 140–41, n. 5.
9. ICC International Maritime Bureau, p. 16, n. 6.
10. Prabhakaran Paleri, pp. 140–41, n. 2.
11. ICC International Maritime Bureau, p. 17, n. 6.
12. See website of Vantage Systems Inc, Hamilton, MT: "Facing the Black Cloud of Piracy: A Captain's Point of View," p. 9.
13. ICC International Maritime Bureau, *Piracy and Armed Robbery Against Ships, Report for the Period January 1–December 31*, 1998, p. 13.
14. Ibid.
15. "Police Find 15 Dead Men on Bangladesh Fishing Boat," *Agencies*, 28 October 2004.
16. "India, Bangladesh Discuss the Possibility of Joint Naval Exercises," *Press Trust of India*, 12 Oct 2004. The issue came up for discussion when Bangladesh Navy Chief Shah Iqbal Mujtaba called on Admiral Arun Prakash. This was the first visit by a Bangladesh Chief of Naval Staff since 1998. Admiral Prakash stressed the need for more frequent navy-to-navy

interaction to build mutual confidence and trust, while Admiral Mujtaba appreciated the support being given by the Indian Navy to train Bangladesh naval personnel in India.

17. Rohan Gunaratna, "The Asymmetric Threat From Maritime Terrorism," *Jane's Navy International*, 1 October 2001.
18. Reference Number: 1999-54, 1999. Anti-Shipping Activity Messages (ASAM) available at http://www.fas.org/irp/world/para/docs/ASAM-1999.htm
19. Xinhua (Beijing), "Report on Ship attack in Sri Lanka," FBIS, 11 September 1997.
20. Rohan Gunaratna, "Trends in Maritime Terrorism — The Sri Lanka Case," *Lanka Outlook*, Autumn 98, p. 13.
21. Captain R. Sawhney and Commander N.A. Mohan, "Role of Indian Navy in Combating Piracy," Paper presented at the *IMO Seminar and Workshop on Piracy and Armed Robbery Against Ships* (Mumbai, India: 22–24 March 2000).
22. For more details see http://www.sai.uni-heidelberg.de/workgroups/bdlaw/1994-a26.htm.
23. Cited in Prabhakaran Paleri, pp. 137–40, n. 5.
24. Ibid.
25. Vijay Sakhuja, "Maritime Order and Piracy," *Strategic Analyses*, vol. 24, no. 1, August 2000.
26. Ibid.
27. Commodore RS Vasan, "Alondra Rainbow Revisited. A Study of Related Issues in the Light of the Recent Judgment of Mumbai High Court," *Paper No. 1379*, available at www.saag.org/papers1379.html.
28. Ibid.
29. Ibid.
30. Ibid.
31. Vivian Louis Forbes and Vijay Sakhuja, "Challenging Acts of Marine Trans-Boundary Transgressions in the Indian Ocean," *MIMA Issue Paper*, vol. 1/2004, Maritime Institute of Malaysia, p. 9.
32. Ibid.
33. See "PM Calls For Institutionalisation of Co-operation Between Navies" at the website of *Rediff* at http://rediff.com/news/2001/feb/18fleet.htm.
34. Ibid.
35. Vijay Sakhuja, "Malabar to Malacca: Indo-US Naval Cooperation," *Indian Defence Review*, New Delhi, August 2002.
36. Ioannis Gatsiounis, "Malacca Strait: Target for Terror," *Asia Times*, 11 August 2004. http://www.atimes.com/atimes/Southeast_Asia/FH11Ae02.html.
37. Ibid.
38. Peter Chalk "The Tamil Tiger Insurgency in Sri Lanka," in Abdul Musa (ed.), *Over a Barrel: Light Weapons and Human Rights in the Commonwealth* (New Delhi: Commonwealth Human Rights Initiative, 1999) available at http://www.nisat.org/publications/armsfixers/Chapter6.html.
39. B. Raman, "Maritime Terrorism: An Indian Perspective," *Paper no.1154*, 10 October 2004; available at http://www.saag.org/papers12/paper1154.html.

3
Piracy in Maritime Asia: Current Trends

GRAHAM GERARD ONG-WEBB

Introduction

As a study couched in the field of security and criminology, this chapter makes two arguments, stemming from an epistemological and methodological problematic. Part of the problematic relates to the tendency to mistake certain enduring features of "historical" piracy (until the end of the nineteenth century) and "modern" piracy (roughly within the twentieth century but more specifically after the end of the World War II) for a set of overarching trends joining the historical past and the contemporary present. The argument is that while modern piracy and its historical precedent are phenomena driven by certain enduring factors and drivers, modern piracy possesses a set of distinctions important enough for security and criminological analyses to jettison any undue reference to the past. In other words, the continuities between "piracy" of the past and contemporary or "modern piracy" should not be overstated. In fact, for the security analyst and criminologist, the search for cultural and historical links is not entirely helpful for current security analyses and can even be detractive. The work of historians on piracy as it had existed through the ages preceding the twentieth century has been able to delve beneath what Ger Teitler calls its "public appearance" — the opposite, which would be the "private" or opaque aspects of pirates — including:

> [F]acts about their organisations, international ramifications, culture, management style, financial style, financial support structure, patterns of expenditure, forms of recruitment and relations to receivers and officials in legal, police or harbour circles.[1]

However, to use Carolin Liss's argument, the "structurally different role[s]" of "historical" and modern piracy mean that much of what we know about the former in phenomenal terms will not apply to current research efforts on the latter.[2] In clearing the ground for making the case about current trends in maritime Asia, this chapter justifies the case for structural difference while teasing out the aforementioned factors and drivers that are relevant to any current analysis of modern piracy in maritime Asia (and perhaps elsewhere).

The second part of the problematic relates to the stunted, repetitive, and superficial research program that has come to plague "piracy studies" or any analyses of piracy within the various subfields of the social sciences, in terms of qualitative and quantitative material as well as research methodology. Even the exercise in rudimentary statistics on reported piracy attacks and the lack of a more powerful synthesis of collected data continues to be problematic. While it is not the scope of this chapter to solve these problems, it hopes to shed some light on the path in that direction with Liss's notion of structural difference as a starting point and by taking seriously Teitler's call for the unmasking of the opacity of modern piracy. Considering the outstanding lack of information described by Teitler, we must continue to clarify the public appearance of modern piracy with greater rigor as we endeavor toward a better understanding. This would include facts about pirates' behavior and evolution, including scale, modus operandi, choice of prey, types of violence employed, and the means of application. Inferences that shed light on the operational strengths and weaknesses of maritime piracy may allow criminologists and security analysts to make more effective and prudent policies and strategies despite incomplete information and finite resources.

This chapter uses an underlying framework that is both qualitative and quantitative in nature. Drawing upon the prevailing qualitative scholarship, the phenomenon that is modern piracy in maritime Asia can be epistemologically "divided" into three overlapping subperiods: "early modern" piracy, from the 1970s until 1991 (or the end of the Cold War); "late modern" piracy, from 1991 until between 2000 to 2001; and — inspired by Warren's reference to the rise of "space-age" piracy since the 1970s — "postmodern" piracy from 2000/2001 to the present. With regard to the "postmodern" era, the chapter clarifies that while piracy in Indonesian waters and the Malacca Straits has become a growing risk to regional and international trade — by increasing the chances of an inter-ship collision along the traffic congested waterway brought about by disrupting the navigation and safety of the host vessel when the latter is violently boarded and/or hijacked — the phenomenon as such has undergone two "waves" of securitization that have removed the foundational notions of traditional piracy. The first wave in the 1990s was initiated by certain states such as Japan which sought to politicize piracy as a policy and security problem. The second wave at the turn of the twentieth century was mostly initiated by Singapore, following the embellishment by analysts and pundits of the supposed analogy between maritime terrorism and piracy since the terrorist attacks of 11 September 2001 in the United States and the consequent focus upon global terrorism by militant Islamic groups such as Al Qaeda and in Southeast Asia, the Indonesian-based *Jemaah Islamiyah*.

In terms of the quantitative literature, this chapter uses the statistical data on piracy attacks worldwide from the International Chamber of Commerce's International Maritime Bureau (IMB) from 1981 until the middle of 2005 (that is, at the time of writing), with the intention of further clarifying the trends within and across "early modern," "late modern," and "postmodern" piracy, the chapter performs a simple "ground-clearing" exercise:

1. Aggregating and disaggregating the data sets for "maritime Asia" where possible
2. Creating graphical trend-lines by "joining the dots" between the figures covering the various aspects of piracy incidents so as to extract greater descriptive value from the raw statistics

The aim here is to provide a visual illustration to qualify (or disqualify) current "metanarratives" of piracy in maritime Asia since the 1970s, and in particular, from the 1980s and 1990s when statistical data such as the IMB's were made available. Although references will be made to certain cases regarded as significant or "serious incidents" in the IMB reports, this chapter moves away from standard analyses that focus on detailed narratives of reported piracy attacks in terms of individual cases — a task which is excellently accomplished in the IMB reports and by individual scholars such as Liss and Peter Chalk, as well as the dual authorship of William M. Carpenter and David G. Wiencek, and Jason Abbot and Neil Renwick.[3]

Caveat and Limitations of Analysis

As a caveat, it is acknowledged that, as with any set of statistics, the accuracy and representation of the IMB data sets are not free from debate and criticism. Ultimately, the IMB's reports provide the only consistent (and hence reliable) set of figures to date that allow us to make some sense of the current piracy attacks and, following Teitler's advice, "to get these phenomena more sharply into focus, in this way enabling researchers and policy makers to ask new, relevant questions."[4] Critics are mainly concerned that the IMB figures tend to be inflated in their numbers. For example, the littoral states straddling the Straits of Malacca are known to be uncomfortable with the IMB's radical point of departure from the "two-ship requirement" in the commonly accepted definition found in the 1982 United Nations (UN) Convention on the Law of the Sea (UNCLOS II). For the bureau, piracy is:

> An act of boarding or attempting to board any ship with the intent to commit theft or any other crime and with the intent or capability to use force in the furtherance of that act.[5]

This means that attacks from a raft or even a quay are counted as acts of piracy. However, the negation of the "two-ship requirement" is defensible — and the IMB definition by extension — if one accepts the most fundamental description of piracy by I. R. Hyslop in his opening chapter in Eric Ellen's edited volume *Piracy at Sea* (1989), which reflects the unchanging threat perception of ship owners on the ground: "[p]iracy is basically *aggravated* theft."[6] Inferentially, this is regardless of *how* pirates board a ship. Next, it can be assumed that for purposes of basic analysis, the inherent problem of underreporting by ship owners — the bureau estimates that 40 to 60 percent of all attacks go unreported — creates the side effect of minimizing this distortive tendency, *at least at the level of descriptive statistics.*[7]

To be sure, further study and advanced statistical methods — such as regression analyses which can tell us to what extent an independent variable such as the use of knives and small arms can explain the rise in the use of violence against seafarers — are needed to concretely verify the underlying causes that can explain the rise and fall of phenomena as well as the turn toward increasing violence. Such analyses have been avoided in this chapter after preliminary attempts at applying regression analysis — such as the relationship between arms and general violence (which is the total of the IMB's separate categories of violence: total individuals being taken hostage, threatened, assaulted, injured and killed) — generated errant results and significant statistical distortions. Certainly, a "better fit" in regression analyses could be obtained by disaggregating the independent variable for use of arms and the dependent variable for violence against crew and testing specific cases in which guns were used against cases in which both the exercise of a certain type of violence occurred (such as assaults) and guns were present. However, this endeavor would involve studying each and every incident such as those found in the narration of attacks in the annual IMB reports, which exceeds the scope of the preliminary research in this chapter.

Notwithstanding the need to define, qualify, and disaggregate variables more rigorously, the problems with carrying out deeper statistical probes into piracy indicate that the very same factor of underreporting which assists basic analyses may be hampering more advanced statistically based studies. It is highly possible that the approach toward reporting by victims of piracy attacks and their ship owners is plagued by several challenges. First, reporting could be a selective exercise, which can include omissions of certain types of information ship owners fear may affect subsequent security policies and ship countermeasures that may not be in their perceived interest. For example, the reporting of arms in attacks may strengthen the view in some quarters that crews should arm themselves with guns and rifles against pirates, which some seafarers believe only serves to encourage the pirates to use force on top of placing the crew in additional jeopardy by way of shoot-outs or misfiring accidents that can accompany an untrained hand. Second, victims of pirate attacks themselves may not possess complete information about an attack since their observations are often accrued under duress and under the cover of night, hence preventing them from making detailed descriptions such as whether their perpetrators were armed. From 2002 onward, the IMB reports dropped the category for unarmed attacks, which could be a possible reflection of this problem. However, at the same time, the reports are willing to indicate if acts of violence are being exercised against a ship's crew.

The trends in Figure 3.1 may be explained by such challenges that, in statistical terms, may distort more sophisticated analyses. Even though there are strong analogues between the trend in the total number of reported attacks from 1991 to 2004 and the trend in the reported use of arms during the same period, at both the worldwide level and the level of maritime Asia — which is qualified in the next section as a maritime region encompassing Southeast Asia, South Asia, and Northeast Asia — the period of 1996 to 2004 saw the trend in which the presence of arms that could not be verified ("Not Stated") both worldwide and in maritime Asia was becoming too significant to ignore. In the peak years of 2000 and 2003 for reported attacks worldwide, the cases of the use of arms not being stated worldwide comprised 51.8 percent and 37.8 percent respectively. For maritime Asia, the cases of the use of arms not being reported — where the data for cases of arms not being stated in reported attacks only become available from 1997 — was 31.8 percent (in 2000) and 29.1 percent (in 2003) of all reported attacks in the region. Next, the trends also indicate that the number of reported cases of pirates being unarmed in their attacks worldwide has decreased considerably — from 55.1 percent (59 out of 102 cases) in 1991 to 0.9 percent (3 out of 335 cases) in 2001 — while the number of cases in which the presence of arms could not be verified increased from 1.86 percent (2 out of 107 cases) in 1991 to 35.2 percent (118 out of 335 cases); approximately an inversely proportional relationship. On the surface, these trends indicate that victims are increasingly unable to tell us whether pirates are armed or not. However, the trends for violence against crew compels any analysis to infer that force is being applied in order to enact such aggression as indicated in Figure 3.6 later in the chapter. Ultimately, current and future endeavors in the statistical collection of the scale and nature of piracy attacks — through the help of commercial shipping companies and their vessels' crew — must find a way to overcome the obstacles that sustain the problem of incomplete information. In the end, the attempts in this chapter to explicate a set of trends and possible relationships between factors constituting piracy in maritime Asia are not intended to translate into tested assertions about causality.

Defining Maritime Asia

This section conceptualizes the notion of a "maritime Asia" in terms of a geographical subregion of Asia which is distinct from continental Asia and which is in turn a set of smaller (and overlapping) "subregions." These subregions

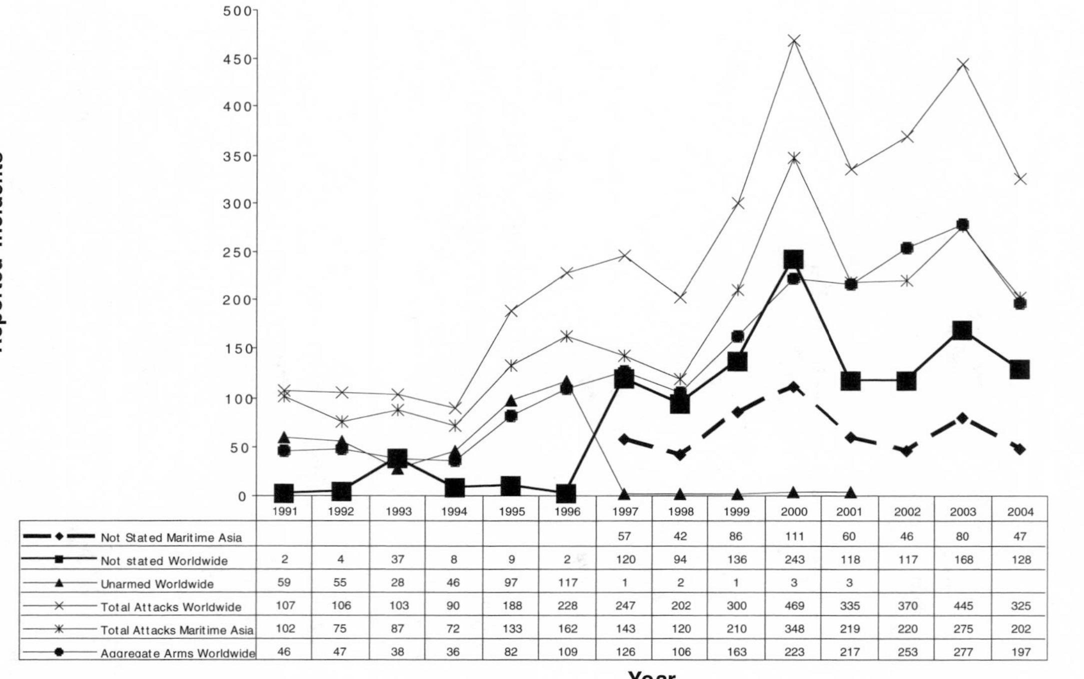

	1991	1992	1993	1994	1995	1996	1997	1998	1999	2000	2001	2002	2003	2004
Not Stated Maritime Asia							57	42	86	111	60	46	80	47
Not stated Worldwide	2	4	37	8	9	2	120	94	136	243	118	117	168	128
Unarmed Worldwide	59	55	28	46	97	117	1	2	1	3	3			
Total Attacks Worldwide	107	106	103	90	188	228	247	202	300	469	335	370	445	325
Total Attacks Maritime Asia	102	75	87	72	133	162	143	120	210	348	219	220	275	202
Aggregate Arms Worldwide	46	47	38	36	82	109	126	106	163	223	217	253	277	197

Figure 3.1 Comparison of (1) cases of arms "not stated" in maritime asia and worldwide, (2) unarmed attacks worldwide against (a) total reported attacks worldwide, and (b) total cases of arms used worldwide, 1991–2004

Source: Note that the figures for reported cases of unarmed attacks and cases in which arms are not stated in maritime Asia appear in the IMB reports only from 1997. However, the cases of unarmed reports in the region are omitted from table and graph in Figure 3.1 as the figures are either dismal or null. Data compiled from various issues of *Piracy and Armed Robbery against Ships: Annual Report,* (Kuala Lumpur: IMB Regional Piracy Centre), from 1997 onwards.

1. Physically conjoin with the sea through coastlines and/or connecting rivers and estuaries
2. Have a historical, sociocultural, and economic relationship with the sea
3. Perceive themselves as either coastal or maritime states whose security and survival depends upon the maritime realm

By virtue of employing the statistical data on reported incidents of piracy by the IMB, this concept of maritime Asia grafts itself closely to the configuration which the bureau has used to carve up the region — "Southeast Asia," the "South Asian subcontinent," and the "Far East" — with several alterations which align the final geographical makeup closer to the way it is conventionally understood. Thus, the IMB's Southeast Asia, while including the waters of Malaysia, Indonesia, Singapore, the Philippines, Thailand, and even the Malacca Straits as a distinct water body, is now expanded to include Vietnam (which the bureau originally categorizes under the "Far East"), which also faces a significant number of piracy attacks annually. The rationale for including Vietnam stems from the defensible claim that "Southeast Asia's maritime realm, the seaward-looking realm, includes the southern part of the Malay[sian] Peninsula and the southeastern coast of Vietnam."

Next, the "South Asian subcontinent" is renamed simply as South Asia, and while including the waters of India, Bangladesh, and Sri Lanka, excludes the IMB's choice of Iran. While it is a Central Asian state, Iran does not tend to figure in the geographical and historical imagination of maritime Asia today. Likewise, the peculiar term "Far East" is renamed as Northeast Asia while keeping to the original inclusion of the Chinese, Japanese, and South Korean waters and the oceanic subregion that is the South China Sea.

Breaking with the Past: The Rise of Modern Piracy in "Maritime Asia"

As common wisdom would have it, maritime piracy is probably the world's third oldest profession among careers of questionable moral standing, since for as long as maritime commerce has existed, this phenomenon has existed with it. Indeed, records of "piracy" have been found even among the Phoenicians and Greeks. "Piracy" in "maritime Asia" dates back to as early as the fourteenth century when Chinese, Japanese, and Malayan "pirates" were recorded to have operated throughout the Indian Ocean, the South China Sea, and waters adjacent to them. "In more common parlance, that translates to mean that the very first time something valuable was known to be leaving a beach on a raft the first pirate was around to steal it," and it is one that further reinforces Hyslop's notion of aggravated theft. This rudimentary description of "piracy," stripped of the conceptual and legal trappings found in UNCLOS II, indicates that the *nature* of the phenomenon has changed little over time.

At the deeper level of heuristics, this means that between the two categories of historical process models — linear and cyclical — which can help "educate our thinking about where [piracy] come[s] from and where [it] might be going," the phenomenon of piracy appears to strongly reflect the latter at first glance.[8] With regard to linearity, some scholars have argued that social relations have been historically evolving in manners such that successive epochs are qualitatively different. That is, history does not repeat itself; it is directional and even possibly teleological. On the other hand, a cyclical process model would assert that the conditions, modes, and outcomes in the relations between people have been historically recurrent. As Donald J. Puchala notes:

> Human experiences do repeat themselves: actors, ideas, and technologies change from epoch to epoch, but patterns and phases of ... cultural interaction relentlessly repeat.[9]

In other words, while there are certain features in modern piracy that have not changed over time, there are new characteristics, which cannot use the past as reference. Adam J. Young's article "Roots of Contemporary Maritime Piracy in Southeast Asia" attempts to articulate the continuities and discontinuities between historical and modern piracy in the subregion, which can mostly be applied to the discussion of maritime Asia (see Table 3.1).[10]

Table 3.1 Piracy past and present — discontinuities and continuities

Discontinuities

1. A distinct definitional and conceptual separation between conditional legitimacy in the past, and complete illegitimacy in the present, has radically changed the nature of piracy.
2. There has been real material, political, social, and cultural change between the nineteenth century and today, which makes the phenomenon called "piracy" in some ways very different.
3. Rigidly defined, static territorial borders have been established through the imposition of Western, Westphalian geopolitical consciousness in maritime Southeast Asia.

Continuities

1. "Piracy" is a complex, diverse phenomenon, lacking contextualization within Southeast Asia, making definition difficult, and therefore problematizing the addressing of the issue.
2. Despite changes, there is a continuous presence of a maritime oriented social-cultural matrix, largely characterized by a marginal socioeconomic existence, where piracy is thinkable.
3. State "control" of "pirates" has relied on providing economic opportunity, and engendering a sense of loyalty to the state; and a state's failure to provide this leaves sea folk to fend for themselves, or seek patronage from alternative sources.

4. Patronage is important for any large-scale organization of piracy.
5. There is a persistence of patron-client relationships.
6. Weak political development is relative to economic expansion.
7. Piracy emerges during times of weak political control, when the state's political hegemony is challenged.
8. The complex physical and cultural geography limits the ability of the state to maintain rigid boundaries. This was a particular concern for colonial states imposing their geopolitical consciousness on the region, and is problematic for the independent successors of those colonial states.
9. Regional and international cooperation is problematic due to competition for resources, and questions of sovereignty and territorial integrity.
10. A rough technological balance, inclusive of "tools" and "knowledge," is to the advantage of "pirates." When the state had a dramatic technological edge, virtually monopolizing access and use of technology vis-à-vis "pirates," such activities were largely brought under control.
11. Piracy is endemic to the maritime world of Southeast Asia, and will always exist in some form.
12. It is highly adaptive, finding weak spots in state control.

However, it is clear that the discontinuous and continuous features that Young has identified only relate to the repeating "patterns and phases of ... cultural interaction" and tell us nothing about the "actors, ideas, and technologies" that have entered and exited the historical stage. The same could be said of James F. Warren's "A Tale of Two Centuries: The Globalisation of Maritime Raiding and Piracy in Southeast Asia at the end of the Eighteenth and Twentieth Centuries" (2000), which posits the role of China in the regional economic network. Operating on a cyclical heuristic, it argues that there is a repeating narrative in the rise of Iranun maritime raiding from 1768 to 1800 and the rise of regional piracy and sea armed robbery again between 1968 to 2000; the "interconnective relationship" being between the ascendancy of "piracy" on a regional scale and the development of an economic boom in Southeast Asia in both periods. The intervening variable would be the "China connection" — the "initial opening of China to the [W]est" (via the colonial powers in the region at the time) in the first instance and "China's recent momentous economic transition" in the second instance.[11]

Indeed, while scholars have been able to describe the lives and actions of well-known "pirates" of Southeast Asia — such as the ferocious Iranun[12] of the late eighteenth to the nineteenth centuries — or tally historical similarities and differences in piracy since antiquity, the enduring factors (which also serve as lessons for security analysts) to be gleaned from these narratives boil down to mainly four and explain why piracy is historically endemic to maritime Southeast Asia and maritime Asia at large:

- *Economics.* Piracy is to a significant degree the action of social groups marginalized as a result of economic and political developments in the region. It is a product of economic competition driven by survival.
- *Sociology.* Piracy is often rooted in a society's tradition and experiences. There must exist a large group of maritime oriented and skilled sea folk for piracy to be "thinkable" as an alternative livelihood.
- *Politics.* The scale of piracy is inversely related to the political will and capability of states to control, secure, protect, and enforce laws over their sovereign territories, waters, and borders against perceived threats, either individually or collectively.
- *Geography.* The inherent "curse of geography" of a maritime Asia comprising states with (1) broad coastlines (Bangladesh, China, India, Indonesia, Japan, Malaysia, and Thailand), (2) an archipelagic makeup (Indonesia, Japan, and the Philippines), (3) punctuated with numerous islands and coves (Malaysia and Indonesia), (4) under the cover of dense tropical (and temperate) vegetation — these factors work in the favor of pirates (and other transnational criminal activities such as drug, people, and arms smuggling as well as illegal fishing) and against states. This curse is starkest at maritime Asia's geographical jugular called the Malacca Straits — an extremely long and narrow waterway that sees the congruence of *all* four geographical descriptions.[13]

Lastly, following Warren, Liss et al., globalization in all its manifestations — economic, sociocultural, political, and technological — serves as a significant driver cutting across some or all the above factors over time.[14]

However, as established in the beginning of this chapter, there exists a linear heuristic undercutting its cyclical counterpart. For Liss, what has come to distinguish "piracy" of the past and the present is the "structurally different role" that the phenomenon has played in "global and local interactions" over time. Citing Warren, Liss notes that what the European colonizers had labeled as "pirates" in Southeast Asia were actually maritime raiders whose activities — such as the capturing of people for the slave trade — helped to sustain and strengthen chiefdoms and sultanates relative to the growing and competing colonial powers that began to establish a significant regional presence since the end of the eighteenth century until the outbreak of World War II in 1943. The label "pirate" was assigned by these foreign powers so as to render illegitimate what was generally accepted as legitimate activity by the indigenous societies in the same way that Europe during the sixteenth and seventeenth centuries gave such activities — called privateering — official sanction due to the hiring of pirate vessels by European states for hostile purposes. While William MacFee would argue that the difference between maritime raiders, privateers, and pirates has really always been an academic one, Liss is correct to add a structural quality to the distinction. This is because the change in labels had both the effect of changing and reflecting the discourse and perception of piracy.

For Europe, the most decisive change in the discourse on piracy occurred when privateering was outlawed on the high seas through the Declaration of Paris in 1856. Internationally, piracy as aggravated theft for whatever purpose was deemed illegitimate. Thus, piracy became contemporary or "early modern" to the European consciousness after the second half of the nineteenth century as soon as it was explicitly "criminalized" through the Paris Declaration; hence internationalizing piracy as a criminal activity within an international system that comprised mainly the Western world at the time.[15] Subsequently, through the 1932 Harvard Research Draft, the 1958 Geneva Convention on the High Seas, and finally, the 1982 UNCLOS II (which only came into full force in 1994 after complete ratification), the "criminalization" of piracy became complete by the late twentieth century within an international system that encompassed the entire globe, including the non-Western world in the post–World War II era. Overall, two waves of criminalization could be said to have occurred within the late nineteenth century and the twentieth century; the first wave in a largely European international system through the Paris Declaration and the second wave from 1932 to 1994, which encompassed the postwar international system whose domain (including its body of international law) was almost global in reach.

"Early Modern" Piracy in Maritime Asia, 1970s to 1991

Hence, as compared to Europe, the "early modern" period of piracy in maritime Asia could be said to have occurred about a century within the period when the criminalization of the phenomenon was undergoing its second wave. The mid-twentieth century marked an era when Asian societies and polities transformed themselves into independent and sovereign states of the Westphalian mould after the end of World War II — especially during the period of massive decolonization in the region during the 1960s and 1970s. Firstly, statehood ushered in the implementation of national laws (largely modeled upon those of its European counterparts) that enforced the criminalization of theft and violence within a country's territory (land and sea), thus forging a new discourse on piracy in the region which Europe embraced since 1856. Statehood also significantly ended the economic disruption of World War II by embellishing Asia's participation in the world economy. Consequently, both the trappings and tribulations of economic participation have exacerbated the rise of modern piracy in maritime Asia from the 1960s to the present. The trappings: economic growth, the rise of ports and commercial maritime traffic. The tribulations: simultaneously, (1) the widening gap between the haves and have-nots — the result of the fragmentary effects of economic globalization — reinforcing the conditions that compel marginalized maritime-oriented communities and sea folk to turn to piracy, and (2) the same rises in commercial maritime traffic since the 1970s (due to the containerization of global maritime commerce) making piracy an even more lucrative trade. Most importantly, notwithstanding the lack of available research on piracy in maritime Asia during the period after World War II until at least the end of the 1970s — which may change current assertions about the phenomenal rise of modern piracy in the region — t he available literature (such as the work of Warren and Liss for example) regarding its general magnitude suggests the 1970s as the genesis of its modernity in phenomenal terms. To be sure, Liss's work does tell us that the attacks of the 1970s (and even the 1980s, as is discussed below) …

> were often still small-scale and rarely involved physical injuries to those who were attacked — except for attacks on Vietnamese boat people in the Gulf of Thailand, which often featured violence and cruelty.[16]

However, by the early 1980s, the rising perception was that "armed attacks on merchant vessels had increased to the extent that concern was being expressed both by shipping interests and by governments," with the Malacca Straits in Southeast Asia as the "world's 'growth point'."[17]

According to the IMB, from 1981 to 1987 the Straits saw 245 "confirmed" reported attacks — a label which the IMB then used to refer to "real," piratical attacks, which have a recognized element of potential violence — out of a worldwide total of 733 such reports; a proportion of 33 percent. To be sure, as can be seen in the *linear* trend lines in Figure 3.2, the number of both "total" attacks, which includes confirmed attacks and "attacks … about which either few details are known, or perpetrators of which are unobserved by their victims," actually decreased in absolute terms over this seven-year period. However, both the raw and linear trend lines reflect a convergence between the total and confirmed reported attacks, which in turn indicates that the level of violence (both the threat to use violence and the actual application of force) had gone up during this period.

In terms of their *modus operandi*, most pirate attacks in the Straits during the 1980s were equated with "petty thefts and housebreakings," and their perceived lack of both organization and sophistication reflected motivations that were impulsive and ad hoc in nature when compared to the "large gang" operations on container cargoes by West African pirates during the same time. The IMB also reported that most attacks used the cover of night to conduct their attacks through fast and small boats, two trends that would become patent features of future attacks. However, the pirates of this decade tended to operate in small groups of two to five individuals, a trend that would change

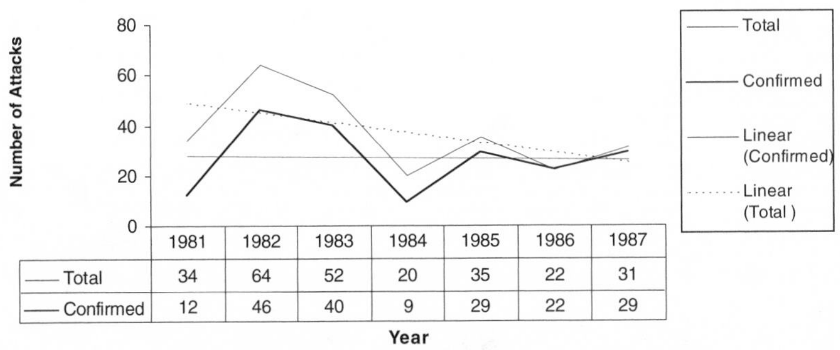

	1981	1982	1983	1984	1985	1986	1987
Total	34	64	52	20	35	22	31
Confirmed	12	46	40	9	29	22	29

Figure 3.2 "Total" and "confirmed" piracy attacks in the Malacca Straits, 1981–1987
Source: The line graph is reproduced from the IMB original which was not accompanied by a separate description of the figures that were used to construct the latter (except for the figures of confirmed attacks in 1982, 1983 and 1987 which were 64, 52 and 29 respectively). However, such figures could be gleaned from a close reading of the "IMB Chronology of Pirate Attacks on Merchant Vessels, 1981–1987" which provides a worded description of the 733 reported pirate attacks worldwide during that period. For the original graph created by the IMB see "The Malacca Straits Area" in Appendix 2, "Analysis of the IMB Chronology," in Eric Ellen ed., *Piracy at Sea* (Paris: ICC Publishing, 1989), p. 275. For the figures provided for 1982, 1983 and 1987 see ibid., p. 12. The "IMB Chronology of Pirate Attacks on Merchant Vessels, 1981–1987" can be found in Appendix 1 in ibid. pp. 241–271.

during the period of "late modern" piracy — the 1990s right through the opening of the twenty-first century — when attacks would be conducted by larger pirate crews.

"Late Modern" Piracy in Maritime Asia, 1991 - 2004

Maritime Asia

One of the chief hallmarks constituting the rise of "late modern" piracy in maritime Asia since the 1990s would revolve around the issues of *scale*. First, there has been a large rise in the number of attacks, especially after 1991 (see Figure 3.3). The trends in worldwide figures are largely driven by the trends in maritime Asia, which form close and strong analogues in their rise and fall and generate a proportional mean of 67.3 percent (from 2,368 cases in maritime Asia against 3,515 cases worldwide). Interestingly, the median year for reported attacks in maritime Asia against the worldwide figures is 2003 with 348 attacks. However, as the absolute figures rose over the years toward the median, the proportion dropped considerably (though inconsistently) with 2004 reflecting a proportion of 62.2 percent as compared to 1991 with 95.3 percent. In turn, the trends in maritime Asia are driven most by the trends in Southeast Asia (a proportional mean of 69.8 percent from 1,655 cases in Southeast Asia against maritime Asia's 2,368 cases) with South Asia as the secondary driver (a proportional mean of 19.9 percent from 472 cases in South Asia against maritime Asia's 2,368 cases). Except for the years between 1993 to 1995 in which the trend in Northeast Asia either exceeded

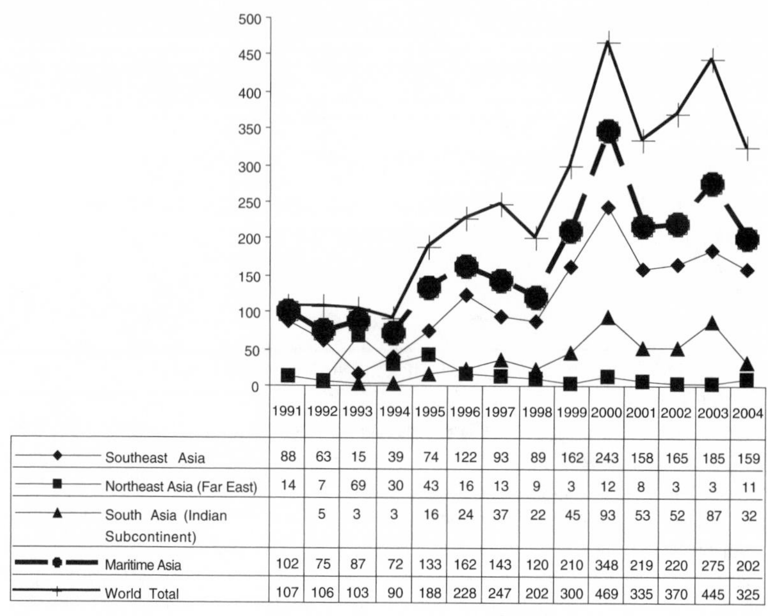

	1991	1992	1993	1994	1995	1996	1997	1998	1999	2000	2001	2002	2003	2004
Southeast Asia	88	63	15	39	74	122	93	89	162	243	158	165	185	159
Northeast Asia (Far East)	14	7	69	30	43	16	13	9	3	12	8	3	3	11
South Asia (Indian Subcontinent)		5	3	3	16	24	37	22	45	93	53	52	87	32
Maritime Asia	102	75	87	72	133	162	143	120	210	348	219	220	275	202
World Total	107	106	103	90	188	228	247	202	300	469	335	370	445	325

Figure 3.3 Total number of reported incidents of piracy/armed robbery at sea among the subregions of maritime Asia, 1991–2004
Source: For total number of attacks for each sub-region reported from 1991 to 2002, which includes all actual and attempted and reported cases, see *Piracy and Armed Robbery against Ships: Annual Report, 1st January – 30th December 2002* (Kuala Lumpur: IMB Regional Piracy Centre, 30 January 2003), p.5, Table 1. For the tabulation of the years between 2003 to 2004, see *Piracy and Armed Robbery against Ships: Annual Report, 1st January – 30th December 2004* (Kuala Lumpur: IMB Regional Piracy Centre, 7 February 2005), p. 4, Table 1.

or converged with Southeast and South Asia, the trend for the former subregion leveled down toward the magnitudes found in 1991 and 1992, forming a relatively weak trend from 1996 to 2004, hence feeding little into the trends in scale for the entire region. Overall, the proportional mean for Northeast Asia from 1991 to 2004 was 10.2 percent (241 cases out of maritime Asia's total). Thus, in terms of general scale, piracy in maritime Asia is largely a Southeast Asian phenomenon.

The assertion about the dominance of Southeast Asia holds equally true for the reported cases of both actual attacks reported in maritime Asia and the world (Figure 3.4) and attempted attacks reported in these two geographical categories (Figure 3.5) from 1997 to 2004. However, while the descending order of magnitude for South Asia and Northeast Asia for overall reported attacks also finds itself in the trends for reported actual attacks during the same period, both subregions roughly match each other for reported attempted attacks in addition to the fact that they contribute little to maritime Asia's tally

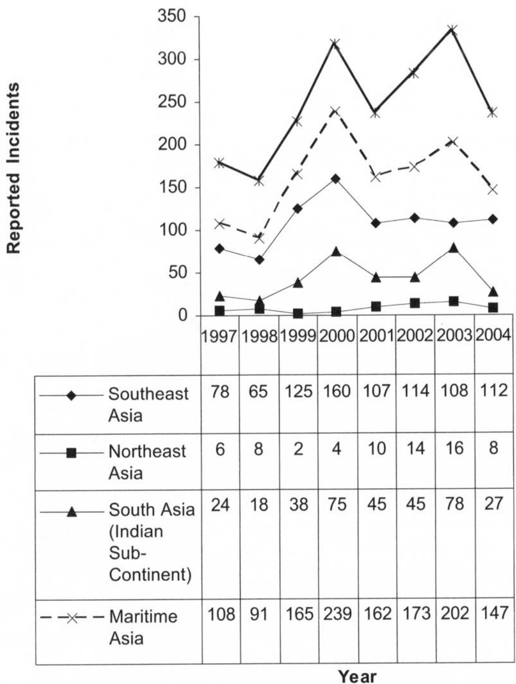

	1997	1998	1999	2000	2001	2002	2003	2004
Southeast Asia	78	65	125	160	107	114	108	112
Northeast Asia	6	8	2	4	10	14	16	8
South Asia (Indian Sub-Continent)	24	18	38	75	45	45	78	27
Maritime Asia	108	91	165	239	162	173	202	147

Figure 3.4 Number of reported incidents of actual piracy/armed robbery at sea among the subregions of maritime Asia, 1997–2004
Source: Data compiled from various issues of Piracy and Armed Robbery against Ships: Annual Report (Kuala Lumpur: IMB Regional Piracy Centre) from 1997 onwards.

for attempted attacks. Thus, this roughly means that Southeast Asia's pirates are more adept at succeeding at an attack within the region of maritime Asia (indeed the world) than their South Asian and Northeast Asian counterparts. There are two possible assumptions to account for this trend. First, pirates in Southeast Asia may be more highly skilled in their trade than their South Asian and Northeast Asian brethren. Second, assuming an equal level of skill among the pirates in the three subregions, the sheer volume of general attacks in Southeast Asia naturally increases the chances for success. The subsequent sections on Southeast Asia, South Asia, and Northeast Asia make further disaggregated comparisons of trends between actual and attempted attacks in these subregions to investigate the issues of success and skill.

Next, there has been a general rise in the use of small arms, automatic weapons, and other paraphernalia in carrying out a pirate attack in maritime Asia, which accounted for a proportional mean of 64.2 percent of such cases worldwide from 1997 to 2004 (1,002 cases out of a total of 1,562) as shown in Figure 3.6. The median year of this eight-year period would be 2002 with 201

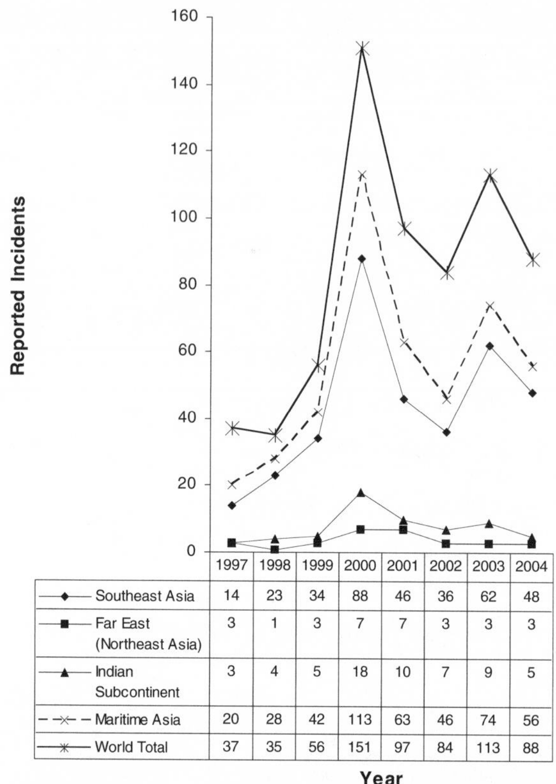

	1997	1998	1999	2000	2001	2002	2003	2004
Southeast Asia	14	23	34	88	46	36	62	48
Far East (Northeast Asia)	3	1	3	7	7	3	3	3
Indian Subcontinent	3	4	5	18	10	7	9	5
Maritime Asia	20	28	42	113	63	46	74	56
World Total	37	35	56	151	97	84	113	88

Figure 3.5 Reported incidents of attempted piracy/armed robbery at sea among the subregions of maritime Asia, 1997–2004
Source: Data compiled from various issues of Piracy and Armed Robbery against Ships: Annual Report (Kuala Lumpur: IMB Regional Piracy Centre) from 1997 onwards.

cases. As with the comparative trends between maritime Asia and the world, the trend in the use of arms in maritime Asia from 1997 to 2004 is largely driven by the trend in Southeast Asia, which generates a mean of 74.9 percent (751 out of maritime Asia's 1,002 such cases) — and to a lesser degree, South Asia with a mean of 21.7 percent (217 cases) during the same eight-year period. Conversely, reported cases of Northeast Asian piracy have been accompanied less by reports on the use of arms from 1999 to 2004, which deviate from their previous parity with South Asian cases in 1997 and 1998. From the 1997 to 2004, the mean for the cases in Northeast Asia against maritime Asia was 3.39 percent (34 cases). Further disaggregations are carried out for the type of arms used within each subregion in the subsequent sections.

As Figure 3.7 shows, in the years between 1997 and 2004, violence in maritime Asia accounted for a range of 61.9 percent (398 out of 643 individuals) to 72.4 percent (289 out of 399 individuals in 2004) of world figures with a mean

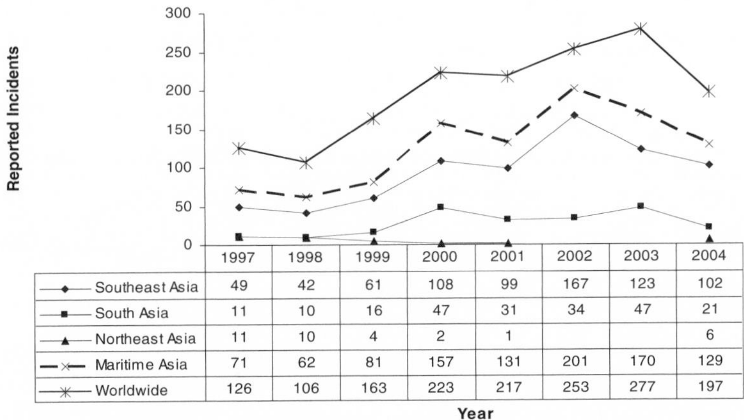

	1997	1998	1999	2000	2001	2002	2003	2004
Southeast Asia	49	42	61	108	99	167	123	102
South Asia	11	10	16	47	31	34	47	21
Northeast Asia	11	10	4	2	1			6
Maritime Asia	71	62	81	157	131	201	170	129
Worldwide	126	106	163	223	217	253	277	197

Figure 3.6 Use of arms in reported attacks in maritime Asia, 1997–2004
Source: Data compiled from various issues of Piracy and Armed Robbery against Ships: Annual Report (Kuala Lumpur: IMB Regional Piracy Centre) from 1997 onwards.

of 58.3 percent. However, while Southeast Asia accounted for a range between 47.5 percent (189 out of 398 individuals in 1997) to 99.1 percent (244 out of 246 individuals in 2003) of individual seafarers subjected to violence in the same time period, or a mean of 76.5 percent in maritime Asia, the same region accounted for a range between 27.2 percent (132 out of 485 individuals in 1999) to 55.4 percent (221 out of 399 individuals in 2004), or a mean of 41.6 percent at the worldwide level. Thus, while the assertion about the statistical dominance of Southeast Asia in the overall trends in maritime Asia also holds true for the increasing use of piratical violence against seafarers, the former region loses salience in accounting for the majority of the violence in the rest of world, validating the quantitative observations of significant violence in regions elsewhere such as Africa vis-à-vis Nigeria and Somalia. To be sure, South Asia exhibited a near-equal magnitude in violence with its Southeast Asian counterpart in 2003 (236 and 246 individuals respectively) — a spike that is analogous to the overall peak in worldwide figures — though it reflects an anomaly when compared to the years between 1997 and 2002 and again in 2004.

Southeast Asia: Indonesia and the Malacca Straits

This section focuses mainly on attacks in Indonesian waters and adjacent Malacca (and neighboring Singapore) Straits. The rationale is clear: Figure 3.8 illustrates how the total reported attacks in Indonesian waters are driving the scale of the phenomenon in this subregion — the proportional mean from 1991 to 2004 was 59.1 percent from 975 cases against Southeast Asia's 1,651 cases. The Malacca Straits is the secondary subregional driver with a proportional mean from of 13.8 percent from 228 cases against Southeast Asia's total. In addition, though the attacks in the Straits receive the most media coverage

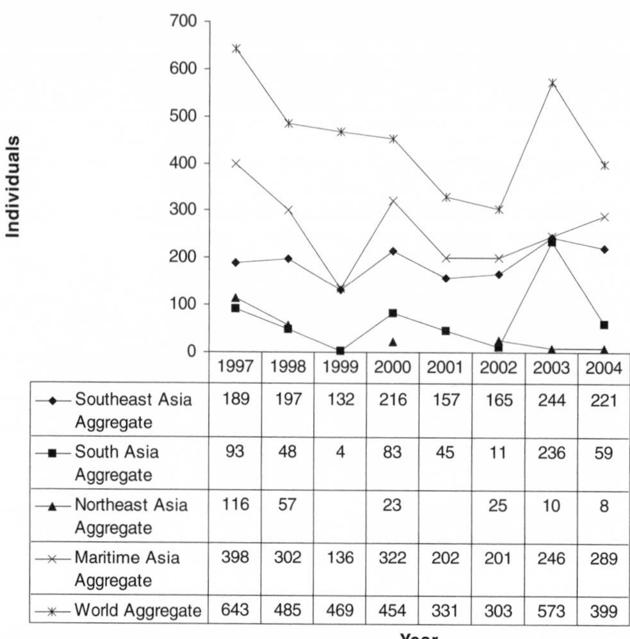

	1997	1998	1999	2000	2001	2002	2003	2004
Southeast Asia Aggregate	189	197	132	216	157	165	244	221
South Asia Aggregate	93	48	4	83	45	11	236	59
Northeast Asia Aggregate	116	57		23		25	10	8
Maritime Asia Aggregate	398	302	136	322	202	201	246	289
World Aggregate	643	485	469	454	331	303	573	399

Figure 3.7 Violence reported against crew among the sub-regions of maritime Asia, 1997–2004
Source: Data compiled from various issues of Piracy and Armed Robbery against Ships: Annual Report (Kuala Lumpur: IMB Regional Piracy Centre) from 1997 onwards.

among all other areas experiencing the phenomena (as later sections will show), they generated a proportion of only 6.5 percent (228 cases out of the total of 3,505 cases) of world figures during this period.

The availability of the disaggregated data on reported actual and attempted attacks in Southeast Asia collected by the IMB since 1997, provides analysts with further clues on the nature of the phenomenon in the region (see Figures 3.9 and 3.10). For example, the figures on reported actual attacks (Figure 3.9) produces a graphical indication that piracy in Indonesia accounts for the majority of all successful attacks in the subregion; a mean proportion of 67.3 percent from 1997 to 2004 (569 out of 845 regional cases in this category). In contrast, piracy in the Malacca Straits, Malaysia, the Singapore Strait, Thailand, Vietnam, and the Philippines forms the "background noise" behind the Indonesian phenomenon. In fact, the rest of Southeast Asia, excluding Indonesia, generates a total proportional mean of only 32.7 percent (276 cases).

However, as Figure 3.10 shows, though Indonesia still takes the lead in the number and proportion of reported attempted attacks in Southeast Asia from 1997 to 2004 (with a proportion of 51 percent or 177 out of 347 regional cases in this category), the rest of Southeast Asia nearly matches this proportion with a figure of 48.9 percent (170 cases).

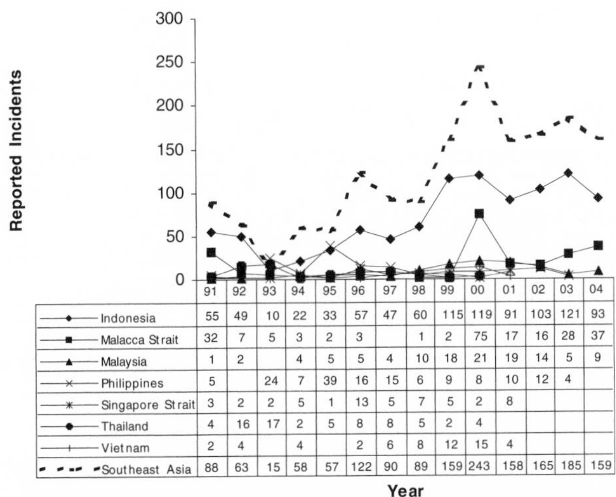

	91	92	93	94	95	96	97	98	99	00	01	02	03	04
Indonesia	55	49	10	22	33	57	47	60	115	119	91	103	121	93
Malacca Strait	32	7	5	3	2	3		1	2	75	17	16	28	37
Malaysia	1	2		4	5	5	4	10	18	21	19	14	5	9
Philippines	5		24	7	39	16	15	6	9	8	10	12	4	
Singapore Strait	3	2	2	5	1	13	5	7	5	2	8			
Thailand	4	16	17	2	5	8	8	5	2	4				
Vietnam	2	4		4		2	6	8	12	15	4			
Southeast Asia	88	63	15	58	57	122	90	89	159	243	158	165	185	159

Figure 3.8 Reported incidents of piracy/armed robbery at sea among Southeast Asian countries, 1991–2004

Source: For the tabulation of the figures 1991 to 2002, see *Piracy and Armed Robbery against ships: Annual Report, 1st January – 30th December 2002* (Kuala Lumpur: IMB Regional Piracy Centre, 30 January 2003), p. 5, Table 1. For the tabulation of the figures 2003 to 2004, see *Piracy and Armed Robbery against Ships: Annual Report, 1st January – 30th December 2004* (Kuala Lumpur: IMB Regional Piracy Centre, 7 February 2005), p. 4, Table 1.

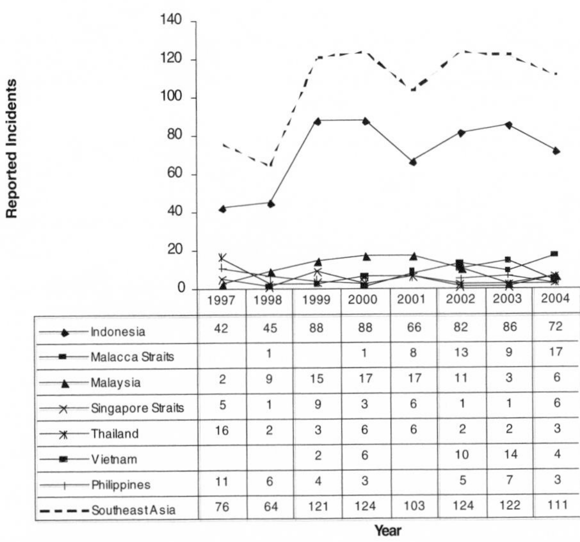

	1997	1998	1999	2000	2001	2002	2003	2004
Indonesia	42	45	88	88	66	82	86	72
Malacca Straits		1		1	8	13	9	17
Malaysia	2	9	15	17	17	11	3	6
Singapore Straits	5	1	9	3	6	1	1	6
Thailand	16	2	3	6	6	2	2	3
Vietnam			2	6		10	14	4
Philippines	11	6	4	3		5	7	3
Southeast Asia	76	64	121	124	103	124	122	111

Figure 3.9 Reported incidents of actual piracy/armed robbery at sea among Southeast Asian countries, 1997–2004

Source: Data compiled from various issues of Piracy and Armed Robbery against Ships: Annual Report (Kuala Lumpur: IMB Regional Piracy Centre) from 1997 onwards.

The main factor for this trend is largely due to piracy reported in the Malacca Straits. While displaying a highly erratic trend-line swinging within a range of 2 to 38 cases during this period, the high number of cases of failed attacks — 38 incidents in 2000, 19 incidents in 2003, and 20 incidents in 2004 — greatly recompensed the trough years of 1997 and 1998 (with null reports), 1999 (with two cases), and 2002 (three cases). All in all, the Straits accounted for 26.2 percent (91 cases) of the failed piracy attempts in the region. In addition, as Figure 3.9 indicates, the Malacca Straits only accounts for 5.79 percent of successful attacks in the region (49 cases). Figure 3.11, which shows the comparison between reported attempted and actual attacks in the Malacca and Singapore Straits between 1998 and 2004 (77 and 85 cases respectively), generates a proportion of 90.6 percent and indicates that while the number of general attacks in the Straits may be relatively low, when they do occur, pirates in these waters have about a 91 percent probability of succeeding in an attack.

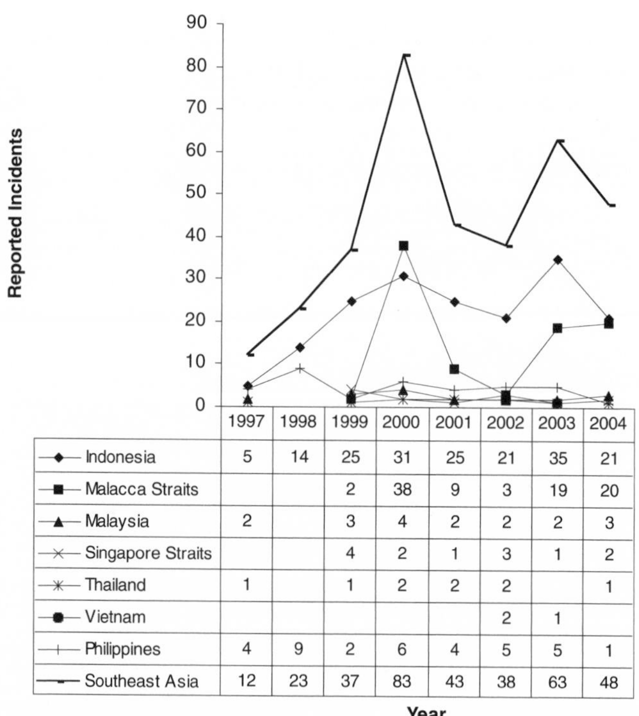

	1997	1998	1999	2000	2001	2002	2003	2004
Indonesia	5	14	25	31	25	21	35	21
Malacca Straits			2	38	9	3	19	20
Malaysia	2		3	4	2	2	2	3
Singapore Straits			4	2	1	3	1	2
Thailand	1		1	2	2	2		1
Vietnam						2	1	
Philippines	4	9	2	6	4	5	5	1
Southeast Asia	12	23	37	83	43	38	63	48

Figure 3.10 Reported incidents of attempted piracy/armed robbery at sea among Southeast Asian countries, 1997–2004

Source: Data compiled from various issues of Piracy and Armed Robbery against Ships: Annual Report (Kuala Lumpur: IMB Regional Piracy Centre) from 1997 onwards.

In the case of Indonesia, the comparison between reported attempted and actual attacks between 1998 and 2004 (171 and 525 cases respectively), as illustrated in Figure 3.12 generates a proportion of 32.5 percent. Hence, pirates operating in the Malacca Straits are more successful than those operating in Indonesian waters, where the most number of attacks occur in the subregion of Southeast Asia year on year.

In terms of the status of ships attacked — steaming, berthed, and anchored — during the period of 1998 to 2004, pirates in Southeast Asia showed that they may have been getting increasingly adept and inclined toward successfully attacking berthed and steaming vessels especially from 2002 to 2004, achieving a proficiency near to their consistent success and inclination toward taking anchored craft from 1998 to 2004, as the linear trend-lines generated from the raw trend-lines in Figure 3.13 seem to indicate.

However, the trends involving the status of ships in attempted attacks in Southeast Asia (Figure 3.14) add nuance to the earlier assertion by showing that failed attacks tend to occur highest when pirates in this region prey upon steaming ships, followed by anchored vessels, followed by berthed craft. The IMB reports do not currently provide disaggregated data on the summary statistics on ships attacked in actual and attempted incidents in each of the areas under Southeast Asia such as Indonesia and the Malacca (and Singapore) Straits — as for the South Asian and Northeast Asian subregions as well — which could help shed light on the exact trends in particular areas of concern by policy makers and analysts.

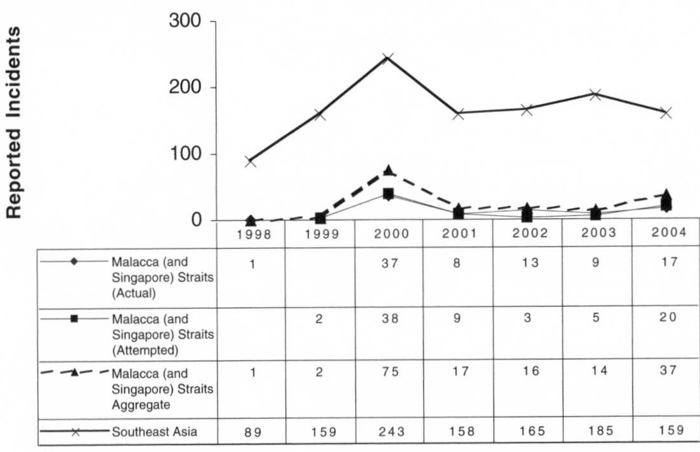

	1998	1999	2000	2001	2002	2003	2004
Malacca (and Singapore) Straits (Actual)	1		37	8	13	9	17
Malacca (and Singapore) Straits (Attempted)		2	38	9	3	5	20
Malacca (and Singapore) Straits Aggregate	1	2	75	17	16	14	37
Southeast Asia	89	159	243	158	165	185	159

Figure 3.11 Comparison between actual and attempted attacks in the Malacca (and Singapore) Straits, 1998–2004
Source: The total number of reported actual attacks and reported attempted attacks in the Malacca Straits, as well as the aggregate of the two sets of figures, are derived from Figures 3.9 and 3.10.

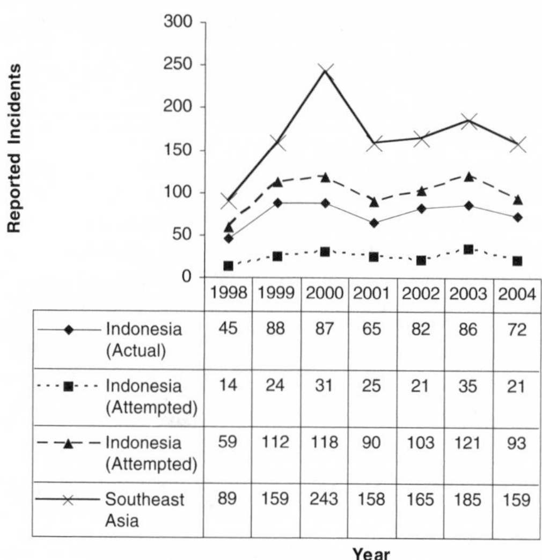

	1998	1999	2000	2001	2002	2003	2004
Indonesia (Actual)	45	88	87	65	82	86	72
Indonesia (Attempted)	14	24	31	25	21	35	21
Indonesia (Attempted)	59	112	118	90	103	121	93
Southeast Asia	89	159	243	158	165	185	159

Figure 3.12 Comparison between actual and attempted attacks in Indonesia, 1998–2004
Source: The total number of reported actual attacks and reported attempted attacks in Indonesia, as well as the aggregate of the two sets of figures, are derived from Figures X and Y.

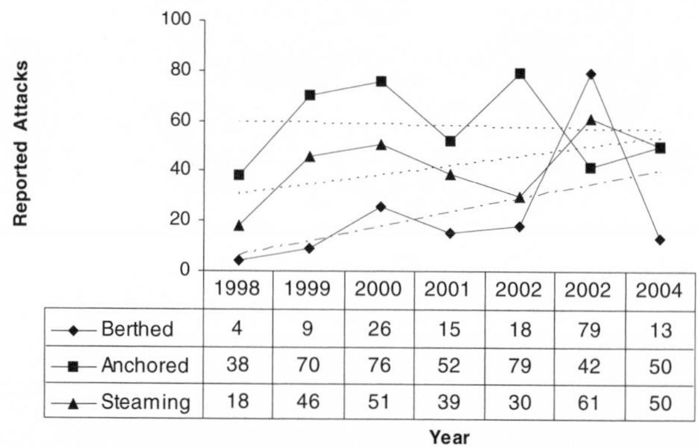

	1998	1999	2000	2001	2002	2002	2004
Berthed	4	9	26	15	18	79	13
Anchored	38	70	76	52	79	42	50
Steaming	18	46	51	39	30	61	50

Figure 3.13 Status of ships in reported actual attacks in Southeast Asia, 1998–2004
Source: The 'Status of Ships' as a category appears in the IMB reports from 1998 onwards. See the tables in *Piracy and Armed Robbery against Ships: Annual Report*, (Kuala Lumpur: IMB Regional Piracy Centre), from 1997 onwards.

As it was discussed earlier in reference to Figure 3.7, Southeast Asia accounted for a range between 47.5 percent (189 out of 398 individuals in 1997) to 99.1 percent (244 out of 246 individuals in 2003) of individual seafarers subjected to violence in the same time period, or a mean of 76.5 percent in maritime Asia from 1997 to 2004. As Figure 3.15 shows, except for

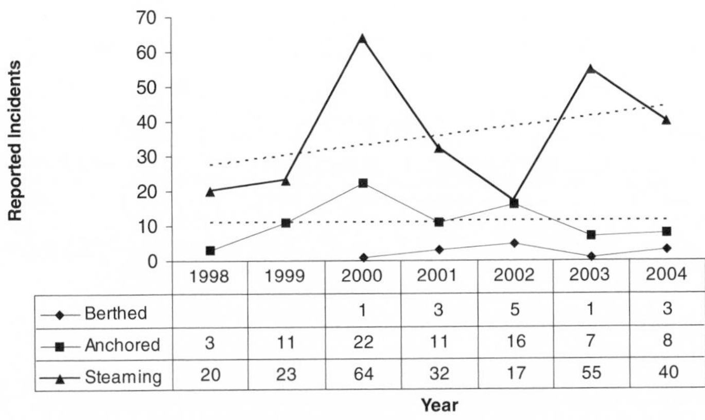

	1998	1999	2000	2001	2002	2003	2004
Berthed			1	3	5	1	3
Anchored	3	11	22	11	16	7	8
Steaming	20	23	64	32	17	55	40

Figure 3.14 Status of ships in reported attempted attacks in Southeast Asia, 1998–2004
Source: Data compiled from tables in Piracy and Armed Robbery against Ships: Annual Report, (Kuala Lumpur: IMB Regional Piracy Centre), 1997 passim.

hostage-taking, the cases for crew being threatened, killed, injured, assaulted, or made to go missing form baseline figures of around 100 and below against the worldwide scale of 3,657 individuals experiencing an act of violence. However, disaggregations against the 1,521 individuals experiencing a form of violence by their perpetrators within the Southeast Asian region itself from 1997 to 2004 reflect a different interpretation in proportional terms for some types of violence: 58.5 percent for hostage-taking (890 individuals), 14.1 percent were threatened (215 individuals), while 9.27 percent were killed (141 individuals), 6.64 percent were injured (101 individuals), 5.33 percent were assaulted (81 individuals), and 3.29 percent went missing (50 individuals).

As with the previous sets of relationships between piracy in Indonesia and Southeast Asia, Indonesia accounted for 60.4 percent of the individuals taken hostage in Southeast Asia during this period (538 out of 890 individuals), with the crew threatened at 34.4 percent (74 out of 215 individuals threatened) as Figure 3.16 demonstrates. However, it is clear that other than hostage-taking, the cases of individuals being threatened, killed, injured, assaulted, or made to go missing form the baselines of the trends for this country.

For the Malacca and Singapore Straits (Figure 3.17), the assertion about increasing violence against individuals along this waterway may be slightly tenuous beyond the trend in hostage-taking, which comprises 20 percent of individuals taken hostage in Southeast Asia (178 out of 890 individuals): 8.91 percent were injured (9 out of 101 injured), 7.91 percent were threatened (17 out of 215 threatened), 4.96 percent were killed (7 out of 141 killed), 2.47 percent were assaulted (2 out of 81 assaulted), and 2 percent went missing (3 out of 50 missing). In 2004, which is the year the IMB began collecting information on kidnappings, the debut statistic for the Malacca (and Singapore) Straits is

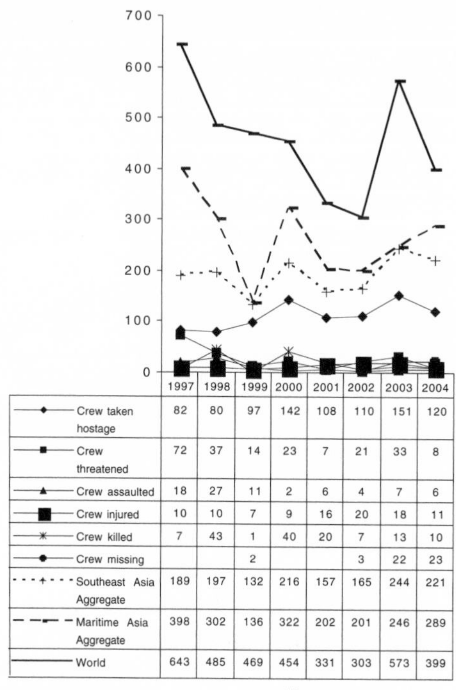

	1997	1998	1999	2000	2001	2002	2003	2004
Crew taken hostage	82	80	97	142	108	110	151	120
Crew threatened	72	37	14	23	7	21	33	8
Crew assaulted	18	27	11	2	6	4	7	6
Crew injured	10	10	7	9	16	20	18	11
Crew killed	7	43	1	40	20	7	13	10
Crew missing			2			3	22	23
Southeast Asia Aggregate	189	197	132	216	157	165	244	221
Maritime Asia Aggregate	398	302	136	322	202	201	246	289
World	643	485	469	454	331	303	573	399

Figure 3.15 Types of violence reported against crew in Southeast Asia, 1997–2004
Source: Data compiled from tables in Piracy and Armed Robbery against Ships: Annual Report, (Kuala Lumpur: IMB Regional Piracy Centre), 1997 passim.

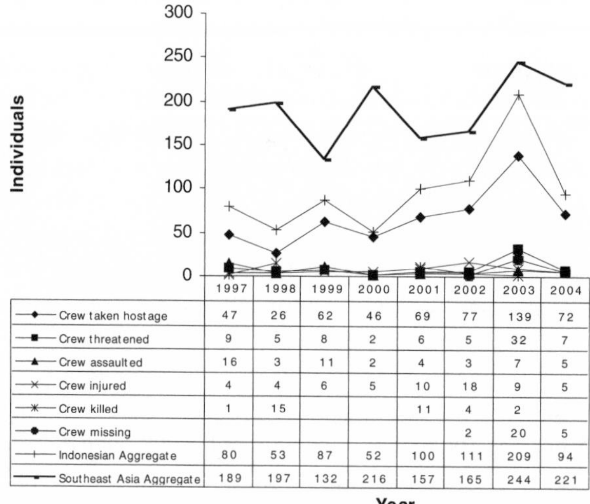

	1997	1998	1999	2000	2001	2002	2003	2004
Crew taken hostage	47	26	62	46	69	77	139	72
Crew threatened	9	5	8	2	6	5	32	7
Crew assaulted	16	3	11	2	4	3	7	5
Crew injured	4	4	6	5	10	18	9	5
Crew killed	1	15			11	4	2	
Crew missing						2	20	5
Indonesian Aggregate	80	53	87	52	100	111	209	94
Southeast Asia Aggregate	189	197	132	216	157	165	244	221

Figure 3.16 Types of violence used against crew in Indonesia, 1997–2004
Source: Data compiled from tables in Piracy and Armed Robbery against Ships: Annual Report, (Kuala Lumpur: IMB Regional Piracy Centre), 1997 passim.

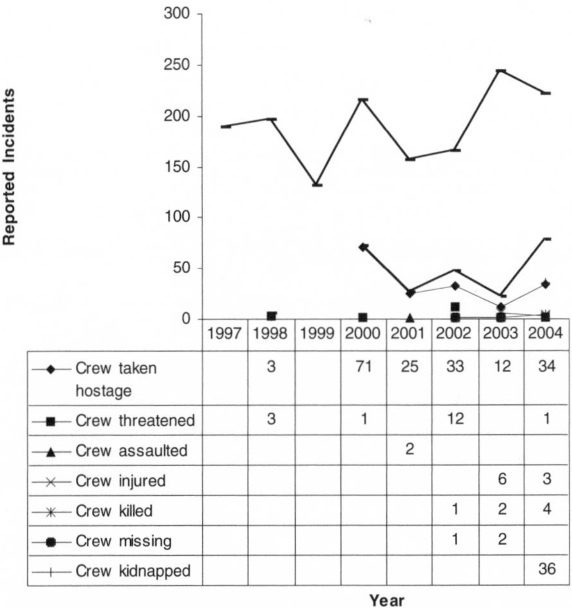

	1997	1998	1999	2000	2001	2002	2003	2004
Crew taken hostage		3		71	25	33	12	34
Crew threatened		3		1		12		1
Crew assaulted					2			
Crew injured							6	3
Crew killed						1	2	4
Crew missing						1	2	
Crew kidnapped								36

Figure 3.17 Types of violence used against crew in the Malacca and Singapore Straits, 1997–2004
Source: Data compiled from tables in Piracy and Armed Robbery against Ships: Annual Report, (Kuala Lumpur: IMB Regional Piracy Centre), 1997 passim.

36 individuals being taken or 83.7 percent of the total number of kidnapping in Southeast Asia (36 out of 43 individuals) or 59 percent (36 out of 61 individuals) against that of the total kidnappings in maritime Asia.[18] However, the judgment on kidnapping needs to be suspended until more statistics become available in the unfolding years.[19]

Notwithstanding the problems in establishing the relationship between reported use of arms and the reported exercise of violence against individual crewmembers in the IMB reports outlined in the beginning of the chapter (specifically the issue of increasing cases of unspecified descriptions concerning the presence of weapons in pirate attacks), statistical analyses of the residual figures on the type of arms reported in each subregion within maritime Asia can produce significant information. Most interestingly, pirates in Southeast Asia appear to include traditional weapons such as knives and machetes (reminiscent of historical piracy) in the array of weapons reported. From 1997 to 1998 (Figure 3.18), the use of knives accounted for 47.9 percent (360 out of 751 cases) of arms being reported in Southeast Asia with the median year being 2000 with 79 cases. In contrast, guns and rifles constitute 31.6 percent (237 cases) of arms reported in the subregion. Other kinds of weapons, which have included batons and sticks, encompass a proportion of 20.5 percent (154 cases) with the median year being 2003 with 58 cases. Note that there were only two reported cases of pirates being unarmed while there were 520 cases of unstated reporting in this period.

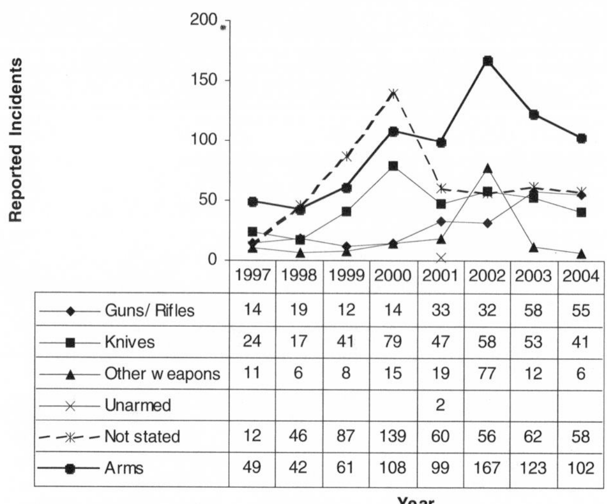

	1997	1998	1999	2000	2001	2002	2003	2004
Guns/ Rifles	14	19	12	14	33	32	58	55
Knives	24	17	41	79	47	58	53	41
Other w eapons	11	6	8	15	19	77	12	6
Unarmed					2			
Not stated	12	46	87	139	60	56	62	58
Arms	49	42	61	108	99	167	123	102

Figure 3.18 Types of arms used in reported attacks in Southeast Asia, 1997–2004
Source: Data compiled from tables in Piracy and Armed Robbery against Ships: Annual Report, (Kuala Lumpur: IMB Regional Piracy Centre), 1997 passim.

In the case of Indonesia (see Figure 3.19), the incidences of arms being used amounted to 58.4 percent of total cases in Southeast Asia (439 out of 751 respectively) from the period 1997 to 2004 with the median year being 2003 with 85 cases. Also, knives constituted 61.5 percent of the total cases of arms used in Indonesia (270 out of 439 total cases of arms used in the region) with 2000 as the median year with 51 cases — which matches the median year for unstated reporting — while the use of guns and rifles constituted 24.8 percent (109 cases) against the total cases of arms in the country, with the median year in 2003 with 35 cases. Other weapons comprised 13.6 percent (60 cases) with the median year being 2002 with 14 cases.

However, compared to the Indonesian trend, from Figure 3.20, the Malacca and Singapore Straits show a different picture when it comes to the use of guns and rifles, which topped the list of weapons used from 1997 to 2004. The generated proportion is 58.8 percent of all cases in the Malacca (and Singapore) Straits: 70 out of 119 cases. In addition, knives constituted 34.4 percent (41 cases) while other weapons led to 5.76 percent (8 cases).

South Asia

As demonstrated earlier, South Asia has served as the secondary driver behind the scale of piracy attacks in maritime Asia after Southeast Asia. Still, the comparison between the scales in South Asia and maritime Asia within Figure 3.21, reflects the diminutive proportion of reports in the former compared to the latter during this period, translating into a figure of 0.04 percent (472 cases out of the regional total of 2,368). However, notwithstanding the

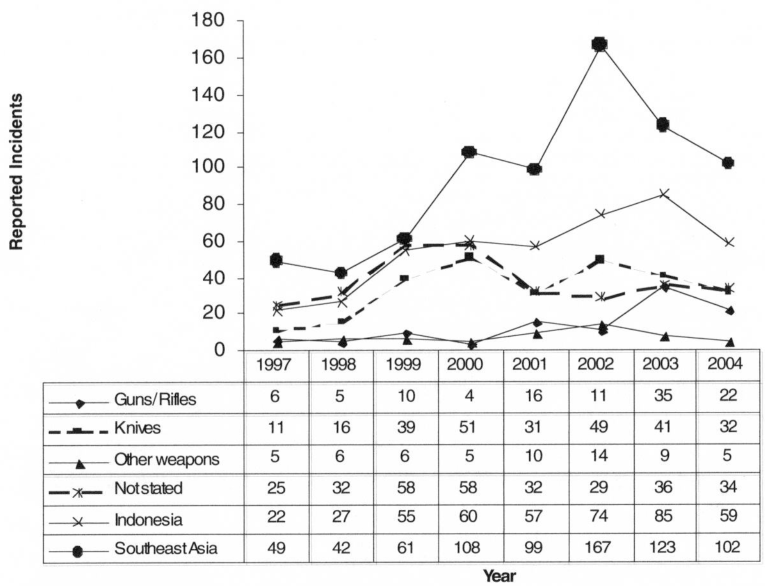

	1997	1998	1999	2000	2001	2002	2003	2004
Guns/Rifles	6	5	10	4	16	11	35	22
Knives	11	16	39	51	31	49	41	32
Other weapons	5	6	6	5	10	14	9	5
Notstated	25	32	58	58	32	29	36	34
Indonesia	22	27	55	60	57	74	85	59
SoutheastAsia	49	42	61	108	99	167	123	102

Figure 3.19 Types of arms used in reported attacks in Indonesia, 1997–2004
Source: Data compiled from tables in Piracy and Armed Robbery against Ships: Annual Report, (Kuala Lumpur: IMB Regional Piracy Centre), 1997 passim.

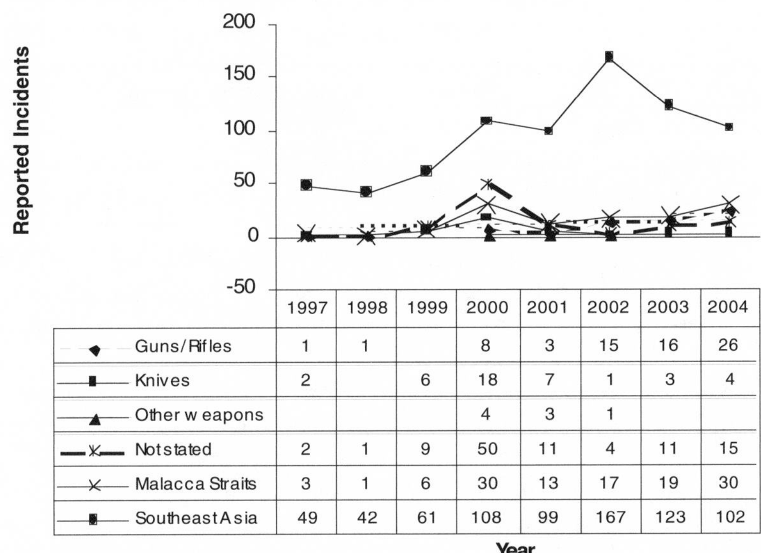

	1997	1998	1999	2000	2001	2002	2003	2004
Guns/Rifles	1	1		8	3	15	16	26
Knives	2		6	18	7	1	3	4
Other w eapons				4	3	1		
Notstated	2	1	9	50	11	4	11	15
Malacca Straits	3	1	6	30	13	17	19	30
SoutheastAsia	49	42	61	108	99	167	123	102

Figure 3.20 Types of arms used in reported attacks in the Malacca and Singapore Straits, 1997–2004
Source: Data compiled from tables in Piracy and Armed Robbery against Ships: Annual Report, (Kuala Lumpur: IMB Regional Piracy Centre), 1997 passim.

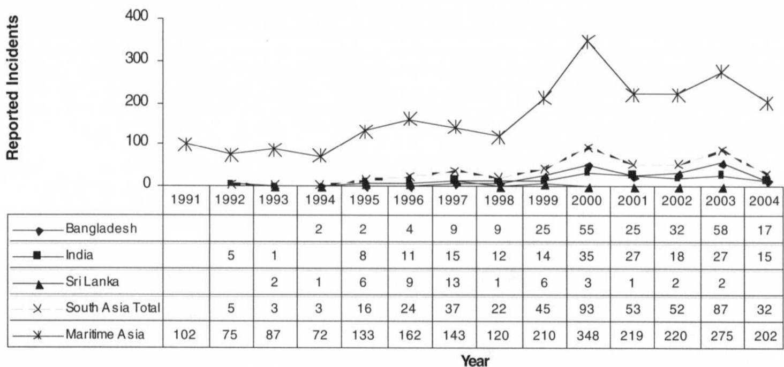

	1991	1992	1993	1994	1995	1996	1997	1998	1999	2000	2001	2002	2003	2004
Bangladesh				2	2	4	9	9	25	55	25	32	58	17
India		5	1		8	11	15	12	14	35	27	18	27	15
Sri Lanka			2	1	6	9	13	1	6	3	1	2	2	
South Asia Total		5	3	3	16	24	37	22	45	93	53	52	87	32
Maritime Asia	102	75	87	72	133	162	143	120	210	348	219	220	275	202

Figure 3.21 Reported incidents of piracy/armed robbery at sea among South Asian countries, 1991–2004

Source: For the tabulation of the figures from 1991 to 2002, see *Piracy and Armed Robbery against Ships: Annual Report, 1st January – 30th December 2002* (Kuala Lumpur: IMB Regional Piracy Centre, 30 January 2003), p. 5, Table 1. For the tabulation of the figures from 2003 to 2004, see *Piracy and Armed Robbery against Ships: Annual Report, 1st January – 30th December 2004* (Kuala Lumpur: IMB Regional Piracy Centre, 7 February 2005), p. 4, Table 1.

weak analogue between reports in South Asia and maritime Asia along 1996, 1997, and 1998 — as reflected in the arching trend-line and negative trend-line respectively — their analogue virtually corresponded from 1998 to 2004 with the mean year of attacks in 2000 and the second highest year of attacks in 2003 corresponding for both geographical groupings. Correspondingly, the South Asian trend is driven mainly by piracy in Bangladeshi waters, which accounted for 50.4 percent of attacks in the subregion during this period (238 out of 472 subregional cases) with the mean year also being 2000 and the second highest year of attacks in 2003. Piracy in India, having a tertiary rank of 39.8 percent (188 cases) in South Asia, also reflected the same trends in terms of its analogy with the next two aggregate levels and the corresponding mean year and second highest year of attacks. In contrast, piracy in Sri Lanka, in addition to presenting the lowest proportion of attacks in South Asia with 9.74 percent (46 cases), also shows a rather even trend-line albeit a weak rise and fall especially from 1999 to 2004.

The dominance of the total number of reported cases of piracy in Bangladesh within South Asia from 1991 to 2004 finds itself in the reported cases of actual or successful cases of pirate attacks from 1997 to 2004 (see Figure 3.22), which generated a proportion of 55.2 percent (192 out of 348 cases of success in the subregion). Just like the mean year for overall piracy reported in Bangladesh, the mean year for its actual variant was also 2000. To be sure, piracy in India and Sri Lanka (in descending order) did exceed their Bangladeshi counterpart from 1997 to 1998. Reported cases of actual piracy in Bangladesh and India also nearly matched in 2001. All in all, the analogue between reported actual cases of piracy for Bangladesh and South Asia is

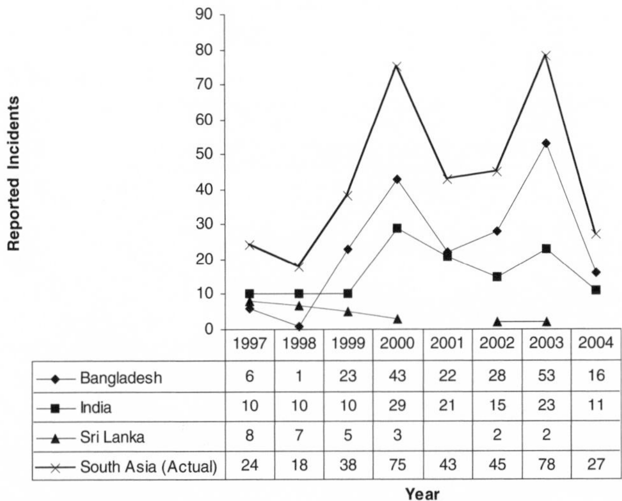

	1997	1998	1999	2000	2001	2002	2003	2004
Bangladesh	6	1	23	43	22	28	53	16
India	10	10	10	29	21	15	23	11
Sri Lanka	8	7	5	3		2	2	
South Asia (Actual)	24	18	38	75	43	45	78	27

Figure 3.22 Reported incidents of actual piracy/armed robbery at sea among South Asian countries, 1997–2004
Source: Data compiled from tables in Piracy and Armed Robbery against Ships: Annual Report, (Kuala Lumpur: IMB Regional Piracy Centre), 1997 passim.

similarly as strong as the general trends between them demonstrated earlier. It reflects the assertion that *actual* piracy has been the key driver for overall piracy in South Asia during this period. On the contrary, the analogue for India and South Asia is invariably weak. Also, reported cases of actual attacks for Sri Lanka was both dismal and with absent reporting or no actual attacks in 2001 and 2004.

The situation for reported cases of attempted or failed attacks in South Asia is remarkably different from the trends in actual attacks (Figure 3.23). First, India accounted for 48.4 percent of cases (31 out of 64 cases), the highest in the subregion, followed by Bangladesh at 42.1 percent (27 out of 64 cases), and then Sri Lanka at 9.38 percent (6 cases). Second, the trend for failed attacks in South Asia did not obtain much of its explanation from the erratic trends in India and Bangladesh as well as the near nontrend in Sri Lanka. This tells us that there is a lack of relative consistency in pirates in these waters at failing in an attack as compared to their Southeast Asian counterparts. The reference between Figure 3.22 and Figure 3.23 indicates that on average, pirates in South Asian waters are invariably better at succeeding in an attack than in failing. This is confirmed in Figure 3.24, which shows the probability of success in a graphical expression reflecting the statistical description that form a proportion between 59 failed attacks and 150 successful attacks between 1998 to 2004, pirates in South Asia had a 60.7 percent chance of succeeding in an attempt.

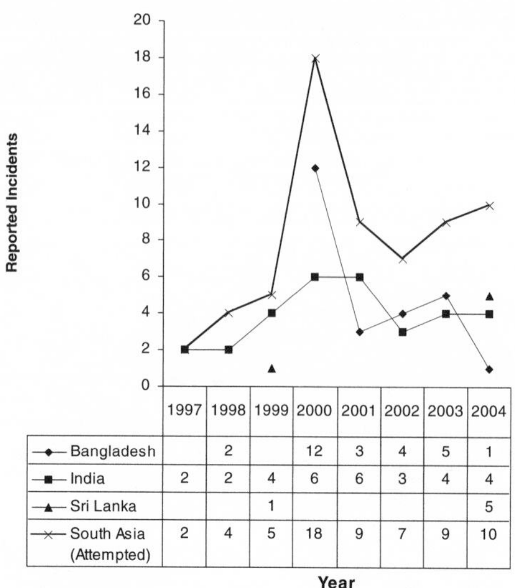

	1997	1998	1999	2000	2001	2002	2003	2004
Bangladesh		2		12	3	4	5	1
India	2	2	4	6	6	3	4	4
Sri Lanka			1					5
South Asia (Attempted)	2	4	5	18	9	7	9	10

Figure 3.23 Reported incidents of attempted piracy/armed robbery at sea among South Asian countries, 1997–2004
Source: Data compiled from tables in Piracy and Armed Robbery against Ships: Annual Report, (Kuala Lumpur: IMB Regional Piracy Centre), 1997 passim.

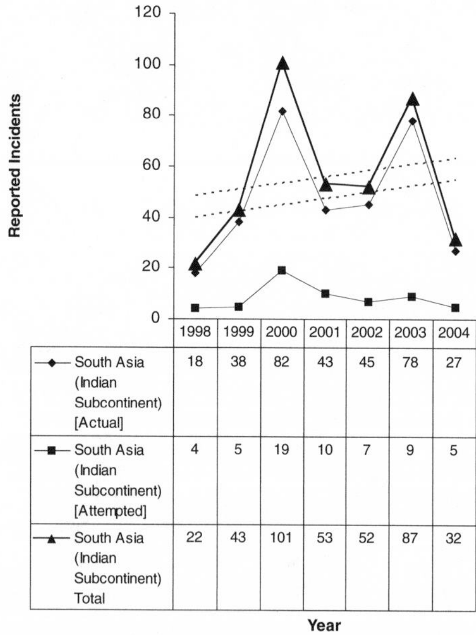

	1998	1999	2000	2001	2002	2003	2004
South Asia (Indian Subcontinent) [Actual]	18	38	82	43	45	78	27
South Asia (Indian Subcontinent) [Attempted]	4	5	19	10	7	9	5
South Asia (Indian Subcontinent) Total	22	43	101	53	52	87	32

Figure 3.24 Comparison between actual and attempted attacks in South Asia, 1997–2004
Source: The total number of reported actual attacks and reported attempted attacks in South Asia, as well as the aggregate of the two sets of figures, are derived from Figures 3.22 and 3.23.

Compared to their Southeast Asian counterparts, South Asian pirates are adept at successfully attacking anchored vessels, as Figure 3.25 indicates. In contrast, the latter are relatively weak at succeeding with berthed and steaming vessels, which they have been able to attack with equal proficiency. However, while South Asian pirates are also adept in failing to attack anchored vessels followed by steaming vessels as Figure 3.26 shows, they are shown to rarely fail with berthed ships when they actually do make an attempt.

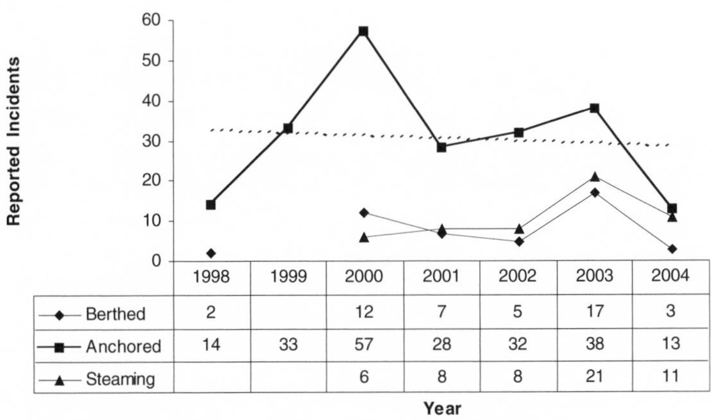

	1998	1999	2000	2001	2002	2003	2004
Berthed	2		12	7	5	17	3
Anchored	14	33	57	28	32	38	13
Steaming			6	8	8	21	11

Figure 3.25 Status of ships in reported actual attacks in South Asia, 1998–2004
Source: Data compiled from tables in Piracy and Armed Robbery against Ships: Annual Report, (Kuala Lumpur: IMB Regional Piracy Centre), 1997 passim.

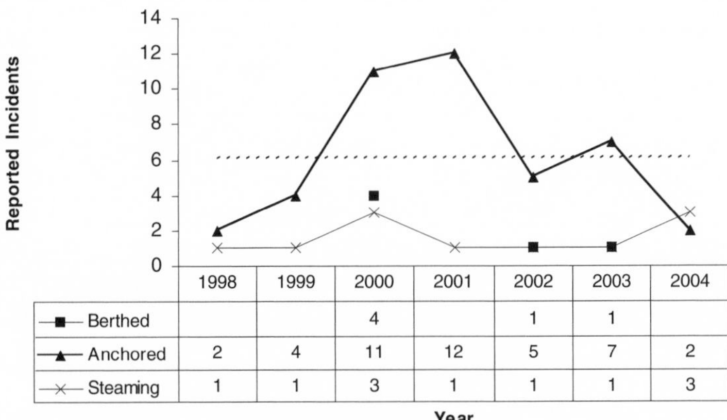

	1998	1999	2000	2001	2002	2003	2004
Berthed			4		1	1	
Anchored	2	4	11	12	5	7	2
Steaming	1	1	3	1	1	1	3

Figure 3.26 Status of ships in reported attempted attacks in South Asia, 1998–2004
Source: Data compiled from tables in Piracy and Armed Robbery against Ships: Annual Report, (Kuala Lumpur: IMB Regional Piracy Centre), 1997 passim.

In South Asia, hostage-taking comprised 38.9 percent or 225 out of 579 individuals which experienced some form of violence in the subregion (Figure 3.27). In other instances, 27.8 percent were injured (161 individuals), 9.33 percent were threatened (54 individuals), 8.9 percent were killed (52 individuals), 7.25 percent went missing (42 individuals), and 4.7 percent were assaulted (27 individuals). In 2004, which is the year the IMB began collecting information on kidnappings, the debut statistic for South Asia was 18 individuals being taken or 3.1 percent of the total number of kidnappings in the subregion or 29.5 percent (18 out of 61 individuals) against that of the total kidnappings in maritime Asia.[20]

Like their Southeast Asian counterparts, pirates in South Asia appear to favor the use of knives among the array of weapons reported (Figure 3.28). From 1997 to 1998, the use of knives accounted for 66.8 percent (145 out of 217 cases) of arms being reported in Southeast Asia with the median year being 2003 with 35 cases. However, unlike their Southeast Asian brethren, South Asian pirates do not tend to use guns and rifles as their secondary weapon of choice, which encompasses only 11.5 percent (25 cases) of the arms reported

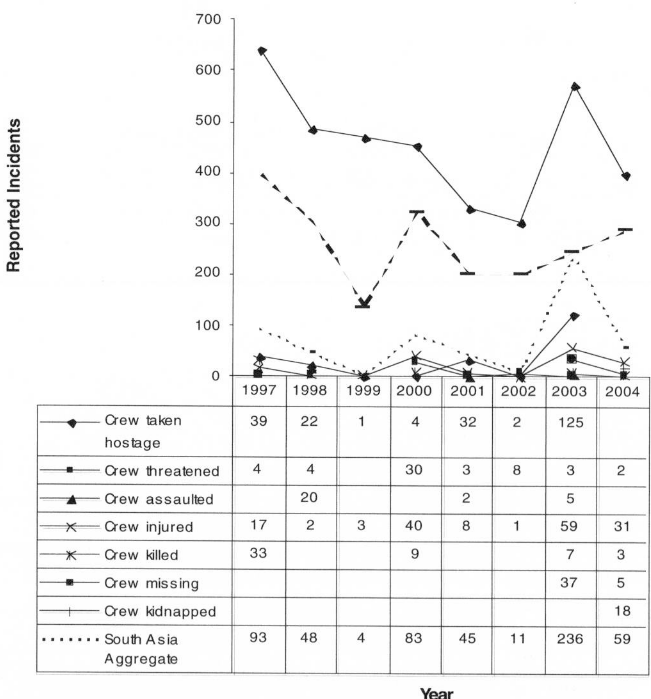

	1997	1998	1999	2000	2001	2002	2003	2004
Crew taken hostage	39	22	1	4	32	2	125	
Crew threatened	4	4		30	3	8	3	2
Crew assaulted		20			2		5	
Crew injured	17	2	3	40	8	1	59	31
Crew killed	33			9			7	3
Crew missing							37	5
Crew kidnapped								18
South Asia Aggregate	93	48	4	83	45	11	236	59

Figure 3.27 Types of violence against crew in South Asia, 1997–2004
Source: Data compiled from tables in Piracy and Armed Robbery against Ships: Annual Report, (Kuala Lumpur: IMB Regional Piracy Centre), 1997 passim.

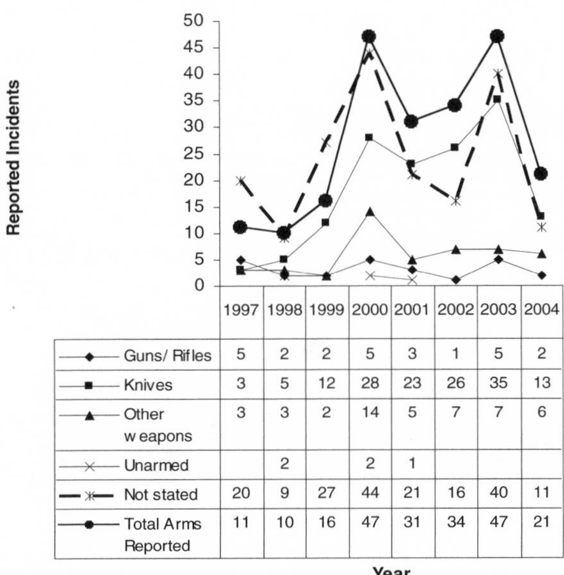

	1997	1998	1999	2000	2001	2002	2003	2004
Guns/ Rifles	5	2	2	5	3	1	5	2
Knives	3	5	12	28	23	26	35	13
Other weapons	3	3	2	14	5	7	7	6
Unarmed		2		2	1			
Not stated	20	9	27	44	21	16	40	11
Total Arms Reported	11	10	16	47	31	34	47	21

Figure 3.28 Type of arms used in reported piracy attacks in South Asia, 1997–2004
Source: Data compiled from tables in Piracy and Armed Robbery against Ships: Annual Report, (Kuala Lumpur: IMB Regional Piracy Centre), 1997 passim.

in the latter subregion, while other kinds of weapons constitute a proportion of 21.7 percent (47 cases) with the median year being 2003 with 58 cases. Note that there were only 5 reported cases of pirates being unarmed while there were 188 cases of unstated reporting in this period.

Northeast Asia

As was mentioned earlier, the trends in piracy in Northeast Asia provides a tertiary account of the phenomenon in maritime Asia, after Southeast Asia and South Asia. As Figure 3.29 illustrates, reports in the South China Sea account for the bulk of the attacks from 1991 to 2004, with a proportion of 41.4 percent (99 out of a total of 239 cases) with the mean year in 1993 (31 attacks). This is followed by reports in the China-Hong Kong-Macau (CHM) area with 25.1 percent (60 cases) and a mean year of 1995 (31 attacks), and the Hong Kong-Luzon-Hainan (HLH) area with 21.3 percent and a mean year of 1993 (27 attacks). Both the East China Sea and Taiwan have exhibited a modest number of reports at 9.6 percent (23 attacks) and 3.4 percent (6 attacks) respectively. However, while the mean year of attacks for the East China Sea was in 1993 (10 attacks) as in the other adjacent areas within Northeast Asia, Taiwan's mean years were in 1995 and 2001 with two attacks in each case while there was a null report in 1993. In fact, there were null reports in ten years out

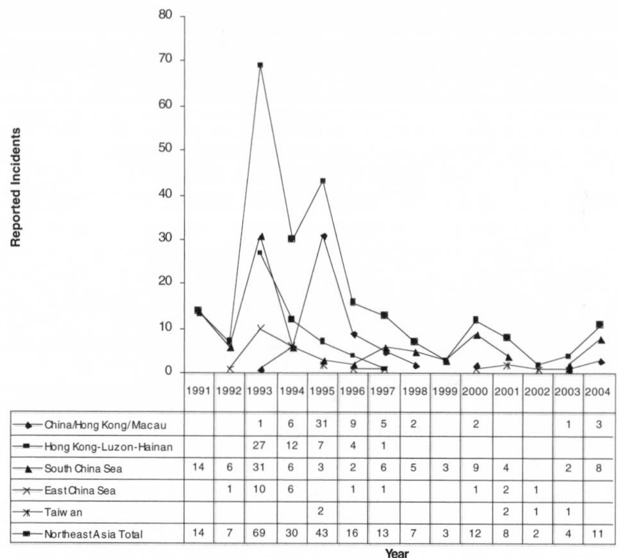

	1991	1992	1993	1994	1995	1996	1997	1998	1999	2000	2001	2002	2003	2004
China/Hong Kong/Macau			1	6	31	9	5	2		2			1	3
Hong Kong-Luzon-Hainan			27	12	7	4	1							
South China Sea	14	6	31	6	3	2	6	5	3	9	4		2	8
East China Sea		1	10	6		1	1			1	2	1		
Taiwan					2						2	1	1	
Northeast Asia Total	14	7	69	30	43	16	13	7	3	12	8	2	4	11

Figure 3.29 Reported incidents of piracy/armed robbery at sea among Northeast Asian countries, 1991–2004

Source: For the tabulation of the figures from 1991 to 2002, see *Piracy and Armed Robbery against Ships: Annual Report, 1st January – 30th December 2002* (Kuala Lumpur: IMB Regional Piracy Centre, 30 January 2003), p. 5, Table 1. For the tabulation of the figures from 2003 to 2004, see *Piracy and Armed Robbery against Ships: Annual Report, 1st January – 30th December 2004* (Kuala Lumpur: IMB Regional Piracy Centre, 7 February 2005), p. 4, Table 1.

of the fourteen-year period, which is most likely to be explained by an overall lack of significant piracy in this region rather than underreporting.

As compared to Southeast and South Asia, there is a relatively weak number of reported cases of both actual and attempted piracy attacks in Northeast Asian waters from the available data between 1997 to 2004. As Figures 3.30 and 3.31 demonstrate, there were only 32 reported cases of actual attacks and 26 reported cases of attempted attacks in Northeast Asia from 1997 to 2004. The South China Sea accounted for 56.3 percent (18 cases) of all actual attacks and 73.1 percent (19 cases) of all attempted incidents. While the CHM area accounted for 37.5 percent (12 cases) of actual attacks, it had a null report for the entire eight-year period for attempted piracy; raising the weak inference that pirates operating here almost never fail in their attacks. Lastly, as an extension of the low number of overall attacks, both Taiwan and the East China Sea area show a dominant trend in null-reporting for actual and attempted piracy that prevents the analysis from making preliminary assertions about the level of skill of attacks in these areas. However, as a regional aggregate (see the statistics in Figure 3.32), the tenuous claim could be made that pirates in Northeast Asia have a 73.3 percent chance of succeeding in an attack (74 successful cases out of an aggregate of 101 cases).

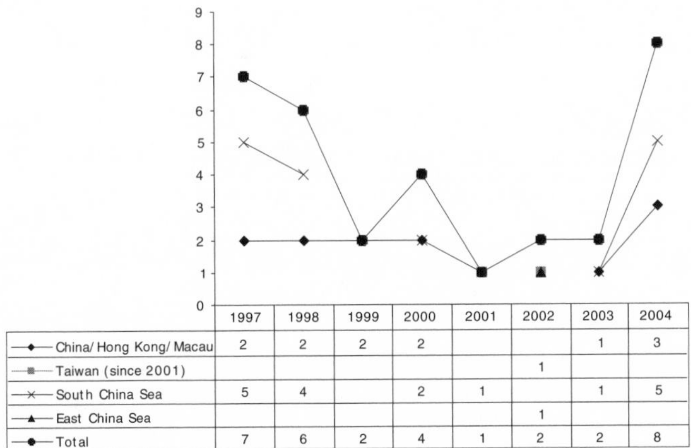

	1997	1998	1999	2000	2001	2002	2003	2004
China/ Hong Kong/ Macau	2	2	2	2			1	3
Taiwan (since 2001)						1		
South China Sea	5	4		2	1		1	5
East China Sea						1		
Total	7	6	2	4	1	2	2	8

Figure 3.30 Reported incidents of actual piracy/armed robbery at sea among Northeast Asian countries, 1997–2004
Source: Data compiled from tables in Piracy and Armed Robbery against Ships: Annual Report, (Kuala Lumpur: IMB Regional Piracy Centre), 1997 passim.

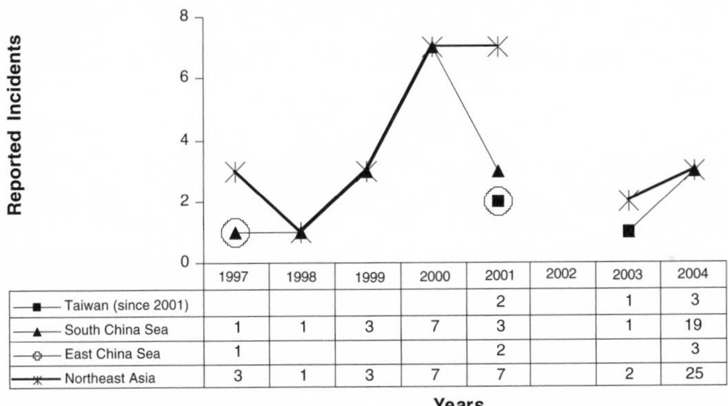

	1997	1998	1999	2000	2001	2002	2003	2004
Taiwan (since 2001)					2		1	3
South China Sea	1	1	3	7	3		1	19
East China Sea	1				2			3
Northeast Asia	3	1	3	7	7		2	25

Figure 3.31 Reported incidents of attempted piracy/armed robbery at sea among Northeast Asian countries, 1997–2004
Source: Data compiled from tables in Piracy and Armed Robbery against Ships: Annual Report, (Kuala Lumpur: IMB Regional Piracy Centre), 1997 passim.

Notwithstanding the weak number of reports for Northeast Asia, a perceptible trend can be ascertained on the disposition of a vessel and its relationship with the success or failure of an attack. From Figure 3.33, it can be inferred that steaming and anchored ships constitute the bulk of successful attacks from 1997 to 2004, with proportions of 55.9 percent (19 cases of anchored vessels out of the aggregate of 34) and 38.2 percent (13 cases of anchored vessels) respectively. Judging from the frequency of attacks, steaming ships are

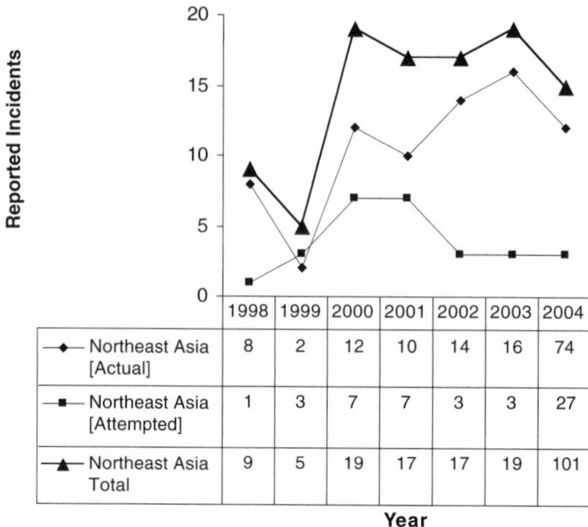

	1998	1999	2000	2001	2002	2003	2004
Northeast Asia [Actual]	8	2	12	10	14	16	74
Northeast Asia [Attempted]	1	3	7	7	3	3	27
Northeast Asia Total	9	5	19	17	17	19	101

Figure 3.32 Comparison between actual and attempted attacks in Northeast Asia, 1997–2004
Source: The total number of reported actual attacks and reported attempted attacks in Northeast Asia, as well as the aggregate of the two sets of figures, are derived from Figures 3.30 and 3.31.

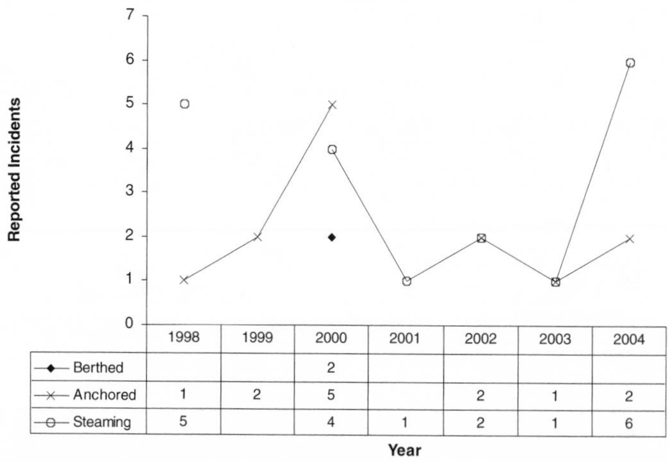

	1998	1999	2000	2001	2002	2003	2004
Berthed			2				
Anchored	1	2	5		2	1	2
Steaming	5		4	1	2	1	6

Figure 3.33 Status of ships in reported actual attacks in Northeast Asia (Far East), 1998–2004
Source: Data compiled from tables in Piracy and Armed Robbery against Ships: Annual Report, (Kuala Lumpur: IMB Regional Piracy Centre), 1997 passim.

likely to be the mainstay of both successful and failed cases from the repetition of peak attacks in 1998, 2000, and 2004 with a range of 4 to 6 cases in the first instance and a repetition of a similar scale of attacks in 2000 and 2001 in the second instance (six and seven cases respectively). In comparison, the mean number of successful attacks involving anchored ships was five cases in 2000 in contrast to a range of between one to two attacks in the other years.

Lastly, unlike their Southeast Asian and South Asian counterparts, pirates in Northeast Asia do not tend to attack berthed ships (Figure 3.34). There were only two cases of berthed ships being attacked successfully in 2002, and a null report for attempted attacks during the seven-year period.

In comparison to Southeast Asia and South Asia as well as the aggregate trend-line for maritime Asia, there is a lack of any trend with regard to the types of violence exercised against crew in the reported number of individuals harmed in Northeast Asia (see Figure 3.35). It is difficult to apply the concept of the mean in this category as the entire spectrum of reported violence from 1998 to 2004 is interspersed with null reporting. To be sure, reports on hostage taking showed the lowest number of null years (three) and hence, the most compelling case for expressing a significant mean of 89 individuals in 1997, corresponding with the proportion of 56.5 percent (135 out of 239 individuals harmed in maritime Asia). Next, making crew disappear constituted 20.9 percent (50 individuals), followed by threatening (13 percent or 31 individuals), and killing (10 percent or 24 individuals) over the eight-year period. Notwithstanding the pervasiveness of null reporting in these subcategories, the injury and assaulting of crew constituted four and two cases respectively, reflecting the lack of a tendency toward these activities as compared to Southeast Asia and South Asia. In sum, the figures on reported violence do reflect the disproportionate number of individuals being attacked against the low number of vessels attacked.

Despite the high number of unstated reports (see Figure 3.36), the case of disproportionate violence upon individuals in Northeast Asia may be explained in part by the significant proportion of guns and rifles — 64.7 percent among the total arms reported (22 out of 34 cases) — being used among

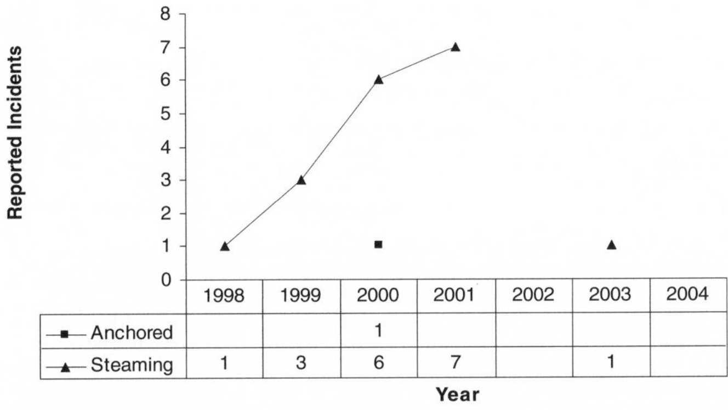

	1998	1999	2000	2001	2002	2003	2004
Anchored			1				
Steaming	1	3	6	7		1	

Figure 3.34 Status of ships in reported attempted attacks in Northeast Asia (Far East), 1998–2004
Source: Data compiled from tables in Piracy and Armed Robbery against Ships: Annual Report, (Kuala Lumpur: IMB Regional Piracy Centre), 1997 passim.

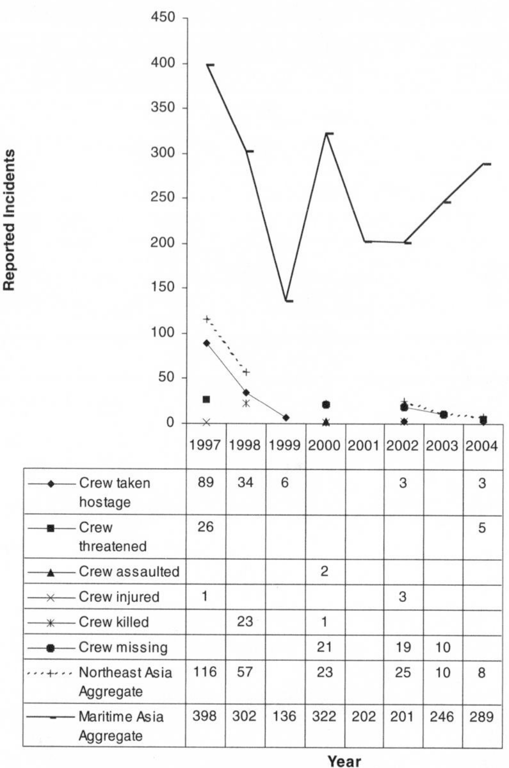

	1997	1998	1999	2000	2001	2002	2003	2004
Crew taken hostage	89	34	6			3		3
Crew threatened	26							5
Crew assaulted				2				
Crew injured	1					3		
Crew killed		23		1				
Crew missing				21		19	10	
Northeast Asia Aggregate	116	57		23		25	10	8
Maritime Asia Aggregate	398	302	136	322	202	201	246	289

Figure 3.35 Types of violence reported against crew in Northeast Asia (Far East), 1997–2004
Source: Data compiled from tables in Piracy and Armed Robbery against Ships: Annual Report, (Kuala Lumpur: IMB Regional Piracy Centre), 1997 passim.

the range of weapons categorized. Also, in comparison to the other subregions of Southeast and South Asia, there are no significant figures and trends for the use of knives (three cases) and other weapons among the total number of arms reported in Northeast Asia. In addition, both subcategories saw six and five years of null reporting respectively out of the eight year period in comparison to the use of guns and rifles, with three years devoid of reports.

Other Trends

Several other trends of piracy in maritime Asia can be obtained from both the IMB reports and the prevailing body of scholarship. First, if maritime Asia accounts for 67.3 percent of the reported attacks worldwide as shown earlier, then the IMB's aggregate tally of the kinds of vessels that are attacked annually can be used to make strong inferences about the trend in maritime Asia as compared to other regions. From Figure 3.37, it can be seen that generally, bulk carriers, general cargo vessels, and container ships have become the ships

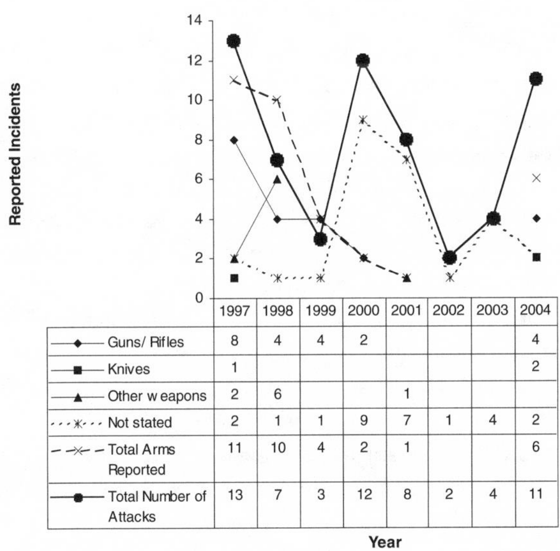

	1997	1998	1999	2000	2001	2002	2003	2004
Guns/ Rifles	8	4	4	2				4
Knives	1							2
Other weapons	2	6			1			
Not stated	2	1	1	9	7	1	4	2
Total Arms Reported	11	10	4	2	1			6
Total Number of Attacks	13	7	3	12	8	2	4	11

Figure 3.36 Type of arms used in reported piracy attacks in Northeast Asia, 1997–2004
Source: Data compiled from tables in Piracy and Armed Robbery against Ships: Annual Report, (Kuala Lumpur: IMB Regional Piracy Centre), 1997 passim.

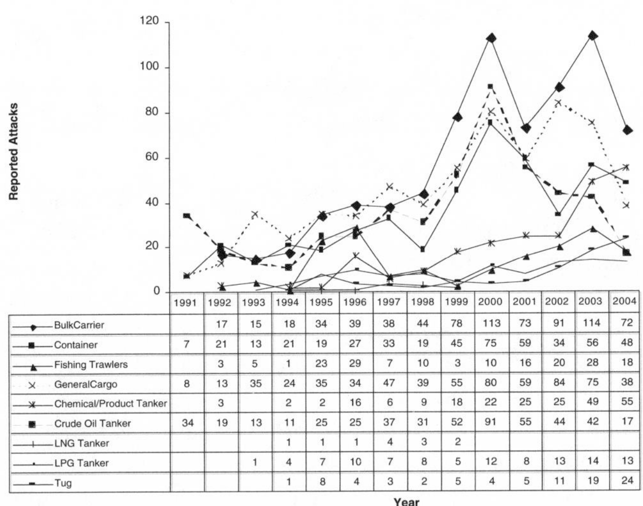

	1991	1992	1993	1994	1995	1996	1997	1998	1999	2000	2001	2002	2003	2004
BulkCarrier		17	15	18	34	39	38	44	78	113	73	91	114	72
Container	7	21	13	21	19	27	33	19	45	75	59	34	56	48
Fishing Trawlers		3	5	1	23	29	7	10	3	10	16	20	28	18
GeneralCargo	8	13	35	24	35	34	47	39	55	80	59	84	75	38
Chemical/Product Tanker		3		2	2	16	6	9	18	22	25	25	49	55
Crude Oil Tanker	34	19	13	11	25	25	37	31	52	91	55	44	42	17
LNG Tanker				1	1	1	4	3	2					
LPG Tanker			1	4	7	10	7	8	5	12	8	13	14	13
Tug				1	8	4	3	2	5	4	5	11	19	24

Figure 3.37 Top nine vessel types attacked worldwide, 1991–2002
Source: For the figures from 1991 to 1992, see *Piracy and Armed Robbery against Ships: Annual Report, 1st January – 30th December 2002* (Kuala Lumpur: IMB Regional Piracy Centre, 30 January 2003), p. 13, Table 12. For 1993 to 2004, see *Piracy and Armed Robbery against Ships: Annual Report, 1st January – 30th December 2004* (Kuala Lumpur: IMB Regional Piracy Centre, 7 February 2005), p. 12, Table 11.

of choice over the 11-year period. Attacks on tugs have also risen to some degree, and the IMB attributes this to the high market value of the palm and gas oil they carry.[21] To some alarm, attacks upon chemical tankers have been on the rise while attacks on crude oil tankers have been on the decline, from around 91 attacks in 2000 to 17 in 2004. Lastly, and perhaps most significantly, there has not been an attack upon LNG (liquefied natural gas) tankers since 1999, in addition to the extremely low number of attacks upon this kind of ship from 1994 to 1999. This runs against the grain of media reports and analyses that bank on the possibility of a "floating bomb" scenario caused inadvertently by an act of piracy or intentionally by maritime terrorists, as is discussed later in the chapter.

Second, from the IMB statistics represented in Figure 3.38, the trends on the timing of attacks by pirates in maritime Asia tend to fall within the window of 1800 hours to 0900 hours. Interestingly, the data shows that while piracy starts to peak between 1800 hours to 2200 hours, there is a slight drop from 2201 hours to midnight before a more intense rise starts to unfold between 0001 hours to 0400 hours, a period when antipiracy watches by crew on the graveyard shift tend to be more difficult to exercise due to natural lapses in human vigilance during such interludes. Equally interesting, the year 2004 shows a sudden rise in the number of attacks in the daylight from 0900 hours to 1100 hours; reflecting increased audacity.

Third, the IMB as well as Liss underscore the general profile of pirates in maritime Asia in the late modern period, of which there exist the following categories, roughly in the ascending order of scale of their operations and in relation to the class of ships they are capable of apprehending:

1. Hit-and-run robbers operating in small groups who are generally not predisposed toward violence which the IMB terms as "Asian piracy" — perpetrators who attempt to slip aboard a ship under the cover of darkness and to leave with the booty unnoticed, using force only when their escape is blocked or when they are confronted by the crew.[22]
2. Hit-and-run robbers operating in small groups who tend to employ violence in their attacks; perpetrators who intend to take a ship by force and to confront the crew with violence.[23]
3. "Social" pirates — Liss argues that these are a variation of Eric Hobsbawm's notion of "social bandits" who are driven by the poverty of their villages and societies to turn to piracy to generate income and material gain for their communities, most notably on Indonesia's Riau islands and in Manila Bay in the Philippines.[24] They appear to straddle the two categories above.
4. Organized pirate gangs — characterized by a much higher level of organization and sophistication, and where the use of overwhelming force and violence is expected.[25]

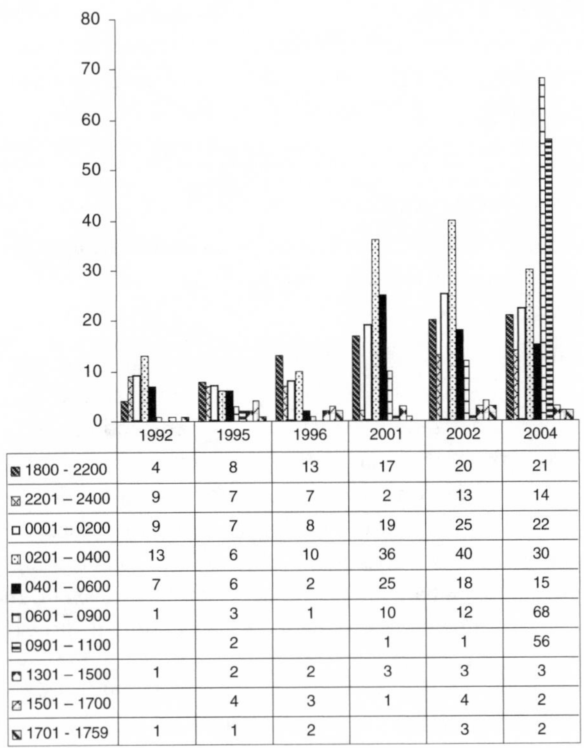

	1992	1995	1996	2001	2002	2004
1800 - 2200	4	8	13	17	20	21
2201 – 2400	9	7	7	2	13	14
0001 – 0200	9	7	8	19	25	22
0201 – 0400	13	6	10	36	40	30
0401 – 0600	7	6	2	25	18	15
0601 – 0900	1	3	1	10	12	68
0901 – 1100		2		1	1	56
1301 – 1500	1	2	2	3	3	3
1501 – 1700		4	3	1	4	2
1701 - 1759	1	1	2		3	2

Figure 3.38 Time of attacks in maritime Asia, 1992–1996, 2001–2002, and 2004
Source: The schema for the time bands used in Figure 3.38 is based on one used by the IMB which they employed only once in their 1992 report. While it not clear whether the IMB gives treatment to the issue of the timing of attacks in their report in 1993 (which is not available to this author), the IMB becomes inconsistent with this issue between 1994 to 2004 (or 2005 excluded from this particular analysis). In 1994, the IMB drops the use of a detailed summary table and summarizes that "[w]hile it is generally the case that attacks occur during the hours of darkness, it should be remembered that 11 out of the 90 attacks in 1994 were conducted between 0900 and 2100 hours." From 1995 to 1996, the IMB does not make any comment on the timing of attacks and places the information in the detailed narration of attacks for each year. The timing of attacks is then dropped in subsequent reports until it reappears from 2001 onwards. The author conducted a tally of the timing of attacks from the narrations for these years except 2003, which was not available to the author at the time of writing.

5. Piracy that has political connections with the state on the one hand and counterstate movements on the other, such as secessionist and rebel groups. In terms of state-sponsored piracy, Peter Chalk describes in some detail the controversy surrounding the suspected role of the Chinese state in officially sanctioning piracy against foreign vessels as a way of asserting Beijing's sovereignty over the South

China Sea.[26] In terms of secessionist and rebel groups, Liss discusses the role of the Free Aceh Movement (GAM) in Indonesia and the Abu Sayyaf Group in the Philippines in carrying out pirate attacks as an economic mode of financing their separate political and militant activities.[27]

General Drivers Behind Late Modern Piracy in Maritime Asia

Because piracy is a criminal activity that preys on maritime trade, it is clear that the rise of late modern piracy in maritime Asia is strongly linked to three interrelated sets of developments:

1. The intensification in global maritime trade and the rise in commercial maritime traffic paralleling (1) the further intensification of economic globalization particularly after the end of the Cold War which saw the shift from "battlefields to markets" and (2) further advancements in containerization since the 1970s, including the shift from ocean carrier to total logistics system; greater concentrations of trade flows of traditional commodities such as sugar, wood and grain; the globalization of production facilities; and the development of supply-chain management. Since the end of the twentieth century, 80 percent of world trade (or about six billion tons of cargo) is being pushed by sea, supported by a massive maritime trade network supported by 46,000 commercial vessels and 1.25 million seafarers calling at 4,000 ports. Ninety percent of general cargo is now transported in containers with 15 million of them in circulation, amounting to 232 million container moves annually.
2. The dynamic growth and development of maritime Asian economies has attracted greater volumes of commercial maritime traffic passing through the region. Notwithstanding the Asian financial crisis of 1997–1998, the region has witnessed relatively high growth in the past few decades. Continuing industrialization and trade, increasing regionalization and economic integration, and the growth of trade between Asia, Europe, and the United States has led to the rise of new Asian hub ports such as Malaysia's Tanjung Pelepas, Thailand's Laem Chabang, and China's Port of Shanghai on top of Hong Kong and Singapore as established ports which serve as key container choke points with connectivity in a "hub-and-spoke system" to regions worldwide.
3. The increasing divide behind the haves and have-nots in the world and maritime Asia as a result of the fragmentary forces of economic globalization. As Liss points out, while many people benefited from the economic developments of the 1990s, others were left behind in the boom:

For some of the more desperate of those left behind, a pirate attack can be an alternative source of income to feed a hungry family. Since the 1997 economic crisis, poverty, unemployment, and uncertainty spread even more widely in Southeast Asia, and more people were forced to seek alternative sources of livelihood and income.[28]

4. The proliferation of small arms among transnational criminal syndicates since the end of the Cold War who are now able to take advantage of a huge array of sophisticated weaponry left over from past wars in Afghanistan and Cambodia as well as from the former Red Army.

However, it is not entirely clear if the growth of military and naval operations such as antipiracy patrols in maritime Asia — especially in Southeast Asia — or if conversely, the "reduction in the number of superpower naval vessels patrolling Asian sea-lanes" can be regarded as a significant development or driver to explain the fall and rise of piracy. Two counterfactual cases exist to place the role of military and naval operations into question. The first case is the implementation by the littoral states of Malaysia, Indonesia, and Singapore of round-the-clock coordinated naval patrols in July 2004, codenamed Operation Malsindo, comprising 17 vessels patrolling the 900-kilometer stretch constituting the Malacca Straits, hence, by far, the largest patrolling exercise to be undertaken in the Straits. There has been no tangible evidence, at the time of writing, to suggest that the coordinated naval patrols by the littoral states since July 2004 have done much to reduce the scale of piracy attacks in these waters. The inference is drawn from the third and fourth quarter results for 2004 and the first and second quarter figures for the Malacca Straits, which show no concrete decrease in the number of attacks. The second quarter 2005 figures show a rise for Indonesia as well (see Table 3.2):[29]

The second case refers to the apparent lull in piracy in Indonesian waters and the Malacca Straits in the wake of the Asian tsunami on 26 December

Table 3.2 Total number of reported incidents of piracy/armed robbery at sea in the Malacca Straits and Indonesia in the last quarters of 2004 and the first two quarters of 2005

	2004		2005	
	3rd quarter	4th quarter	1st quarter	2nd quarter
Malacca Straits	3	5	2	6
IndonesianWaters	17	16	16	26
Malaysian Waters	1		2	
Singapore Straits			2	4

2004 which some analysts deduced as a possible factor to explain the lack of reported attacks to the IMB in the first two months of 2005. The IMB was reported to have asserted that the "[pirate] gangs could have been quiet because of the presence of multinational naval contingents engaged in tsunami relief operations in Aceh." However, though the last of the naval contingents departed from the region by 16 March, a string of attacks occurred from late February to early March. The opening attack took place in the Malacca Straits on 28 February involving an attack by pirates against a tugboat towing a barge. The attackers captured the tug's captain and chief officer, who were then freed a week later. On 12 March, 35 armed pirates attacked an Indonesian-registered tanker, the *Tri Samudra*, fully laden with highly flammable cargo off Port Dickson, before boarding it and taking two hostages: the Indonesian captain and chief engineer. The hijackers demanded a ransom of two billion Indonesian rupiah (S$350,200 [US$220,700, ed.]) from the ship's firm. The third reported attack occurred on 14 March 2005, when 14 armed pirates fired on a Japanese tugboat, the *Idaten*, when it passed by Penang to tow a barge. Four pirates boarded the vessel and took three hostages — two Japanese and a Filipino — with a ransom demand of about 800,000 yen (S$12,470 [US$7,860, ed.]). In the final analysis, just as an editorial in the *Straits Times* argued that "[i]t is guesswork whether the tsunami ... took with it pirate gangs," the same assertion about "guesswork" applies to the impact of the multinational military and naval presence.[30] Further study, fieldwork, and more rigorous methods of analysis are needed to investigate the causal relationship between military and naval patrols and maritime piracy.

In the final analysis, despite the rise of piracy in areas such as the Malacca Straits, the concern that this threat can disrupt maritime shipping through an intership collision borne out by a hijacked vessel must be placed in some perspective. In 2004, there were a total of 37 attacks in the Straits. When placed against the grain of 50,000 ships transiting the Strait, the probability of an attack is 0.07 percent. Even if we double the figures to take account of the 40 to 60 percent of all attacks which the IMB says goes unreported, this produces a probability of 0.1 percent.

However, these low statistical probabilities hide the manner in which piracy victimizes and brutalizes a vessel's crew and its shipping company, by way of kidnapping for ransom activities increasingly undertaken by pirates in maritime Asia. It has been reported that about US$1 million in ransom was paid out by ship owners in the region in 2004, with an average ransom fee negotiated at an estimated range between US$50,000 to US$100,000. In that year, 40 sailors were kidnapped in about 20 incidents. Four seafarers were killed because of botched negotiations. As of the end of June 2005, there have already been five ransom-driven kidnappings in the Strait. In July 2005, it was announced that the Joint War Committee (JWC) of Lloyd's

Market Association had declared the Strait a war risk area, along with 20 other locales worldwide, in jeopardy of conflict, strikes, terrorism, and other related dangers.[31]

"Postmodern" Piracy in Maritime Asia, 2001 — Present

As the preceding analysis has shown, notwithstanding the exogenous factor of poor regional law enforcement, the increasing role of organized crime in piracy activities — which has led to attacks accompanied by better planning and equipment — and the availability and use of small arms and other ordinance are key endogenous factors that partly explain the increasing violence that accompanies these attacks. Warren sums up the current trend in Southeast Asia vis-à-vis the Malacca Straits running up from the 1970s:

> In the last three decades of the twentieth century, these space-age raiders have used computers and the Internet to select vessels and itineraries; they have relied on radar to locate targeted vessels; they have gathered intelligence from radio transmissions and informers and carried out night attacks using swift, small motorised boats and automatic weapons ... While they have not been ignored, between the late 1970s and 2000 and as a major feature of an emergent globalised culture, the pirates and criminals on the high seas of Southeast Asia have become more numerous, more dangerous and equipped with more sophisticated crime technology.[32]

Though the conjecture that certain piracy syndicates use computers, the Internet, radar systems, and intercept the radio transmissions of commercial maritime traffic is warranted by a mix of limited evidence and informed guesswork, the usage of the phrase "space-age" to denote the "modernity" of contemporary "pirates and criminals" in Southeast Asia relative to the capacities of state authorities and their maritime forces is problematic. First, historical pirates of the organized kind such as privateers and raiders of the eighteenth and nineteenth centuries were just as "modern" as their state and state-sponsored naval counterparts, in terms of the weapons, ships, and maritime crew they used. Thus, the use of the label "space-age" does not produce any distinctive power for the purposes of academic analysis.

Second, and more importantly, while the implicit referent object of the description may be organized piracy syndicates, the loose interchange with the general label of "pirate" and "criminal" has lent a blanket quality to the overall phenomenon of piracy in the region being "space age" in nature. To be sure, ad hoc or less organized and relatively poorer bandits are just as capable of conducting the same "swift" armed attacks, and using small boats may be attributed not necessarily to prudent maritime tactics (of evading detection and capture) and sound operational planning, but to an inherent lack of long-projection capabilities as well as a lack of supplies and navigational equipment needed for longer excursions. As the then Royal Malaysian Navy Chief Admiral Datuk Ilyas Din observed of the Malacca Straits from Malaysia's counterpiracy experience:

> Piracy is usually only focused in [a] certain area because they do not have sophisticated boats to stay long at sea. They only used small boats when committing robberies because they do not have boats equipped with sophisticated or high-technology equipment and their targets are usually not far from their operating base.[33]

Thus, it is likely that a large proportion of piracy attacks in Southeast Asia, and the Malacca Straits in particular, are generated by common sea banditry committed by people in the fringes of the maritime economy, such as poor fishermen and taxi-boat drivers, who are accredited in turn with the same degree of sophistication as their organized counterparts especially in media reports, which may gloss over the details behind the IMB's oft-quoted statement that since 2000 "modern piracy is violent and ruthless" and which may overemphasize the adjective ("modern") over the noun ("piracy").[34]

The "Securitization" of Piracy: The "First Wave," Mid-1990s to 2001

In fact, the endowment of an added mixture of sophistication and ruthlessness upon piracy at the turn of the twenty-first century, has played a key role in the social (re)construction, "politicization," and indeed, the unprecedented "securitization" of contemporary piracy in maritime Asia, leading to what could in turn could be called the rise of "postmodern" piracy in maritime Asia: a phenomenon that has been reinterpreted and reconstituted outside of its traditional archetype to the point where it has been dislocated from its foundational, historical, and sociological leanings. Emmers neatly summaries the epistemology that comprises "securitization" in his *Non-Traditional Security in the Asia-Pacific: The Dynamics of Securitisation* (2004). He argues that a transnational criminal phenomena such as piracy can be transformed — at least in terms of discourse — into a nontraditional security threat through a process captured by the Copenhagen School in the field of Security Studies, founded by Barry Buzan, Ole Waever, and Jaap de Wilde in the late 1990s. Briefly, security is a socially constructed concept where security problems are generated out of issue areas that have run the course of being nonpoliticized, politicized, and then securitized. The dynamics of securitization are underpinned by securitizing actors which are often "political leaders, bureaucracies, governments, lobbyists, and pressure groups" and their referent objects to be securitized.[35] As Emmers elaborates at length:

> A securitising actor articulates an already politicised issue as an existential threat to security and asserts that it needs to be removed from the ordinary norms of the political domain due to its declared

> urgency. Securitisation therefore refers to the classification of certain issues, persons or entities as existential threats requiring extraordinary measures ... The Copenhagen School stresses the importance of the speech act in the process of securitisation. Speech informs and influences our perception of reality and has a direct impact on human behavior and outcomes. Consequently, it does much more than just represent "reality." Securitising actors use language to articulate a problem in security terms and to persuade a relevant audience of its immediate danger. The articulation in security terms conditions public opinion and provides securitising actors with the right to mobilise state power and move beyond traditional rules.[36]

On top of the discursive speech act, Emmers adds that the necessary final step toward complete securitization requires the nondiscursive act of policy implementation and action: "the implementation of extraordinary measures to address the so-defined threat to security."[37]

Indeed, there could be said to be two "waves" of the securitization of piracy in maritime Asia from 1999 to the present. First, there has been a synchronic mix of politicization and a "first wave" of securitization driven by both international media reports and governmental undertakings (driven mainly by Japan) from 1995 to 2001. According to John J. Bradford, "[I]n the mid-1990s, Japanese researchers had identified Southeast Asian piracy as a potential threat to Japan, and successfully politicized the issue by bringing it into the policy discourse." However, Bradford adds that "the piracy threat was not securitized [in Japan and the region] until [late] 1999," "given Japanese antimilitarist norms and hesitancy to take a direct role in regional security."[38] In early 1999, an international media agency such as the BBC could carry an article about the findings of a seminar organized by the United Nation's International Maritime Organization (IMO), which had found that piracy had become a growing problem, especially in Asia, hence fueling the regional politicization of the issue. On 24 April 2000, the BBC carried an article on the release of the IMB's piracy report for 1999 and the bureau's opinion that the phenomenon had turned violent and ruthless.[39] At the November 1999 ASEAN+3 Summit in Manila, Japan then surprised other Asia-Pacific members (and created much opposition from countries such as China) when Prime Minister Keizo Obuchi announced Japan's desire for its Japan Coast Guard to conduct joint antipiracy patrols with Southeast Asia maritime forces.

"Second Wave" Securitization: The Conflation Between Piracy and "Maritime Terrorism," 2001 to the Present

Next, a "second wave" of securitization from around 2000/2001 to the present (driven mainly by Singapore and the United States) was promulgated by three sets of developments:

1. The rising threat of "maritime terrorism" — which can be roughly defined as attacks on vessels or fixed platforms at sea or in port including suicide bombings and/or vessel hijackings leading to such bombings —from 2000 to 2002[40]
2. The rise of global terrorism waged by the militant Islamic network known as the Al Qaeda which became fully apparent in the wake of Al Qaeda's terrorist attacks against the United States on 11 September 2001 (henceforth referred to as 9/11)
3. The "Jemaah Islamiyah" bombings in the Indonesia island of Bali on 12 October 2002

With regard to the first set of developments, the following list of successful and attempted maritime terrorist attacks worldwide and in the region, as well as new intelligence markers that unveiled Al Qaeda's possible maritime operations between 2000 to 2002, had the effect of ushering in the second wave:

- The Al Qaeda explosive-laden dingy attack on the USS *Cole* at the port of Aden in Yemen in October 2000 killed 17 sailors and injured 39 others.
- The discovery by analysts that Al Qaeda had dispatched the masterminds of the USS *Cole* attack to Kuala Lumpur, Malaysia, to plan another attack on a another U.S. ship visiting a Malaysian port in 2000.
- The suicide bombing of the French-flagged tanker *Limburg*, anchored approximately 5 miles from the port Mina al-Dhabah off Yemen on 6 October 2002, where a small boat carrying a large amount of explosives rammed the ship's hull, wounding four persons.[41]
- Malaysia's Special Branch disruption of a plan by the Kumpulan Mujahidin Malaysia (KMM) to ambush a U.S. ship in 2001.
- Singapore's Internal Security Department (ISD) disruption of an Al-Qaeda and JI plot to attack a U.S. ship docked in Singapore in 2002.
- The Philippine's based ASG claimed responsibility for an explosion sinking the *SuperFerry 14*, a large RoRo (roll on-roll off) ferry sailing from Manila to Bacolod and Davao, and killing over 100 people.
- Senior al-Qaeda operative Omar al-Faruq's indication of plans to attack an American naval ship in Surabaya, Indonesia's second largest port, during his interrogation after he was taken into U.S. custody when arrested by Indonesian intelligence in June 2002.[42]
- Though Abdul Raheem an-Nashiri, the so-called Prince of the Sea, has been captured, the fact that Al Qaeda possessed a chief of naval operations confirms that maritime attacks form a serious component of their spectrum of operations.
- At the level of technological capabilities, dual-use technologies such as the Global Positioning System (GPS), satellite communications

systems, sea sport scooters, scuba diving equipment, and mini-submarines are either being added to the network's inventory list or are within their purchasing power.

Still, despite the burgeoning threat of maritime terrorism setting the initial tone of the second wave, the peak in this succeeding process of piracy securitization was driven in part by 9/11, which produced two subsequent effects. First, it had the effect of exposing the vulnerability of every conceivable piece of social, political, and economic infrastructure of value to terrorism. Thus, it broadened the scope of terrorism, which on top of direct maritime attacks such as the USS *Cole* bombing, has come to include what Michael Richardson has termed "maritime-related terrorism", the financing of terrorism and the supply and shipment of weapons of mass destruction (WMD), explosives, suicide bombers, and other resources through the global maritime supply chain and trading network via commercial vessels, containers, and seafarers.[43] In a very short time, concerns over maritime-related terrorism led to the implementation of the US-led Container Security Initiative (CSI) in January 2002, the Customs-Trade Partnership Against Terrorism (C-TPAT), and the Proliferation Security Initiative (PSI) in May 2003, supported by various participating countries.

In maritime Asia itself, the third set of developments initiated by the Bali bombings by the JI in 2002 — which analysts interpreted at the time as a shift in the strategy of groups such the JI toward regional economic targets, which by extension, could include commercial shipping lanes such as the Malacca Straits — buttressed what Adam J. Young and Mark Valencia have termed as the "conflation" of piracy and terrorism by the international media and certain maritime powers: "in the charged political atmosphere, the mass media and governments have blurred the line between piracy and acts of terrorism."[44] For example, certain writers were already referring to "piracy as terrorism" in Southeast Asia a few months prior to the 2002 Bali bombings. They employed the trends in regional piracy to make a case for what the prevailing security lexicon call the "experienced vulnerability" of regional waterways such as the Malacca Straits to other similar threats such as maritime terrorism, which as past attacks have shown, also tend to deploy small motorized boats for their operations.[45] Indeed, after the 2002 Bali bombings, Richard Halloran posed the question "What if Asia's pirates and terrorists joined hands?" in an opinion editorial of the *South China Morning Post* in May 2003.[46] Young and Valencia suspect that the conflation may be a political device to "persuade reluctant developing countries to let maritime powers pursue pirates and terrorists in their territorial and archipelagic waters"[47] and as the author argues below, to pressure these countries to initiate their own alternative regional arrangements.

Like Japan, which led the first wave of piracy securitization in the late 1990s, Singapore became the key initiator of the second wave by the middle of 2003. At a key Asian security conference known as the Shangri-La Dialogue in June

2003, Singapore's Deputy Prime Minister and then Defence Minister Dr. Tony Tan acknowledged the forewarning of the media and analysts mentioned earlier on maritime terrorism: "Some security analysts have warned that with the hardening of land and aviation targets, the threat of maritime terrorism is likely to shift to maritime targets, particularly commercial shipping."[48] Dr. Tan also recognized the claims for a nexus between maritime terrorism and regional piracy:

> We have been dealing with the problem of piracy for some time, and there are methods and tactics associated with terrorism which we can identify, and put in place several preventive measures.[49]

It is clear that in addition to the roughly similar modus operandi of employing small motorized boats and the tendency toward hijacking operations, the technological imperative constituting Warren's notion of the space-ageness of regional piracy and perceived technological capabilities of Al Qaeda in the maritime realm had reinforced the possibility of a nexus, though it was not entirely clear what exact form it would take.

It would take the infamous *Aegis Terrorism Report 2003* released by the London-based Aegis Defence Services, a private military/security company, a few months after Dr. Tan's debut statement, for a more developed notion of a nexus to become adopted in subsequent regional threat assessments. Chiefly, the report claimed that the attack and boarding of a chemical tanker *Dewi Madrim* off the coast of Indonesia's island of Sumatra by ten "pirates" — armed with machetes, guns, and VHF (Very High Frequency) radios — who took the helm and steered the vessel for around half an hour before abducting the ship's captain and first officer (who are still missing), were actually

> terrorists learning to drive a ship, and the kidnapping (without any attempt to ransom the officers) was aimed at acquiring expertise to help the terrorists mount a maritime attack. In other words, attacks like that on the *Dewi Madrim* are equivalent of the al-Qaeda hijackers who perpetrated the September 11th attacks going to flying school in Florida.[50]

Following the *Dewi Madrim* incident, Dr Tan commented to the press that:

> Piracy is entering a new phase; recent attacks have been conducted with almost *military precision*. The perpetrators are well-trained, have well laid out plans ... The increased frequency of piracy, attacks, the changing pattern of how the attacks are carried out, lead us to fear the worst, that an operation is being planned, the preliminary preparation is taking place, and the vessels are being readied.[51]

Subsequently, Singapore's media devoted a full-page spread to the Aegis report and highlighted its generation of three possible "maritime spectacular" scenarios that would disrupt shipping in the Suez Canal, the Panama Canal, the Straits of Gibraltar, or the Malacca Straits:

- The exploding of a liquid petroleum gas (LPG) tanker, or the rupturing of an oil tanker inside or near these sea-lanes
- The blocking of a port or restriction of a seaway while simultaneously causing the spillage of a toxic cargo to pollute the sea, the shoreline or the atmosphere
- Setting fire to a VLCC (very large crude carrier) inside a major port[52]

Hence, through the discursive speech-act, Dr. Tan articulated the issues of maritime terrorism and piracy as a security problem, to persuade a relevant audience of its immediate danger and to legitimize the right to mobilize state power and move beyond traditional rules. It set the general tone for Singapore's maritime security agenda for the next few years, rearticulated through a host of other statements by Singaporean ministers and officials, as well by the country's media. Even subsequent investigations into the attack on the *Dewi Madrim* by the IMB and by Liss in 2004, which both came to the conclusion that terrorists were not involved in the incident, had done nothing to change the tide and momentum of the second wave of piracy securitization as of the time of writing.[53] In fact, the article "Terrorism Goes to Sea" by Gal Luft and Anne Korin in the November/December 2004 issue of *Foreign Affairs* makes reference to the *Dewi Madrim* incident, as it originally stood in the Aegis report, and under the subheading entitled "A New Nexus" argues that "piracy on the high seas is becoming a key tactic of terrorist groups."[54]

Not surprisingly, the idea of a maritime terrorist threat in Southeast Asia and the nexus between piracy and maritime terrorism generated controversy among the other two littoral states of Indonesia and Malaysia (which maintains that there is no credible evidence to suggest such a nexus) articulating similar charges to those of Young and Valencia of a Singaporean agenda of wanting to draw in the support of external maritime powers — especially the United States — in the patrolling of the Malacca Straits which straddles the territorial boundaries of the littoral states. Indeed, this is exactly what happened when commander-in-chief of U.S. Pacific Command Admiral Thomas B. Fargo's testimony to the U.S. House of Representatives in March 2004 revealed that the Pentagon was formulating a Regional Maritime Security Initiative (RMSI) to combat piracy, maritime terrorism, and sea trafficking in people and narcotics in the Malacca Straits. The main point of controversy when the proposal became public was that the RMSI would involve not only closer intelligence sharing with Southeast Asian states, but also deployment of U.S. Marines and special forces on high-speed vessels to interdict maritime threats, particularly from terrorists. In April, Al Qaeda carried out a successful multi-boat attack on an oil terminal off the southern city of Basra in United States-occupied Iraq, killing two U.S. sailors and wounding four others, hence adding further brevity to the RMSI.[55]

While Admiral Fargo secured immediate support for the RMSI from Singapore (a day after the Basra attack), Indonesia and Malaysia strongly objected to the initiative and asserted that security in the Straits was the responsibility of the coastal states. Consequently, both the pressure of the RMSI and the significance of Indonesian and Malaysian support (or objection) to enable any multilateral initiative in the Straits to succeed compelled Singapore (which desired any undertaking rather than none) to shore up support for Indonesia's suggestion for the littoral states to hold round-the-clock coordinated naval patrols implemented in July 2004.

By the middle of 2005, Malaysia's and Singapore's perspectives on managing regional maritime security converged further when Malaysia's Deputy Prime Minister Najib Razak at the Shangri-La Dialogue articulated a rudimentary maritime security "doctrine" for the littoral states at the Shangri-La Dialogue in June that year.[56] Most significantly, he proposed the Eyes in the Sky initiative (EiS), which entailed the conducting of joint maritime air patrols over the Malacca Straits by the littoral states. In a matter of three months, Malaysia, Singapore, and Indonesia launched their maiden EiS patrol in September 2005 (with Thailand as an observer and additional contributor of aircraft).[57]

The Demise of Maritime Terrorism, the "Desecuritisation" of Piracy, and "Back to the Future" in Maritime Asia?

However, while there has been a moment of unprecedented cooperation among the littoral states and indeed the rest of Southeast Asia as well Japan, China, and India (which made their own proposals for various patrolling and escorting contributions in the South China Sea and the Malacca Straits), there appears to be a countermoment heralding the possible decline of the threat of maritime terrorism. On balance, since the series of plans and foiled attempts at maritime terrorism in Malaysia, Singapore, and Indonesia between 2000 and 2002, there have been no further indications that the Al Qaeda, the JI, or other terrorist groups still intend to conduct maritime terrorist operations globally and in the region. While global and regional terrorism continues to pose a significant threat at the time of writing, the U.S.-led war against global terror has led to a general attrition in the leadership, manpower, resources, and the financing of the Al Qaeda network to the point where it has been compelled to concentrate its limited resources to its campaign in the Middle East, specifically in U.S.-occupied Iraq. In Southeast Asia, recent analyses indicate that the JI network also intends to focus its future attacks in Indonesia.

In fact, the recent pattern of attacks by these groups — including the Al Qaeda-linked attacks in the Spanish city of Madrid in March 2004 and the London bombings on 7 July 2005, and JI-linked bombings of the Marriot Hotel in Jakarta in August 2003 and of Australia's Jakarta embassy in September

2004, as well as the second Bali bombings in October 2005 — reinforces the claim that that terrorist organizations prefer to hedge their bets on land-based targets which are tried and tested in their success, against maritime-based ones. Since 1961, only approximately 40 maritime terrorist incidents have been documented.[58] In contrast, from 1981 to just prior to the 9/11 attacks alone, there were about 9,000 international terrorist attacks (excluding intra-Palestinian violence).[59] Lastly, all things being equal, it is also possible that current efforts at securing vital sea-lanes and major ports that run along the Straits are finally generating a deterrence dividend (in terms of perception) against maritime terrorism. It is also equally likely that terrorist organizations may be ruling out an attack in the maritime theater because current state awareness and responses have removed the element of shock and surprise which terrorists appear to prize highly in their operations.

To be sure, after the *SuperFerry 14* bombing, the ASG maritime terrorist operations still remain significant amid the volatile situation between the central government and Mindanao. In May 2004, officials from the country's defense and energy departments signed an agreement to strengthen the security of the Malampaya gas field in the southern portion of the archipelago in light of the indications that the ASG (in possible collaboration with the JI) intended to sabotage and attack the facility. There were renewed indications of a possible attack in April 2005. In Sri Lanka, the rebel Sri Lankan Liberation Tigers of Tamil Eelam (LTTE), who have been fighting for a separate Tamil homeland in the country's north and east since 1976, is reputed to be the world's preeminent organization with regard to maritime terrorist operations. In the end, while the threat of maritime terrorism may persist in the southern Philippines and Sri Lanka, it is possible that the threat of maritime terrorism could become "desecuritized" in the Malacca Straits should it fail to materialize in the this waterway over the medium to long term. The implications of such a development are shared by piracy scholars John Kleinen and Manon Osseweijer, who rightly question whether "the issue of maritime piracy [which has existed through the ages] will remain on the international research agenda after the imminent link with terrorism and cataclysm has faded away."[60]

Already, regional governments and commercial shippers may be attempting to distance themselves from their earlier claims about the rise of piracy and its impact after the Joint War Committee (JWC) of Lloyd's Market Association declaration in July 2005 that the Malacca Straits was deemed a war risk area, along with 21 other locales worldwide, in jeopardy of conflict, strikes, terrorism, and other related dangers, which led to fears that insurance risk premiums were set to increase substantially, a partial reflection from the private sector that the littoral states are not doing a satisfactory job in securing the Straits. This placed the Malacca Straits, as well as other areas within Indonesian waters such as the ports of Dumai and Belawan, in notorious company with war-torn Somalia, insurgency-stricken Iraq, and a politically unstable

Lebanon. However, Malaysian Transport Minister Chan Kong Choy lashed out at the declaration, claiming that the Straits is one of the safest shipping lanes in the world by citing a statistical probability for a piracy attack similar to one cited in an earlier section of this chapter.

In the final analysis, it is clear that piracy is a nontraditional security threat that cannot be solved through military solutions. As Mak Joon Num suggests, it requires better policing on land. If there is anything to be learned from counterterrorism, piracy should be rooted out by attacking sources of their strength on land, disrupting their organizational structure, and isolating them from their sources of support. In particular, this means destroying their bases and hideouts; cutting off their sources of capital, technology and recruitment; and crippling the middlemen and markets that allow them to dispose of their loot. Mak reiterates the long-held argument that as a long-term solution, governments would have to employ socioeconomic measures such as poverty alleviation and good governance in order to deal with piracy (and even terrorism) effectively.[61] Mak explains that the principles of success for countering pirates in the past have not changed over the last few centuries. For example, during the Spanish-Dutch-British campaigns in the Sulu seas in the eighteenth to the nineteenth century, the British and Dutch colonial powers had failed to suppress Balangingi-Samal and Iranun raiders of the Sulu area for more than 70 years between 1760 to 1830 as they had relied mainly on patrols to protect trading routes. They did not attack Iranun-Balangingi strongholds and left the initiative to the raiders, who also possessed a superior knowledge of the local maritime terrain. Similar to the situation in the Malacca Straits today, the colonial borders of the period were not demarcated and hampered effective regional cooperation in the fight against raiders. However, these lessons were quickly learned, and subsequent colonial attacks on the strongholds of the raiders explain the success of their subsequent campaigns from 1845 to 1878.[62] At the 2005 Shangri-La Dialogue, Minister Najib acknowledged the importance of directing stronger enforcement, regional cooperation, and a better use of technology toward the effort of detaining pirates "at source."[63] If the current climate of regional cooperation in maritime Asia in fighting piracy, potential maritime terrorism, and other maritime-based threats can be sustained, the question of greater effectiveness will revolve around questions of sovereignty and international law as the possibility of attacking pirates at their source depends on overcoming legal and sovereign barriers.

Notes

1. Ger Teitler, "Piracy in Southeast Asia: A Historical Comparison," *Maritime Studies*, vol. 1, no. 1, 2002, p. 68 (avalable at http://www.marecentre.nl/mast/documents/GerTeitler.pdf).
2. Carolin Liss, "Maritime Piracy in Southeast Asia," in *Southeast Asian Affairs 2003* (Singapore: Institute of Southeast Asian Studies, 2004), p. 57.
3. Carolin Liss, op. cit., pp. 52–68; Peter Chalk, *Non-Military Security and Global Order: The Impact of Extremism, Violence and Chaos on National and International Security* (London: Macmillan Press, 2000), especially, "Contemporary Maritime Piracy," pp. 57–76.

William M. Carpenter and David G. Wiencek, "Maritime Piracy in Asia," in William M. Carpenter and David G. Wiencek, eds., *Asian Security Handbook: An Assessment of Political Security Issues in the Asia-Pacific Region* (New York: M.E. Sharpe, 1998), pp. 79–88; Jason Abbot and Neil Renwick, "Pirates? Maritime Piracy and Societal Security in Southeast Asia," *Pacifica Review*, vol. 11, no. 1, February 1999, pp. 7–24.

4. Ger Teitler, op. cit.
5. This definition can be found on p. 3 of *Piracy and Armed Robbery Against Ships: Report for the Period 1 January to 30 June 2005* (released 17 July 2005), used during the writing of this chapter.
6. I. R. Hyslop, "Contemporary Piracy," in Eric Ellen, ed., *Piracy at Sea* (Paris: ICC Publishing, 1989), p. 6.
7. Stefan Eklof, "Piracy: a critical perspective," *International Institute for Asian Studies Newsletter*, No. 36, March 2005, p. 12. See also Cleopatra Degas, "The Problem of Under Reporting," http://www.geocities.com/cdelegas/PIRACYWEBSITE_probUnder_reporting.html (accessed on 4 August 2005).
8. Donald J. Puchala, *Theory and History of International Relations* (New York: Routledge, 2003), chap. 4, "International Theory and Cyclical History," especially p. 53.
9. Ibid.
10. Adam J. Young, "Roots of Contemporary Maritime Piracy in Southeast Asia," in Derek Johnson and Mark Valencia, eds., *Piracy in Southeast Asia: Status, Issues and Responses* (Singapore: International Institute for Asian Studies [The Netherlands] and the Institute of Southeast Asian Studies, 2005), pp. 15–24 and p. 16, Table 1.1.
11. James F. Warren, "A Tale of Two Centuries: The Globalisation of Maritime Raiding and Piracy in Southeast Asia at the end of the Eighteenth and Twentieth Centuries," *Asia Research Institute Working Paper Series*, no. 2, June 2003, National University of Singapore, p. 1.
12. For an elaborate description of the Iranun, see James F. Warren, op. cit., pp. 6–11.
13. Elsewhere, Warren describes geography as the "sinister ally" of past and modern pirates. See James F. Warren, op. cit., pp. 1–30.
14. *See* James F. Warren, op. cit., pp. 1–30; Carolin Liss, "Maritime Piracy in Southeast Asia," in *Southeast Asian Affairs 2003* (Singapore: Institute of Southeast Asian Studies, 2004), p. 57.
15. Ralph Emmers defines the act of criminalization of transnational crime as "the practice of legislating and enforcing existing laws against its different categories [such as a piracy]. In such a process, transnational criminal issues are confronted within the realm of domestic legal systems that are meant to ensure the rights suspected criminals and follow standard legal procedures." See Ralph Emmers, *Non-Traditional Security in the Asia-Pacific: The Dynamics of Securitisation*. Non-Traditional Security Series (Singapore: Eastern Universities Press, 2004), p. 83.
16. Carolin Liss, op. cit., p. 55.
17. I. R. Hyslop, "Contemporary Piracy," in Eric Ellen, ed., *Piracy at Sea* (Paris: ICC Publishing, 1989), p. 3, 12.
18. *Piracy and Armed Robbery against Ships: Annual Report, 1 January - 30 December 2004* (Kuala Lumpur: IMB Regional Piracy Centre, 7 February 2005), p. 10, Table 8.
19. By the end of June 2005, there have been nine kidnappings in the Straits. The figure may preliminarily indicate a drop for 2005. See *Piracy and Armed Robbery against Ships: Report for the Period, 1 January - 31 June 2005* (Kuala Lumpur: IMB Regional Piracy Centre, April 2005), p. 10, Table 8.
20. *Piracy and Armed Robbery against Ships: Annual Report, 1 January - 30 December 2004* (Kuala Lumpur: IMB Regional Piracy Centre, 7 February 2005), p. 10, Table 8.
21. *Piracy and Armed Robbery against Ships: Annual Report, 1 January - 30 December 2002* (Kuala Lumpur: IMB Regional Piracy Centre, 30 January 2003), p. 16.
22. Carolin Liss, op. cit., p. 59.
23. Ibid., p. 59.
24. Ibid., p. 60. See also the fieldwork based analysis of Liss's "social pirates" and hit-and-run robbers by Eric Frecon, "Piracy and Armed Robbery at Sea in Southeast Asia: Initial Impressions from the Field," in Graham Gerard Ong, ed., *Piracy, Maritime Terrorism and Securing the Malacca Straits* (Singapore: Institute of Southeast Asian Studies, 2006), forthcoming.
25. Ibid., pp. 62–63.

26. Peter Chalk, *Non-Military Security and Global Order: The Impact of Extremism, Violence and Chaos on National and International Security* (London: Macmillan Press, 2000), pp. 69–70.
27. Carolin Liss, op. cit., p. 64.
28. Carolin Liss, op. cit, pp. 57–58.
29. The quarterly figures are tabulated by counting the number of reported cases within each quarter of the year from the annual narration of actual attacks found at the end of the IMB reports.
30. "What the pirate attacks mean," *The Straits Times*, 18 March 2005.
31. Graham Gerard Ong, "The Threat of Piracy and Maritime Terrorism," in *Regional Outlook 2005–2006* (Singapore: Institute of Southeast Asian Studies, 2005), forthcoming.
32. James F. Warren, op. cit., p. 22. Warren borrows heavily from John J. Brandon's "High-seas piracy is booming: It's time to fight harder," *Christian Science Monitor*, 27 December 2000 http://csmonitor.com/cgi-bin/durableRedirect.pl?/durable/2000/12/27/p11s1.htm (accessed on 28 June 2005).
33. "Malaysian navy chief: North and South ends of Malacca Strait focus of piracy," BBC Monitoring Asia Pacific, 8 June 2005.
34. "Modern pirates: Armed and ruthless," BBC News, 24 April 2000, http://news.bbc.co.uk/1/hi/world/asia-pacific/724753.stm (accessed on 20 June 2005).
35. Ralph Emmers, op. cit., pp. 3–4. The author would add the media as another significant actor in the securitization of an issue area, which is best exemplified in the securitization of piracy and simultaneous conjecture that a "nexus" can and does exist between piracy and maritime terrorism.
36. Ralph Emmers, op. cit., pp. 4–5.
37. Ralph Emmers, op. cit., p. 6.
38. John Bradford, "Japanese Anti-Piracy Initiatives in Southeast Asia: Policy Formulation and the Coastal State Reponses," *Contemporary Southeast Asia* vol. 26, no. 3 (2004), p. 488.
39. "Modern pirates: Armed and ruthless," BBC News, 24 April 2000, http://news.bbc.co.uk/1/hi/world/asia-pacific/724753.stm (Accessed on 20 June 2005).
40. To date, there is no official definition of maritime terrorism.
41. One person drowned when the burning ship was evacuated.
42. Tanner Campbell and Rohan Gunaratna, " Maritime Terrorism, Piracy and Crime," in Rohan Gunaratna ed., *Terrorism in the Asia-Pacific: Threat and Response* (Singapore: Eastern University Press, 2003), p. 78; Graham Gerard Ong, "Taking the fight against terrorism to the high seas," *The Straits Times*, 2 December 2002, p. 13; "Pre-empting Maritime Terrorism in Southeast Asia," *ISEAS Viewpoints*, 29 November 2002, Institute of Southeast Asian Studies http://www.iseas.edu.sg/viewpoint/ggonov02.pdf. Faruq escaped from Bagram jail in Afghanistan on 10 July 2005, a fact that was only released to the public on 1 November 2005. See "Faruq's great escape," *Asia Views*, volume 44, issue 2, November 2005 http://www.asiaviews.org/?content=25889s1dddt33gf&colcom=20051110023921 (accessed on 28 November 2005).

    Regarding the attack on the *SuperFerry 14*, see Simon Elegant, "The Return of Abu Sayyaf," *Time*, 23 August 2004 http://www.time.com/time/asia/magazine/article/0,13673,501040830–686107,00.html (accessed on 28 June 2005).
43. Michael Richardson, *A Time Bomb for Global Trade: Maritime-Related Terrorism in an Age of Weapons of Mass Destruction* (Singapore: Institute of Southeast Asian Studies, 2004).
44. Adam J. Young and Mark J. Valencia, "Conflation of Piracy and Terrorism in Southeast Asia: Rectitude and Utility," *Contemporary Southeast Asia*, vol. 25, no. 2 (August 2003), p. 269. Young and Valencia are right to argue that there are enough requisite distinctions to separate the two phenomena, which are especially important in implementing the long-term solutions in eliminating piracy and terrorism.
45. As examples of such journalism, see John J. Brandon, "Piracy as terrorism," *Journal of Commerce*, 3 (June 2002), *United States Council for International Business* http://www.uscib.org/\index.asp?documentID=2153 (accessed on 22 July 2003); and John J. Brandon, "Protect Asia's Shipping," The PacNet Newsletter, 24 May 2002, *The Centre for Strategic and International Studies*, http://www.csis.org/pacfor/pac0221A.htm (accessed on 14 April 2003). The author first employs the term "experienced vulnerability" in Graham

Gerard Ong, "The Threat of Piracy and Maritime Terrorism," in *Regional Outlook 2005–2006* (Singapore: Institute of Southeast Asian Studies, 2005), forthcoming.
46. Richard Halloran, "What if Asia's pirates and terrorists joined hands?" *South China Morning Post*, 17 May 2003, http://www.uscib.org/index.asp?documentID=2636.
47. Adam Young and Mark J. Valencia, "Piracy, terrorism threats overlap," *The Washington Times*, http://www.washingtontimee.com/world/20030706-104801-9949r.htm (Accessed on 15 April 2005).
48. Dr. Tony Tan cited in Ralph Emmers, *op. cit.*, pp. 37–38.
49. Dr. Tony Tan quoted in "3 S'pore ideas for boosting maritime security," *The Straits Times Interactive*, 2 June 2003, http://www.straitstimes.com.sg/storyprint-friendly/0,1887,192467,00.html? (accessed on 30 June 2003).
50. "Peril on the sea," *The Economist*, 4 October 2003, p. 59.
51. Dr Tan cited in B. Rahman, "Taming terror on the high seas," *Asia Times*, 9 June 2005 http://www.atimes.com/atimes/Southeast_Asia/GF09Ae05.html .
52. Felix Soh, "Terrorism will take on a new face," *The Straits Times*, 15 November 2003, p. 24.
53. Carolin Liss, *Private Security Companies in the Fight against Piracy in Asia*. Murdoch University Asia Research Centre Working Paper No. 120, June 2005 (Revised September 2005), p. 11. Available at http://wwwarc.murdoch.edu.au/wp/wp120.pdf. See also Keith Bradsher, "Attacks on Chemical Ships in Southeast Asia Seem to Be Piracy, Not Terror," *The New York Times* (On the Web), http://www.uscib.org/\index.asp?documentID=2527.
54. Gal Luft and Anne Korin, "Terrorism Goes to Sea," *Foreign Affairs*, November/December 2004, pp. 61–71, especially p. 61 and p. 67.
55. Jason Burke "Suicide bombers in boat attack on Iraq oil terminal," *The Observer*, 25 April 2004, http://observer.guardian.co.uk/iraq/story/0,12239,1202976,00.html.
56. See Graham Gerard Ong, "Charting a unified course for a safer seas," *The Straits Times*, 25 June 2005, p. S10.
57. For details on the operational aspects of the EiS, *see* Graham Gerard Ong and Joshua Ho, "Maritime Air Patrols: The New Weapon Against Piracy in the Malacca Straits," *IDSS Commentary*, 75/2005, Nanyang Technological University, Singapore http://www.idss.edu.sg/publications/Perspective/IDSS702005.pdf.
58. Kubiak lists nearly 40 incidents of maritime terrorism from 1961 to 2002. See Krzystof Kubiak, "Terrorism is the New Enemy at Sea," *Proceedings*, December 2003, p. 70.
59. "Patterns of Global Terrorism," released by the Office of the Coordinator for Counterterrorism, 21 May 2002, US Department of State, http://www.state.gov/s/ct/rls/pgtrpt/2001/html/10266.htm.
60. John Kleinen and Manon Osseweijer, "Piracy and robbery in the Asian seas," *International Institute of Asian Studies Newsletter — Theme: Maritime Piracy* no. 36 (March 2005), p. 8.
61. Mak Joon Num, "Going on the Offensive: Taking the Fight to Pirates and Terrorists," a presentation made at a Public Seminar by the Institute of Southeast Asian Studies (ISEAS), entitled "Securing the Malacca Straits: Developments, Challenges and Opportunities," 23 August 2004, ISEAS, Singapore.
62. Ibid.
63. See Graham Gerard Ong, "Charting a unified course for a safer seas," *The Straits Times*, 25 June 2005, p. S10

4

Compound Piracy at Sea in the Early Twenty-First Century: A Tactical to Operational-Level Perspective on Contemporary, Multiphase Piratical Methodology

RUPERT HERBERT-BURNS

Introduction & Methodology

At 1249 on 10 April 2005, in position 03° 24.0'N 048° 17.0'E, approximately 60 nautical miles off the coast of Somalia, the 19,240 DWT bulk carrier M/V *Tim Buck* loaded with urea from Jeddah, Saudi Arabia, was assaulted by two four-man pirate teams in high-speed boats, all of them armed with AK-47 assault rifles and RPG-7 grenade launchers. At 1250 local time, as the two assault teams approached the starboard quarter, the master sounded the general alarm and the engineers brought the vessel up to maximum power in an attempt to evade boarding. Realizing the defensive measure, the pirates opened fire on the bridge, bridge wings, and superstructure with small arms fire and rocket propelled grenades. The master, Captain Sergey Potemkin, now suffering from acute chest pains, sent a distress signal via Inmarsat-C. Following another grenade volley aimed at the No. 1 lifeboat and another at the bridge, the pirates boarded the vessel on the starboard side adjacent to the No. 5 and No. 6 holds. After a failed attempt to gain access to the accommodation spaces, which were locked down (the vessel was sailing under ISPS Level 2 security), the pirates were later found to have fled the vessel by search teams and crews fighting fires on the lifeboat deck. Tragically, at 1520 the master suffered a heart attack and died shortly after. The rest of the crew were unhurt. The vessel, now under the command of the chief officer, Tischenko Konstantin, sailed for Dar es Salaam, its intended destination.[1]

This type of startlingly violent attack, while certainly not commonplace, is reflective of the brazen attacks perpetrated by the most well-armed and determined of modern pirates. Though the attack failed, it is indicative of the level of preparedness, tactical flair, and skill-at-arms demonstrated by experienced and determined pirates operating in the more dangerous littoral waters and shipping lanes in parts of Southeast Asia, the Bay of Bengal, off the coasts of West and East Africa. An analysis of piratical methodology at the tactical and (where applicable) the operational level, such as that revealed in the synopsis above, is the focus of this chapter.

Compound piracy is a term used by the author as a means to capture and convey the multifaceted nature of contemporary piracy incidents, in particular, the complex and multiphase nature of more sophisticated operations involving deception, multiple assault craft approach, mother ships, kidnap and ransom demand operations, and hijackings involving organized crime syndicates. The term is particularly germane to pirate operations designed to bring about deliberate vessel devolution, commonly (and colloquially) referred to as "phantom ship" incidents. Devolution operations can begin months before the assault itself during the "intelligence development" phase when vessels are deliberately selected by criminal elements on the basis of information concerning vessel type, routing, and cargo typology passed to them from contacts within the shipping world that are in collusion with the criminals. The tactics and methodology explicit in the operations will be discussed in greater detail elsewhere in this paper.

The content and orientation of the analysis is intended only as a utilitarian examination of a broad range of piratical methodologies that have occurred over many years. Though some of the tactics and approaches embraced by the more accomplished operators are often violent and sophisticated, this chapter will not engage in extrapolation for the generating of hypotheses pertaining to putative maritime terrorist activity as has been suggested by other commentators. Notwithstanding the latter caveat, the chapter is intended to identify and assess the effectiveness and implications of the methodologies employed by all types of pirates, whether they are engaged in the straightforward robbery of ship's stores from an anchored fishing vessel or the creation of a "phantom ship" that will be used for arms smuggling or human trafficking. To this end, the project will be split into deliberately sequential sections that address: generic piracy typologies; target vessel selection and outcome objective; the assault phase; ordinary robbery of vessels at anchor or alongside; vessel seizure and situation control; hostage-taking and ransom demand operations; and deliberate acts of vessel devolution, also known colloquially as "phantom ship" operations. Where applicable, concise case studies will be used to further illustrate methodology, so as to better set the tactics used in a broader operational context.

Each section will be broken down into its salient components; for example, the section addressing "assault phase" will comprise: methods of approach and withdrawal, and vessel boarding and access (to include weapons used and ammunition types). Intrinsic to the examinations at every level of analysis will be commentary on effectiveness, lethality (where applicable), inventiveness, and methodological flair. This is not to extol the virtues of these criminals; however, it is recognized that the structured and rigorous appraisal of contemporary piratical methodology is useful, indeed often essential, in devising and applying counter strategies and practical contingency planning. Moreover, a holistic appreciation of piracy in terms of tactics or methodology is frequently insightful in developing further understanding of the geographical origins of pirate gangs, investigating putative links with far-flung organized criminal syndicates, or recognizing instances of symbiotic actors which are at once either members of a legitimate armed force or law-enforcement agency, or perhaps members of an established insurgency group. In other words, recognizing the specific weapons and tactics used in an incident can be helpful in attempting to establish what kinds of pirates were involved (by virtue of the operation's level of sophistication), or even their parent organization. Nevertheless, it would be fair to convey that to date this has typically been more that just a little problematic for law-enforcement and security forces in the majority of instances.

Obtaining generic commentary on incidents of piracy, especially pertaining to those attacks that occur in Southeast Asian waters, presents little difficulty. The increased attention being paid to this phenomenon in the wake of increasing concern over global maritime security and the implementation of the International Ship and Port Facility Security (ISPS) Code, the growing velocity of maritime trade, increased numbers and lethality of piratical incidents, and increasing concern over the putative (and highly speculative) links between piracy and maritime terrorism, has ensured a wealth of nonspecific material reported in the media. However, detailed data was gathered on specific incidents and vessel identities from Lloyd's List and Lloyd's Marine Intelligence Unit casualty archives.

Types of Piracy and Armed Robbery at Sea: Distinctions and Definitions

The classifications offered in this section are not intended as a fresh set of definitives to shape onward discussion outside of this chapter; they merely serve as points of reference for the examination of tactics at various levels of piratical competence and ambition. On the subject of classification, brief mention of definitions is also warranted, however, for the purposes of clarity. This essay concerns itself with the practical methodology of modern piracy and armed robbery at sea and does not encompass the debate surrounding the various definitions. The UN has one, the IMB another, which highlight distinctions such as: acts of *piracy* occur in international waters, while *armed robbery* occurs in waters that lie within a sovereign state's jurisdiction. Significantly, however, mention must also be made that according to Article 101 of UNCLOS, piracy is "committed for *private* ends" (my emphasis) not political ends. This is important because within current discourse on the subject of piracy, particularly sensationalized reporting in the media, the more sophisticated and violent strains of piracy have been irresponsibly conceived of as augury to (or even synonymous with) acts of maritime terrorism, which are conducted for *political* ends. Because this chapter examines violent practice at sea this must not be misinterpreted as anything but violent piracy. Nevertheless, it would be fair to say that the tactical methodology and practical application of violent coercion and firepower and kidnapping used by some of the most sophisticated and determined pirate teams are indeed methods reflective of the *tactical* approach embraced by various terrorist cells in pursuit of their objectives. Simply put, what works for a terrorist also works for a criminal in the very practical sense of getting what they want. Nevertheless, it is vital to highlight that though the means may be very similar, the ends, and by inference the phenomena, are very distinct from one another and must not be confused or synthesized into something they are not.

The classification levels used in considering the tactics and methodologies used by pirate teams are as follows:

Simple robbery of ship stores and valuables from vessels at anchor/moored at a buoy/berthed alongside
Armed/violent robbery against vessels at anchor/moored at a buoy/berthed alongside
Armed/violent robbery against vessels underway or making way
Armed attacks against ships underway or making way for purposes of hostage-taking and ransom demand
Deliberate vessel hijacking and devolution — "Phantom ship" operations

A large number of the tactics used in contemporary pirate attacks cut across several of the above forms of assault, such as target selection, access, weapons, command and control, and withdrawal; thus, the assessment that follows will be sequential and thematic. There will be separate sections, however, addressing levels 1, 4, and 5; levels 2 and 3 will be discussed across most of the examination pertaining to target selection, assault, and command and control.

Target Vessel Identification/Selection

Pirate teams capable of longer reach into littoral waters and beyond into the shipping lanes are well equipped on every level: transport, communications, means of access, suitable weapons, and, significantly, a definitive objective and a plan of execution. The first step in a successful operation is "target selection"; locating and in some cases deliberately identifying a target vessel. Before discussing the more sophisticated targeted operations, it is worth noting that the assault of *targets of opportunity* is the most common "at sea" operation. Pirates will be induced to particular vessels for a variety of reasons: vulnerability — slower vessels such as ULCCs, VLCCs, product tankers, older general cargo vessels, fishing vessels, and tug and barge tow combinations are attractive for the obvious reason that masters have no capacity to outrun a pursuing pirate team, particularly if there are more than one attacking craft. Vessels *restricted in their ability to maneuver* or vessels *constrained by their draft* are also easy prey, namely ULCCs, VLCCs; and bulk carriers, especially when in confined waters, pilotage waters, or traffic separation schemes, are also attractive as targets as they will also be unable to maneuver sufficiently to evade pursuit.

Vessels laden with high-value dry or liquid bulk cargoes; refined petroleum fuels (diesel, gasoline, and kerosene), organic oils such as palm oil (which is particularly valuable), or aluminum ingots can be sold on the black market in their entirety provided the operation has been sufficiently well planned and the pirates have the correct contacts in order to source out the appropriate buyer. Alternatively, general cargo vessels may be targeted for their finished manufactured goods. Clearly, vessels that are berthed, particularly those ships at anchor in poorly patrolled or isolated working/commercial anchorages, present attractive targets of opportunity simply because they are static and thus easier to board. The large numbers of vessels in this state open up the possibility of piracy to a far wider audience, many of whom possess only the rudimentary skills necessary for straightforward robbery of ship's stores, or the theft of crew belongings and cash for the rather more adventurous. Fishing vessels are also very vulnerable to attack by virtue of their slow speed, their inability to maneuver quickly (especially when carrying out trawling operations) and small crews.

Ease of approach — slower vessels, vessels *constrained by their draft* or those ships *restricted in their ability to maneuver* are favored, not only because they cannot evade pursuit but also because it means that those operators that do not have access to high-speed boats can also conduct successful assaults. Vessels that fall into this category are bulk carriers, VLCC and ULCC tankers, product tankers, tug and barge combinations, fishing boats (especially those with gear deployed), and some older general cargo vessels. Some vessels, even in piracy-prone waters, will neglect to take adequate antiassault precautions such as turning on all available upper-deck and external superstructure lighting and having a visible lookout presence on the upper deck and bridge wings; these ships are especially attractive as they afford the assailants valuable time in making their approach and effecting the boarding itself.

Tug and barge tow combinations present particularly tempting targets given their slow speed, their inability to maneuver to avoid the approach and boarding of agile pirate boats, and their often very small crew sizes (thereby further reducing opportunities for sufficient antipiracy watches and ultimately confrontation). Tugs and the barge (or barges) being towed are also identifiable as such on radar; moreover, at night these vessels must display distinctive lights that identify them as such, thereby making them readily discernable to seasoned pirates knowledgeable of Part C of Collision Regulations governing lights for ships at sea steaming at night. In regions of the world where there is significant offshore oil and gas production, tugs are used to tow platforms into position or away from fields back to shore facilities for maintenance or decommissioning; these structures are very easy to identify and very ponderous.

The vulnerability of these tows renders them attractive to the more sophisticated operators, as was demonstrated on 3 November 2004 when a Netherlands-registered tug, M/V *Smitwijs London*, towing an oil rig (Ocean Sovereign), was attacked in position 05°02'N 99°11'E in the Malacca Straits at 1900 hrs. Witnesses onboard reported that several small craft disguised as fishing boats took up position 250 m on either side of the tug and fired into the wheelhouse and superstructure using assault rifles, causing significant damage to the bridge windows and the navigation equipment. The tug's crew reacted by switching on the upper deck lighting, activating fire hoses, and even firing rocket flares at the attackers. The pirates continued to fire, moving to within 50 m of the tug; however, the master used this proximity to take aggressive evasive maneuvers that eventually forced the pirates to withdraw. Surprisingly, considering the physical damage inflicted upon the *Smitwijs London*, there were no injuries.[2] This incident is revealing not merely for its ferocity but for the pirates' use of deception to shadow the target by masquerading as a small local fishing fleet, and the selection of a conspicuous but vulnerable target that but for the brazen actions of the crew would have been seized with little difficulty.

Separately, on 14 March 2005, pirates armed with M-16 5.56 mm assault rifles and rocket-propelled grenade launchers (RPG-7s) fired upon, and subsequently boarded, the 498 DWT Japanese-registered salvage tug M/V *Idaten*, which was towing an accommodation barge, the 14,661 GT *Kuroshio N0.1*, with 156 workers onboard.[3] The attackers, numbering between 10 to 14, approached the vessel combination at dusk in three fishing boats some 75 nm southwest of Penang in position 04°17'N 99°46'E. This kind of barge, like the rig noted above, is an awkward tow and renders the towing vessel an ideal target, especially when the light is fading. It is interesting to note that the attackers confined their attention to the tug and not the barge. It is impossible to know whether the pirates were aware of how many people were aboard the barge; however, they knew that there would be a sufficiently large number to have made operational control once aboard far more complex. Thus they sought to confine their kidnap to members of the tug's much smaller crew. Nevertheless, the attackers would have assumed that given that the barge was ferrying personnel, even if the tug had managed to sever the tow in order to attempt evasion, the master would have been unlikely to leave his human cargo adrift. On reflection, it seems astonishing that the company (Nippon Marine International S.A.) did not request some protection for the barge given that its was transiting through waters well known for piracy attacks on tugs and barge tows. (Kidnapping operations will be covered in greater detail in a subsequent section.)

In seeking vulnerable prey, pirates have been known to attack vessels that are stopped in the water, usually because of the need to make repairs to the main machinery. Clearly, in these circumstances, with the main engine stopped and the shaft locked, the vessel in question is totally unable to maneuver to avoid the impending assault (especially if it has also anchored if in sufficiently shallow water), rendering the successful seizure of the ship almost a *fait accompli* if the attackers are sufficiently armed and determined. Repairs to machinery can be forced upon the master in waters not necessarily of his choosing, far from assistance (should it be needed) and sometimes in dangerous waters, such as those off the coast of Aceh on the northern tip of Sumatra, Indonesia. Well-equipped operators will be monitoring VHF radio traffic for target information and may even have access to radar and AIS receiving equipment that offer precise target location and identification.

It was in these waters that the Indonesian-flagged product tanker, M/V *Tirta Niaga IV* (now the M/V *Brothers-4*), was attacked by pirates while it was stopped in the water effecting repairs to a seized main engine.[4] The 3,108 DWT tanker, which was lifting palm oil and bound for India, was spotted off the coast of Aceh on 27 June 2001, boarded by pirates presumed to have come from Aceh. The assailants subsequently kidnapped the master and demanded a Rp.1 billion (US$88,000), which was later paid. Captain Mukundan from the International Maritime Bureau (IMB) later stated that the attackers had precise knowledge of its latitude and longitude prior to the assault.[5] It is very likely that the pirates learned this by monitoring vessel VHF radio transmissions coming from the vessel as it was reporting its status to coastal authorities. This practice of pirates monitoring radio traffic to identify targets is well known; in this instance it would have enabled the attacking unit to learn not only the vessel's position but also that it was effectively immobilized and thus an ideal target. This incident prompted Captain Mukundan to say that "The advice the Royal Malaysian Police are giving to masters is that if you have engine problems in the Malacca Strait, and you are still mobile, you should try to get your vessel into Malaysian waters for repair ... it is dangerous to anchor in areas just outside Aceh."[6] It is interesting to note that he did not suggest going into Indonesian waters, and for good reason.

Fishing vessels are also very vulnerable to attack by virtue of their slow speed, their inability to maneuver quickly (especially when carrying out trawling operations), their small crews, and, not surprisingly, their sheer ubiquity; simply put, fishing vessels represent among the most numerous and easily seized targets on the water. Indeed, given their multiplicity, pirates often use their own fishing boats (or ones they have seized) to prey on others (see section on deception).

By the end of 2004, pirates using, and directing attacks against, fishing boats in the northern reaches of the Bay of Bengal had reached alarming proportions as the following incident illustrates. On 11 November 2004, in the

Sundarbans off the coast of Bangladesh, it was reported that 15 fishing trawlers had been looted in four days, 11 fishermen were thrown into the sea, and 27 others hurt in attacks. All but two of the fishermen were rescued by other fishermen. The pirates looted fish, nets and other equipment, diesel fuel, and about Taka 2 million (roughly US$30,000) from the 15 trawlers. The survivors reported that hardly a day passes without piracy in these areas, and incidents have increased because there is no patrol by the Coast Guard in these waters. Armed pirates move on the water in and around fleets posing as other fishermen. At the opportune moment, they attack trawlers, loot them, and again move on to the next one.[7]

Simple Robbery of Ship Stores and Valuables from Vessels at Anchor/Berthed

From 1 January 2004 to 31 December 2004, the International Maritime Bureau's Piracy and Armed Robbery Against Ships Annual Report revealed that of the 237 actual and 88 attempted incidents of piracy and armed robbery reported, 183 were against vessels either berthed or at anchor in roads,[8] which constitutes 56.3 percent in total. Of this proportion, 13 percent of incidents involved vessels berthed alongside, and 44 percent involved those ships at anchor in roads. These figures are revealing in a number of ways; pirates and criminals in 2004 were still more inclined to target immobile vessels than those underway or making way, and of these, a much greater proportion of criminals favored vessels at anchor. This is not surprising; vessels at anchor do not benefit from dock-side security, endemic lighting at night, the ability to call upon rapid-reaction police units, and CCTV surveillance at the berths (at the larger high-activity facilities). Vessels at anchor can be physically isolated (from harbor-based security support) yet proximate to both shipping lanes, large volumes of peripatetic harbor traffic, and a myriad of coastal enclaves, all of which are ideal incubators of waterborne criminals and pirate teams keen to use the cover of busy commercial and working anchorages to effect boardings unimpeded.

Though vessels at anchor in piracy-prone areas will have most, if not all, upper-deck lighting on, these criminals will take advantage of the opportunity to scale the anchor chain (which on large merchant vessels is of sufficiently large link diameter to render climbing that much more straightforward). One of the clear advantages of gaining access via the forecastle (other than the obvious ease of climbing from the waterline where the approach boat can stand by unobserved under the flair of the bow) is that compared to the deck surrounding the superstructure and the cargo-handling gear, the stem of a vessel does not tend to be as well lit at night, is not heavily manned except during anchor stations, and has a good deal of deck equipment and machinery (such as the windlass) that can serve as initial cover once the pirate has emerged from the casting.

Straightforward robbery of vessels is often accomplished by thieves who are unarmed, relying upon stealth, the cover of darkness, the distraction of cargo-handling operations, and, frequently, simply being undetected. However, incident reports in recent times detail that increasingly thieves are arming themselves for these more straightforward actions, typically with knives and bludgeoning instruments, but also increasingly frequently with firearms. There are several reasons for this. If thieves have been discovered and the general alarm has been raised, it then becomes far easier to maintain items already pilfered and indeed solicit valuables and cash if one is armed. Also, thieves are arming themselves because vessel crews are far better prepared and frequently maintain standing antipiracy watches and deck patrols even at anchor; thus pirates are expecting to be encountered and even challenged by several crew members if the attack has occurred during a watch change or during normal working hours when all crew not ashore will be working.

Unarmed thieves tend to confine their actions to stealing stores situated in the forecastle area, from inside pump rooms, lifeboats, paint stores, the carpenter's shop, or other poorly secured stowages on the weather deck, tank deck, or poop deck. Large tankers or bulk carriers can be particularly attractive for those seeking to steal from stores in the forecastle area because there will be few if any crew there to challenge the thieves; even if they were spotted from the bridge or accommodation spaces, the need to travel a long distance enables the pirates sufficient time to make their escape.

Armed operators are better equipped to enter into the superstructure and accommodation spaces to seek out valuables and cash. Instances involving armed thieves encountering crew members frequently result in violence as a means of instilling compliance, control, and fear. The key here for the assailants is aggression, speed, surprise, and control. If the pirates are seeking to make off with a sizeable amount of the crews' belongings, and cash and perhaps even cash from the master's safe, they will need to use intimidation and aggression to obtain what they want (including the necessary keys); however, a "bulk" theft will require control of the crew during the time of the assault (perhaps in a central location such as the mess) and reasonable knowledge of a modern vessel's superstructure and accommodation layout so that time is not wasted and operators do not become disoriented.

It is worth bearing in mind that even piracy methodology at the comparatively prosaic level of the robbing of static vessels is being executed by the increasingly experienced; knowledge regarding vessel deck and superstructure layouts, dimensions, upper deck lighting, access points, and even antipiracy watches increases with each successive robbery. Pirates, many of whom have grown up near or working within fishing communities, earn (or at least supplement) their income by utilizing and improving upon skills they already have. Though many may only have rudimentary or even no formal education, their ability to improve their skill set and adapt to countermeasures should not be underestimated.

Assault Phase

In assessing pirate assaults upon vessels under way or making way, a critical consideration is the approach. There are two main facets to this phase of the operation; the type of craft used and the method of approach, which takes into account vectoring (speed and direction of approach to the target), the use of deception (if adopted), the adoption of "multiples" as a means of approach and assault, and the use of "mother ships."

The types of craft used vary widely, depending on the preparedness and sophistication of the teams involved, the region in which the assault was executed, and operational necessity (for example, the need for high-speed extraction and evasion or a large force complement). Often the craft used will be the types of craft available, such as relatively narrow, open wooden coastal/inshore fishing boats common in Indonesia and the Philippines. Such craft have a squared transom and a tapered stem, and are powered by either single or sometimes twin outboard motors. These craft are also made from glass fiber, though these are less common. Outboard motor powers vary. Single or twin 25–50 hp (tiller-controlled) Yamahas are common in Asia and Africa. Better-equipped (or financed) operators will have access to single or twin (wheel-controlled) 150–250 hp U.S.-manufactured variants, which can enable speeds of up to 40 to 50 kts in favorable sea states, which are sometimes mounted on modern center-console craft that have very good sea-keeping qualities. The smaller, low-riding inshore craft are favored because of their very small or even negligent radar cross-sections, which enables them to approach from the target vessel's quarters or astern with little or no chance of being detected at night. If they have them, pirates will switch off any navigation running lights during the approach and extraction phases to reduce chances of detection and tracking.

In an attempt to mitigate or even eliminate chances of their approach being detected, the more sophisticated pirates will make full use of the very small radar signatures of their low-lying boats. The minimal return radar echo is easily lost in the wave clutter, effectively obliterating the trace of a small wooden or glass-fiber boat on the screen of even the modern S- or X-band ARPA, EPA, or ATA set displays found on modern bridges. Some operatives will even be aware of how to take further advantage of "sector blanking," a phenomenon referring to the blind arc azimuths astern of a vessel. In this instance, the pirate team (or teams) will approach from astern in the tract of water that is not swept effectively by the radar transmission, which has been scattered or "blanked" by the superstructure and the ship's funnel.

In busy shipping lanes in narrow waters (such as the southeastern extent of the Malacca Strait) where there is a great deal of crossing traffic and service boats, the sheer quantity of radar contacts on the bridge watch-keeper's radar screen could easily enable even a small contact to go unnoticed during a busy eight-to-midnight watch in the Phillips Channel, especially during times of heavy weather or sea states when radars produce more echo clutter. Naturally, some operatives will seek to take advantage of the cover of darkness to make their approach, though night operations are more complex and more hazardous; calm sea states would be preferable for these approaches, though it would be fair to say that any approach in heavy weather would present serious challenges to even the most determined and experienced pirates.

Larger blue-water fishing boats (or boats behaving like them) have been used by pirates to approach their target, using their seemingly innocuous presence and acknowledged ubiquity. (To the endless irritation of merchant navy and naval watch-keepers, fishing boats are often notorious for sailing and operating exactly how they please even in very congested waterways and channels; however, though a nuisance, they are expected.) Fishing vessels are ideal as a means of attacking other fishermen and, if they are fast enough, those slower merchant vessels making way. Pirates' embrace of deception as a means to diminish or even eradicate suspicion on the part of bridge watch-keepers and other crew members working on the upper deck is well known. Indeed, the use of coastal fishing vessels as cover has been particularly effective, as sizable pirate teams (occasionally operating as a "pack" in several vessels) approach closer to unsuspecting merchantmen in keeping with seemingly benign trawling operations. Conversely, pirates have been observed approaching fishing vessels in small boats under the pretext of attempting to buy some the day's catch.[9]

Deception has also been used in slightly more sophisticated ways; in one incident, pirates disguised their assault craft as offshore support vessels (ships that service oil-drilling and production platforms). On 8 August 2003, pirates attacked the Taiwanese-flagged M/V *Dong Yih* bound for Singapore in the waters off Aceh. The fact that the boats appeared to be oil-rig support vessels caused the crew to ignore them initially. The attack started in daylight at 1745, local time, when one vessel's team opened fire with automatic weapons. After 40 minutes; a second vessel joined in the attack that lasted over two hours, leaving the Taiwanese ship riddled with over 200 rounds. Despite heavy fire, the pirates never managed to board the *Dong Yih*.[10] Though the assault ultimately failed, the incident illustrates that the use of deception can be very effective in the approach phase of an operation, especially if circumstances do not allow for the attack to be executed under cover of darkness.

This incident also highlights the effectiveness of the use of "multiples" when attempting to approach and assault a merchant vessel, especially one sailing at full economic speed. Pirate operations involving more than one approach craft offer the assailants more scope for situation control, sea room denial, more angles and volume of weapons fire, the ability to bring more attackers to the fight, additional transport space for hostages, and operational redundancy

— if one of the boats is compromised, damaged in some way, then the other can continue with the assault.

The final approach to the target vessel is, as mentioned previously, likely to come from astern. Some operators will favor a boarding at the stern using bamboo poles or ladders or grappling hooks and line, especially if the vessel typically has a high freeboard (even when laden) such as container vessels, general cargo vessels, refrigerated cargo vessels and crude tankers, and bulk carriers sailing in ballast. For the aforementioned ships, the poop deck is the part of the vessel nearest the waterline and thus more attractive as an access point. The difficulty with an astern assault is the turbulence in the water caused by the ship's wake, which can make station-keeping by the pirate boat driver highly problematic, sometimes prohibitively so. Also, given that the majority of modern merchant vessels are configured to have the accommodation superstructure aft, there tend to be more off-watch crew members on the upper deck in the poop deck area; this clearly raises the chances of premature detection before the boarding phase is complete.

Alternatively, the pirates can proceed ahead of the quarters to the waist of the vessel and effect a boarding using grapnel hooks and line or ladders on the vessel's port and/or starboard side amidships. This method is particularly effective (and thus favored) if the vessel is a product, chemical, or parcel tanker, which typically has tank decks that are low to the waterline. This reduced freeboard (especially when the ship is laden) makes a flank boarding the easiest method of gaining access.

Another method that has been used, albeit infrequently, is for the pirates to tether two boats together with a long line, placing them abeam of the passing ship. As the ship catches the line in the water, the two boats are drawn in toward the port and starboard sides of the ship amidships and the pirates can then effect a boarding from either side. Clearly, this tactic requires a great deal of skill, luck, and not a little daring; if the target vessel is steaming at full economic speed and alters course for whatever reason, this method can result in disaster (for the hapless pirates). Given the problems of this method, not least its inherent lack of flexibility, the use of tethered craft is not common.[11]

The majority of offshore pirate assaults are executed using relatively small open craft, which though agile and well suited for most forms of inshore and littoral work, have limited fuel endurance and are vulnerable in larger sea states, especially when heavily laden with large boarding teams of ten or more. Given these limitations, and for the purposes of greater operational flexibility and even deception, some of the most sophisticated operators have used "mother ships." Mother ships are larger blue-water fishing boats or even small coastal general cargo vessels (perhaps those previously hijacked) equipped with either dedicated or retrofitted cargo loading derricks that can carry several smaller assault craft which can be lowered into the water at the optimum time for the assault, often during fading light at the beginning and end of the day or at night. This enables the teams' leaders to wait far offshore for passing targets, gain proximity to other merchantmen posing as another "legitimate" vessel in the shipping lane, and support the smaller assault craft that would otherwise have neither the range nor the facilities required for a long range approach with many men on board. Moreover, such an arrangement also allows whole-scale deployment in heavy weather, as the operation's leadership waits for favorable assault conditions farther out to sea, an option unavailable to pirates in small open boats. This tactic has more typically been used by pirates operating off the Somali coast of the Horn of Africa.[12] This increasingly dangerous body of water has long been synonymous with particularly violent and accomplished pirate attacks. Given this, masters have been warned to sail at least 50–100 nm offshore to avoid being attacked; some reports even warn masters to steam further out to nearer 200 nm. These precautions make the use of mother ships not only practical but even essential for those that have the means.

Vessel Boarding

As mentioned above, pirate teams will board target vessels that are making way from astern or from the sides. (Static targets at anchor are more likely to be boarded at the forward part of the vessel; see below.) Scaling the sides of the ship will be accomplished using poles, ladders, or ropes. The key to this phase of the operation is control, keeping a small boat alongside or astern of a large moving ship is not easy, especially if it is a full economic speed (for a modern container vessel or general cargo ship this could be 18–22 kts or faster). The bow wash, side wave and wake patterns, though anticipated, make keeping a small open boat in position a skilled and often dangerous undertaking. Clearly, the intent, thus, is to keep the time required for the actual scaling phase to a minimum; pirates who undertake these assaults tend to be experienced, fit, and have good upper body strength. Clearly, this phase is best executed in calm weather when the sea state is minimal or at least reduced. Moreover, assaults, regardless of the actual site chosen for boarding, are best effected under cover of darkness; indeed, it is reckoned that 95 percent of all at sea pirate attacks happen at night and in calm weather.[13] Additionally, given the challenges of boarding vessels that are making way, slower vessels such as tankers, bulk carriers, and fishing boats are favored. However, in an attempt to minimize the risks of failure or injury, pirate teams have been known to board ships that have just disembarked a pilot and are thus at reduced speed.

A well-used method of boarding vessels at anchor (on larger vessels with sufficiently wide hawse pipes) is to scale up the anchor chain from the waterline and gain access to the forecastle via the hawse pipe.[14] This mode of access is also used on occasion for exfiltration. Access to, and escape via, the forecastle is ideal when the vessel is at anchor, at a buoy, or even moored alongside, at night or in poor visibility, or when the vessel's crew are otherwise occupied in cargo-loading operations. In an example of how brazen pirates have become, 10 assailants boarded the bulk carrier M/V *Mallika Naree* in Balikpapan Anchorage in Indonesia while the vessel was undergoing cargo operations with two barges alongside port and starboard and with stevedores aboard.[15] This is exemplary of criminals taking advantage of operational distraction such as cargo loading and discharge to effect a robbery even, paradoxically, when this results in more personnel on the weather deck who could in theory complicate the assault. In an attempt to reduce the likelihood of initial discovery, and to add to the potential for inducing confusion, pirates have also been known to mingle with stevedores during cargo operations.

Vessel Seizure and Situation Control

The seizure, operational control of the vessel, and the subjugation of its crew is arguably one of the most complex and dangerous parts of a pirate attack both for the assailants and especially the crew. Nevertheless, in reviewing the more sophisticated incidents in recent years, especially those involving entire cargo-theft operations and hostage-taking scenarios, it becomes clear that operators are highly experienced and some are very well trained. In his book *Dangerous Waters,* John S. Burnett reveals that officers from the Royal Malaysian Marine Police (RMMP) have encountered pirates in the shipping lanes in the Malacca Straits with levels of tactical competence and equipment (M-16 5.56 mm assault rifles, flack jackets, helmets, and low-reflective and black assault-type fatigues) that strongly suggested they were members of the Indonesian Navy supplementing their meager military salaries by "moonlighting" as pirates.[16] Though RMMP inspections of vessels following violent pirate attacks have revealed spent 5.56 mm casings, which they suggest offer conclusive proof that the weapons used could only have been in the hands of Indonesian naval personnel, I would argue that this is not necessarily the case.[17] The M-16, though not nearly as common as the ubiquitous AK-47, is still relatively easy to get hold of by criminals, and the weapon is common in Southeast Asia.

The effective, efficient, and ultimately successful seizure of a vessel's crew, taking the vessel under operational command and the subsequent control of the onboard situation requires essential components: a skilled and experienced team, surprise, speed, aggression, coordination of effect, the credible threat and use of violence, language skills, leadership, and often detailed knowledge of vessel layout and ship systems. The complexity of full assault operations for the purposes of a hijacking and hostage operation or a complete cargo seizure has given rise to specialized assault teams that are subcontracted by organized criminal syndicates (particularly those in Southeast and East Asia) to perform such composite operations.[18]

A concise review of some the salient features of the assault and seizure of the M/T *Petro Ranger* on 17 April 1998 is revealing of the preparedness of the assailants. The team members, wearing balaclavas, assaulted the key parts of the tanker — the bridge, radio room, and machinery control room (MCR) — virtually simultaneously. The assailants quickly located and lashed the crew with preprepared lengths of nylon cord and secured them centrally. Also the team numbered two (press-ganged) marine engineers and a leader who spoke several Asian languages and perfect English.[19] However, good as they were, the pirates still required some instruction on the bridge control and navigation systems and knew nothing about the operation of the cargo pumping systems. (The latter oversight was surprising given that the hijacking of the vessel was carried out for the sole purpose of transferring the entire cargo of diesel and kerosene jet fuel).

The team that seized the *Petro Ranger* was well armed, reflective of current trends of piratical *modus operandi*. Though this incident mercifully did not result in the intensive use of lethal weapons fire, other vessels' crews have not been so fortunate. On 8 August 2003 the 3,455 DWT M/V *Dong Yih* was attacked by some 50 pirates in a classic example of a "multiple"-style operation involving two boats. The teams, armed with assault rifles, fired over 200 rounds of automatics weapons fire at the wheel house and superstructure in an hour-long attempt to force the master to stop the vessel.[20] Though the ship eventually evaded seizure, the master received a bullet wound to the leg.

In a separate incident, at 0930 hrs on 15 June 2002, off the Alula Cape in the Arabian Sea, 20 men armed with concealed automatic weapons boarded the M/V *Panagia Tinou* posing as Somali maritime officials. The attackers, from a group calling itself the "Armed Tribal Coast Guard of Somalia," had managed to board the Cypriot-flagged 25,402 DWT bulk carrier, which was lifting 21,000 tons of muriate potash fertilizer, because it was stopped in the water while effecting repairs to its main machinery. After taking control of the vessel, the assault team mounted a .50 caliber heavy machine gun on the hatch cover of No. 3 hold in preparation to fend off rival attackers. During the period that the crew was taken hostage, the assailants engaged in two protracted firefights with rival gangs in high-speed boats that had surrounded the M/V *Panagia Tinou* in an attempt to seize the vessel for themselves.[21] The ferocity of this incident and the sophistication of the overall operation, which involved a hostage-for-ransom phase even in the presence of NATO warships, ensured that the incident was entered in a UN Security Council report pursuant to a resolution (UNSCR 1425) pertaining to an arms embargo on Somalia.[22]

In attempting to take a vessel under command, (or even in instances requiring the fighting off of competing pirates as indicated above), requiring on occasion firing upon it prior to boarding and the ensuing subjugation of its crew, the use of assault weapons can be a lethally effective form of portable coercion. Indeed, for operations requiring prolonged presence aboard to effect ransom demands or to dissuade resistance, small arms could be viewed as essential equipment by modern pirates. It should be born in mind, however, that the lethal use of firearms is not as frequent as perceived in the more alarmist press reports and analyses. Specifically, the firing of RPGs upon vessels is very rare, and incidents when they do occur tend to be more common in the waters of Somalia rather than in Southeast Asia.[23] In contextualizing the use of weapons by pirates at sea it is important to note that though seemingly common, using small arms and particularly heavy machine guns and anti-armor weapons *effectively,* that is to say accurately against moving targets (especially at longer range), is difficult on platforms that are moving, such as small boats. Those operators that are proficient will have experience of effective ranges of their assault rifles, minimum safe distances of explosive effect (for example, 4 meters for an anti-armor RPG round),[24] allowances for firing at night, and of course weapon limitations (such as the virtual ineffectiveness of the smaller caliber rifle ammunition against steel superstructure bulkheads and armored-glass bridge windows). Furthermore, the use of small arms in a tactical sense in accommodation spaces and below decks is dangerous, requiring confidence, discipline, and a thorough appreciation of spatial awareness and adjacent team-member positions and intentions. Few pirates will have all of the skill-at-arms and sense of tactical acumen mentioned above. This is perhaps why there are few mass casualty incidents involving pirate assaults and firearms. Nevertheless, there are experienced operators out there, and it can only be hoped that their sense of tactical discipline is commensurate with their prowess in handling the weaponry examined in this essay so as to avoid unnecessary bloodshed.

Table 4.1 reveals the generic range of small arms and light weapons that have been used by the most well-equipped and determined pirates in recent years. These weapons can be found all over the world, and their availability has proliferated to the extent that these weapons can be acquired on the black market and through organized criminal syndicates with increasing ease. The specifications listed alongside each firearm reveal criteria such as caliber, muzzle velocity; and rates of fire so as convey as sense of lethal potential. A sizable team of pirates armed with a combination of assault rifles or submachine guns, rocket propelled grenade launchers, and pistols has the capacity to lay down withering, sustained fire if adequately equipped with large scales of ammunition. It must be stressed that the weapons listed below represent a reasonably comprehensive selection of those that have been used over the years but by no means all.

Other weapons favored by pirates either due to their inherent effectiveness, or more often due to availability, include: long knives, Parangs (a form of machete common to Malaysia and Indonesia), axes, crowbars, swords, steel bars, and clubs.

Supplementary equipment will vary depending on the area in which the pirates are operating, the type of operation and the level of external support.

Table 4.1 Small arms and light weapons used by pirates in recent years

Weapon		Specifications
Pistols	Caliber:	9 mm
	Muzzle velocity:	approx. 375 m/s
	Magazine capacity:	10–15 rounds
Submachine Guns (SMGs)	Caliber:	9 mm
	Muzzle velocity:	approx. 400 m/s
	Cyclic rate:	approx. 800 rpm
	Magazine capacity:	20–30 rounds
AK-47 Assault Rifle (Russian)	Caliber:	7.62 mm
	Muzzle velocity:	700 m/s
	Cyclic rate:	600 rpm
	Magazine capacity:	30 rounds
	Max. effective range:	approx. 400 meters
AK-74 Assault Rifle (Russian)	Caliber:	5.45 mm
	Muzzle velocity:	900 m/s
	Cyclic rate:	600–650 rpm
	Magazine capacity:	30 rounds
	Max. effective range:	500 meters
56–1 Assault Rifle (Chinese)	Caliber:	7.62 mm
	Muzzle velocity:	710 m/s
	Cyclic rate:	600 rpm
	Magazine capacity:	30 rounds
	Max. effective range:	approx. 400 meters
M-16 A1/A2/A3 Assault Rifle (U.S.)	Caliber:	5.56 mm
	Muzzle velocity:	945 m/s
	Cyclic rate:	650–750 rpm
	Magazine capacity:	20/30 rounds
	Max. effective range:	460–550 meters
RPG-7 Grenade Launcher (Russian)	Warhead:	fin-stabilized 40 mm armor-piercing antiarmor or high-explosive antipersonnel grenades
	Max. effective range:	300 meters (single mobile target)
		500 meters (single stationary target)
		920 meters (area target)

The following items constitute a sample of what might be expected: plasticuff wrist bonds, nylon cord for binding limbs, dark nonreflective combat clothing, spare ammunition, mobile phones, portable VHF radios, grappling hooks and lines, bamboo poles, bamboo ladders, balaclavas, flack jackets, helmets, and a range of false vessel documentation (bills of lading, registration papers, crew manifests, invoices, port clearance papers, safety construction certificates, oil-pollution-prevention certificates, load line certificates, and classification survey papers).

Hostage-Taking and Ransom-Demand Operations

This form of piracy constitutes the boldest, and potentially most complex, of piratical incidents with the exception of vessel devolution operations (see next section). These attacks bring together all of the phases and features of piracy tactics and methodology discussed thus far, and as such, excepting the ransom-for-hostage exchange process, require no further elaboration. In recent years, there has been a disturbing rise in the frequency of hostage-for-ransom incidents. In addition to their other tactical skills, operators are skilled at selecting the most rewarding hostages — typically the senior officers onboard (master, chief officer, chief engineer, and second engineer), often able to covertly transfer the captives ashore, and diligent in conducting the negotiation and ransom collection phase. Many operations are revealing as indication of the level of likely "inside information" pertaining to the "anticipated" negotiating behavior of the shipping company responsible for the vessel and the crew. Operators in the Malacca Straits area often target "local" vessels (those owned/operated by Indonesian companies).

These incidents, thus, involve somewhat "local-to-local" negotiations,[25] as shown by the following incident, involving the attack on the 1,289 GT product tanker M/T *Tri Samudra* on 12 March 2005. Following an assault by over 30 men armed with assault rifles and RPGs, the master and chief engineer were kidnapped and removed from the vessel which was lifting methane gas bound for Belawan. The pirates later demanded a ransom of 2 billion rupiah (US$211,449). The fate of the two officers is still unknown and it is unclear whether the ransom was paid.[26] Days later, on 14 March three crew members were abducted from the Japanese-owned tug *Idaten* in the Malacca Strait northeast of Pulau-Berhala. The Japanese master and chief engineer and Filipino chief officer were released six days later off the coast of southern Thailand after the owner paid the ransom of 50 million yen (US$461,000).[27] The latter example is revealing for the speed of completion of the deal and its international dimension, which involved a multinational crew, a Japanese shipping company, and Malaysian negotiators and law-enforcement officials. Only a group of experienced operators with sophisticated international support and good negotiating skills, to say nothing of having the tactical awareness to change their location through international waters and into different sovereign waters, could have executed such an operation successfully.

On 27 June 2005, in an incident that generated international media attention, Somali pirates seized the 992 DWT general cargo vessel M/V *Semlow* in the waters 300 km northeast of Mogadishu. The vessel, under charter to the United Nations World Food Programme (WFP), was lifting 850 tons of rice for the Somali victims of the Tsunami. The pirates kept the vessel at sea and initially demanded a ransom of US$500,000 for the release of the 10 crew. After protracted negotiations between the pirates and the UN, the vessel's crew still had not been released at the beginning of October; indeed, the captured vessel was used to attack a second vessel, the M/V *Ibn Batuta*, in the waters off Mogadishu with the captured crew still onboard.[28] Though the incident remains unresolved at the time of writing, the incident reveals the increasing danger to vessels off the Horn of Africa, the brazenness and endurance of the pirates, their ability to negotiate at the highest levels, and the capacity to gain intelligence enabling them to target a high profile target.

Vessel Devolution Operations and Vessel Hijacking for Cargo Sale

Of all the forms of piracy that constitute the contemporary form of the phenomenon, an operation involving vessel devolution, the so-called phantom ship variant, is the most elaborate and intriguing. Commensurate with the sense of the title itself, a strict conceptual definition of phantom shipping is unsurprisingly rather elusive, not least because there are a variety of ways in which these acts can arise. Nevertheless, in following the stream of work concerning the study of piracy started by Eric and Shao Lin Ellen (formerly of the International Maritime Bureau — IMB) and the current director of the IMB, P. K. Mukundan, a workable definition has emerged; "phantom ships" are described as those vessels "without legal registry plying the seas for illegal purposes."[29]

There are a number of ways to "create" a phantom ship, which have implications for methods of target selection. Aside from an act of piracy, a vessel owner can be complicit in creating a phantom ship, or indeed be entirely responsible for instigating the act. During a lean shipping market when freight rates are exceptionally low or when there are simply no charter parties for the ship, instead of bearing the burden of bank loan or mortgage repayments the owner may simply decide to erase the vessel's existence — in a virtual sense. The vessel selected for this may be one that due to its advanced age has become more of an economic liability — costly and problematic to sell. Alternatively, it may be under investigation for links to fraudulent activity or trafficking and thus has become a liability from the point of view of potential litigation for the owner. However, the owner may have calculated that the vessel may yield a short-term large "cash value" return if both the hull and cargo are sold on the black market; to greatly reduce the chances of subsequent investigations it is advantageous to get the crew to alter its name, flag, superficial appearance, routing, and documentation. In some situations it is decided to report the vessel missing at sea. After a sufficient time lapse to allow for "transformation," a new ship appears at a new destination and sells the cargo. Clearly, the owner will select the timing for the "disappearance" and sale with care; seeking to benefit from the sale of a high value cargo such as palm oil, other refined fuels, expensive consumer goods, alloys, or exotic ores.

Crews themselves can create and benefit from a phantom ship, an act known as barratry. According to admiralty law, barratry is defined as "a fraudulent act committed by a master or crew of a vessel which damages the vessel or its cargo, including desertion, illegal scuttling, and theft of the ship or cargo"[30] This is, in effect, an act of "self-piracy." In this instance, the opportunity to induce operational control is ideal: the crew has unsurpassed knowledge of the vessel and can thus effect precise physical modifications; the crew also has time on their side to change itineraries, paperwork, and cargo manifests. Additionally, given the comparative ease with which registries can be changed and the availability modern onboard Inmarsat communications, a master could rename and reregister a vessel while at sea if he deemed this kind of "legitimate" operational cover beneficial for the time needed to complete the voyage, discharge and sell the cargo, and even arrange to load another. Currently, a favorite destination for pirates that have managed to create a phantom ship is the southern Chinese coast and the Gulf of Tonkin.[31]

Vessel hijackings for a cargo or composite vessel-cargo sale on the black market do occur; however, the deputy director of the IMB at Maritime House in Barking, London claims they are far less common than they were ten years or so ago. A decade ago one might see 10–12 incidents per year; in 2005 this figure is down to nearer 1–3 per year.[32] Nevertheless, as with the subcontracting out of hostage-for-ransom operations to highly skilled teams, crime syndicates based in Singapore, Bangkok, Hong Kong, Sumatra, and the Philippines will find specialist subcontractors to seize specially selected vessels so as to sell entire cargos such as petroleum distillates, rubber, palm oil, finished steel, copper, and aluminum.[33] Even if these vessels are later discovered, the pirates will create a "phantom vessel" at least for the duration of the initial operation so as to avoid detection by police forces and naval units (patrol vessels and maritime patrol aircraft). Those vessels that do manage to remain undiscovered are used again and again to traffic narcotics and other contraband. The smuggling of people, sometime across considerable distances such as the Pacific, is particularly profitable. The *She-tou* syndicate is known to have used hijacked vessels to ferry illegal immigrants from China to the United States and Canada.[34] The ability of syndicates and the onboard operators to maintain a covert operation and continue to operate the seized vessel in an ostensibly legal fashion for protracted periods without attracting attention is testament to their levels of sophistication, maritime acumen and daring.

"The hijacking of a whole ship and the resale of its cargo requires huge resources and detailed planning," said Pottengal Mukundan, Director of ICC's Commercial Crime Services.[35] "It typically involves a mother ship from which to launch the attacks, a supply of automatic weapons, false identity papers for the crew and vessel, fake cargo documents, and a broker network to sell the stolen goods illegally." The director goes on to say that: "Individual pirates don't have these resources. Hijackings are the work of organized crime rings."[36] Intelligence is critical to hijacking the correct cargoes; crime syndicates and their pirate subcontractors are known to have precise knowledge of the contents of containers so that precision vessel assaults can be executed in order to steal cargoes to order.[37]

The most reported and notorious instances of phantom ship operations are those that result from an act of violent piracy. These operations are often as cavalier as they are complex; and it is these operations that have most concerned security officials from the point of view of a potential maritime terrorist operation because of the concerns over attempting to find and track a vessel seized by a terrorist cell that has effectively vanished.

Table 4.2 offers a sample of some incidents of "phantom ships" involving pirate hijackings.

Conclusions and Extrapolations

This essay is an exposure and discussion about the tactics and methodology used by contemporary pirate teams at a tactical and, occasionally, an operational level (when operations are of a hijacking and/or vessel devolution nature). The chapter has examined methods of target vessel identification, ordinary robbery of static target vessels, team approach and deception methods, boarding tactics, vessel seizure and situation control, weapons and equipment, and some of the critical elements that pertain to vessel hijacking, hostage-taking for ransom, and vessel devolution or "phantom ship" operations.

What becomes clear in assessing the various methods and tactics used by modern pirates, especially the more sophisticated teams, is that they are very good at what they do. These criminals are experienced, highly skilled (especially those teams that work as specialist assault subcontractors), motivated, intelligent, adaptable and, on occasion, willing and experienced in using modern firepower to achieve their objectives. This analysis, it is hoped, could be of potential value in complementing other analyses regarding piratical tactics and methodology in pursuit of advancing understanding of the phenomenon and refining counterstrategies. However, it must be stressed that much of what has been examined represents the zenith of piratical capabilities, particularly when it comes to hijacking operations and the use of assault weapons. Thus, prudence demands a cautionary note that not all piracy be viewed in its most exceptional manifestations, especially considering that as a proportion of total shipping activity, even in elevated risk areas, piracy remains a comparatively infrequent menace and not a high intensity existential threat as suggested by some media reports and so-called maritime security experts.

This is particularly important given the tendency in recent times to erroneously view pirate operations and capabilities as somehow synonymous with maritime terrorism. Nevertheless, it would be fair to suggest that the very high degree of competence and ruthlessness of some pirate operators raises concerns regarding the best approach to countermeasures. Defensive precautions and vigilance by crew members in high threat areas remains essential; however, the use of armed counterforce by those not properly trained is likely

Table 4.2 Selected incidents of "Phantom Ships" involving pirate hijackings

Vessel Name (Original)	IMO Number	Flag	Date	Vessel Type	Incident Narrative
Petro Ranger	7115086[38]	Malaysia	24 April 1998	Product Tanker	Vessel lifting 9,600 tons of jet fuel and diesel, attacked north of the Horsburgh Light by large pirate team in fast boat. Following successful approach through the radar blind arc astern, armed team boarded and captured the tanker and disabled all communications equipment. Pirates renamed vessel "Wilby" by painting over original name welds fore and aft. Pirates had preprepared false documentation such as bills of lading, crew manifests, and registration papers. Pirates captured off Hainan Island in southern China after transferring cargo to other vessels offshore.[39]
Fu Tai	3516713[40]	Belize	5 Aug. 1998	General Cargo	Hijack while at anchor off Bantam Island. Crew ordered to jump overboard. Chief engineer kept hostage. Pirates changed vessel's identity to unknown name. Reports indicate vessel was used to smuggle narcotics between Bangkok, Philippines, and Hong Kong. Vessel still at large and chief engineer still missing though did call at Hong Kong under original name on 5 November 1998.[41]
Suci	7903354[42]	Malaysia	19 Nov. 1996	Product Tanker	Pirates assaulted the 4,924 DWT tanker when it was six hours out of Singapore, bound for Sandakan on the island of Borneo with a cargo of diesel oil. In a professional operation, the team took over the bridge, secured the crew below decks, painted out the ship's

					name, and repainted the funnel in new colors. The following day, the crew was forced into a lifeboat and the renamed M/V *Glory II* sailed on. The crew was soon rescued, but the tanker vanished.[43]
Windsor III	6904507[44]	Honduras	14 Oct. 1995	General Cargo	Disappeared, presumed hijacked, 14 October 1995, but later found docked at Beihai, China, with a new name painted on it. Incident proved to be cargo fraud and Chinese authorities seized cargo. Vessel escaped. Cargo returned in July 1995.
Alondra Rainbow	9178094[45]	Panama	22 Oct. 1999	General Cargo	Japanese-owned vessel hijacked by pirates off Sumatra and sailed NW into to the Andaman Sea and renamed Mega Rama while at sea. Vessel intercepted by Indian navy on 16 November, pirates detained. Pirates attempted to scuttle ship after having been fired upon by canon from naval patrol boat and corvette.[46]
Global Mars	8502731[47]	Panama	22 Feb. 2000	Edible Oil Tanker	Vessel was reported missing, feared hijacked, in the Malacca Straits, after sailing from Port Klang, Malaysia, on 22 February 2000. Owners lost contact with it on 23 February. Eventually all 17 crew members were found safe on an island near Phuket in Thailand on 10 March. Crew confirmed that vessel had been seized by pirates. Detained in southern China on 1 June.

(Continued)

Table 4.2 Selected incidents of "Phantom Ships" involving pirate hijackings (*Continued*)

Vessel Name (Original)	IMO Number	Flag	Date	Vessel Type	Incident Narrative
Han Wei	7530547[48]	Belize	15 March 2002	Product Tanker	The Han Wei became a phantom ship after pirates seized it on a voyage from Singapore to Rangoon. They set adrift the 11-man crew, who were later found marooned on the coast of Sumatra. The Belize-registered ship was carrying 1,950 tons of gas oil. When Thai marine police caught up with it last month and boarded the vessel, it had been renamed Phaeton. The original black-and-white hull had been painted yellow and blue, its cargo unloaded at an unknown destination.[49]
Tenyu	8514241	Panama	13 Oct. 1998	General Cargo	*Tenyu*, lifting Alumina Ingots, was hijacked by pirates following its departure from Kuala Tanjung bound for Inchon, South Korea, on 8 October. The vessel was still missing on 16 November, but was eventually located at Zhangjianang, under false name (*Sanei 1*)[50] on 21 December. Returned to owners by Wuhan Maritime Court on 28 April 1999.
Anna Sierra	7117955[51]		13 Sept. 1995	General Cargo	Hijacked by armed pirates at position 11°15′N 102°00′E. Crew set adrift on pontoon and a life raft but later rescued. Pirates repainted vessel superstructure and changed its name illegally (to Artic Sea which could still be read). Arrived Beihai 20 September. Detained 25 September Pirates eventually abandoned vessel 10 months later in July 1996.[52]

to have seriously inimical consequences for the crew. Counterpiracy action is best addressed by marine police units and naval forces. Highly experienced, vetted operators (such as ex-military personnel) from private military/security companies protecting vessels and crews arguably represent a viable alternative under the correct circumstances and with proper sanction, although this is not by any means certain, and clearly not practical as a form of endemic protection for merchant shipping in high threat areas.

Finally, as previously raised, it is very important that the obvious tactical capabilities of some modern pirates be viewed in a straightforward sense for what they are — capabilities. The skill set of the most accomplished operators is a function of criminal intent and high stakes. However tempting to do so, this must not be confused with the intent of terrorists, which is very distinct from that of pirates.

Notes

1. Lloyd's Marine Intelligence Unit, casualty archives.
2. International Maritime Organization, MSC.4/Circ.61, 16 December 2004: Reports on Acts of Piracy and Armed Robbery Against Ships. http://www.imo.org/includes/blastDataOnly.asp/data_id%3D11500/61.pdf.
3. Lloyd's casualty database and Lloyd's List.
4. Daily Shipping Newsletter. http://www.ibiblio.org/maritime/Scheepvaartnieuws/Pdf/scheepvaartnieuws/2001/juni/28-06-2001A.PDF.
5. Ibid.
6. Ibid.
7. Lloyd's List, November, 2004.
8. ICC International Maritime Bureau, *Piracy and Armed Robbery Against Ships Annual Report 1 January-31 December 2004* (London: ICC International Maritime Bureau, 2005).
9. ICC International Maritime Bureau, *Piracy and Armed Robbery Against Ships Annual Report 1 January-31 December 2004* (London: ICC International Maritime Bureau, 2005), p. 30.
10. Lloyd's Marine Intelligence Unit, casualty archives.
11. Interview with IMB Deputy Director Jayant Abhyankar, September 2005.
12. Ibid.
13. Ibid.
14. ICC International Maritime Bureau, *Piracy and Armed Robbery Against Ships Annual Report 1 January-31 December 2004* (London: ICC International Maritime Bureau, 2005), p. 29
15. Lloyd's Marine Intelligence Unit, casualty archives.
16. John S. Burnett, *Dangerous Waters: Modern Piracy and Terror on the High Seas* (Harmondsworth, England: Dutton, 2002), pp. 166–167.
17. Ibid.
18. Interview with IMB Deputy Director Jayant Abhyankar, September 2005.
19. Captain Ken Blyth, *Petro Pirates, The Hijacking of the Petro Ranger* (St Leonards, Australia: Allen & Unwin, 2000), pp. 10–15.
20. Farah Abdul Rahim/Joanne Leow Bron: http://www.channelnewsasia.com, 11 August 2003, 2257 hrs (SST) 1457 hrs (GMT).
21. http://www.bridgedeck.org/mmp_htmlcode/mmp_news_archive/2002/mmp_news020829.html.
22. Report of the Panel of Experts on Somalia pursuant to Security Council Resolution 1425 (2002). http://www.somali-civilsociety.org/downloads/UN%20Panel%20of%20Experts%20Report%20-%2025%20March%202003.pdf.
23. Interview with IMB Deputy Director Jayant Abhyankar, September 2005.
24. http://www.d-n-i.net/fcs/iraq_and_the_RPG-7.htm.

25. Ibid.
26. Lloyd's Marine Intelligence Unit, casualty archives.
27. Ibid.
28. BBC News, 10 October 2005.
29. Peter C. Unsinger, "Phantom Ships, A Growing Menace." http://www.councilcea.org/articles/global/phantomships.html.
30. http://thestarport.org/people/steve/Doc/Songs/barratry.html.
31. Vivek Narain, Iffco Tokio General Insurance Company Ltd. http://www.assocham.org/events/recent/ev199/284,1,Risks Associated With Fraud In International Trade & Their Insurability.
32. Interview with IMB Deputy Director Jayant Abhyankar, September 2005.
33. John S. Burnett, *Dangerous Waters...*, pp. 218–219.
34. Ibid.
35. "Organized crime takes to the high seas, ICC piracy report finds." http://www.iccwbo.org/home/news_archives/2002/piracy_report.asp
36. Ibid.
37. Interview with IMB Deputy Director Jayant Abhyankar, September 2005.
38. Lloyd's Marine Intelligence Unit, casualty archives.
39. John S. Burnett, *Dangerous Waters...*, p. 227.
40. Lloyd's Marine Intelligence Unit, casualty archives.
41. Ibid.
42. Ibid.
43. Helen Gibson. http://home.wanadoo.nl/m.bruyneel/archive/modern/plague.htm.
44. Lloyd's Marine Intelligence Unit, casualty archives.
45. Lloyd's Marine Intelligence Unit, casualty archives.
46. William Langewiesche, *The Outlaw Sea, A World of Freedom, Chaos, and Crime* (New York: North Point Press, 2004), pp. 74–75.
47. Lloyd's Marine Intelligence Unit, casualty archives.
48. Lloyd's Marine Intelligence Unit, casualty archives.
49. http://scotlandonsunday.scotsman.com/international.cfm?id=759242002.
50. Captain Ken Blyth, *Petro Pirates...*, p. 148.
51. Lloyd's Marine Intelligence Unit, casualty archives.
52. Lloyd's Marine Intelligence Unit, casualty archives.

5
The Abu Sayyaf Group: Threat of Maritime Piracy and Terrorism

ROMMEL C. BANLAOI

Introduction

On 27 February 2004, MV *Superferry 14*, a commercial vessel carrying 899 passengers, exploded shortly after it left Manila Bay. The explosion resulted in the gruesome death of 116 people and the serious wounding of at least 300 others. This tragic incident in Philippine waters apparently converted the MV *Superferry 14* into a dreadful floating inferno. It was also the most violent man-made disaster in Philippine waters since 11 September 2001 and the worst terrorist attack in Asia since the 2002 Bali bombing.

The Abu Sayyaf Group (ASG) proudly claimed responsibility for the explosion and stressed that the incident was a "just revenge" of the group for the "brutal murder" of Bangsa Moro people amidst the "on-going violence" in Mindanao. Since the 1970s, the Philippine government has been agonizing with the internal armed challenges posed by Filipino Muslim radicalism. Among Muslim radical groups, the ASG has received international notoriety as the most violent group in the Philippines despite its small number. The administration of President Gloria Macapagal Arroyo initially denied ASG's involvement in the incident. But an ASG spokesperson, Abu Solaiman, identified passenger 51, Arnulfo Alvarado (pseudonym of Redendo Cain Dellosa), as the suicide bomber of the vessel. ASG Chief Khadafy Janjalani arrogantly confirmed Solaiman's claim and strongly warned that the "best action" of ASG was yet to come."

On 10 October 2004, the Marine Board Inquiry tasked to investigate the explosion submitted a report to President Arroyo. This report confirmed that based on the confession of Dellosa, the ASG had indeed deliberately planted the bomb that sank the MV *Superferry 14*. Dellosa admitted during investigation that he placed around eight pounds of TNT in a television set that he carried onto the ferry.

The bombing of the commercial vessel was an excellent case of a maritime terrorist attack in Southeast Asian water in the post-9/11 era. It was also watershed event not only in the Philippines but also in the international community as it revealed the hitherto unknown capability of the ASG to wage maritime terrorism by adopting some pirates' tactics.

This chapter aims to describe the capability of the ASG to conduct piracy and to wage maritime terrorism. It endeavors to analyze the fine line between piracy and terrorism, using the ASG as an example. Specifically, this chapter attempts to address the dual role that ASG members play as both pirates and terrorists in Philippine waters, the use of maritime piracy to fund terrorist operations, and the potential for ASG to transform the knowledge it has gained through piracy into a tool of terrorism.

Nexus Between Piracy and Terrorism

In reaction to the growing number of attacks on ships and tankers passing through the sea-lanes of Southeast Asia, particularly in the congested Strait of Malacca, Singaporean Minister for Home Affairs Wong Kan Seng once opined that pirates roaming the waters of the region should be declared terrorists.[1] Minister Wong argued, "we do not know whether it's pirates or terrorists who occupy the ship so we have to treat them all alike."[2] But describing the nexus of piracy and terrorism is conceptually problematic because many experts and policy makers are unsure at which point piracy becomes terrorism.[3]

The distinction between piracy and terrorism[4] is blurred because "pirates collude with terrorists, terrorists adopt pirate tactics and policymakers eager for public support start labeling every crime as maritime terrorism."[5] Terrorists can also use piracy as a cover for maritime terrorist attacks.

Motives of pirates and terrorists are arguably different from a conventional perspective. Pirates pursue economic gains while terrorists advance political objectives.[6] But it is said that terrorists have developed some capabilities to either adopt pirates' tactics or "piggyback" on pirates' raid.[7] It is also viewed that maritime terrorists, rather than simply stealing, could either blow up the ship or use it to ram into another vessel or a port facility.[8] Terrorist groups even regard seaports and international cruise liners as very attractive terrorist targets because they reside in the nexus of terrorist intent, capability, and opportunity.[9] Thus, nontraditional security studies consider the fine line between piracy and terrorism.

There is no doubt that maritime piracy is becoming a preferred method of funding for some terrorist groups with strong maritime traditions. This makes the threat of maritime piracy and terrorism overlapping, particularly in the tactics of ship seizures and hijackings. The ASG is one of those Southeast Asian terrorist groups which have a demonstrated capability to use piracy both as a camouflage to wage maritime terrorist attacks and as a means to fund terrorist ventures.

Brief Background of the ASG

The ASG is one of the internationally known but continue to be one of the least understood terrorist organizations in Southeast Asia.[10] Though the public has been informed, through various media reports, of the virulence of the threat posed by ASG, little is still known about the nature and scope of this threat, particularly in the area of piracy and maritime terrorism. In fact, there has been no uniform view of the ASG. The United States has listed the ASG as one of the Foreign Terrorist Organizations (FTO), while the United Nations has designated the ASG as one of the three most dangerous terrorist organizations operating in Southeast Asia along with Al Qaeda and the Jemaah Islamiyah (JI). Some see the ASG as part of the international fundamentalist movement, linked to Osama bin Laden, which aims to establish an independent Islamic state in the Philippines.[11] Others regard the ASG as the agent provocateur of the Philippine military and the Central Intelligence Agency (CIA).[12] The Philippine government continues to condemn the ASG as a mere bandit gang, which aims to amass funds through piracy, kidnap-for-ransom, extortion, and other criminal activities. But its members and sympathizers claim that the ASG represents the desire of all Muslim resistance groups in the Philippines to establish a separate Islamic state.

This mixed understanding of the ASG may also be attributed to its very nebulous beginning.[13] According to the various intelligence briefings of the Armed Forces of the Philippines (AFP), the formation of the ASG could be traced from disgruntled members of the Moro National Liberation Front (MNLF) formed in 1974. Some founding members of the ASG also came from the Moro Islamic Liberation Front (MILF), a splinter group of the MNLF organized in 1977. Existing reports, however, always point to Abdurajak Abubakar Janjalani as the founder of ASG. Janjalani organized the ASG after the Soviet-Afghan War in the 1980s. But there remains an uncertainty on the exact founding date of the ASG. What is certain is that Janjalani used the nom de guerre *Abu Sayyaf* while fighting in the 1980s in Afghanistan. Janjalani used this name in honor of Afghan resistance leader and Islamic professor Abdul Rasul Sayyaf, who adheres to Wahhabi theology, which regards other interpretations of Islam as a heresy. Professor Sayyaf's Wahhabism greatly influenced Janjalani's concept of an Islamic state. Janjalani formed the movement to propagate his fanatical belief of an Islamic state in the Philippines.

Despite the nebulous origin of the ASG, what is exactly known is that in 1990, Janjalani formed the Mujahideen Commando Freedom Fighters (MCFF) to establish an independent Islamic State in the Philippines through *jihad*. The MCFF may be regarded as the forerunner of the ASG. When the MCFF attracted some "hard core" followers in Basilan, Zulu, Tawi-Tawi, and Zamboanga, it became known as the ASG.

According to the Southern Command of the AFP, it was in 1991 when the name ASG was first publicly used by Janjalani in connection with the bombing of *M/V Doulos*, a Christian missionary ship docked at the Zamboanga port in the Southern Philippines.[14] The ASG gained international notoriety on 20 May 1992 when it assassinated Fr. Salvatorre Carzedda, an Italian missionary working in Zambonga City. These two major events prompted some observers to conclude that the ASG was founded sometime in 1991–1992.[15] But a recent study states that the ASG first emerged in 1989.[16] Based on intelligence reports, Janjalani renamed the ASG to Al-Harakatul Al-Islamiya (AHAI) in 1994 to solicit funding support from fellow radical Muslims abroad. The AHAI reportedly drew financial, material, and ideological support from the extremist element in Iran (Hezbollah), Pakistan (Jamaat-Islami and Hizbul-Mujahideen), Afghanistan (Hizb-Islami), Egypt (Al Gamaa-Al-Islamiya), Algeria (Islamic Liberation Front), and Libya (International Harakatul Al-Islamia). The International Islamic Relief Organization (IIRO) was also known to have provided financial support to AHAI. Because of repeated media reports, the name ASG became more popular than the AHAI. Western sources, however, tend to use and even interchange both names.[17]

Despite the lack of agreement about the exact founding date of the ASG, there is a need to emphasize that when Janjalani formed the ASG, his original vision was to form a highly organized, systematic, and disciplined organization of fanatical secessionist Islamic fighters in the Southern Philippines. To elaborate his intention in establishing the ASG and dispel misconceptions about the objectives of the organization, Janjalani issued an undated public proclamation, presumably written between 1993 and 1994. In this proclamation, he stressed the "Four Basic Truths" about the ASG, to wit:

- It is not to create another faction in the Muslim struggle which is against the teaching of Islam, especially the Quran, but to serve as a bridge and balance between the MILF and MNLF whose revolutionary roles and leadership cannot be ignored or usurped.
- Its ultimate goal is the establishment of a purely Islamic government whose "nature, meaning, emblem and objective" are basic to peace.
- Its advocacy of war is necessity for as long as there exist oppression, injustice, capricious ambitions, and arbitrary claims imposed on the Muslims.
- It believes that "war disturbs peace only for the attainment of the true and real objective of humanity — the establishment of justice and righteousness for all under the law of the noble Quran and the purified Sunnah."[18]

Like leaders of the MNLF and MILF, Janjalani regards ASG's Muslim radicalism as an expression of legitimate grievances of Muslim communities in Mindanao.[19] Thus, Janjalani's ultimate solution to Muslim problems in the

Philippines is the establishment of separate Islamic state in the Philippines. His death, however, resulted in the severe factionalization of the ASG and the eventual demise of ASG's original theological and ideological passion. At present, the ASG is no longer a homogenous organization. Rather, the ASG is a very loose coalition of many groups of radical Muslim leaders commanding their own loyal followers in the Southern Philippines. These groups have mixed objectives from Islamic fundamentalism to mere banditry. Members of these groups pay allegiance mostly to their respective leaders rather than to ASG doctrines.

Not all groups associated with the ASG are truly committed to the idea of a separate Islamic state in the Southern Philippines, though there is no doubt that some groups are really committed to the cause. Some Muslim bandit groups in the Southern Philippines want to be associated with the ASG for prestige, political expediency, and economic gains. But the dynamics of most these groups share common feature: they are highly personalistic rather than ideological groups of Muslim radicals and bandits.

According to various military reports, there were two major factions of the ASG operating independently in two major areas in the Southern Philippines: Basilan and Sulu. Other AFP reports mentioned another faction of ASG operating in Zamboanga City, but local government leaders in the city denied the existence of this faction. The Basilan-based and Sulu-based factions of the ASG were further divided into various autonomous groups with their own leaders and followers. As of 2002, the Basilan-based faction had 10 armed groups while the Sulu-based faction was composed of 16 armed groups. Because of intensified military campaigns of the Philippine government, some groups have already been dismantled with the capture, death, and neutralization of their leaders. But to date, the exact number of surviving groups has not been openly reported by the AFP or the Philippine National Police (PNP). What is known is that as of 2004, ASG strength was placed at 440, a substantial decrease from its peak of 1,269 in 2000. Based on the official briefing of the Anti-Terrorism Task Force (ATTF), ASG strength has been reduced to not more than 380 combatants as of the second quarter of 2005. According to the Department of National Defense (DND), "the ASG is presently factionalized and its remnants have splintered and are constantly on the move due to continued military pressures."

Despite its small number, the ASG can still wreak huge terrorist havoc because of its tremendous ability to solicit strong local support from among the Muslim population such as relatives, friends, classmates, and neighbors of ASG fighters. Moreover, the ASG continues to have effective alliances with rogue factions of the MNLF, MILF, and some JI personalities operating in the Philippines. A police intelligence report reveals that ASG has forged alliances with some gunmen loyal to jailed MNLF leader Nur Misuari.[20] Captured ASG members even admitted during police interrogation that they hired some rogue factions of the MNLF to mount some piracy and terrorist attacks in Mindanao. MNLF members acted as mercenaries of the ASG for an amount of US$1,000 each and provided sanctuaries for ASG members during hot military pursuits. Intelligence sources also revealed that ASG and MILF members have shared fighters in some of their major operations. According to Ruland Ullah, a former ASG member and now a state witness, "Sometimes the MILF would plant a roadside bomb against soldiers and the Abu Sayyaf would shoot the soldiers wounded in the blast." MILF and ASG members also receive joint training with JI operatives, particularly in the area of bomb making. JI-ASG linkage, therefore, remains intact and operational. The Philippine National Police Intelligence Group (PNP-IG) estimates that the number of JI operatives in the Philippines may be placed at 60 as of April 2005.[21] These JI operatives continue to exploit local Muslim secessionist rebels in the Philippines by sharing their demolition skills.

From the foregoing, the ASG has developed a strong capability to mount terrorist attacks in the Philippines. But what is not popularly known is the ASG's inherent capability to conduct piracy and wage maritime terrorism.

The ASG and the Threat of Piracy and Maritime Terrorism

Piracy and maritime terrorism are inherent in the capability of ASG. Most ASG members and followers belong to Muslim families and communities of fishermen with a century-old seafaring tradition. Because ASG members live close to the waters of Basilan, Sulu, and Tawi-Tawi, they have gained tremendous familiarity of the maritime environment. In fact, most Muslim Filipinos living in coastal communities are experienced divers. ASG members' deep knowledge of the maritime domain also gives them ample capability to conduct piracy and wage maritime terrorist attacks.[22]

Because of its embedded seaborne abilities, ASG's first terrorist attack was, in fact, maritime in nature. As mentioned previously, on 24 August 1991 the ASG bombed the *M/V Doulous*, both a Christian missionary ship and a European floating library docked at the Zamboanga port. At that time, the missionaries were holding their farewell program after conducting their evangelization project. Two foreign missionaries were killed and eight others were wounded in the blast.

The ASG waged this particular attack purely for political reasons. According to Abdurajak Janjalani, the bombing of M/V *Doulous* was a reaction of the group to the continuing military offensive against Muslims in the Southern Philippines. Janjalani even warned of more future violence to match if not surpass the violence inflicted by the Philippine military on the Muslim people. But the Philippine government was clueless of the maritime terrorist capability of the ASG during this time. Initially, the Philippine Coast Guard (PCG), the Philippine Navy, and the PNP Maritime Group did not even regard this incident as an act of maritime terrorism. It was only recently that Philippine authorities realized that the ASG has developed capability to wage maritime terrorism.

Three years after the M/V *Doulous* attack, ASG Secretary General Abu Abdu Said issued a document in 1994 explaining in detail the objective of the group in bombing the ship. This document denies that the ASG was a creation of the military as alleged by various media reports. It explains that the ASG is an organization of radical Bangsa Moro people to seek *kaadilan* (justice) for Filipino Muslims through the establishment of separate Islamic state.[23] The document also states that the ASG had bombed the ship because foreign Christian missionaries aboard the ship "spoke against Islam" and even called Allah a "false God." These missionaries also described Prophet Muhammad "a liar" and the Quran a "man-made book."[24] According to University of the Philippines professor Samuel K. Tan, "The desire to avenge the insult against the sacred values of Islam started the motive force of the Abu Sayyaf."[25]

On August 1993, the ASG abducted Mr. Ricardo Tong, a prominent shipyard owner in Zamboanga City. The abduction of Mr. Tong demonstrated that during its infancy stage, the prime target ASG was the maritime sector. The ASG was more familiar with the maritime rather than with the mountainous terrain. Mr. Tong was released only on 17 January 1995 after paying a ransom of 5 million Philippine pesos (roughly US$93,000). The Philippine military considered the kidnapping of Mr. Tong a criminal act because of ransom payments. But it was also a political act because the ASG issued some political demands prior to the abduction when it kidnapped, in April 1993 Luis Biel, a five-year-old grandson of a bus-company owner in Basilan. Among its demands was the removal of all Catholic symbols in Muslim communities and the banning of all foreign fishing vessels in the Sulu and Basilan seas. The ASG continued its terrorist and criminal activities afterward. From 1991 to 2000, the ASG engaged in a total of 378 terrorist activities, resulting in the deaths of around 288 civilians. During the same period, the ASG also conducted a total of 640 kidnapping activities victimizing at least 2,076 individuals.[26]

Because of the spate of kidnapping activities of the ASG, Philippine government officials and foreign analysts said that the group had already degenerated into a criminal organization. But Khadafy Janjalani is presently attempting to revive the original Islamic agenda of the ASG. The ASG resorted to kidnapping activities not merely to commit crimes but to deliberately raise funds from ransom payments, which the organization used to buy arms and explosives for its terrorist activities. The Philippine law-enforcement authorities recorded several arms shipments to Basilan and Sulu to supply ASG with explosives, mortar tubes, high-powered firearms, and ammunition.[27] With huge ransom money in its possession, the ASG was able to purchase powerful weapons. ASG's stock of firearms increased at an annual average rate of 12 percent from 230 in 1994 to 390 in 2000. In 2003, the AFP reported that the

ASG possessed at least 300 firearms, not to mention its illegal possession of explosives and communication equipment being used for urban terrorism.

The ASG also used part of its huge ransom money to build up its manpower and to lure local communities into providing mass support to the organization. The ASG succeeded in recruiting some MNLF and MILF leaders and followers to join the group. The most prominent of these leaders was Sakiruddin Bahjin, or Commander Ullom, who served as Deputy Secretary for Political Affairs of the MNLF Central Committee. MNLF Commanders Radullah Sahiron and Hadji Sulaiman Hadjirul also joined the ASG. With the huge amount of money in its possession as a result of a series of kidnap-for-ransom activities from 1991–2000, the ASG was able to offer monetary compensation to those parts of the local population who opted to become core members of its mass-based support system.[28] As stated earlier, ASG membership rapidly expanded from less than 100 fighters in 1991 to around 1,269 fighters in December 2000. According to the Philippine Naval Intelligence Group, most of these fighters possessed a mastery of the maritime domain because they belonged to families of fishermen with a deeply rooted maritime tradition. Thus even before 11 September 2001, the ASG had already developed the capability to conduct piracy and wage maritime terrorism based on this maritime tradition. In fact, "piracy" has even been embraced in the Southern Philippines as part of the local culture, a "normal" though "illegal" means of making money.

ASG proved its maritime terrorist mettle when it waged another attack on 23 April 2000, kidnapping some 21 tourists, including ten foreigners, from a Malaysian beach resort in Sipadan. These foreigners included three Germans, two Japanese, two Finns, two South Africans, and a Lebanese woman. The hostages were eventually taken to Jolo Island of Mindanao. This incident demonstrated ASG's capability to operate outside its usual maritime turf. It also displayed ASG's creativity in waging maritime terrorist attacks because some of its members were disguised as diving instructors. ASG member Ruland Ullah, who is now a state witness to the Sipadan hostage crisis, was successfully disguised as a diving instructor in this Malaysian resort prior to the incident. An intelligence source revealed that Ullah trained some ASG members in scuba diving prior to the attack. In fact, the Philippine military recently confirmed that ASG members were trained in scuba diving to prepare for possible seaborne terror attacks not only in the Philippines but also outside of the country.

Based on the interrogation of Gamal Baharan, a captured ASG member involved in the 2005 Valentine's Day bombings of three major cities in the Philippines, some ASG members took scuba diving lessons in southwestern Palawan as part of a plot for an attack at sea. Baharan said that the training was in preparation for a JI bombing plot on unspecified targets outside the Philippines that require underwater operation.[29] Baharan also said that ASG Amir Khadafy Janjalani and ASG spokesman Abu Solaiman were on top of the maritime training.

The Sipadan hostage drama was a serious maritime terrorist attack with clear political objectives because ASG issued several demands. These demands included recognition of separate Islamic State in the Southern Philippines, an inquiry into the alleged human rights abuses against Filipino Muslims in Sabah, and the protection of their ancestral fishing grounds in Mindanao. The Sipadan incident was also considered as an "act of piracy" because the ASG eventually demanded a US$2.6 million ransom for the hostages. The ASG even threatened the Philippine government to behead hostages if their demands were not met. A few months later, ASG members kidnapped another three Malaysian nationals in Pasir Beach Resort in Sabah on 30 September 2000 using a speedboat. This incident showed the fine line between maritime piracy and terrorism.

The April 2000 Sipadan kidnapping incident was only resolved in 2001 when the ASG reportedly received a US$15 million ransom from the Philippine government. But the payment of ransom money was marred by controversies.[30] The September 2000 kidnapping, on the other hand, was resolved when the Philippine government troops in Talipao, Sulu, successfully rescued the three Malaysian nationals under the operation Trident.

But the maritime terrorist attacks of the ASG did not end there. On 22 May 2001, ASG guerrillas raided the luxurious Pearl Farm beach resort on Samal island of Mindanao. This incident resulted in the killing of two resort workers and the wounding of three others. Though no hostages were taken during this attack, the Samal raid demonstrated anew the willingness of ASG to pursue maritime targets. On 28 May 2001, the ASG waged another maritime terror when it abducted three American citizens and seventeen Filipinos spending a vacation at the Dos Palmas resort in Palawan.

Thus far, the Dos Palmas incident had been the most notorious and the most sensationalized attack of the ASG. The incident received international coverage because several of the victims were murdered and beheaded, including an American citizen. The Philippine government declared a no-ransom policy and imposed a news blackout about the incident. But the Dos Palmas incident served as a wake-up call for the United States to get involved in antiterrorism cooperation with the Philippines.[31] Because two American hostages were involved, the U.S. military sent U.S. Army special forces to the Philippines to train AFP forces in counterterrorism. The U.S. Pacific Command even extended a US$2 million assistance to the Philippines from its regional security assistance program as a result of the Dos Palmas incident. But when the lives of the two American hostages were put in danger, the U.S. Army special operation forces changed the scope of their mission in the Philippines by facilitating the rescue of American citizens. During a rescue operation mounted by the AFP in 2002, two victims, including an American missionary, Martin Burnham, were killed. His wife, Gracia Burnham, the well-known survivor of the kidnapping incident, later wrote a memoir of her captivity in the hands of the ASG.[32]

The Dos Palmas incident convinced the American government that the ASG was a deadly foreign terrorist organization. To increase the capability of the Philippine military to destroy the ASG, American and Filipino forces conducted the controversial joint military exercise called Balikatan 02–1.[33] *Balikatan,* literally meaning "shouldering the load together," is the largest joint and combined military exercise of Philippine and U.S. forces. The conduct of this exercise is based primarily on the 1951 Mutual Defense Treaty (MDT), requiring the two countries to undergo this type of exercise to develop their capacity to resist aggression and to combat common adversaries.

The Philippines and American forces conducted the Balikatan 02–1 primarily in the island province of Basilan, the haven of the ASG. Other troops held their exercises in and near Zamboanga City, the headquarters of Philippine Southern Command. Balikatan 02–1 originally involved 3,800 Philippine military personnel and 660 U.S. special forces and support personnel. The United States augmented its force five months later with 340 U.S. Navy and Marine construction engineers and 176 Navy and Army engineers to implement some civil engineering projects in support of the exercise. Admiral Dennis Blair, former commander-in-chief of the U.S. Pacific Command (CINCPAC), described Balikatan 02–1 as the "largest military operation against terrorism [outside of Afghanistan]."[34] However, at this occasion, the number of American troops was relatively small compared to past Balikatan exercises, which usually involved 1,500 to 3,000 American troops. The conduct of Balikatan 02–1 resulted in the neutralization of many ASG members, including the reported death of notorious ASG spokesman, Abu Sabaya and the eventual capture of Sulu-based ASG leader Galib Andang, also known as Commander Robot. Galib Andang met his untimely death on 16 March 2005 during a foiled jail break incident.

But the neutralization, capture, and death of some ASG leaders and members did not prevent the group from continuing its operations. In September 2003, the ASG threatened to hijack some vessels of Sulpicio and WG&A lines passing through Sarangani Bay to generate funds while trying to recover from the severe impact of Balikatan 02–1. According to PCG officials, they received intelligence reports that the ASG planned to attack one of the passenger vessels of WG&A and Sulpicio lines plying the Mindanao route. Hence, the PCG intensified its patrol operations in Sarangani Bay and adjacent coastal areas to thwart any possible hijack attempt by the ASG.

The ASG, however, has a strong determination to pursue its maritime terrorist operation. An intelligence source reported that during the last quarter of 2003, the ASG kidnapped four Indonesian nationals and one Filipino in the Borneo Paradise Eco-Farm Beach Resort in Lahad Datu, Sabah/Malaysia, to raise funds. Reportedly, the hostages were divided into groups and separately brought to Patikul and Indanan in Sulu using speed boats. In April 2004, just two months after the *Superferry 14* incident, the Philippine National Police Maritime Group reported that the ASG hijacked a boat and kidnapped two Malaysian and one Indonesian in the Southern Philippines near Sabah. Their abduction came on the heels of the escape of 23 ASG members from a Basilan jail.

The foregoing cases clearly demonstrated the capability of ASG to conduct piracy and wage maritime terrorism. The ASG has resorted to piracy not merely to commit crimes but to fund itself while at the same time wage maritime terrorism to deliver political messages. The Filipino Coast Guard officials even admitted that the Philippines was seen increasingly under threat of piracy and maritime terrorism posed by the ASG.[35] Manila has even been identified as among 26 city ports and anchorages vulnerable to such maritime attacks.[36]

Though it has been known that the ASG has already developed capability to wage various terrorist attacks in both the land and maritime domain, we have yet to conduct further research on its capability to use piracy as a tool of terrorism. Based on its records of various maritime attacks, beach resorts were usual targets of the ASG. Though the ASG has threatened to hijack commercial vessels after 9/11, none of these threats were carried out except the bombing of the *Superferry 14* and the seizure of small boats to kidnap Indonesian and Malaysian nationals in April 2004. Though ASG members have undergone training to mount an attack at sea, plots have been foiled by the Philippine law-enforcement agencies. Sadly, details of these plots have not been publicly disclosed by law-enforcement authorities for further analysis.

Combating the ASG: The Philippine Counterterrorism Strategy

The Philippine government has adopted a multilevel approach to combat the terrorist threat posed by the ASG, in particular, and international terrorism, in general.

At the international level, the Philippine government signed UN Security Council Resolutions 1373, 1368, 1267, and 1333 in September 2001. At the regional level, the Philippines signed the Asia Pacific Economic Cooperation (APEC) Leaders Statement on Counter-Terrorism in 2001 and the ASEAN Regional Forum (ARF) Statement on the Prevention of Terrorism in 2002. It also signed all ASEAN statements and declarations related with counterterrorism.[37] At the trilateral level, it signed the Trilateral Agreement on Information Exchange and Establishment of Communication Procedures with Malaysia and Indonesia on 7 May 2002. At the bilateral level, the Philippine reinvigorated its security relations with the United States and forged strategic bilateral partnership with Australia, China, India, and Japan on counterterrorism.

At the national level, the Philippine government formed the Inter-Agency Task Force Against International Terrorism on 24 September 2001 under the direct supervision of the Office of the President. This Inter-Agency Task Force aimed to coordinate intelligence operations and to facilitate the identification and neutralization of suspected terrorist cells in the Philippines. To freeze the financial assets of international terrorists, the Philippine Congress passed the Anti-Money Laundering Act on 29 September 2001. President Arroyo also announced on 12 October 2001 its 14-pillar approach to combat terrorism. Through the Operation Center of the Cabinet Oversight Committee on Internal Security (COCIS), formed on 19 June 2001 through Executive Order No. 21, the Philippine government formulated the National Plan to Address Terrorism and its Consequences as Annex K to the National Internal Security Plan (NISP). The Philippine government approved the NISP on 26 November 2001 through Memorandum Order 44.

The COCIS was tasked to implement the national antiterrorism plan by involving all national government agencies, local government units (LGUs), and the private sectors in the campaign. But the Philippine government abolished the COCIS in October 2004. The task of managing and implementing the antiterrorism plan was transferred to the ATTF, which was originally formed on 24 March 2004 under the COCIS. The ATTF is now operating under the office of the president with the executive secretary as the chair. The ATTF is now based in Malacanang Palace in Manila.

The ATTF aims to establish an extensive antiterrorism information system and accelerate intelligence fusion among all intelligence units in the Philippines in the identification of terrorism personalities, cells, groups, and organizations in various LGUs. It also aims to conduct an extensive information drive at both national and local levels "to prepare the public and all stakeholders to get involved in the national antiterrorism campaign." With the creation of ATTF, the Philippine government adopts the 16-point counterterrorism program to operationalize the 14-point antiterrorism policy of the national government.

At the local level, the Philippine government also pursues a local government approach and urges all local government units (LGUs) in the country to cooperate in the Philippine campaign against international terrorism.[38] As a result, the League of Municipalities of the Philippines (LMP) passed a resolution in November 2002 condemning terrorism in strongest terms. Presently composed of 1,500 member municipalities, LMP regards terrorism as "a serious threat to the security and well-being not only of the Filipino people but also of the whole civilized world."[39] The LMP also established closer partnership with defense establishment in order to implement its antiterrorism plan at the municipal level. During its major island conferences and general assemblies, LMP involved various defense officials in its programs and activities in order to increase the awareness of municipal chief executives on terrorism and counterterrorism.

The League of Cities of the Philippines (LCP) also joined the fight against terrorism when it expressed its unwavering support on the passage of the antiterrorism bill. It even supported the passage of the controversial national identification system and vowed to acquire modern equipment such as metal detectors and train bomb-sniffing dogs that would be utilized against terrorist threats.[40] The LCP is presently composed of 116 member cities.

The League of Provinces of the Philippines (LPP), on the other hand, asked the national government for the timely release of internal revenue allotment (IRA) to LGUs in order to finance its drive against terrorism. But President Arroyo urged Philippine provinces to take the initiatives in raising their own funds.[41] The LPP comprises 79 member-provinces to date.

To fight terrorism at the grassroots level, the *Liga ng mga Barangay sa Pilipinas* (LBP or League of Philippine Villages) also launched its antiterrorism campaign when it forged closer partnership with the ATTF. On 8 June 2004, the League and the ATTF published an advocacy material, *Gabay ng Barangay Laban sa Terorismo* (Villages Guide Against Terrorism), to increase local-government awareness about the gravity of terrorist threats. This advocacy material contains fundamental discussions on the definition of terrorism and how to respond to terrorist threats at the village level. The League promotes what it calls "4A's to Fight Terrorism": Awareness, Alertness, Action, and Advocacy.[42] The League is composed of more than 42,700 members.

Through its unrelenting efforts to combat terrorism in the Philippines at various levels, the Philippine government has effectively reduced the strength of the ASG. As stated earlier, ASG strength has been reduced to not more than 380 combatants in the second quarter of 2005, which can be regarded as a great achievement of the Philippine government in the global fight against terrorism.

It is very sad to note, however, that as of the time of writing, there is no specific antiterrorist law in the Philippines. As a result, some terrorist leaders captured by the Philippine law-enforcement authorities for illegal possession of explosives were able to bail out, since under the Philippine law, illegal possession of explosives is a "bailable" offense.

As of May 2005, nine antiterrorism bills were filed at the Philippine House of Representatives while five were filed at the Philippine Senate. President Arroyo declared antiterrorism bills to be priority bills. But most of the bills filed in both houses of the Philippine Congress are identical. It is very sad to note that all antiterrorism bills remained at the Technical Working Group (TWG) level for consolidation. No bills filed have reached the First Reading in both Houses of the Philippine Congress. As of April 2005, the TWG in charged of consolidating all antiterrorism bills in the Philippine House of Representatives is still in the snail-pace stage of "consultation in aid of legislation." Philippine Senate President Franklin Drillon even opined that "antiterrorism bill is not and may no longer be a senate priority."[43] The absence of an antiterrorism law in the Philippines is the weakest link in the Philippine's antiterrorist efforts. Because of the absence of such a law in the Philippines, at least five terror suspects who took part in terrorist attacks since 2002 have been released on bail by local authorities.

Toward A Maritime Security Strategy to Combat ASG's Maritime Terrorist Threats

Despite heavy military operations and amidst government pronouncements that the ASG has become a "spent force," it continues to wreak terrorist havoc in the Philippines. The bombing of *Superferry 14* on 27 February 2004 and the three simultaneous bombings in Makati City, General Santos City, and Davao City on the eve of Valentine's Day celebration in 2005 were recent indications that the ASG is alive and kicking. In a telephone interview pertaining to the *Superferry 14* incident, ASG spokesperson Abu Soliaman even taunted the Philippine government by saying, "Still doubtful about our capabilities? Good. Just wait and see. We will bring the war that you impose on us to your lands and *seas*, homes and streets. We will multiply the pain and suffering that you have inflicted on our people" (italics mine).[44]

As a result of the 2005 Valentine's Day bombing, the PCG increased the security of major ports in the Philippines. Intelligence operatives in plainclothes were deployed in various ports in the country. The PNP Maritime Group also tightened its security measures in the Visayas and Mindanao following the bombing. At least six sea marshals were also assigned to ensure the safety of passengers in every ship sailing in Philippine waters. Philippine Marines have also been on foot patrol in various ports since the aftermath of this bombing attack.

To combat piracy and maritime terrorism in the Philippines, the Philippine Navy has pursued its Naval Modernization Program despite serious budgetary constraints. It sought the assistance of the United States for its modernization program. On 8 March 2004, for example, the United States transferred to the Philippine Navy the ownership of a Cyclone Class ship that aims to enhance the Philippines' coastal patrol and counterterrorism capabilities. The United States refurbished the patrol ship, which has been renamed BRP General Mariano Alvarez after a Philippine hero, at the cost of US$7 million, including a two-year supply of spare parts. The transfer costs a total of US$30 million. President George W. Bush offered this ship to President Gloria Macapagal Arroyo during her visit to the White House in November 2001.

Though the Philippine maritime authorities are serious in their efforts to curb piracy and maritime terrorism in the country, they are crippled by the absence of an antiterrorism law. Worst of all, the Philippines does not have an updated national maritime security law. Although the Philippine government created the Office for Transportation Security (OTS) to make a draft of the national maritime security law that will comply with the requirements of the International Ship and Port Facility Security (ISPS) Code, nothing has been heard of the draft since the OTS was created on 30 January 2004 by virtue of Executive Order No. 277.

Conclusion

There is no uniform view of the ASG. Though many studies have been written about the ASG, little work has been done to examine the maritime terrorist capability of the ASG. This paper initially described the maritime terrorist threat posed by the ASG and its ability to use piracy as a tool for terrorism.

After examining the record of maritime terrorist attacks, this paper observed that most targets of the ASG were beach or coastal resorts. Though it has threatened to hijack commercial vessels, Philippine law-enforcement authorities have thwarted these attacks, except for the bombing of the *Superferry 14* and the seizure of small boats in April 2004. Despite the Philippine government's declaration of the ASG as a spent force due to intensified military operations and hot pursuits, it continues to wreak terrorist havoc because of its ability to solicit local support and to link with JI, the MILF, and the MNLF. The absence of an antiterrorism bill in the Philippines aggravates the situation. Sadly, the Philippines does not even have a maritime security law that will impose severe punishment to groups and individuals engaged in piracy and maritime terrorism.

Notes

1. Graham Gerald Ong, "Southeast Asian Pirates Bear the Marks of Terrorists," *Institute of Southeast Asian Studies Viewpoints* (1 January 2004), p. 1 at http://www.iseas.edu.sg/viewpoint/ggojan04.pdf. Also see Agence Prance Presse "Piracy and Equals Terrorism in Troubled Waters: Minister" (21 December 2003) at http://www.singapore-window.org/sw03/031221af.htm (accessed on 26 April 2005).
2. Ibid., p. 3.
3. Bantarto Bandoro, "When Piracy Becomes Terrorism in the Strait," *The Jakarta Post* (29 July 2004).
4. This section is largely based in Rommel C. Banlaoi, "Maritime Security Outlook for Southeast Asia" in Joshua Ho and Catherine Zara Raymond, eds, *The Best of Times, The Worst of Times: Maritime Security in the Asia-Pacific* (Singapore: World Scientific, 2005).
5. Rubert Herbert-Burns and Lauren Zucker, "Malevolent Tide: Fusion and Overlaps in Piracy and Maritime Terrorism" (Washington DC: Maritime Intelligence Group, 30 July 2004), p. 1.
6. Tamara Renee Shie, "Ports in a Storm? The Nexus Between Counterterrorism, Counter-proliferation, and Maritime Security in Southeast Asia," *Issues and Insights*, Vol. 4, No. 4 (Pacific Forum CSIS, July 2004), p. 13.
7. Patrick Goodenough, "Maritime Security Takes Center Stage in SE Asia," *CNSNews.COM* (29 June 2004) at http://www.cnsnews.com/ (accessed 27 July 2004).
8. Ibid.
9. Tanner Campbell and Rohan Gunaratna, "Maritime Terrorism, Piracy and Crime" in Rohan Gunaratna, ed., *Terrorism in the Asia Pacific: Threat and Response* (Singapore: Eastern University Press, 2003), p. 72.
10. This section is largely based on Rommel C. Banlaoi, "Leadership Dynamics in Terrorist Organizations in Southeast Asia: The Abu Sayyaf Case" (paper presented at the international symposium, "The Dynamics and Structures of Terrorist Threats in Southeast Asia" organized by the Institute of Defense Analyses in cooperation with the Southeast Asia Regional Center for Counter-Terrorism and the U.S. Pacific Command, Kuala Lumpur, Malaysia, on 18–20 April 2005), pp. 1–21.
11. See Eusaquito P. Manalo, *Philippine Response to Terrorism: The Abu Sayyaf Group* (MA Thesis: Naval Post Graduate School, Monterey, CA, December 2004).

12. See International Peace Mission, *Basilan: The Next Afghanistan?* Report of the International Peace Mission to Basilan, Philippines (23–27 March 2002), p. 11. Also available at the following website: http://www.bwf.org/pamayanan/peacemission.html (accessed on 30 August 2004).
13. Glenda Gloria, "Bearer of the Sword: The Abu Sayyaf Has Nebulous Beginnings and Incoherent Aims," *Mindanao Updates* (6 June 2000).
14. "Special Report on the Abou Sayyaf" Briefing of MIG9 during the Southern Command Conference, 19 January 1994.
15. Marites D. Vitug and Glenda M. Gloria, *Under the Crescent Moon: Rebellion in Mindanao* (Quezon City: Ateneo Center for Social Policy and Public Affairs, Institute for Popular Democracy and Philippine Center for Investigative Journalism, 2000) and Mark Turner, "The Management of Violence in a Conflict Organization: The Case of the Abu Sayyaf," *Public Organization Review*, vol. 3, no. 4 (December 2003), p. 388.
16. Manalo, p. 31.
17. See for example, Angel Rabasa, "Southeast Asia: Moderate Tradition and Radical Challenge" in Angel Rabasa, et al. *The Muslim World After 9/11* (Santa Monica, RAND: Rand, 2004), Chapter 8. Also see "Inside Abu Sayyaf" at http://www.inq7.net/specials/inside_abusayyaf/2001/features/formative_years.htm.
18. Quoted in Samuel K. Tan, *Internationalization of the Bangsamoro Struggle* (Quezon City: University of the Philippines Center for Integrative and Development Studies, 2003), revised edition, p. 96.
19. For a good contextual analysis of the rise of Abu Sayyaf, see Charles Donnely, "Terrorism in the Southern Philippines: Contextualizing the Abu Sayyaf Group as an Islamist Secessionist Organization" (Paper presented to the 15th Biennial conference of the Asian Studies Association of Australia in Canberra 29 June–2 July 2004) at http://coombs.anu.edu.au/ASAA/conference/proceedings/Donnelly-C-ASAA2004.pdf. (Accessed on 27 April 2005).
20. Jim Gomez, "Filipino Terror Group's Reach Grown Nationally," *Associated Press* (8 March 2005).
21. Interview with Police Chief Superintendent Ismael R. Rafanan, director of the Philippine National Police Intelligence Group, held at Camp Crame, Quezon City, on 1 April 2005.
22. Rommel C. Banlaoi, "Maritime Terrorism in Southeast Asia: The Abu Sayyaf Threat," *U.S. Naval War College Review*, vol. 58, no. 4 (Autumn 2005).
23. Tan, *Internationalization of the Bangsamoro Struggle*, p. 95.
24. Ibid., p. 94.
25. Ibid.
26. Department of National Defense, "Info Kit on the Abu Sayyaf Group" (Submitted to the Committee on National Defense and Security of the Philippine Senate on 24 August 2001).
27. Ibid.
28. Ibid.
29. See Associated Press, "Terrorist Train for Seaborne Attacks" at http://www.ldslivingonline.com/stories/30_ds_330924.php. (Accessed on 27 April 2005.)
30. For an eyewitness account of the issue including the controversial payment of ransom, see Roberto N. Aventajado, *140 Days of Terror: In the Clutches of the Abu Sayyaf* (Pasig City: Anvil Publishing, Inc., 2004).
31. Larry Niksch, "Abu Sayyaf: Target of Philippine-US Anti-Terrorism Cooperation," *CRS Report for Congress* (25 January 2002).
32. Gracia Burnham and Dean Merrill, *In the Presence of my Enemies* (Wheaton, IL: Tyndale House Publishers, 2003).
33. For further discussions, Rommel C. Banlaoi, "The Role of Philippine-American Relations in the Global Campaign Against Terrorism: Implications for Regional Security, *Contemporary Southeast Asia*, vol. 24, no. 2 (August 2002), pp. 294–312. Also see Rommel C. Banlaoi, "Philippine-American Security Relations and the War on Terrorism in Southeast Asia" in *International Relations of the Asia Pacific After 9/11 and China's Accession to WTO*, Wang Xingsheng, ed. (Guangzhou: Zhongshan University Institute of Southeast Asian Studies, 2003), pp. 80–95.

34. Admiral Dennis C. Blair, "The Campaign Against International Terrorism in the Asia-Pacific Region" (Remarks to Asia Society Hong Kong Center on 18 April 2002) at http://usinfo.state.gov/regional/ea/easec/blair1802.htm. (Accessed on 27 April 2002.)
35. Agence France-Presse, "Philippines Seen Increasingly Under Threat from Maritime Terrorism" (8 September 2003) at http://quickstart.clari.net/qs_se/webnews/wed/ao/Qphilippines-apec-attacks.RBWM_DS8.html (accessed on 30 August 2004).
36. Ibid.
37. Rommel C. Banlaoi, *War on Terrorism in Southeast Asia* (Quezon City: Rex Book Store International 2004).
38. Rommel C. Banlaoi, "Local Government Response Against Terrorist Threats in the Philippines: Issues and Prospects" (Paper presented to the 12th International Conference of the East and Southeast Asia Network for Highly Performing Local Governments organized by the Konrad Adenauer Foundation and the Local Government Development Foundation, Rendezvous Hotel, Singapore on 2–3 December 2004).
39. League of Municipalities of the Philippines, Resolution Number 001–2002 (12–14 November 2002).
40. "Mayors Vow to Lead Fight Vs Terrorism, Support National ID System," *Philippine Star* (22 October 2002).
41. Jayme Arroyo, "Local gov t officials use 10–10–10 to clamor for release of IRA," *Cuberdyaryo* at http://www.cyberdyaryo.com/features/f2001_1023_03.htm (accessed on 26 October 2004).
42. Liga ng mga Barangay sa Pilipinas (League of Philippine Villages), *Gabay ng Barangay Laban sa Terorismo* (*Villages Guide Against Terrorism*), 8 June 2004.
43. Ruth Mercado, "Maritime Enraged on Drillon Barb," *The Freeman* (6 April 2005) at http://www.thefreeman.com/local/index.php?fullstory=1&issue=articles_20050406&id=28938. (Accessed on 29 April 2005.)
44. Marco Garrido, "After Madrid, Manila?" *Asia Times* (24 April 2004) at http://www.atimes.com/atimes/Southeast_Asia/FD24Ae01.html (accessed on 28 August 2004).

6

The Emerging Nexus between Piracy and Maritime Terrorism in Southeast Asia Waters: A Case Study on the Gerakan Aceh Merdeka (GAM)

JEFFREY CHEN

Introduction

Dr. Tony Tan, Singapore's deputy prime minister and coordinating minister for security and defence, said the following at the 2004 Institute of Defence and Strategic Studies Maritime Security Conference held in Singapore on 20 May 2004: "The possible nexus between piracy and maritime terrorism is probably the greatest concern to maritime security. … What is more disturbing is the prospect that pirate attacks might be linked to terrorist organizations as they are conducted with increasing sophistication and precision."[1] He went on to give the example of the boarding of the *Dewi Madrim* in March 2003, when pirates who were well armed boarded the tanker. Instead of looking for valuable items onboard the vessel, the pirates took control of the helm of the vessel, steering the vessel for an hour in the Malacca Straits before they fled, with the vessel's crew all tied up.

It has been suggested that when it comes to acts of piracy in Southeast Asia, one finds at least two groups with a political agenda embarking on such acts: the Abu Sayyaf Group (ASG) in the Southern Philippines and Gerakan Aceh Merdeka (GAM) on the Aceh Peninsula, in the northern part of Sumatra, Indonesia. Unlike the ASG, GAM is deemed to be more likely to be involved only in maritime piracy, rather than having maritime terrorism intentions like the ASG, which actually did carry out one devastating bombing onboard of a Philippine domestic ferry, the *Super Ferry 14*. GAM is essentially a "separatist movement" fighting for self-governance in the Aceh peninsula. They are likely to have committed acts of piracy to fund their separatist war with Jakarta, though there is no certainty that this is the case. Maritime piracy is different from maritime terrorism in the sense that essentially pirates are interested in the value of the loot (for economic gain) while maritime terrorism tends to have an ideological bent, trying either to discredit the domestic government and/or cause disruption to international economic commerce (for political gain).

The attack on the Japanese tugboat *Idaten* on 14 March 2005, 45 nautical miles west of Tanjung Hantu, Lumut, was reported in newspapers to be the work of GAM. It was reported that pirates in fishing boats carrying machine guns and rocket-propelled grenades were responsible for kidnapping and ransoming the ship's captain and crew. GAM denied responsibility. In a similar incident two days earlier, the *Tri Samudra*, an Indonesian owned methane tanker was stormed by heavily armed pirates who briefly took control of the ship. Similar to the case of the *Idaten*, the ship's captain and the chief engineer were taken hostage and held until ransom was paid. Again, some press reports alleged that GAM was responsible.[2] The question remains, is GAM really responsible?

It is interesting that in reports of the two attacks mentioned, geographical and logistical issues are often missing. The attacks were carried out some 45 nautical miles off the coast of Sumatra, meaning that the location of the attacks was actually closer to the Malaysian coast. Executing such an attack would involve considerable logistical support if it originated from the Aceh Peninsula. While we cannot rule out Aceh-based GAM operatives having been involved, the huge geographical distance and the amount of logistics involved makes it less than likely.

In making the case that GAM is responsible for acts of piracy, there are claims from some quarters that GAM is not only responsible, but has more sinister motives than simply using the revenues from piracy to help finance their insurgency. Rather, their motive is acquiring maritime expertise in navigating and steering a big ship as preparation for an act of maritime terrorism, like attacking the port of Singapore or blocking the Strait of Malacca. Therefore, GAM is treated as a proof of a nexus between (maritime) terrorism and piracy. But is this analysis accurate or is it misplaced concern?

Analysts need to be very careful in drawing the conclusion that GAM is involved in the above-mentioned cases. This is because it is in the interest of some elements in Indonesia to term GAM a terrorist organization that has both economic as well as political motives, inasmuch as it is in the interest of GAM to portray itself as oppressed freedom fighters. Both parties will often employ disinformation to forward their cause. The truth may be found somewhere between their public rhetoric and what a close examination of individual cases reveals.

Objective

There are two sets of interrelated questions. First: is GAM responsible for the various incidents of highly armed piracy in the Malacca Straits? If the answer to that is an unequivocal yes, what is their motive for piracy? Profit? Is it only to support their guerilla activities against the Indonesian government? Could these acts of piracy be carried out by rogue or splinter elements within GAM for personal gain? Or are these acts committed by elements linked to the Indonesian government to discredit GAM? Or are they committed by others who copy the modus operandi of GAM? Second: does GAM actually harbor more sinister motives besides the desire to conduct piracy, such as acquiring expertise in navigating large vessels to conduct acts of maritime terrorism?

To answer these questions and to decide whether there is an emerging nexus between piracy and maritime terrorism in Southeast Asian waters, GAM has to be analyzed on several levels. First, an understanding of the organization is required, in particular GAM's aims and ideology. This is an important aspect in discussing the validity of assertions that GAM is proof of an existing nexus between (maritime) terrorism and piracy.

Again, this is important because a good understanding of how GAM internationalizes their cause — combined with the fact that only the Indonesian government and those who are conspiring with the Indonesian government are legitimate targets of GAM — would provide better clarity when discussing the connection between (maritime) terrorism and piracy.

Third, with an understanding of GAM's ideology and the way GAM fights, what then is the role of piracy in this fight? If the role of piracy is strictly to fund GAM's guerilla war targeted specifically against the Indonesian government, then is there a likelihood that GAM will carry out maritime terrorism in the Malacca Straits targeting a vessel or ports of nations other than Indonesia or those belonging to multinational companies operating in Aceh?

Fourth, it is also important to look at the current "peace process" between GAM and the Indonesian Government and how it will affect the incidence of piracy, assuming that GAM is responsible for some of these acts of piracy to fund its ongoing guerilla war against Indonesia. More importantly, does it mean that an act of maritime terrorism in the Malacca Straits against the interest of the international community will not take place regardless of the outcome of the peace process between GAM and Jakarta?

In conclusion, it is assessed that GAM is likely to be responsible for maritime piracy for the purpose of profit to fund its struggle against Jakarta. But even that is difficult to prove with a high degree of certainty. Moreover, since GAM's ultimate goal is territorial and requires the support of the international community to help it forward its aim of self-governance in Aceh, the movement is unlikely to have a more sinister motive behind its piratical acts. If and when GAM does commit acts of maritime terrorism, it is very much limited to targeting Indonesian government assets. GAM knows that it would be unwise to commit a heinous act of maritime terrorism damaging the interest of the international community who are likely to withdraw support for GAM's agenda.

Gerakan Aceh Merdeka (GAM)

What were the origins of the conflict between the Indonesian government and GAM? Four reasons can be found. They are political alienation, history, perceived economic exploitation by Jakarta, and the harsh security measures adopted by Jakarta in dealing with the insurgency.[3]

The first reason behind the conflict is the political alienation of Aceh from Jakarta. Central to this conflict is the center/periphery relations and profound Acehnese alienation from Jakarta. The Acehnese had always wanted to safeguard their strong regional and ethnic identity, which was derived from Aceh's adherence to Islam and its history of having been an independent sultanate until the Dutch invasion in 1873.

In terms of history, in the 1950s, then-President Sukarno tried to make "secular" nation building his agenda for Indonesia and this caused greater disaffection by the Acehnese. Sukarno's successor, Suharto only made matters worse by adopting a highly centralized developmental method. This was antithetical to the desires of the Acehnese who already felt that they were alienated.

The perceived political and historical alienation was exacerbated in the 1970s when multinational companies (MNCs) were granted permission by the central government in Jakarta to exploit the resources of oil-and-gas-rich Aceh. The Acehnese themselves profited little from these activities, thus leading to complaints that the economic activities of the MNCs benefited only the MNCs themselves and the central government in Jakarta. In popular perception, the economic benefits barely trickled down to the Aceh people even though the resources mined were largely of Acehnese origin and, therefore, belonged to the people of Aceh.

The harsh security measures adopted by Jakarta accentuated the problem. GAM originally started as a guerilla group gaining support from the Acehnese population because of the harsh measures undertaken by Jakarta in putting down dissent. GAM began initially as an ideology, but the harsh security and military operations fuelled the hatred for Jakarta, and GAM was able to win much support with the Aceh people and it soon developed into a popular "separatist movement." In addition, those who came to join GAM in its armed struggle were not only motivated by ideology (such as justice and revenge) but by kinship ties, as many had family members who were tortured or killed by Indonesian security forces or had witnessed such brutalities. The sheer repressiveness of Jakarta's counterinsurgency operations from 1989 to 1998 thus enabled GAM to transform from a guerilla force to a popular resistance movement. In addition, Jakarta was perceived to have failed to keep its promise of granting Aceh special-autonomy status, instead proceeding with yet another round of harsh security measures in May 2003 when various rounds of "peace talks" broke down between Jakarta and GAM.

Aims of GAM

In terms of its aims, GAM's objectives since its inception have been the separation of Aceh from the Republic of Indonesia and to establish an independent republic.[4] Their ultimate goal is to establish Acehnese control over Acehnese territory. Some elements within GAM are amenable to increased autonomy as a possible compromise. It appears now that the political leadership within GAM is amenable to self-governance rather than pressing for a separate sovereign and independent republic. This has been a key concession made by GAM with regards to the current ongoing peace process, but it is difficult to ascertain if this is a tactic to draw Jakarta to the negotiating table or if they have given up completely on their aim of becoming an independent, sovereign republic. One notes this has not always been the case for the leaders of GAM. From the onset of the founding of GAM by Hasan Di Tiro, it has expressed hopes for a separate and independent republic. In essence, the ideology is to free Aceh from all political control of the foreign regime of Jakarta. GAM also contends that Aceh did not voluntarily join the Republic of Indonesia in 1945 but was illegally incorporated. The incorporation of Aceh into Indonesia was done without consultation with the people of Aceh.

With the fall of President Suharto in the late 1990s and East Timor being able to gain independence in the post-Suharto era, hopes were renewed for a separate and sovereign Aceh republic. The thinking behind this was that Indonesia was a failed state ready for an implosion.[5] The leaders of GAM thought that post-Suharto Indonesia would soon disintegrate and hoped that independence for Aceh was soon within reach, similar to what had been achieved by East Timor. However, time passed and hopes for independence soon evaporated as Indonesia did not disintegrate but recovered economic and political strength.

The 26 December tsunami tilted the balance in Indonesia's favor as the tsunami brought massive devastation to the Aceh peninsula. Much of Aceh was destroyed by the tsunami and it was estimated that some 165,000 Acehnese were killed by it.[6] The tsunami brought tremendous hardship to Aceh, and it would not have been possible for reconstruction efforts to take place without cooperating with Jakarta and with the international community, or without getting assistance from Non-Government Organizations (NGOs). As such, GAM dropped their claims for independence and opted to restart the fourth round of peace talks in May 2005.

The Way GAM Fights

In terms of how GAM plans to achieve its objective of an independent, sovereign republic free from the Jakarta regime, one has to understand the three-pillars theory of GAM. In essence, the struggle for independence is divided into three distinct but interrelated segments. The first pillar is the Aceh people. There is an overwhelming need to win the support of the Acehnese people.

After all it is from the Acehnese people that GAM is able to draw strength, win support, and fight Jakarta. The support of the people in Aceh is critical.

Second, there is the Indonesian government. This consists of the military (Tentara Nasional Indonesia — TNI), the police (Brigade Mobil — BRIMOB), and officials loyal to Jakarta but working in Aceh. In essence, the Republic of Indonesia is seen as an artificial construct. It is also perceived by GAM to be corrupt and doomed for disintegration. The hatred for Jakarta is mostly centered on Indonesian security forces such as the military and the police, whose excessive use of force and harsh security measures are pushing the Acehnese to support GAM.

Third, there is the international community at large. Just as the local people of Aceh are the support base for GAM, the international community is needed by GAM to internationalize their struggle and achieve their objective of having a sovereign and independent Aceh republic. In short, GAM needs the support of the international community for international recognition as legitimate crusaders for Aceh's independence and also to put pressure on Indonesia.[7]

Organization of GAM

GAM is one of the more coherent groups fighting for independence in Southeast Asia. It is highly structured with a group of leaders in exile in Stockholm, Sweden. In general, it has good command and control of its forces in Aceh by the leaders in Stockholm. GAM forces operating in Aceh are also in general a fairly disciplined force though they are small. It is estimated that there are up to 10,000 GAM members.

It is also common knowledge that there is direct communication between GAM leaders living in Stockholm and their field commanders in Aceh. This is exercised through direct telephone contact.[8] Often, there are suggestions that GAM is not a coherent organization in entirety, and that its exiled leaders in Stockholm have little control over the field commanders located in Aceh. This could be partially true, but it could also simply be disinformation on the part of Jakarta to discredit GAM since the movement is known not to be a rogue group and its field commanders are generally known to be loyal to the Stockholm-based leaders. It is common knowledge that when there is a conflict, it is often difficult to find out which group, such as the Indonesian military, the Indonesian Police, GAM, or some other group is responsible for particular acts of violence. In general, leaders in Stockholm do exercise control over field commanders in Aceh, and the goals and interests of those in Stockholm and Aceh are the same. GAM believes that other groups within Aceh, such as the Republik Islam Aceh (RIA) and Front Mujahidin Islam Aceh (FMIA), as well as Majlis Pemerintahan GAM (Council of the Free Aceh Movement; MP-GAM), are all products of the Indonesian intelligence agency, created to discredit GAM by making it look fanatical and fundamentalist.[9]

GAM is also one of the few groups in Southeast Asia with a proven maritime capability. This is because the local culture of Aceh is maritime in nature. The people of Aceh have long been accustomed to maritime trade and warfare. It is through this maritime nature that the Acehnese have strong cultural and trade links with populations along both sides of the Malacca Straits. GAM is also known to have sympathizers in regional maritime communities, such as the ethnic Acehnese populations in Penang and Perak, Malaysia, and in Muslim-Thai fisher communities in Southern Thailand.[10]

The maritime forces of GAM are capable of brown water (riverine) and green water (coastal) operations. Although GAM maritime vessels can sail the high seas, it has been assessed that GAM's maritime operations are not blue water in nature and that GAM cannot engage in sustained blue water combat operations. GAM's maritime forces have the ability to execute attacks on maritime shipping in its coastal waters and may even be able to strike closer to Malaysian waters. Aside from the *Idaten* and *Tri Samudura* cases, GAM has also been linked to very high profile Strait of Malacca piracy cases such as the *Ocean Silver* in August 2000 and *Penrider* in August 2003, where pirates involved were well armed with automatic weapons and rocket launchers. In both instances, GAM has vehemently denied involvement.

Strategy of GAM

GAM's strategy for winning independence and sovereignty is twofold. One is through the diplomatic struggle and the other via armed conflict. GAM puts more emphasis on the diplomatic struggle, and some 80 percent of its struggle is thought to be diplomatic and only 20 percent is armed struggle.[11]

In terms of diplomatic struggle, GAM's agenda is to internationalize the conflict. For example, GAM regularly approaches supranational organizations such as the UN; regional organizations such as the EU and ASEAN; and governments sympathetic to its cause, such as the United States, the Swedish, and the Finnish governments. GAM's aim is to get them involved and to recognize GAM as legitimate freedom fighters rather than condemning them as a "terrorist group" as purported by Jakarta. In this diplomatic struggle, both GAM and Jakarta are trying to convince the international community of their respective views and to win the international community over. Disinformation plays a crucial role in this struggle.

GAM is interested in using the international community to put pressure on the Indonesian government. They do this by highlighting various related issues, such as human rights abuses committed by Indonesian security forces, economic exploitation by Jakarta and the unequal payoffs received by the Aceh people, and the harsh security measures adopted by both Jakarta and its security forces in Aceh that cause undue hardship for the population in Aceh. GAM knows that they have little to gain from direct talks with Jakarta and are not interested in direct negotiations with Jakarta. GAM understands they have more to gain talking through mediators such as the Crisis Management Initiative (CMI) who can then convince Jakarta to come to the negotiating table to negotiate for a cease-fire and to implement the peace process.

Concurrently, GAM continues to wage guerilla warfare to render Aceh ungovernable in order to make Jakarta pay the highest price for retaining the territory.[12] GAM fully understands that its forces are no match for Jakarta and will not engage Jakarta via conventional warfare. Instead it chooses to adopt guerilla warfare tactics similar to the Vietcong during the Vietnam War. The armed faction of GAM is much smaller and less well armed than the Indonesian military. Hence, the aim of GAM is to continue to wage guerilla war to exhaust the Indonesian government politically, economically, psychologically, and socially.

Targets of GAM

GAM has been to date fairly consistent in targeting the following in their armed struggle against Jakarta:

- The Indonesian political structure
- The state education system
- The economy (structure, U.S. corporations, and MNCs)
- The Javanese (who are seen as colonial masters and collaborators)
- The Indonesian military and security forces

1. The Political Structure and Civil Servants[13]

GAM specifically targets local politicians and civil servants loyal to Jakarta with the aim of either turning them over or eliminating them. In essence, by threatening these local politicians and civil servants who criticize GAM, GAM is effectively trying to make the region of Aceh as ungovernable as possible and at the same time trying to strengthen its rule over Aceh by forcing those local politicians and civil servants to switch loyalty.

2. The State Education System in Aceh

GAM often has been blamed for a number of school-burning incidents. It is likely that GAM is responsible for some of these incidents because GAM believes that the education system in Aceh is the battlefield for the next generation of supporters. GAM believes that the education system is the key to Aceh's past and the hearts and minds of future generations. Simply put, it is an ideological battle and GAM does not want the next generation of Acehnese to grow up as Indonesians.[14] There are also practical aspects of burning down schools. One is that by burning down schools, the children are forced into rural Islamic boarding schools, most which are under GAM control. Second, schools are often used by TNI forces on patrol in the area for rest and shelter. However, not all school-burning incidents can be attributed to GAM, as it is noted that the TNI could also be responsible for school-burning incidents to avenge the killing of their soldiers, in anger with the local villagers for being uncooperative, or simply to pin the blame on GAM.[15]

3. The Economy

GAM also targets those sectors of the economy that Indonesia and its security forces stand to benefit from. GAM would often target workers of foreign multinationals through intimidation, kidnapping for ransom, or even death. GAM targets multinational companies operating in Aceh for two reasons. One is that these MNCs are seen as stealing Aceh's wealth. And secondly, they are seen as collaborators with the Indonesian military, who provide security for their premises. For instance, GAM leaflets have been known to call upon foreign workers of Mobil and Bechtel to leave because these two companies have made themselves "coconspirators" with the "Javanese colonialist thieves" and GAM cannot guarantee their safety.[16] GAM has been known to attack near the LNG complex in Paja Bakong area "to protect their gas resources from being stolen by the Javanese invaders and their foreign accomplices." In addition, some members in GAM also believe that MNC facilities have been used not only as military bases but also as torture camps, particularly during the Daerah Operasi Militer (Military Operations Zone; DOM) period, when TNI forces were responsible for massive military operations against the surrounding villages in the North Aceh subdistricts.[17]

4. The Javanese

Though GAM does not overtly state that they specifically target the Javanese who settled in Aceh owing to Indonesia's transmigration program, the evidence on the ground proves otherwise. GAM equates Indonesia with Javanese neocolonialism and has systematically tried to cleanse Aceh of Javanese presence. GAM sees Javanese migrants not only as neocolonialists who are there to exploit Aceh, but also there to demographically "soften up" Aceh. Moreover, the Javanese are perceived to be collaborators with Jakarta as they often play the role of informers to the Indonesian security forces and on occasion act as militias for Jakarta.[18]

5. Indonesian Security Forces

GAM sees Indonesian security forces such as the TNI and the police as an occupation force. In the earlier part of the armed struggle, GAM was unable to pose much of a threat to the Indonesian security forces, but they gradually became more proficient and more effective in forcing the Indonesian security forces onto the defensive. GAM fights a guerilla war as they know that, from a military perspective, they are not in a position to defeat the Indonesian security forces in open battle. Hence, their aim is tie down as much of Indonesian security forces in Aceh as possible to force Jakarta to expend more money in fighting the insurgency and finally to exhaust it. As such, GAM resorts to hit and run tactics, by "ambushing troops, planting bombs and launching grenades near military installations, executing off duty personnel, disrupting enemy communications, intercepting and destroying Indonesian military vehicles."[19] Though the capacity for and the frequency of the attacks have increased, GAM tactics have changed little.

Piracy and Kidnapping for Ransom?

The reason behind acts of piracy and kidnapping for ransom in this fight is a financial one: in essence, such acts are used to put money into the war coffers of GAM to fight the war against Jakarta.

It is likely that acts of piracy target specific vessels that contain valuable raw materials such as oil and even certain types of vessels themselves, which are then sold for a profit on the black market to finance the guerilla war against Jakarta. Though it is hard to prove with certainty that GAM is involved in acts of piracy that specifically target vessels or equipment for sale on the black market, it is likely that certain people in GAM could be responsible as there is a need for resources to fight the Indonesian security forces.

In terms of kidnapping for ransom, there has been evidence indicating that GAM is responsible for maritime kidnappings such as the *Penrider* case, where pirates were reported to wear uniforms, speak Acehnese and where the hostages were held captive in Sumatra.[20] Although these reports could demonstrate that acts of piracy or maritime kidnapping for ransom are indeed committed by GAM, such "proof" is far from being conclusive. Not all Acehnese speakers are GAM members and those committing such acts could easily be working for Jakarta as "agents provocateurs" to discredit GAM. However, what is true is that since 7 September 2001 all vessels passing between Sumatra and Malaysia must get the movement's permission, and GAM has reiterated on occasion that it threatens to attack ships in the Malacca Straits that have not sought its permission for transit.[21]

Kidnapping for ransom of personnel working for MNCs such as oil workers, business people, and local legislators also takes place, although it is hard to ascertain whether such kidnappings have the official sanction of GAM leaders in Stockholm, or were simply carried out by rogue elements within GAM for personal gain or even committed by groups posing as GAM. The case of *Ocean Silver*'s crew members being abducted was attributed to GAM, which had demanded US$33,000 for their release, but GAM has denied responsibility. Another case in point is the reported kidnapping of nine crewmen servicing the offshore oil industry from their ship, *Pelangi Frontier*.[22]

Other Sources of Revenue for GAM

Piracy and kidnapping for ransom are just two ways in which GAM raises money for its guerilla war against Jakarta. GAM has several other streams of revenue: through taxes, through donations by sympathizers (overseas Acehnese in South Thailand and Malaysia,) and through criminal activities like smuggling (people and arms) and drug trafficking.[23]

In regard to taxes, GAM levies an Aceh state tax on all elements in society. These taxes, known as "pajak nanggroe," [Bahasa Indonesia (Malay) for "state tax", ed.] have been collected since GAM was first established. The second is based on the Islamic principle of alms giving. GAM has no qualms about collecting such taxes and has stated that it only became an issue because Jakarta had made it an issue. In fact, GAM asserts that just as Jakarta has the right to collect taxes in Aceh, GAM is also entitled to collect taxes. This is based on the view that Jakarta collects these taxes to finance military operations against the Acehnese, while GAM collects them to lend protection to the Acehnese.

GAM is also noted to collect "taxes" from wealthy Chinese merchants, contractors operating in Aceh, and local civil servants. These groups are all perceived to be legitimate targets as they are seen as collaborators or as working for the Indonesian government. These groups are often intimidated and threatened.[24] In certain cases, such as those in the newly acquired territories of the Lhokseumawe industrial complex, GAM has actually resorted to force to extract money.

Another source of funding for GAM is through foreign donations, such as the Acehnese expatriate community. The biggest donors of money probably originate from Malaysia. Up to some 5,000 Acehnese living in Kuala Lumpur are estimated to provide GAM with regular donations.[25]

Yet another source of revenue is from criminal activities, such as drug trafficking. Thirty percent of all of Southeast Asia's marijuana is believed to originate from Aceh. It is also interesting to note that though the TNI and GAM are sworn enemies on one level, on another they are business partners. This is the case as drugs are sold to various criminal syndicates and the drug money is used to obtain weapons not only from Thailand but also certain elements from the Indonesian security forces, Indonesia's main arms manufacturer, Pindad, and also from former pro-Jakarta militias.[26]

The Current Peace Process and Its Implications

There have been some bright sparks amidst the fighting between GAM and Jakarta. Firstly, the Emergency Rule in Aceh was lifted by Jakarta in May 2005 since it was implemented two years before, in May 2003, after the last round of peace talks broke down.[27] However, little has changed on the ground as Indonesian security forces are still conducting military operations against GAM and GAM is still ambushing Indonesian security forces.

What could perhaps be called the silver lining in the "negotiation process" is the fact that there have been major concessions by GAM, who have dropped claims to complete independence and sovereignty. GAM now is looking to more self-governance in Aceh with participation in the local political parties.[28]

The Crisis Management Initiative (CMI) mediators were upbeat with the completion of the fourth round of talks that ended in May 2005 as 90 percent of the issues in contention had been agreed upon. But the most important aspect relating to self-governance in Aceh seems to be far from agreement. The sticking point is that GAM wants local elections in Aceh and a permission for GAM to participate in the local elections as a political party. Jakarta rejects this, as Indonesian law requires all political parties to be nationally based and have extensive organization in at least half of the nation's 33 provinces.[29] Jakarta has emphasized that changes to the Indonesian constitution and to Indonesian electoral laws would be required if they were to accommodate GAM's demands.[30]

In general, the peace talks are going well. In terms of monitoring the peace accord, disarmament process and withdrawal of Indonesian security forces, the idea of asking for mediators neutral to this conflict, such as the EU and ASEAN, to monitor the peace agreement, disarmament process, and withdrawal of Indonesian troops has been broached with little objection from Jakarta.[31]

While it is hard to discern if GAM is sincere by dropping its staunch claims to independence and sovereignty, it is certain that GAM is not keen on getting anything directly from Indonesia but wants international support to pressure Indonesia to concede and perhaps to show how uncompromising Jakarta is to the international community.[32]

Meanwhile, the Indonesian security forces continue to wage war on GAM, trying to root out GAM fighters from Aceh. At the same time, both sides are making preparations for the fifth round of peace talks to be scheduled for 12 July.[33] The TNI has a vested interest in pursuing the war against GAM. The TNI is alleged to be involved in the illegal logging and marijuana trade, while ordinary soldiers are involved in collecting illegal tolls on highways in Aceh where GAM is in the way.[34] Moreover, the TNI perceives that any let-up in military operations against GAM would only increase future resistance by GAM, which would take the opportunity during the cease-fire period to regroup and reorganize.[35] In addition, TNI does not see the ongoing military offensive operations to root out GAM forces as affecting the peace process. In fact, Jakarta is probably aware that the 26 December 2004 tsunami was a "godsend" as it gave the upper hand to Jakarta in its military operations against GAM and the government is likely to exploit the current advantage to the hilt.

This also begs the question, since the Indonesian security forces have an interest in fighting the war, could it be a deliberate move by the military to "sabotage" the peace process? Could it also be the case that Jakarta does not exercise complete control over TNI commanders in the field?

Again, this is hard to discern as President Yudhoyono argues that "it is clearly wrong to view the Aceh problem purely from a security point of view and it is extremely dangerous to give priority to military methods. That is why we have developed comprehensive measures."[36] But Yudhoyono has also ordered security operations to be intensified, and he described GAM as a "terrorist organization." He could presumably be hoping that the United States will place GAM on its list of terrorist organizations.[37] Perhaps Yudhoyono believes the way to the peace accord is to have it strongly backed by the use of force, thereby convincing GAM to give up its armed struggle.

The fundamental reason why peace talks have produced so few results so far is because of a huge gap between Jakarta and GAM in respect to their goals. Both sides are not willing to abandon their respective positions. For Jakarta, it is for GAM to give up its armed struggle, dissolve itself and abandon the struggle for a sovereign Aceh. On the other hand, GAM, who until now fought for an independent Aceh, is willing to settle for self-governance status but wants to participate in local elections, a demand Jakarta would not agree to. What will be achieved in the fifth round of peace talks on 12 July 2005? It remains to be seen if any real breakthrough is possible. Any major breakthrough in the peace process is highly unlikely, unless Jakarta allows for local election with GAM participation in the local political process. Conversely, it is also difficult for Jakarta to withdraw security forces from Aceh as demanded by GAM.[38]

Conclusion

In conclusion, the validity of the assertions that GAM is proof of an existing nexus between (maritime) terrorism and piracy is assessed to be unlikely for now. GAM does not have the intention (though it is likely they have the capability) to commit maritime terrorism against the international community. GAM needs international support for its agenda since internationalizing its cause is the mainstay of GAM's strategy. In addition, GAM has seen its efforts paying off in being able to bring Indonesia to the negotiation table. It is thus unlikely to intentionally commit maritime terrorism to hurt the economic interest of the international community. Moreover, the ultimate goal of GAM is territorial, not ideological like the goal of the Jemaah Islamyiah. However, one should not rule out the possibility that factions within GAM, for whatever reasons, in the near future will have the intention of committing maritime terrorism in Southeast Asia.

There is no certainty that GAM is responsible for all the reported cases of piracy that have been attributed to by GAM, though it is plausible. Other activities such as kidnapping for ransom of workers from MNCs and smuggling bears the imprints of GAM. Since GAM still needs money to buy arms and fund its guerilla effort against Jakarta, such activities are likely to continue. GAM is likely to be careful in whom it targets, and GAM operators are probably mindful of possible implications, especially if such an act will affect the interest of the international community. GAM would also be mindful of public perceptions, such as those of the international community as well as the Acehnese people.

But it is hard to say with certainty if acts of piracy and kidnapping for ransom will have unintended effects resulting in a maritime incident in the Malacca Straits. For instance, an act of piracy that involves tying up the entire ship's crew and leaving the ship without effective control could lead to a major maritime incident, such as that of the *Nagasaki Spirit* in the Malacca Straits.[39] In short, one cannot be certain of the unintended effect of an act of piracy that goes awry.

In addition, one cannot be certain that in the future GAM will continue to exercise discipline in only attacking MNCs' oil and port facilities within Aceh, or close to the coastal region of Aceh and to specifically targeting Indonesian interests. One could speculate that out of sheer frustration in being unable to use the international community to leverage Indonesia, certain elements in GAM could actually harm the international community's economic interests by either directly involving themselves in maritime terrorism or by employing indirect methods, such as sharing its maritime capabilities with other groups such as the Jemaah Islamyiah (JI) who are known to harbor maritime terrorist intentions. To date, there have been no confirmed reports of GAM lending its knowledge to, or training members of, the JI, unlike the situation in the Philippines, although it is likely that GAM and other groups in Southeast Asia have fraternal links.

It is likely too that GAM will continue to fight the Indonesian government, ambush Indonesian security forces, and engage in guerilla warfare. But again it is hard to tell whether GAM starts the fight or whether it acts in self-defense. It is also likely that GAM will continue to attack MNC facilities and kidnap foreign personnel for ransom. Will it all be the handiwork of GAM? Or will the Indonesian military be responsible for some of these actions as a means to convince the United States that its assets are in jeopardy to win U.S. approval of continued military actions against GAM? Again, it will be difficult to discern without examining each incident closely.

It is assessed that for now, though GAM is likely to be responsible for some acts of piracy in the Malacca Straits, such acts are committed with the aim of securing funding, and/or trying to shame the Indonesian government by demonstrating that Indonesia as a littoral state is unable keep the Malacca Straits safe for international shipping. This is plausible as it may lead to the international community putting pressure on Jakarta to resolve the situation in Aceh. However, such a move may backfire as it could also legitimize Jakarta's use of force to quell the insurgency in Aceh.

To date, GAM had been very focused in their choice of targets for their attacks. The international community and global commerce are not targets for two reasons. One is that GAM knows that it needs international support for its agenda. The second reason is GAM is not a transnational terrorist group like Jemaah Islamyiah that is fighting an "ideological" war. GAM's goals are territorial. GAM is first and foremost interested in the armed struggle against

Indonesia and against MNCs who are perceived to be robbing Aceh of its wealth and to be conspirators of Indonesia.

The situation may change and one grey area is the policy of the United States. If GAM continues to kidnap personnel belonging to U.S. corporations or sabotage U.S. corporation facilities in Aceh, what will be the position of the United States? Will the United States perceive U.S. economic interests as being threatened and react by sending their special forces to either directly fight GAM or lend support to Indonesian security forces? If it does, then will the United States get directly drawn into conflict with GAM? The other scenario is as discussed: elements in GAM become disillusioned with the international community who would be perceived to be unable to leverage Indonesia and, out of frustration, such elements could hurt international economic interests with a maritime terrorist incident in the Malacca Straits committed intentionally.

Another possible scenario would be that GAM hijacks vessels containing diving gear and sells them for profit to would-be terrorist groups who then use this equipment to commit an act of maritime terrorism in the Malacca Straits. After indirectly and unknowingly being "connected" to a maritime terrorist incident, what would the international community's view of GAM be? How would it affect policies of both the littoral states as well as that of user states such as the United States, South Korea, Japan, and China?

Whatever the case may be, it is in the international community's interest to encourage GAM and Jakarta to continue their peace talks since it clearly has a stake in a solution to this three-decade-old problem. Otherwise, the unthinkable in the form of a major maritime terrorist incident in the Malacca Straits might just become a reality, either committed by GAM directly or indirectly by abetting maritime terrorism intentionally or unintentionally.

Notes

1. Speech by Dr. Tony Tan Keng Yam, Deputy Prime Minister and Co-ordinating Minister for Security and Defence, Singapore, keynote address at the 2004 Institute of Defence and Strategic Studies Maritime Security Conference held on Thursday, 20 May 2004 at the Marina Mandarin Hotel, Singapore. Keynote address is available online at http://app.sprinter.gov.sg/data/pr/2004052001.htm.
2. Report from Background Asia Risk Solutions, dated 8 April 2005.
3. Schulze Kirsten, "The Free Aceh Movement (GAM): Anatomy of a Separatist Organisation," East West Center Policy Studies 2, Washington 2004, pp. vii–ix.
4. ASNLF 1976 as quoted in Schulze Kirsten, "The Free Aceh Movement (GAM): Anatomy of a Separatist Organisation," East West Center Policy Studies 2, Washington 2004, p. 6.
5. Schulze Kirsten, "The Free Aceh Movement…", p. ix.
6. BBC News, 8 September 2003. Available online at http://newsvote.bbc.co.uk/mpapps/print/news.bbc.co.uk/2/hi/asia-pacific.
7. Johanson 1999, as quoted in Schulze Kirsten, "The Free Aceh Movement…", p. 20.
8. Schulze Kirsten, "The Free Aceh Movement…," p. 13.
9. Schulze Kirsten, "The Free Aceh Movement…," p. 23.
10. Interview with a Malaysian Researcher.
11. Aspinall and Crouch, "The Aceh Peace Process: Why It Failed," East West Center Policy Studies 1, Washington 2003, p. 12.
12. Schulze Kirsten, "The Free Aceh Movement…", p. 34.

13. Ibid. pp. 34–35.
14. ICG 2003, as quoted in Schulze Kirsten, "The Free Aceh Movement...", p. 36.
15. Schulze Kirsten, "The Free Aceh Movement...", pp. 36–37.
16. Hasan Di Tiro 1982: 108, as quoted in Schulze Kirsten, "The Free Aceh Movement...", p. 37.
17. AGAM Field Report, 8 February 2002, as quoted in Schulze Kirsten, "The Free Aceh Movement...", p. 39.
18. Schulze Kirsten, "The Free Aceh Movement...," pp. 39–40.
19. Hasan Di Tiro 1982: 162, as quoted in Schulze Kirsten, "The Free Aceh Movement...", p. 40.
20. BBC News, 8 September 2003. Available online at http://newsvote.bbc.co.uk/mpapps/print/news.bbc.co.uk/2/hi/asia-pacific.
21. Report by www.MaritimeSecurity.com dated 10 October 2001. Also see Daniel Cooney, "Indonesian Rebels Threaten Straits," Associated Press. 2 September 2001.
22. Agence France Presse, 2 July 2002 as quoted in Schulze Kirsten, "The Free Aceh Movement...", p. 29.
23. Schulze Kirsten, "The Free Aceh Movement...," p. 24.
24. Schulze Kirsten, "The Free Aceh Movement...," p. 25.
25. Interview with a Malaysian Researcher.
26. *Joyo Indonesian News*, 9 June 2002; see also *Jakarta Post*, 10 June 2002, and 15 June 2002, as quoted in Schulze Kirsten, "The Free Aceh Movement...", p. 28.
27. Reuters, 18 May 2005. Available online at http://www.alertnet.org/printable.htm?URL=/thenews/newsdesk/JAK212828.htm.
28. World Socialist Web Site, 15 June 2005. Available online at http://www.wsws.org/articles/2005/jun2005/aceh-j15_prn.shtml.
29. Ibid.
30. *Arab Times*, 8 June 2005. Available online at http://www.arabtimesonline.com/arabtimes/breakingnews/view.asp?msgID=9213.
31. Reuters, 14 June 2005. Available online at http://alertnet.org/printable.htm?URL=/thenews/newsdesk/L14534009.htm also see Bloomberg.com 30 May 2005, available online at http://www.bloomberg.com/apps/news?pid=71000001&refer=asia&sid=aWOiwyRo8R0w.
32. *Time*, 24 January 2005. p. 21.
33. This chapter was completed in June 2005. For an up-to-date article on the International Crisis Group, see "Aceh: Now for the Hard Part," Asia Briefing No. 48, 29 March 2006. Available online at http://www.crisisgroup.org/home/index.cfm?id=4049rl=1.
34. *International Herald Tribune*, 7 June 2005. Available online at http://www.iht.com/bin/print_ipub.php?file=/articles/2005/06/06/news/inndo.php.
35. The Jakarta Post, 10 June 2005. Available online at http://www.thejakartapost.com/misc/PrinterFriendly.asp.
36. Aspinall and Crouch, "The Aceh Peace Process: Why It Failed," East West Center Policy Studies 1, Washington 2003, p. 22.
37. Ibid. p.30.
38. World Socialist Web Site, 15 June 2005. Available online at http://www.wsws.org/articles/2005/jun2005/aceh-j15_prn.shtml.
39. En route to Australia from Brunei, the *Nagasaki Spirit* exploded and was destroyed by fire, and the crude oil flowed out after it collided with the *Ocean Blessing* (Panama registered container ship. 22,600DWT). However, the damage was minor because the oil was light oil, which evaporated, diffused, and disappeared rapidly in the tropical climate.

7

Piracy and UNCLOS: Does International Law Help Regional States Combat Piracy?

MARTIN MURPHY

Introduction

Any reasonable observer will recognize that the United Nations Convention of the Law of the Sea is a remarkable achievement. It has established a legal framework for two-thirds of the Earth's surface; what some have called "a constitution for the oceans." However, no human act is perfect. Each bears the marks of its maker and the time of its gestation. Treaties are not immune from this law and UNCLOS is no exception.

This chapter will look only at the piracy provisions of this long and complex treaty:

It will review their history and background; in other words, it will describe why they are what they are. In so doing it will touch on the SUA Convention and customary international law relating to piracy. This will serve as a prelude to asking how useful they are under present conditions.

It will then review whether, and if so how, these provisions in particular and other UNCLOS articles more generally, can be used to aid or facilitate regional cooperation between states in their efforts to suppress or control this vicious, criminal practice.

Finally the chapter will, in the light of the answers to these two questions, attempt to draw some conclusions about the direction of individual state and regional antipiracy policy in the future and the role UNCLOS could play in both.

UNCLOS and Piracy Suppression

The piracy provisions of UNCLOS are concerned solely with piracy on the high seas. They do not address piracy in territorial or inland waters. For this reason such acts have now come to be referred to as "armed robbery at sea" and, legally, are not acts of piracy at all. The problem of course is that, from the perspective of the victims, this is a distinction without a difference.

UNCLOS, although concerned with the sea, did not spring fully formed from the waves like Venus. It opened for signature in 1982 but the preceding negotiations began eleven years earlier and took account of negotiations and unilateral changes that stretched back to the Truman Proclamation of 1947. The treaty as a whole consists of three hundred and twenty articles and nine annexes of which *only seven are concerned with piracy.* The remainder cover the breadth and extent of the territorial sea, navigation rights of naval and commercial shipping, states' rights over the ocean's economic resources and the resources of the sea bed, a comprehensive regime for environmental and pollution control, scientific research, and the settlement of disputes. Arguably only the UN Charter is a more important international legal regime.

Naturally, any treaty that is as comprehensive as UNCLOS must involve many compromises. It was born in an era when the number of states was growing rapidly as a consequence of decolonialization, and when resource scarcity appeared to be a very real possibility. While the maritime interests of most states in the "developing world" — which was often referred to then as "the third world" — were generally limited and local, many were attracted to the negotiations for two reasons. The first was a desire to limit the military activities of the major powers and increase their own security. This sometimes found expression in the creation of zones of peace. The second was economic. They believed it would give them greater control over their own resources and a share in the mineral deposits that it was thought were to be found in abundance on the seabed, under waters that had traditionally not been regarded as the preserve of any state. Some, indeed, saw the treaty as the partial realization of the "New International Economic Order," a redistributive agenda that started life in 1948 and reached its high water mark in the late 1970s. The control of fish stocks was also a major concern, one that was shared if not driven by developed nations such as Canada and Iceland. For the United States, on the other hand, the primary benefit of the treaty was to restrict and standardize the breadth of territorial waters to ensure freedom of navigation for the U.S. fleet. As Elliott Richardson has pointed out, the participants (of the Conference) "understood from the outset that the accommodation of navigational and resource interests must be at the core of any eventual 'package deal'."[1]

The interest in natural resources might have been of recent origin but the piracy provisions were born out of older concerns. England passed the first domestic law against piracy specifically in 1698.[2] This reflected the view, which was beginning to be shared by other European states at the same time, that piracy was an international problem. Despite being a shared view, from the very beginning international law and domestic laws were inconsistent. It therefore came as little surprise that in the twentieth century the newly formed League of Nations chose piracy to be one of the first offences to be codified.

In 1926 the League's Committee of Experts for the Progressive Codification of International Law published its *Draft Provisions for the Suppression of*

Piracy. These provisions were arranged in eight articles that restricted piracy to the high seas, limited it to private acts, exempted politically motivated attacks, and allowed states to make certain determinations about the status of belligerents.[3]

The *Draft* was not put before the Codification Conference, in part because it did not secure universal agreement. Instead the baton passed to Harvard Law School, which agreed to research the whole subject. In 1932 they published the answer to their central question: "What significance does piracy have in the law of nations?"[4] Many commentators have asserted that the Harvard Group aimed to codify the international public law on piracy. Its aim was, in fact, much larger. The Group's members were at pains to point out the many differences that had existed and continued to exist between international and municipal law, and to gather into one document most (but not all) of the ideas and suggestions about piracy they could uncover.

A fair-minded reading of the Harvard Draft would lead to the conclusion that the Group's appreciation of the obstacles to piracy suppression was remarkably contemporary and that the problems they sought to resolve were different in perhaps only one respect, albeit a crucial one, from the problems that are faced today. The Group wrote:

> The reason for the startling lack of international case authority and modern state practice is apparent, as soon as one remembers that large scale piracy disappeared long ago and that piracy of any sort on or over the high sea(s) is sporadic except in limited areas bordered by states without the naval forces to combat it. Piracy lost its great importance in the law of nations before the modern principles of finely discriminated state jurisdictions and freedom of the seas became thoroughly established. Indeed, the former prevalence of piracy may be assigned as a principal cause of the old reluctance of states to accept the doctrine of the freedom of the seas. Formerly naval powers fought pirates with little regard for the sort of problems that would trouble our modern world of intense commerce and strongly asserted national claims of numerous states, and with an acquiescence of the commercial interests which needed protection against those dangerous common enemies.[5]

The crucial difference is that large-scale piracy has gone, in the sense that pirate ships prowled the high seas looking for prey and that most merchant ships left harbor armed not only to defend themselves but also to prey opportunistically on their weaker brethren. However, it has reappeared in some parts of the world in what is, for many observers, a new form. Instead of cruising the oceans, modern pirates operate in coastal waters relatively close to shore. It is a phenomenon that can be observed around the globe: in the Caribbean, off Ecuador, off Africa mainly in the vicinity of Nigeria and Somalia, around the Bay of Bengal, and in Southeast Asia in particular, where it is far from sporadic and engenders the same fears, dangers, and threats as it did in the past. However, the claim that this form of piracy is new should be treated with caution: even though it is now to be found elsewhere, it in fact bears a close resemblance to the form of piracy that has been practiced in Southeast Asia for centuries.[6] As with so many naval and maritime matters much of the discussion about piracy, and many of the prescriptions advocated for its suppression, have been colored by European and American experience (and practice) and, consequently, evince a certain Western-focused ethnocentricity.

In 1949 the newly formed International Law Commission picked up where the Harvard Group had left off. The aim of the ILC was to prepare a draft of a comprehensive maritime law that would prove acceptable to the states that would attend the ensuring Conference. Piracy, therefore, was not the sole subject; it was now just one issue among several that needed to be woven together.[7] Where the writers of the Draft were keen to lay out the options and point out the theoretical and practical difficulties of piracy suppression, the Commission was looking for solutions to numerous items that would be accepted by a large group of disparate and disputatious states. Although the Harvard Draft formed the basis of articles 14–21 of the eventual High Seas Convention (HSC), in the end the 1958 Law of the Sea Conference adopted only those parts of the Draft recommended by the Commission, and the Commission recommended only those that it thought the Conference would accept. Despite this the HSC, arguably at least, codified the international law of piracy. It is unfortunate that in the process many useful ideas from customary international law that had been included in the Harvard Draft were modified or dropped.

Codification all too often leads to crystallization.[8] The HSC piracy provisions were incorporated almost without amendment into the 1982 UNCLOS treaty (Articles 100–107). This transition without alteration and with little apparent thought illustrates two consistent assumptions that run through the consideration of piracy in the twentieth century:[9]

- That it was an old problem — a problem out of history — that had largely disappeared; where it had not, activity was minimal and could be dealt with by the large fleets that still patrolled the world's seas.
- That the sovereign rights of states always and everywhere had precedence over the measures to prevent and suppress it.

The consequence was that all the work on piracy in the last century lacked urgency, regardless of whether it was undertaken by the League's Committee, the Harvard Group, the ILC, or for UNCLOS.

The 1982 Convention increased the breadth of territorial waters from 3 miles up to a limit not exceeding 12 miles. This shrunk the high seas, the only area where piracy could be called piracy and dealt with as piracy. This change and the introduction of the idea of the Exclusive Economic Zone (EEZ) were driven by the primary motivation of most participants to control and exploit the natural resources that they believed existed in abundance in and under the sea. Barry Dubner turns one of the great rhetorical flourishes of the treaty on its head when he writes: "Greed — the common heritage of mankind — (overcame) the theme of the Convention."[10] UNCLOS not only preserved the HSC piracy provisions and their attendant problems in legal aspic, ready to confront a problem that barely existed, but, by reducing the size of the high seas, made them even less relevant to the suppression of the new form of piracy that was beginning to emerge.

The difficulties with the piracy provisions of the 1958 High Seas Convention (and, thus, the 1982 UNCLOS) are well known:

- The limitation of piracy to "private" as opposed to "public" or "political" acts.
- The geographical restriction of piracy to the high seas.
- The issue of "reverse hot pursuit."
- The "two-ship" requirement that excludes internal seizure.
- The lack of a requirement on states to enact comparable domestic laws.
- The lack of a requirement on states to cooperate.
- The lack of an enforcement mechanism.
- The lack of a disputes procedure.

These difficulties could be found in every twentieth-century piracy proscription beginning with the League of Nations' *Draft* of 1926. Although as a consequence of the rise of the "new" piracy they may well be regarded as contentious judgments today, they were not regarded as such when they were made. After all, by the 1920s piracy was considered more or less obsolete. On the contrary, they were consistent with the broad understanding of piracy as it existed at the time and had evolved over the previous century.

"Private Ends"

The requirement that a pirate act had to be committed for "private ends" had its origin in the distinction between piracy and privateering. The latter was piracy under license. In practice there was little to distinguish between the two if you were a victim, although it is arguable that privateers, because they had to justify the attack before a Prize Court in order to establish a rightful claim to the goods they had stolen, had less incentive to engage in gratuitous brutality and the elimination of witnesses. On the other hand, the distinction was important for privateer captains: provided they abided by the conditions set out in their letter of marque, they gained immunity from prosecution that was recognized by all states (including the flag states of their victims). It was also important for states, partly because they received a cut of the proceeds and partly because they avoided the expense of maintaining a standing fleet as privateers acted as a substitute navy.[11]

The Declaration of Paris abolished privateering in 1856, but the distinction between private and public ends was maintained because courts (and states) wanted to differentiate between piracy and acts of maritime depredation carried out by insurgents or rebels. This distinction was drawn repeatedly by jurists and in court judgments and Timothy Goodman has drawn particular attention to the importance of the case of *Bolivia v. Indemnity Mutual,* a case heard before the English Courts in 1909. As he writes: "The *Indemnity Mutual* court refined the definition of piracy for 20th century international jurisprudence." It affirmed that a loss as a result of a rebel incident was not piracy, as public ends were being pursued not private. It was this definition that was eventually taken up by the League of Nations Committee.[12] The Committee's successors in the Harvard Group retained the "private ends" requirement although they did not define it. Dubner describes their decision as one of "expediency" because it meant that they could avoid such difficult political questions as immunity, asylum, insurgency, and belligerency. On the other hand, they clearly did not intend to limit piracy to acts of actual or intended robbery (*animus furandi*) even though there is a widely held misapprehension that such intention is essential. Perhaps Dubner's description is correct, but it was also the case, as he acknowledges, that the Harvard Group never imagined that what they wrote would be the last word on the subject. Its members believed it was almost certain that their work would be changed in response to new circumstances.[13]

The prime difficulty with the "private ends" requirement is that it excludes politically motivated acts. In the view of most commentators today this means that the Convention cannot be used against terrorists. It also excludes acts carried out by warships or other recognized government vessels. Such ships can, of course, become pirate ships if they are seized unlawfully and then used to perpetrate piratical acts.

Consequently, it is to be regretted that the Committee and its successors chose this formulation and not the one that stems most logically from the pirate-privateer distinction: that is to say piracy is an act undertaken *without due authority.* After all, the insurgents that customary law and in turn the Committee and then the Group sought to protect were bodies that had won some form of recognition, or whose acts would have been legal if they had been recognized, and who directed their depredations solely against the vessels of the country whose government they sought to overthrow. In 1927, for example, the Permanent Court of International Justice held that "the distinctive mark of piracy is independence or rejection of State or equivalent authority." The issue of unauthorized action also underlay the 1937 Nyon Agreement, which was drawn up between a limited number of states in response to the use of submarines during the Spanish Civil War. In the words of the British representative, Sir Gerald Fitzmaurice, "the real basis of the agreement reached at Nyon was the assumption that the acts had been unauthorized because no government would accept responsibility."[14] D. H. N. Johnson, when discussing the work of the ILC, argued "that it would be better to emphasize the lack of due authority as the essence of piracy, rather than … the fact that piracy is an act committed for private ends."[15]

High Seas

One of the tensions that runs through much of the discussion about piracy — and much of its history — is that between universality and particularity. It was Cicero who first expressed the idea that has come down to us as *hostis humani generis* or, as Blackstone put it, "a pirate … by renouncing all the benefits of society and … by declaring war against mankind, all mankind must declare war against him … " This concept was not based on natural law principles. As Kontorovich has demonstrated, piracy was not condemned for its heinousness. Therefore, to draw parallels between it and modern crimes such as genocide is inaccurate. Instead, it was a practical response to a shared problem. States were prepared to accept what amounted to an encroachment on their sovereignty because pirates attacked ships of all states and answered to no one in a part of the world that was beyond the jurisdiction of any state. This universality made sense in an era of few states and great empires, most of which shared a common heritage, with a largely common interest in trade and peaceful passage to distant colonies. Freedom of navigation was central to the success of these ventures. Gradually the notion of *Mare Liberum,* declared so elegantly by Grotius on behalf of his employers at the Dutch East India Company, overwhelmed the opposing notion of *Mare Clausum* which had been driven, in part at least, by concerns about the need to control piracy. Freedom of navigation internationalized the problem. It was no longer the responsibility of a few states but of all states that used the sea. These states enacted domestic legislation broadly in line with international norms. Their ships captured pirates and dealt with them, including summary justice if so allowed, in accord with their own domestic laws. In fact, of course, this universal jurisdiction existed more in theory than reality. Most pirates were hunted down by their own countrymen.

So, while they made it plain that "(I)n a place not within the territorial jurisdiction of another state, a state may seize a pirate ship … ," the Harvard Group grounded their analysis and articles very much in sovereign rights and domestic law.[16] For its members, and in keeping with the view at the time, international law was law between states. Piracy was an act conducted by individuals and there was no international court to try them. Therefore, because it could not be an offence against international law in the technical sense, the Group characterized it as an offence with a special, common basis of jurisdiction.[17] This was fine providing a) that states enacted the necessary domestic legislation and enforced it vigorously or b) the territorial waters of states were sufficiently narrow to leave pirates at risk of arrest on the high seas by interested powers. Both conditions pertained at the time but are questionable now.

As noted already, UNCLOS greatly expanded the area of sea under territorial control. It exacerbated this to a degree by permitting the use of straight baselines such that states could enclose bays and use offshore islands, islets, and even rocks that remained dry above the high water mark as reference points. In the years following World War II, many states had unilaterally increased the breadth of their territorial waters. In some case these claims included straits used by international shipping; the Straits of Malacca was one example. The Convention legitimized these claims but also qualified them. It made clear that they were open to free navigation — including transit by warships — by the creation of a special straits regime. However, while the rights of coastal states were constrained by the right of transit passage (a constraint which several of the states concerned resented), what are often critical waterways are now included within territorial waters and the states that have control of these waters have the sole responsibility for maintaining good order.[18]

This enclosure movement was particularly egregious in the case of the archipelagic regime. This was an important political objective for Indonesia, the Philippines, Mauritius, and Fiji. It enabled these island states, and subsequently others, to bring vast areas of ocean under their territorial control. Although this was qualified significantly not only by the right of innocent passage but by the new concept of archipelagic sea-lane passage, the major maritime powers failed to foresee "the extent and possible consequences of extensive archipelagic sea space enclosure" and, as a result, the measures "were not as fully or widely thought through as other issue areas" such that, in the case of Indonesia, significant variances have developed between its national maritime policy and the Convention.[19]

The Convention also created even larger areas, the EEZs, which have a status all of their own: they are neither territorial waters nor part of the high seas.[20] Most commentators agree that, in accordance with Article 58(2), the piracy provisions apply fully in the EEZs and that all states are therefore allowed to arrest and arraign any pirate found in them under the provisions of the Convention and their own domestic laws.[21] Other commentators are less certain. In their view, although traditional transit rights are maintained, in other respects they are more akin to territorial waters, because Article 58(3) states that in exercising the high seas rights that apply in the EEZ, that is, those permitted under Articles 88–115, states must pay due regard to the rights and duties, laws, and regulations of the coastal insofar as these are not incompatible with the Convention.[22] This ambiguity is rooted firmly in the origins of the EEZ concept.[23] The maritime powers continue to be disturbed by what has been called the "creeping jurisdiction" of coastal states. As Galdorisi and Kaufman write: "As a relatively new regime in international law, the precise nature and full extent of coastal and other nations' rights and responsibilities in the EEZ are still evolving."[24] It is fair to say that few states have tried to expand their territorial sovereignty beyond 12 nautical miles;

nonetheless, either through declarations or domestic legislation, many more states have asserted or attempted to assert interpretations of the EEZ that are not wholly compatible with that in the Convention.[25] If the application of the piracy provisions were also to become a matter of dispute or modification, and their application consequently circumscribed, then, as Birnie has pointed out, should such a limitation spread globally, only 7–15 percent of incidents previously classified as piracy would be still be classified as piracy under UNCLOS.[26] However, it is the potential for restrictions on the right to conduct military activity within the EEZs that is of greater concern to the maritime powers.[27] This concern may not appear to be directly relevant to piracy suppression but there is a growing recognition that piracy is just one aspect of a general trend toward might be described as disorder at sea which includes weapons proliferation, other aspects of criminality — such as illegal migration, drugs and arms smuggling — and terrorism. Clearly the navies of the maritime powers have an important contribution to make in suppressing this disorder and if they are prevented from doing so within the EEZs (which cover between 30 and 34 percent of the world's oceans depending on how the baselines are measured), particularly the EEZs of states that lack the will or resources to suppress disorder, then this will encourage it to grow.

"Reverse Hot Pursuit"

"Hot pursuit" of pirates from territorial waters onto the high seas has been recognized since the concept of territorial seas began to be accepted in the eighteenth century. "Reverse hot pursuit," on the other hand, is the right of ships of one state to pursue pirates from the high seas into or across the territorial waters of another state. Territorial waters that are poorly monitored and patrolled are, in effect, pirate sanctuaries if the pursuing ships of interested states do not have this right. Where this is the case, the contraction of the high seas has clearly given pirates greater freedom of action. A sanctuary with a 12-mile limit offers pirates greater opportunities for escape and evasion than one with a 3-mile limit.

However, it is not axiomatic that such sanctuaries are sacrosanct. If piracy is a universal crime, then it should merit a universal response. Article Seven of the Harvard Draft proposed that pirates could be pursued into or across the territorial waters of another state. In their "Comment" the writers acknowledged that opinion was divided: some experts held that reverse hot pursuit was permissible if the coastal state did not have the means on hand to deal with the pirates (and did not prohibit it); others argued that it was legal even against the protests of the coastal state.[28] Regrettably, the opportunity presented by this proposal was another one lost because the ILC did not regard piracy as a pressing problem. Alternatively it might be possible to invoke customary international law, but only providing it is accepted that it has not been superseded by UNCLOS. The U.S. view has been that pirates could be pursued into or through foreign territorial waters and either held and tried under U.S. jurisdiction or handed over to the coastal state once caught (unless that state demanded the chase be broken off).[29] Secondly, states could invoke self-defense: if, for example, a U.S. warship spied a U.S.-flagged ship under attack by pirates in foreign territorial waters, it could go to its assistance. This assertion is certainly justified under Article 98 of UNCLOS, which requires the master of any ship to render assistance with all possible speed. However, any unarmed ship would be rightly cautious about approaching pirates, and several states, including states in Southeast Asia where pirate problems are particularly acute, would argue that no warship could enter the territorial seas of another state without permission.

"Two Ships"

The "two-ship" requirement has given rise to some confusion, if not legally then practically. It stems from the notion that any ship is always under the jurisdiction of its flag state. Therefore, any offence committed on board, or in some cases against a ship, falls under domestic not international law. When pirates came aboard they might, very loosely, be described as conducting a form of seizure. Many writers, the drafters of UNCLOS Article 101 included, have tried to draw a distinction between piracy and the takeover of a ship from within either by the crew (mutiny) or the passengers (internal seizure), which are domestic offences, but the line is far from clear. One manifestation of maritime robbery that is not addressed in the Convention is the case of passengers who come aboard with the express intention of hijacking the ship, stealing the cargo or from the passengers, or committing some other form of larceny.

The SUA Convention

In the wake of the *Achille Lauro* seizure, the International Maritime Organization (IMO) prepared a study of the problem of terrorism on board or against ships. This led to the Convention for the Suppression of Unlawful Acts Against the Safety of Maritime Navigation in 1988, now referred to more generally as the SUA, or sometimes the "Rome Convention."

Although there is a widespread assumption that the SUA is concerned solely with terrorist acts, despite its origins this is not the case; the word "terrorism" does not occur in the text. Instead it addresses specific acts such as ship seizure and violence by those on board that could result in physical injury, or damage to the ship or its cargo. Therefore the SUA arguably has some utility against criminal hijackings even though the drafters made no attempt to enlarge the definition of piracy to include acts prejudicial to maritime safety; in fact they viewed piracy as a separate issue. Instead, they took as their models The Hague and Montreal Conventions against aircraft hijacking, which led to two important differences compared to the piracy provisions: first, the SUA Convention is applicable everywhere, even in territorial waters, *providing* the ship under attack is coming from or proceeding to an international destination. Second, state parties must enact domestic legislation to make Convention offences punishable under their laws. However, it also suffers from some unfortunate weaknesses: the main aim of the Convention is prosecution, not prevention; its central purpose is to ensure that states either prosecute or extradite. Consequently, and in contrast to treaty and customary law on piracy, the SUA does not recognize or authorize preventive constabulary activity at sea. It is not applicable if the violence on board is insufficient to compromise maritime safety. It is also inapplicable to the intra-state coastal traffic that accounts for so many maritime movements in the territorial and archipelagic waters of Southeast Asia. Nonetheless, it should be noted that, at the instigation of the United States, draft amendments have been prepared for adoption in October 2005. These are discussed below.

Summary

The piracy provisions of UNCLOS (Articles 100–107) show their pedigree. Soundly based on history they stand ready to confront a high seas scourge whose time has passed. The new (or renewed) form of piracy operates usually no more than a few miles from a coastline and often in the congested waters of straits used for international navigation. It occurs, in other words, in waters where the piracy provisions of UNCLOS have no effect. The Convention has encouraged the growth of this new scourge, albeit inadvertently, by entrenching the sovereign rights of states over these waters and, arguably at least, over vast ocean areas beyond. Where these waters fall under the jurisdiction of states that have the will and the means to police them, piracy has not gained a foothold. In the case of states that are unwilling or unable to discharge their security responsibilities — and where opportunities for piracy present themselves — the result has been the creation of what are, in effect, pirate sanctuaries.

It is true that the first signs and early growth of the new (or renewed) piracy emerged before UNCLOS came into effect. Nonetheless, most states operated on the assumption that the Convention would come into force and altered their behavior beforehand. The argument is not that UNCLOS *caused* the rise of the new piracy but that it has brought about a combination of circumstances whereby those states that have the means to combat it are generally reluctant to breach the Convention's articles on coastal-state sovereignty of territorial waters, while some coastal states that lacked the means necessary to patrol their waters effectively when they were limited to three miles have been given control of even larger areas that have strained their resources still further. Therefore, while it is also true that the major naval powers have reduced significantly their presence on the world's oceans, this is a coincidence, not a cause of the new piracy's rise. Even if these navies had been maintained at their cold war levels, they would not have had an appreciable deterrent, preventative or constabulary effect on the new piracy because, except when transiting straits (which under UNCLOS they had to do expeditiously), they sailed further from coasts and therefore well outside the pirates' main operating areas.

UNCLOS and Regional Cooperation

Piracy is no longer piracy when it takes place in territorial waters. According to the IMO definition it is armed robbery at sea. Armed robbery at sea is the unambiguous responsibility of coastal states. However, pirates have shown no propensity to respect national boundaries that in any case are often hard to locate and sometimes disputed. Pirates are prepared to exploit these difficulties by moving between jurisdictions, to avoid capture if they are being pursued, but also in the knowledge that states differ in the priority they assign to piracy suppression and the resources they allocate to it. In other cases state boundaries do not always reflect cultural or community boundaries; peoples that may well have practiced piracy for centuries have sometimes found themselves divided by a border that was laid down in the colonial era and which means little or nothing to them practically or in terms of allegiance. The consequences of all these factors — pirate mobility, the differences in political will and resources, the cultural commonalities, and community links — mean that in areas such as the Caribbean and Southeast Asia where pirates can flee from one jurisdiction to another the problem is best combated on a regional basis. However, the individual state remains the fundamental unit and the focus of international law.

Comparable Domestic Law

UNCLOS is based on the assumption that states have the appropriate domestic legislation in place to be able to prosecute offences that are considered piracy under international law. As the historical work of the Harvard Group made clear, states have always defined piracy and enacted domestic legislation in the light of their own circumstances. Consequently, there were wide divergences in definitions and coverage. In some cases these divergences still exist. India, for example, found that its legislation, which was a carryover from the earlier colonial legislation, hampered its ability to deal expeditiously with the *Alondra Rainbow* incident. Japan, another example, has not enacted the necessary legislation for constitutional reasons. Legislation against piracy (armed robbery) in domestic waters can also be inadequate. The first step in any form of regional cooperation is the enactment of uniform legislation by all interested states, coupled with a demonstrable will to prosecute or extradite (not merely deport) perpetrators when they are caught. The IMO and the CMI have prepared model legislation to fill this gap.

Inter-State Cooperation

UNCLOS places no obligation on states to cooperate to suppress piracy. Admittedly it does *encourage* states to cooperate but this is limited to the high seas and does not extend to territorial waters. It certainly does not suggest that encouragement implies a *duty* to take action against piracy. Even the Harvard Group made it clear that this was not the case.[30] Concomitantly it includes no mechanism to facilitate even the limited cooperation it does encourage. Therefore, except insofar as it has helped to stabilize maritime boundaries and rights of passage, and given states a mechanism for resolving their wider maritime disputes over issues such as fishing and mineral extraction, UNCLOS is of no direct relevance to states wishing to cooperate in piracy suppression or to cajole recalcitrant states to fulfill their obligations.

Cooperation between states requires the conjunction of perceived self-interest and political maturity. The primary obstacle that inhibits inter-state cooperation anywhere is concern over sovereignty. This is a concern that is felt acutely in Southeast Asia. The states of the region are young and artificial, to the extent that they are based on colonial-era territories. Neither is conducive to political self-assurance. The consequence is that cooperation can be seen as a possible diminution of hard-won sovereignty, and a move by one state in the region can arouse suspicions in others based on concerns such as:

- Maritime boundary disputes
- Overlapping claims
- The continuous striving for advantage and access to resources.

Concerns that are compounded by:

- Ethnic differences
- Suspicion of the motives and unbalancing effects of external powers.

This state sensitivity may also be motivated by a desire to distract attention from internal problems such as political corruption, poor policing, and, as far as piracy is concerned, direct involvement by members of the armed forces. Whatever its origins, the effect is that even as they strive to cooperate in the maritime sphere, the states of Southeast Asia view each other with mutual suspicion.

That said, there are other powerful motivations driving the states of the region toward cooperation. The most obvious is geography. First, the region is made up of thousands of islands ringed by thousands of miles of coastline, much of it edged by mangrove swamp, indented with small bays, cut through by narrow straits, and set in seas cluttered with reefs, shallows, and sandbanks. These features provide pirates with cover and impede pursuit. Second, the complexity of the region's boundaries makes it relatively easy for pirates to flip from one jurisdiction to another, leaving their pursuers stymied.[31] Third, all the states in the region have a common interest in trade and economic development; although piracy does not amount to a major threat currently, it could do if suppressive measures fail and control is lost. Finally, piracy is an advertisement of state weakness. It can only flourish in states that lack the will or resources to enforce their own laws; states that obviously cannot enforce their own laws attract disorder; states that are weak stimulate the predatory instincts of other states even as they worry that the causes of instability that affect one of their number might spread to others.

It is this point that perhaps best illustrates the marginal utility of UNCLOS as far as piracy suppression is concerned. Piracy is as much a problem of the land as it is of the sea. No state wants its internal workings and practices exposed to external examination, and the states of Southeast Asia are perhaps more sensitive about this than most. From a security perspective most are weak but pretend to be strong; most have, to one degree or another, problems of internal cohesion with minorities that, while they might not be in open rebellion like the Acehenese are against the Indonesian state, have little or no allegiance to central authority; while others are in varying degrees corrupt and want to hide it. Regional cooperation in Southeast Asia is based on the ASEAN precept of noninterference in the internal affairs of other states; without it, cooperation would be impossible rather than merely very difficult. This alone makes antipiracy cooperation problematic because piracy suppression is, ultimately, a matter of land-based policing. Patrolling controls piracy, only policing can eradicate it. If that policing does not take place for whatever reason — lack of resources; corruption; the belief that it is better to continue to allow marginal, coastal communities to earn their livelihoods in the time-honored way rather than risk the political problems that would follow from confrontation — then this manifestly lies outside the remit of UNCLOS, and other means must be found to encourage or pressure recalcitrant states to take whatever action is required.

If, for the time being at least, eradication is an impossible aim because it requires land-based policing to be effective, then control, because it can be exercised at sea, is the only available option. For the reasons outlined already, cooperation at sea is, therefore, essential. But here too there are obstacles.

- Complacency that the problem of piracy has been exaggerated, mainly by foreigners. In Indonesia, at least, this is reinforced by the belief that the benefits of piracy suppression do not justify the costs because most of the shipping that is attacked is foreign owned.
- Resentment that despite the fact that the international community has, in the form of a United Nations agreement, granted states control over critical straits and huge ocean areas with all their resources, the international states that use these waters simply for transit do not contribute to the cost of security.

- Corruption that can exist anywhere on a spectrum from the lowest level, where it might involve port officials supplying information, to the highest, where politically powerful figures can provide protection and can influence what resources are devoted to the fight.
- Political priorities that place the need for national cohesion and economic development ahead of piracy suppression; in fact, that can view piracy suppression as an irrelevance.
- Rivalry between states to demonstrate that the piracy problem lies in another state's waters; this led Indonesia, for example, to accuse Malaysia of conspiring with the IMB to "massage" their piracy statistics by locating the majority of piracy incidents on the Indonesian side of the Straits.[32]
- Fear that what has been won by international agreement can be taken away: that the pressure to adopt definitions of piracy (such as the one put forward by the IMB which, broadly speaking, views sea robbery as piracy wherever it occurs) could, if adopted, lead to the erosion of national sovereignty over territorial waters and the "internationalization" of straits. This, in turn, could be seen internally as a slight on national sovereignty and be used by opponents to stir up political discord.

Indonesia's idea of sea sovereignty is much closer to *Mare Clausum* than to *Mare Liberum*. By permitting archipelagic baselines the Convention, in effect, recreated and legitimized closed seas and erected a useful shield behind which states such as Indonesia could hide. High seas piracy provisions do not extend to archipelagic waters. As Bernard Kent Sondakh, the Indonesian Navy's chief of staff has put it: "Indonesia is always open for cooperation offered by others so long as they do not tend to '*internationalize*' the management of the Malacca Strait and as long as they are consistent with and respect Indonesian sovereignty and sovereign rights as a coastal state."[33] Malaysia, too, shares these concerns, although it rarely expresses them so forcibly, and both place a much lower priority on navigational freedoms and transit rights than do maritime powers.

The issue of resources is an important one. Patrolling against piracy is a cost that bears down hard on poorer states. It demands a substantial initial capital investment in ships, equipment, and training and continuing expenditure on fuel, maintenance, and crew costs. Again taking Indonesia as an example, on its own estimation it needs 300 vessels of various sizes plus support to maintain its maritime security. It actually has only 115 vessels of which a mere 25 are at sea at any one time. These vessels have more than piracy (or what the Indonesians resolutely refer to as armed robbery at sea) to look after: the prevention of internal conflict, illegal fishing, and other illegal acts such as smuggling and illegal migration, and patrolling the archipelagic sea-lanes. In 1999 it was able to spend only 5.9 percent of its budget on defense, which compares favorably to the general level of defense spending worldwide but is nonetheless well below that of the neighboring state of Singapore, which spent 24.9 percent.[34]

It is against this background of limited resources that Indonesia, and to a lesser extent Malaysia, has sought to use Article 43 of UNCLOS as a lever to persuade extraregional states to contribute to the cost of security. This Article encourages states that use straits and the states that border them to cooperate in the provision of navigational and safety aids and other improvements, and the prevention, reduction, and control of pollution. With this Article in mind, conferences were held in Singapore in 1996 and 1999 to discuss the situation in the Malacca and Singapore Straits. They brought user and coastal states together with the IMO and others to discuss cooperative arrangements. It was agreed, consensually, that it was inequitable to expect the coastal states to bear all the responsibility for maintaining the Straits, that the user and coastal states should seek suitable cooperative arrangements and that funding mechanisms should be developed in order to fulfill the Article's requirements.

The IMO and others believe that Article 43 might well offer a useful framework for inter-state cooperation although there is little reason to invoke it in and of itself. After all it encourages cooperation across only a limited range of technical activities that have been funded generously by Japan (and Japan alone) over many years. The reason for this hesitation is simple: although states in the region view countries such as Australia, India, and the United States with varying degrees of suspicion, the power with the greatest interest in regional maritime security is Japan because all of its energy supplies from the Middle East transit the region's waters. Over and above the assistance it has offered on navigational aids and pollution prevention, it has proved willing to offer additional assistance ranging from shared patrolling to financial aid, but its experience has been discouraging. States in the region have responded only as and when it suits them. The reasons for this might be particular: it is possible that most of its overtures have been rejected because the nations of Southeast Asia share a long memory of the brutal Japanese occupation between 1941 and 1945, while Japan has appeared reluctant to acknowledge those brutalities subsequently. Nonetheless, Indonesia's invocation of Article 43 has come to be seen as a useful stick it can wave at external powers while allowing it to shy away from offers of help if they have entailed any reciprocal commitment.[35] It also appears that it is seen as a useful tool to gain some measure of control over whatever they might offer by placing requests in the framework of a UN treaty. Again as Sondakh put it: "The suitable form of assistance for capacity building in the future is burden sharing as *regulated* in article 43 of UNCLOS 1982" (italics added).[36]

Enforcement Mechanism

The HSC and UNCLOS give individual states the responsibility for taking action against pirates. If states do not take action, or if the action they take is inadequate or ineffective, there is no mechanism or procedure in either Convention that other states could use to make them.[37] As with other treaty articles this was not the original intention. The cooperation article in the HSC is Article 14. Its origins lay in the ILC's Article 38. It read: "(A)ny state having an opportunity of taking measures against piracy, and neglecting to do so, would be failing in a duty laid upon it by international law." In Johnson's view this meant that any state that refused or failed to carry out its responsibilities was liable for "the payment of reparation to other States whose shipping was molested by the pirates in question."[38] Both Johnson and the ILC were, of course, referring only to piracy on the high seas. UNCLOS has no mechanism to ensure states combat piracy (armed robbery) within their own territorial waters.

Disputes Procedure

Disputes at sea fall under two broad headings: disputes between states and disputes between states and individuals. Most examples of the latter involve cases of wrongful or, at least, disputed arrest at sea; for example, cases of boats fishing in what they regard as international waters but which the coastal state regards as being part of its domain. It is certainly conceivable that cases of this nature could arise in connection with piracy or the suspicion of piracy, and UNCLOS makes provision in Article 106 for the payment of reparations, by the state that detained or boarded the suspect vessel, to the flag state of the vessel boarded in cases where suspicions prove unfounded.

However, the background to disputes between states and individuals is now immeasurably more complicated than it was during much of the gestation of the Convention's provisions. The two most important changes have been the rise of open registers and the now-often-fiendishly-complex ship ownership arrangements. The global commercial shipping industry is fiercely competitive. Ships are often "flagged out," that is to say removed from closed registers to open registers, otherwise known as "flags of convenience," in order to avoid tax or other costly liabilities such as safety or manning levels, or call-up in time of war. Most of these flag-of-convenience states are in no position to seek reparations from coastal states even if they were willing to do so. The problem is more often the other way around: it is coastal states that can find it difficult to monitor the activity of some "flagged out" ships.

Ownership in general can also be hard to determine. For reasons similar to those that motivate ship owners to use flags of convenience, the beneficial ownership of a ship can be hidden behind a nominee company or even layers of nominee companies. Flags of convenience are a problem but not the only one. The sheer range of flags and the wide spread of ownerships make it difficult to identify the plaintiff.

Summary

Pirates are mobile. Where their mobility gives rise to problems of "hot pursuit," then responses have to be regional. Nonetheless, even if it is a whole region that suffers, one country might be the prime source of the problem. Concern about piracy today is concentrated primarily in one region, Southeast Asia, and on one country, Indonesia. If piracy in Indonesian waters could be eliminated or controlled, then it would largely disappear from most of the Southeast Asia.

UNCLOS recognizes that other maritime problems, such as those connected to natural resources or fisheries, can have a regional dimension. In these cases it encourages cooperation with regional and even extraregional states up to and including the establishment of dedicated organizations. Similar encouragement is provided for pollution control including enforcement of the Convention's provisions. In contrast, only the most limited and general encouragement to cooperate is suggested in the case of piracy. Enforcement of the piracy provisions, like other provisions, is to be achieved through the domestic law of individual states. However, only in the case of piracy does the Convention make no allowance for states that, for whatever reason, fail to enact or enforce the necessary domestic law. States that have passed the necessary legislation and have the resources to implement it can arrest pirates but only on the high seas. In the territorial waters of states that have not passed the necessary legislation, or lack the will or means to enforce it, pirates can in effect run free, safe in the knowledge that no practical means exist under the Convention to force coastal states to fulfill their obligations.

Conclusions

The piracy provisions of UNCLOS are not working. Or, rather, because they were conceived in another age to deal with a problem that was already largely historical when they were written, they are for the most part irrelevant to the fight against the new (or renewed) form of coastal piracy that has emerged since the Convention opened for signature in 1982. If the relevance of international treaty law in the suppression of piracy is to be restored, then the piracy provisions of UNCLOS need to be rewritten. However, anyone who is concerned with the problem of piracy must be realistic. Most states regard UNCLOS as successful. Obviously it is a document of compromise, but it answers the needs of most states tolerably well. It has resolved some maritime issues and created others, but those that remain are — for now at least — not sufficiently serious to create a momentum for renegotiation. It is conceivable that the Convention's shortcomings as far as piracy is concerned could be addressed in a new Protocol. This, however, would only bind the signatories, and unless these included the coastal states where piracy takes place, it would not affect the problem.

The question that then arises is whether or not a solution can be found in customary international law; that is to say, in international law that has been accepted and practiced by a large number of states over a long period of time. The law of the sea was customary law until the High Seas Convention of 1958. Since then the assumption has been that the HSC and, subsequently, UNCLOS have codified customary law but this may not be the case and, even if true, does not necessarily mean that either Convention has superseded it. The judgment of the British Court in *Cameron v. HM Advocate* (1971), for example, was that the HSC supplemented existing domestic law but did not seek to redefine it retrospectively.[39] In addition, the continuing reluctance of the United States to ratify the Convention means that there are also doubts over its universality. No law is static, even treaty law. A specific treaty or a specific provision might freeze a particular agreement in time, but if circumstances change, the law must change or else wither into disuse. The circumstances pertaining to piracy have changed, and states need to ask themselves whether they should turn again to customary law for the suppressive tools they need, or seek new treaties or agreements.

Put another way, should those states that are concerned about piracy and minded to deal with it revisit the concept of *hostis humani generis* and reclothe it in the new universalism that is now associated with slavery and genocide? If customary international law is the chosen route, then, in Dubner's view, recasting piracy in this manner is the only way forward.[40] The alternative is to seek new treaties or other agreements. In other words, to accept the Harvard Group's view that while piracy is a crime against mankind, them should not be so considered for treaty purposes but instead be regarded as a crime with universal jurisdiction. These two approaches reflect, in microcosm, the contrasting visions of cosmopolitanism and pluralism that dominate the current debate over the shape and direction of global society.

The treaty or agreement route is ultimately discretionary. It rests on those states with a piracy problem having the will and resources to do what is necessary to control or eliminate it. This places piracy suppression between a rock and a hard place. In the most piracy-prone region in the world a modus operandi needs to be found between the rock of states that can or will do little about it, and the hard place of their sovereignty. Whenever piracy occurs in coastal waters, states are on their own. UNCLOS has nothing to say about it. Moreover, because pirates are mobile and, like all criminals, prey upon and exploit weakness, individual states are rarely able to control them. They need to coordinate their suppressive efforts with their neighbors and, quite possibly, with external powers. UNCLOS has nothing to say about this either.

Nonetheless, in 1992 Indonesia, Malaysia, and Singapore signed parallel bilateral agreements to coordinate antipiracy patrols in the Straits which were successful in controlling piracy in their area of operation, although the problem grew regionally. When the Asian financial crisis of the late 1990s meant operations had to be curtailed, piracy in the Straits rose again. Indonesia, in particular, encountered problems in finding the necessary resources. Attempts at cooperation in the Straits and across the region since then have come in response to external promptings rather than as a result of new regional initiatives. This comes as little surprise. Although ASEAN, the regional political grouping, was touted as an autonomous new actor on the world stage, it was and remains acutely reliant on the economic and naval power of the United States.

The first initiative was the Regional Cooperation Agreement on Combating Piracy and Armed Robbery against Ships in Asia (ReCAAP) that was initiated by Japan in 2001 and signed at a meeting of ASEAN in 2004. This is significant because all the nations of ASEAN are signatories plus Japan, China, Korea, India, Bangladesh, and Sri Lanka. However, like other agreements in the region, it reasserted the primary concerns of regional states: that it would be implemented in accordance with national laws and would not affect the rights and obligations of states under UNCLOS. Inevitably, disagreements emerged over the definition of piracy and the status of the EEZ. Its purview was also limited to information sharing, and no provision was made for joint training or enforcement.[41]

The second was the Regional Maritime Security Initiative (RMSI), initiated by the United States, which was concerned about reports that terrorists might be tempted by the low level of maritime security in the Straits to attack shipping or attempt an attack on the megaport of Singapore.[42] Indonesia and Malaysia objected to the idea of U.S. Navy warships patrolling the Straits partly for sovereignty reasons, partly because of the tradition opposition to the basing of foreign forces in the region, and partly because they believed the presence of U.S. forces would inflame radical Islamist opinion. Instead they suggested that they should again mount joint patrols with Singapore, an initiative that has now been formalized as the MALSINDO agreement.[43] All the ships involved would stay under their own national commands and there would be no "hot pursuit or reciprocal enforcement but their activities would be coordinated."

Although this revival is a welcome step, it does not remove several concerns. The first is simply a question of numbers: between them the three states are contributing seventeen ships. It is widely recognized that the Straits present unique navigational, surveillance, and communications problems. *Warships International* took the view that, "(M)alaysia, on one side only has 18 Marine Police boats in service at any one time. Indonesia, on the other side, has about 20 coast guard boats and several navy ships in the area, but not all on duty at the same time. Add to this equation the Singaporean boats and it seems doubtful that terrorists or pirates will be greatly deterred."[44] As noted already, antipiracy patrols have not traditionally been high on the Indonesian agenda.

John Bradford has pointed out that while piracy and maritime security are regarded as a security issue in Singapore and a political issue in Malaysia, in Indonesia they are neither.[45] Furthermore, the fact that this latest response has also come about as a result of U.S. pressure does not auger well. Experience from other fields has demonstrated that outside pressure rarely brings about lasting change. The desire for change, particularly if it requires the reordering of national priorities, has to be driven internally. Piracy is a land-based crime. Defeating it requires an honest, effective, and determined police and criminal justice system. Although there have been some promising signs of change since the fall of the Megawati government, the suspicion remains that while the Indonesian government is prepared to sanction patrols (and buy ships that will inflate their overall *military* capacity), they may not be prepared to undertake the political and legal reforms that will fundamentally weaken and possibly eliminate this menace.

Piracy might be a crime, but it is also inseparable from politics. When it comes to regional cooperation, China, for example, has usually rejected multilateral responses, although its stance has softened somewhat of late. It has generally preferred bilateral arrangements in the belief that these arrangements give it more control over the relationship. It has resolutely blocked Japanese maritime aid and assistance to the region, believing it to be an attempt to gain greater political influence. It has also objected to the RMSI saying it is a threat to the sovereignty of small nations. Given the competition between the states of Southeast Asia, the level of suspicion that exists between them and the opportunities for conflict, it is inevitable that doubts about the durability of any antipiracy agreement will persist. Vijay Sakhuja's comment that the absence of an institutional understanding among countries has been largely responsible for perpetuating piracy rings true.[46] However, given the differences and distrust between the countries of the region, and given also the time it takes to build effective institutions at all the requisite levels, institutional understanding appears a long way off.

What of the customary law approach? Could it offer a way forward in those cases where a coastal state, for whatever reason, is unwilling to take action against pirates? After all, if the states that are most affected will do nothing about it, who will?

UNCLOS is again an obstacle. International law, especially treaty law, is a form of international politics. It is one way states achieve what they want without going to war. Many states gained a great deal from UNCLOS. If they believe other states, the major maritime powers in particular, are adopting new practices and attitudes that could undermine their gains they are likely to resist them just as stoutly as they would any attempt to amend the Convention directly.

UNCLOS is the seaward extension of the post–World War II norm of inviolable borders. However, this shield is beginning to buckle under other pressures. The first is the new, Western-inspired interest in universal human rights. This interest has been behind the whole idea of humanitarian intervention and the belief that sovereign rights should not override human rights. It thereby provokes the question: why should seafarers be exposed to danger and death simply because some states value their sovereignty above seafarers' lives? There are good grounds for believing that piracy could be seen as a human rights offence given the widespread, if erroneous, perception that it is already bracketed with genocide and slavery as a crime deserving universal condemnation as well as universal jurisdiction. A state would find it difficult to claim its sovereign rights had been violated if the world community was convinced it had either failed to deal with the problem itself, or had refused the aid and assistance of another state that could. As Dubner points out, the concerns that led the Harvard Group to label piracy not a universal crime but one with a universal jurisdiction have largely been removed:

> Today, an international tribunal and compulsory dispute provisions exist to deal with rights under the 1982 Convention; an international criminal court is in place; and treaty and customary international laws regarding the rights of human beings *vis-à-vis* the rights of states to proceed on individuals' behalf still exist. The doctrine of universality should give every nation the right to try pirates under either treaty or customary law.[47]

The practical response could conceivably take three forms: first, a version of international humanitarian intervention where a coalition of "user" states could mount vigorous patrols and even coastal raids. This, after all, is not dissimilar to the original concept for RMSI: when it was first mooted before a committee of the U.S. Senate, the suggestion was to bring together U.S. Navy ships, Marines, and special forces using fast boats to track down terrorists (who, in the dark, look just like pirates).[48] Second, a concerted policy of patrolling and "reverse hot pursuit" by states bordering the recalcitrant state — or even extraregional powers such as EU states, the presence of whose ships might be seen as less contentious — to ensure that pirates are brought before a court; third, arming commercial vessels so they can defend and help themselves in case of pirate attack. The last is possibly the least attractive option, but one which seafarers may be forced to adopt in the absence of reliable protection and effective law enforcement. In fact, there are signs that it is happening already.[49]

None of these options are likely to appeal to coastal states, but can they avoid them? The coastal states' first line of defense could well be that the number of attacks, and their cost, has been exaggerated; that piracy is a Western fixation that has been blown out of proportion. There is much truth in this. However, the major maritime trading nations *are* worried (Japan most of all), and coastal states could avoid what they perceive as sovereign humiliation by responding more purposefully.[50] Sovereignty is not established by legislative fiat but by power. That power can derive from several sources, but one is the recognition by other states of its legitimacy and another is the strength to keep others out. Put brutally, "(T)he acid test of sovereignty at sea is the ability to exclude others."[51] If a state lacks the capacity to defend peaceful shipping in its own waters, what legitimate right does it have to exclude others who do? It seems disproportionate that innocent people must die in order to uphold sovereign rights. Jesus argues that it is in the best interest of such states to clear their waters of pirates. In customary and treaty law they are acknowledged to be the enemies of all mankind. Perhaps more pertinently they "are always the enemy of every state."[52] This surely is a powerful rationale for accepting foreign assistance and ceding common jurisdiction, perhaps on a time-limited basis.[53] The purpose would not be to diminish coastal state sovereignty but to suppress a problem that affects everyone. As Jesus goes on to say, states in the past were prepared to cede a degree of sovereign protection over their own flag vessels in order to combat piracy, so why cannot coastal states today similarly cede a degree of sovereignty over their territorial waters in order to bring the new breed of coastal pirates to justice?[54]

This is unlikely to happen, overtly at least. The second pressure on sovereignty, globalization, is possibly less resistible. It is forcing states to open their markets and their borders if they wish to be part of the global trading system. It is a conformist process, and the major trading states expect their trading partners to share more and more of their standards many of which are not just economic. A third pressure is the rising concern over weak or failed states. State failure leading to violence and starvation, and state failure leading to the creation of havens for organized crime and terrorism have both eroded the inviolability of state sovereignty and legitimized outside intervention for humanitarian or security reasons. Major states have shown themselves to be less tolerant toward claims of sovereignty if they believe they are being used to hide weapons proliferation, organized criminal activity, terrorism, or crimes against humanity.

At sea there has been evidence of this new activism for some time. The United States has concluded twenty-three agreements with Caribbean and Central American states (plus the UK) that enable it to board flag vessels of those countries if it believes they are being used to smuggle narcotics. Some of these are so-called shiprider agreements whereby an official of a signatory state travels aboard a U.S. ship available to grant immediate permission to board when a suspect vessel is intercepted. In other cases the flag state is asked for permission to board one of its flag vessels, and if it has not responded within a specified time (usually 2 or 4 hours) then permission is deemed to have been given. In the case of the UK, the United States has permission in advance to board any UK flagged vessel within a designated sea area.[55] In 2003 the Aruba Agreement was signed. This was a multilateral agreement that supplemented but did not replace these bilateral agreements. Most Caribbean states were involved in the negotiations that led up to the Agreement plus four external powers, the United States, the UK, France, and the Netherlands. While neither the bilateral agreements nor the multilateral Aruba Agreement cover piracy specifically, communication channels and procedures have been established between states that could make it easier to obtain the permission necessary to board suspect vessels.[56] International law is therefore developing all the time. The Aruba Agreement grew out of the 1988 United Nations "Drug Trafficking" Convention, and if it can be seen as an advance upon it then it can also be seen as a stepping-stone toward the revision of the 1988 SUA Convention as well.

The United States used the experience it had gained forging counternarcotics agreements in the Caribbean to influence the shape of a new protocol to the SUA Convention: this proposes that the ships of signatories can be boarded on the high seas by ships of other signatories if they are suspected of an offence under the Convention, providing the permission of the flag state is granted; again this permission being deemed to have been given if no reply is received after 4 hours. These new Protocols to the SUA are obviously an important step forward, but the question remains: apart from one marginal case, when has the SUA ever been used since its inception in 1988? Perhaps the new Protocols will change that.

The Proliferation Security Initiative (PSI), and subsequent agreements with the most important open-register states, incorporates the same thinking. The objective of the PSI is to enable its signatories to board ships that they suspect of carrying nuclear materials. Although PSI has aroused some controversy, Michael Byers has argued that much of it "involves nothing more than the consistent and rigorous application of existing rights under national and international law." Its aim as a whole, however, is to develop new legal authorities by means of bilateral and multilateral treaties, and could lead to new rights under customary international law.[57]

RMSI was the first example of a possible regional extension of PSI. While PSI is focused on counterproliferation, is global in scope, and its signatories are all established U.S. allies, RMSI looks across a range of maritime security issues, is regional, and aims to include all the states in the region whether they are U.S. allies or not. The link between the two is that both proceed from the idea that the United States can assemble "coalitions of the willing," an idea that has already informed other parts of its foreign policy. These coalitions have been born out of a frustration that some nations have been prepared to accept international obligations — and all the benefits that flow from being counted as a member of the international community — but have been unwilling to fulfill them. The idea is that the "coalitions of the willing" will bring together like-minded states that share this sense of frustration and then draw in other states once the fundamental principles of any action have been established.[58]

PSI represents a controlled erosion of flag-state sovereignty; controlled because it is not in the interests of the United States or any other state to see flag-state sovereignty removed entirely. Although the United States has not adopted the treaty approach for PSI exclusively, it has done so in the main because to gain acceptance for the same legal authorities under customary law could have taken far longer and involved greater uncertainty as to the outcome. The treaty approach also enabled it to circumvent the blockages that have bedeviled negotiations at the UN and other international organizations. What the PSI has shown is that coalitions can be formed and mobilized to tackle specific problems. It is quite possible that the major powers could use a similar approach to effect a controlled erosion of coastal state sovereignty over territorial waters. This could start, quite possibly, with a campaign to win acceptance for a broader definition of piracy, such as the one used by the IMB.

In many ways piracy is a more complex challenge than proliferation. The threat it presents is less dramatic and more diffuse. Piracy is not just about what happens at sea. Its roots lie on land where it is fed by political corruption, poor government, and underresourced and poorly motivated law enforcement. In order to thrive it depends on networks that pass pirates the information they need and others that dispose of the money and goods they steal. The piracy provisions in UNCLOS are locked into a wider treaty that no one wants to renegotiate. It provides states with a predictable basis for cooperation. The piracy provisions, however, have lost much of their relevance. As the world globalizes so does crime. The security of maritime trade is too important to be left to the mercy of outdated provisions and unwilling states.

Notes

1. The author would like to thank Ronald Barston, Sam Bateman, Vaughan Lowe, and Scott Truver for their helpful comments on earlier drafts of this chapter. I would also like to thank Rosalie Balkin, Bill Gilmore, and George Galdorisi for their advice on specific points. All views are my own.

   For a description of U.S. thinking on this issue see Elliot Richardson. 1980. "Power, Mobility and the Law of the Sea." *Foreign Affairs,* Spring, vol. 58, no. 4, pp. 902–19.
2. P. W. Birnie. 1987. "Piracy, Past, Present and Future." *Marine Policy,* July, Vol. 2, No. 3, p. 163.
3. David Scott. 1994. "Piracy, Terrorism, and Crime at Sea" in Peter T. Haydon and Anne Griffiths, eds., *Maritime Security and Conflict Resolution at Sea in the Post-Cold War Era: Proceedings of the June 1993 Colloquium held by the Centre for Foreign Policy Studies.* 1994. Halifax, N.S.: Dalhousie University, Centre for Foreign Policy Studies, pp. 42–43.
4. Harvard Research in International Law (hereafter called the Harvard Draft), 1932. "Draft Convention on Piracy with Comments." *The American Journal of International Law.* Vol. 26, Supplement, p. 749.
5. Harvard Draft, pp. 764–65.
6. See Ger Teitler. 2002. "Piracy in Southeast Asia: A Historical Comparison." *MAST,* Vol. 1, No. 1, pp. 67–83; Leigh R. Wright. 1976. "Piracy in the Southeast Asian Archipelago." *Journal of Oriental Studies,* Vol. 14, pp. 23–33.
7. Barry H. Dubner. 1980. *The Law of International Sea Piracy.* The Hague: Martinus Nijhoff Publishers, p. 38.

8. D. H. N. Johnson draws attention to the difference between "codification" and "progressive development" as defined by the Statutes of the International Law Commission (Article 15). D. H. N. Johnson. 1957. "Piracy in Modern International Law." *Grotius Society Transactions*. Vol. 63, p. 66, note 5.
9. Malvina Halberstam. 1988. "Terrorism on the High Seas: The Achille Lauro, Piracy and the IMO Convention on Maritime Safety." *The American Journal of International Law*. April. Vol. 82, No. 2, p. 284: " … the importance and controversial nature of other matters apparently precluded the consideration of piracy."
10. Barry H. Dubner. 1997. "Human Rights and Environmental Disaster — Two Problems that Defy the "Norms" of the International Law of Sea Piracy." *Syracuse Journal of International Law*. Vol. 23, No.1, p. 2.
11. Eugene Kontorovich. 2004. "The Piracy Analogy: Modern Universal Jurisdiction's Hollow Foundation." *Harvard International Law Review*. Winter. Vol. 45, No.1, pp. 210–15. See also Donald A. Petrie. 1999. *The Prize Game*. New York: Berkley Books.
12. Timothy H.Goodman. 1999. "'Leaving the Corsair's Name To Other Times': How to Enforce the Law of Sea Piracy in the 21st Century through Regional International Agreements." *Case Western Reserve Journal of International Law*. Vol. 31, No.1, pp. 147–48.
13. Barry H. Dubner. 1980, pp. 62–63; Barry H. Dubner. 1997 pp. 19–20.
14. Malvina Halberstam, p. 281.
15. D.H.N.Johnson, p. 77, note 21.
16. Harvard Draft, Article 6, p. 744
17. Harvard Draft, pp. 756 and 757. See also Barry H. Dubner (1997), p. 17.
18. R.R.Churchill and A.V.Lowe. 1999. *The Law of the Sea*. Third Edition. Manchester: Manchester University Press, pp. 102–15; David M. Keithly. "The Law of the Sea Revisited." *Low Intensity Conflict and Law Enforcement*. Winter. Vol. 7, No. 3, pp. 125–26; Mark J. Valencia. 2005. *The Proliferation Security Initiative: Making Waves in Asia*. Adelphi Paper 376. London: Routledge for the IISS, pp. 12–13.
19. Ronald Barston. 1991. "Law of the Sea: Issues and Practice" in Ronald Barston, ed. 1991. *International Politics since 1945*. Aldershot: Edward Elgar, pp. 150–52.
20. See the discussion in Ronald Barston, pp. 145–46. Also R.R.Churchill and A.V.Lowe, pp. 165–66.
21. See, for example, Barry H. Dubner (1997), pp. 11–12; H.E. José Luis Jesus. 2003. "Protection of Foreign Ships against Piracy and Terrorism at Sea: Legal Aspects." *The International Journal of Marine and Coastal Law*. Vol. 18, No. 3, p. 379; Sam Bateman. 2001. "Piracy and the Challenge of Cooperative Security and Enforcement Policy." *Maritime Studies*, March/April, pp. 14–15.
22. See, for example, P. W. Birnie, p. 172; David M. Keithly, pp. 123 and 133; Samuel Pyeatt Menefee. 1999. "Foreign Naval Intervention in Cases of Piracy: Problems and Strategies." *The International Journal of Marine and Coastal Law*. Vol. 14, No. 3, p. 360
23. A thorough review of the history of the EEZ concept can be found in George V. Galdorisi and Alan G. Kaufman. 2002. "Military Activities in the Exclusive Economic Zone: Preventing Uncertainty and Defusing Conflict." *California Western International Law Journal*, vol. 32, pp. 257–68
24. George V. Galdorisi and Alan G. Kaufman, p. 254
25. George V. Galdorisi and Alan G. Kaufman, pp. 281–88 and George V. Galdorisi and Kevin R. Vienna. 1997. *Beyond the Law of the Sea: New Directions for U.S. Oceans Policy*. Westport, CT and London: Praeger, p. 152. See also Marie Jacobsson. 2000. "Sovereignty at Sea: Illusion or Reality?" in R.A. Herr, ed. *Sovereignty at Sea: From Westphalia to Madrid*. Wollongong Papers on Maritime Policy No. 11; University of Wollongong, Centre for Maritime Policy, pp. 41–42 and 56, and Sam Bateman. 2000. "The Regime of Straits Transit Passage in the Asia Pacific: Political and Strategic Issues" in Donald R. Rothwell and Sam Bateman, eds. *Navigational Rights and Freedoms and the New Law of the Sea* (The Hague, Boston and London: Martinus Nijhoff), pp. 108–9, where he writes: "The ambiguity of UNCLOS with respect to coastal States rights in the EEZ creates the opportunity for States to take unilateral actions that could then evolve into accepted State practice."
26. P. W. Birnie, p. 173.
27. George V. Galdorisi and Alan G. Kaufman, pp. 272–80

28. Harvard Draft, pp. 832–83. This suggestion builds on Articles Five and Six of the League of Nations" *Draft Provisions*. League of Nations: Committee of Experts for the Progressive Codification of International Law. 1926. "Questionnaire No. 6: Piracy." *The American Journal of International Law*. April, Vol. 20, No. 3, supplement, pp. 228–29.
29. US Department of the Navy. *The Commander's Handbook on the Law of Naval Operations*. NWP1-14M at 3.5.3.2 "Pursuit of Pirates into Foreign Territorial Seas, Archipelagic Waters, or Airspace," and 3.10.1.1 "Foreign Internal Waters, Archipelagic Waters, and Territorial Seas" available at http://www.nwc.navy.mil/ILD/NWP%201-14M.htm.
30. Harvard Draft, p. 283.
31. Peter Chalk. 1998. "'Contemporary Maritime Piracy in Southeast Asia.'" *Studies in Conflict and Terrorism*, Vol. 21, No. 1, p. 95
32. John F. Bradford. 2004. "Japanese Anti-Piracy Initiatives in Southeast Asia: Policy Formulations and the Coastal State Responses." *Contemporary Southeast Asia*. Vol. 26, No. 3, p. 499.
33. Bernard Kent Sondakh. 2004. "National Sovereignty and Security in the Strait of Malacca." Presentation to the Maritime Institute of Malaysia Conference, Kuala Lumpur, Malaysia, 12 October, pp. 12–13.
34. Hasjim Djalal. 2004. "Piracy in South East Asia: Indonesian and Regional Responses." A paper prepared for the Centre for Strategic and International Studies (CSIS), American-Pacific Sealanes Security Institute Conference on Maritime Security in Asia, Honolulu, Hawaii, 18–20 January, pp. 3–4.
35. John F. Bradford, pp. 493 and 499.
36. Bernard Kent Sondakh, p. 12.
37. Timothy H.Goodman, p. 156; H.E. José Luis Jesus, pp. 380–81.
38. D. H. N. Johnson. Ibid, p. 65; see also Malvina Halberstam, p. 283.
39. D. G. Steel. 1995. "Piracy — Can the Order of the Oceans be Safeguarded?" *RUSI Journal*, October, vol. 140, no. 5, p. 20.
40. Barry H. Dubner (1997), p. 33.
41. John F. Bradford, p. 493. An information centre has been established in Singapore.
42. United States Pacific Command. 2004. "Strategy for Regional Maritime Security." November, JIACG/CT available at http://www.pacom.mil/rmsi/RMSI%20Strategy%20Nov%2004.pdf.
43. "Piracy and Maritime Terror in Southeast Asia: Dire Straits." 2004. *IISS Strategic Comments*, Vol. 10, No. 6, July.
44. Anthony Tucker-Jones. 2004. "War on Terror Update." *Warships International Fleet Review Web Special*, 16 October available at http://www.warshipsifr.com/pages/master-frameset.html; also Ian Storey, ibid, p. 9.
45. John F. Bradford, p. 482.
46. Vijay Sakhuja. 2000. "Maritime Order and Piracy." *Strategic Analysis*, August, Vol. XXIV, No. 5.
47. Barry H. Dubner. 1997, pp. 39–40. David Letts makes a similar argument in 1999. "Piracy: Some Questions of Definition and Jurisdiction." *Maritime Studies*, No. 104, January–February, pp. 26–32.
48. John Burton. 2004. "Antiterrorism patrols planned for the Malacca Strait." *Financial Times*, 19 June.
49. Malaysia and Indonesia have issued stern warnings against such practices, but in the light of continuing demand appear unsure how to respond. "3 Malacca Strait govts weigh allowing ships to carry arms." 2005. *Straits Times*, 15 May.
50. Barry H. Dubner. 1997, p. 40. See also "Malaysia wants closer cooperation with Indonesia to fight piracy. 2005. *Channel News Asia*, 3 April.
51. James Cable. 1989. *Navies in Violent Peace*. London: Macmillan, pp. 85–86.
52. FitzRoy Kelly, British Attorney-General, 1857. Quoted by Samuel Pyeatt Menefee. 1990, p. 46.
53. Sam Bateman makes the case for "soft law agreements, i.e. non-binding agreements that do not create legal obligations." Sam Bateman (2001), pp. 18–19.
54. H.E. José Luis Jesus, pp. 383–85.
55. Michael Byers. 2004. "Policing the High Seas: The Proliferation Security Initiative." *American Journal of International Law*. July, Vol. 98, No. 3, pp. 538–39.

56. For a full discussion of the Agreement see William Gilmore. 2005. "Agreement Concerning Co-operation in Suppressing Illicit Maritime and Air Trafficking in Narcotic Drugs and Psychotropic Substances in the Caribbean Area, 2003." London: The Stationary Office.
57. Michael Byers, p. 528.
58. Michael Byers, p. 544.

8
The International Politics of Combating Piracy in Southeast Asia

CHRIS RAHMAN

The international politics of combating piracy and other threats to maritime security in Southeast Asia are difficult, to say the least. On the one hand, there is a common interest among both regional states and their extraregional partners for an for improved sea line of communication (SLOC) and energy security. On the other, diverging strategic interests and varying political cultures and sensitivities vastly complicate any effort to eliminate the threat in a practical way. The desire to protect national sovereignty usually trumps efforts to effectively combat the threat, a particular shortcoming when dealing with a problem which is inherently transnational in nature and requires multinational cooperation to be overcome. Moreover, the habit of some states of focusing maritime-security cooperation efforts on multilateral institutions rather than on more active cooperation on the water may simply be a politically expedient way to avoid making difficult choices. This chapter identifies and assesses the effectiveness of four leading drivers of maritime security cooperation to combat piracy and related threats in Southeast Asia: the multilateral institutional framework; Japanese-led initiatives; U.S.-led initiatives; and other, nonmultilateral cooperation.

Multilateral Cooperation To Improve Maritime Security in Southeast Asia

The institutional framework for multilateral maritime security cooperation in Southeast Asia comprises a complex network of international and regional organizations, plus other institutions and forums which deal, somewhat redundantly, with identical or similar issues to counter piracy and other threats to maritime security.

IMO

The International Maritime Organization (IMO) is the UN body charged with regulating international shipping.[1] In addition to its existing conventions regulating maritime safety and security (including the International Ship and Port Security (ISPS) Code),[2] the IMO has more recently pursued new technical regulations which will improve the ability to monitor shipping, as well as measures specifically relating to the Malacca and Singapore Straits.

Firstly, the IMO adopted in 2000 a requirement for all ships to be fitted with an automatic identification system (AIS) by 31 December 2004.[3] The AIS is a VHF transponder which automatically provides information on a ship's identity, location and navigational status to shore stations, other ships, or aircraft. There is a real concern, however, that AIS data is freely accessible on the worldwide web, potentially providing vital intelligence data to well-organized pirates or terrorists. The IMO and other parties involved in improving maritime security increasingly are discouraging the open dissemination of such information. Another problem with AIS is the short range of VHF, thus limiting its utility for region-wide monitoring to combat attacks on shipping. To remedy this shortcoming, the IMO is pursuing a new mandatory requirement to allow long range identification and tracking (LRIT) of ships, which would provide global, rather than localized, monitoring of shipping. The most likely technological solution would be to transmit AIS data via satellite, thus transforming the system into a constant, real-time vessel monitoring system (VMS), similar to those already used to monitor fishing vessels. The United States has been a leading driver of LRIT, as it was also with the ISPS Code, prompted by post-9/11 fears of maritime terrorism. Any LRIT system remains politically sensitive, however, with some states within the IMO preferring to limit access to LRIT data to flag states, who would be able to track all ships flying their respective flags; and port states, who would be able to track ships intending to enter their respective ports, to a determined distance or period of time. Such a restrictive interpretation would undermine the U.S. wish to be able to identify and track all merchant traffic on a global basis, irrespective of flag, location, or destination, thus seriously undermining the push for effective regional "maritime domain awareness," to use the current jargon.

Secondly, the IMO Council determined in November 2004 that the IMO should play a role in the protection of vital shipping lanes of "strategic importance and significance." The safety and security of shipping plying the Malacca Strait was identified as a particular concern, with a high-level conference organized to take place in Jakarta in September 2005 to discuss the objective of keeping the Strait open through improved information sharing and technical and capacity-building cooperation. The IMO is promoting its Marine Electronic Highway (MEH) project for the Straits of Malacca and Singapore as a means to fulfill that objective. The MEH was originally conceived in 1996–1997 to integrate different electronic systems and information technologies into a regional marine information network to improve navigational safety in the Straits.[4] The MEH initially had an environmental focus to reduce the incidence of marine pollution caused by collisions and other accidents. However, in the current security environment it has been recognized that information from the MEH project also has the potential to improve maritime security in the Straits against piratical acts and terrorism by networking communications and positioning data from ships. The demonstration phase of the project is expected to be completed for the Straits by late 2007.[5] If successful, there are plans for a second phase to extend the MEH to other priority areas between the Straits and the Sea of Japan, and a third to complete an entire network for the seas of East Asia, especially for the region's oil and gas transportation routes.

APEC

The Asia Pacific Economic Cooperation (APEC) forum,[6] established to facilitate and promote trade among its member states, has created its own complex network of groups and measures to enhance maritime security. The importance of maritime security to APEC members is immediately obvious: trade with, and within, the Asia-Pacific region is overwhelmingly carried via sea. While the impetus to promote maritime security within the APEC forum has been noticeably enhanced by the specter of terrorism, post-9/11, regional piracy remains an important concern. And, as with the case of the security of shipping throughout Southeast Asian seas more generally, it is all but impossible to disaggregate security concerns and response measures to combat piracy from those to combat maritime terrorism or other threats.

Structurally, APEC has two types of interlinked groups dealing with maritime security issues, arranged below the level of the APEC Senior Officials' Meeting (SOM): Working Groups and SOM Special Task Groups. There are, in turn, two relevant APEC Working Groups: the Transportation Working Group (TPTWG) and the Energy Working Group (EWG). The TPTWG includes a Maritime Security Experts Group (MSEG), which has pursued initiatives to assist member states to improve maritime security. It is not clear, however, whether, or how, MSEG initiatives will impact directly upon the scourge of piracy in a practical way. Among other things, the MSEG sponsors capacity-building measures to assist less-developed members, such as a program to help with the implementation of the IMO's ISPS Code. The TPTWG is also negotiating a Memorandum of Understanding with the IMO and improving its cooperation with the International Maritime Bureau's Piracy Reporting Centre,[7] while another of its experts groups, the Intelligent Transportation Systems Expert Group, has been promoting the integration of new technologies to enhance the security of the entire maritime transportation supply chain.

The EWG established an Energy Security Initiative in 2002, with sea-lane security as one of its five focus areas. As part of this process, a simulation exercise was held in Tokyo in April 2002 to identify shortcomings in response mechanisms and contingency plans to deal with sea-lane disruption in Southeast Asia caused by, *inter alia*, piratical attacks. The subsequent recommendations include the establishment of a real-time emergency information-sharing system and the upgrading of navigational aids in Indonesia's Sunda and Lombok Straits, which might be used as alternative routes should the Malacca Strait be closed for any reason. However, the EWG possesses no practical ability to implement such recommendations, and intended simply to report them to the TPTWG and the IMO to encourage their adoption by other such bodies.

The relevant SOM Special Task Group is the Counter Terrorism Task Force (CTTF), established in February 2003, to assist members to identify and assess threats, coordinate capacity-building programs and technical assistance and facilitate cooperation to counter terrorist activity. One of the CTTF's main priorities is to promote the Secure Trade in the APEC Region (STAR) initiative originally agreed to in October 2002, which seeks, *inter alia*, to promote trade by developing measures to better protect ships and their cargoes. STAR has been organized around a series of conferences to improve cooperation between the respective members' official agencies and private sector organizations. The first, STAR I, was held in Bangkok in February 2003. A follow-up initiative established a technology demonstration project using e-seals to allow satellite tracking of security-sealed containers between the ports of Bangkok/Laem Chabang and Seattle.[8] A Working Group on Maritime Security at STAR II, in Chile in March 2004, focused on implementation of the ISPS Code and on technical cooperation for maritime security.

STAR III, held in Seoul in March 2005, addressed three related maritime security issues. First, STAR III addressed issues arising from the implementation of the ISPS Code and promoted the adoption of VMS to provide real-time monitoring of merchant-ship positions and instant reporting of at-sea incidents such as piracy. Second, the conference addressed the need to implement a viable container-security regime. Third, STAR III addressed the need to improve SLOC protection against piracy and terrorist threats. A final initiative of the CTTF has been to encourage each APEC member to compile a national Counter Terrorism Action Plan, which lists measures being undertaken to support the implementation of STAR objectives.

ASEAN

In addition to work carried out on maritime security by its Maritime Transport Working Group, the Association of Southeast Asian Nations (ASEAN) has adopted a Plan of Action to Combat Transnational Crime, with an attached work program that includes a section on countering piracy.[9] The proposed forms of cooperation to combat piracy involve the usual-candidate categories of information exchange, intelligence sharing, capacity building, and technical and training assistance. Interestingly, it also moots the development of legal arrangements to facilitate, *inter alia*, apprehension, investigation, and hot pursuit of pirates among member states, although such arrangements are only at the feasibility study stage. The document also suggests enhancing "programs" for coordinated antipiracy patrols, albeit without including practical measures for that purpose.

ARF

The ASEAN Regional Forum (ARF) was established in 1994 as a cooperative security mechanism to facilitate multilateral dialogues on security issues in the Asia-Pacific region among ASEAN states and other state actors in the region's security architecture.[10] From the outset, one of the areas of particular ARF focus was to have been maritime security cooperation. The scope of such cooperation was to include, *inter alia*, maritime surveillance, maritime safety, maritime-information databases, and the establishment of zones of cooperation in areas such as the South China Sea.

Over the past decade there has been a growing frequency of ARF workshops, seminars, and confidence-building measures on maritime security. The ARF has produced an ARF Statement on Cooperation Against Piracy and Other Threats to Security (June 2003) and an ARF Statement on Strengthening Transport Security against International Terrorism (July 2004). In addition to consideration of the usual low-level means to cooperation, the June 2003 Statement recognized the necessity of cooperation and coordination among navies and other maritime enforcement agencies, and that an effective response to piracy requires "regional maritime security strategies and multilateral cooperation in their implementation."[11] However, no details were provided on just what a regional maritime security strategy might look like and how it might work.

The Statement also endorsed ASEAN's plan for creating a legal framework for regional cooperation to combat piracy and armed robbery at sea.[12] However, it does not provide clear pathways to transform the idea from mere concept to practical, workable reality. The establishment of a regional legal framework for enforcement cooperation has practical precedents, such as the Niue Treaty for cooperative surveillance and enforcement of fisheries in the South Pacific and the Australia-France agreement on maritime boundaries and enforcement in the Southern Ocean. Genuine cooperative enforcement, however, requires sovereignty to be put aside and other legal arrangements to be made for the enforcement of other states' laws and on matters such as extradition of apprehended pirates. Yet the ARF Statement explicitly states that nothing "should prejudice the position of ARF countries with regard to any unsettled dispute concerning sovereignty or other rights over territory."[13] Sensitivity over sovereignty and sovereign rights at sea remains high in a region with many outstanding territorial disputes and undelimited maritime boundaries, and where postcolonial era nationalist sentiments still rein supreme in many states. This places an obvious limitation on effective cooperation in straits and other narrow sea areas where national jurisdiction is either disputed or constrained by political or physical geography.

WPNS

The Western Pacific Naval Symposium (WPNS) is the primary forum for multilateral cooperation and intercourse outside alliance or coalition contexts among the navies of the Asia-Pacific region.[14] The WPNS is slowly evolving to encompass practical multilateral training and exercising, which in 2005, for the first time, included dealing with piracy and terrorist threat scenarios. In May 2005 Singapore hosted the third WPNS Multilateral Tactical Training Centre Exercise. As part of that meeting, the forum also held its inaugural WPNS Multilateral Sea Exercise in the South China Sea and the first Maritime Security Information Exchange Seminar. The sea exercise included efforts to overcome command-and-control interoperability issues and practice information sharing between ships in order to be able to "detect, identify and track ships of interest."[15] This exercise program may represent a small, and belated, step for the WPNS, but in doing so may be providing just the sort of practical training and capacity building needed if regional states are to successfully tackle the piracy problem. In that respect, it may seem disappointing and surprising, then, that neither Indonesia nor the Philippines, as the two Southeast Asian states with the most dangerous waters, sent ships to participate in the sea exercise.[16]

Other Forums

To a large extent the ARF's inability to move beyond mere talk and the "minimalist" approach of "socializing" its members into multilateral security processes may spell its doom over the medium term.[17] Partly, the ARF's current irrelevance results from its relative success in integrating China into the Forum, which allows Beijing, in effect, to veto debate on issues it deems politically sensitive; in the East Asian context, that excludes many of the most pressing security problems from ARF consideration. Secondly, there are serious questions to be asked about the efficacy of cooperative security processes in general. While such processes may have a role to play in the overall regional security architecture, it is surely a mistake to conflate mere process with actual "security." Even as a talk shop, the ARF risks being superseded by other forums such as the Shangri-la Dialogue held annually in Singapore by the London-based International Institute for Strategic Studies. Attended by high-level officials as well as other participants, the Dialogue includes a session on maritime security cooperation. The inaugural East Asia Summit, to take place in December 2005, will match the ASEAN 10 with China, Japan, South Korea, Australia, and New Zealand in a high-level exchange of, as yet, indeterminate content. Potentially, the summit could supplant both the moribund ARF and the sluggish trade enhancement record of APEC. However, the explicit, intentional exclusion of the United States is likely to ensure that the summit will struggle to play a major role in improving regional security problems such as piracy.

In addition to the above-mentioned forums and institutions, there exists a plethora of other Track I (official), Track II (unofficial), academic and commercial conferences, seminars, meetings, workshops, and confidence-building measures in which regional piracy and ways to improve maritime security are discussed. It is probably no exaggeration to suggest that there are almost as many events of this kind held each year in the region as there are actual piratical attacks. It remains to been whether this vast network of interlinked, multilateral, cooperative security processes can ever equal something greater than the sum of its multiredundant parts.

Japanese Counterpiracy Initiatives

Japan and Japanese interest groups (such as foundations and think tanks, defense and commercial shipping interests), have been advancing the cause of sea-lane security, particularly through Southeast Asian waters, consistently for at least a decade. That concern reflects Japan's longstanding dependence on the sea for both its military and economic security, especially its dependence upon imported oil. A very real, and growing, sense of threat from piratical attacks to the security of its oil shipments passing through Southeast Asian choke points, however, is but one driver of Japan's maritime security capacity and coalition-building activities in the region. Other incentives for greater Japanese involvement and even leadership to improve regional maritime security involve two related national interests. Firstly, Japan is slowly emerging from the largely self-imposed constraints on its international engagement to become a so-called normal country. Instead of restricting its diplomacy to primarily economic instruments, Tokyo is expanding the levers of its political influence in Southeast Asia to include security-related assistance and a greater tangible presence in Southeast Asian waters.

Secondly, Japan increasingly views the rise of China and Beijing's own growing influence as a threat to Japanese interests. In particular, China's expanding maritime power and naval presence throughout the semi-enclosed seas of East Asia and beyond pose a direct challenge to Japanese security, which is inextricably bound, due to Japan's insular geography, to the sea and the ability of Japan and its American ally to be able to operate unchallenged in that maritime environment. Tokyo's perception of threat from the projection of increased Chinese influence into maritime East Asia from the Asian mainland therefore is a central factor in the decision to pursue instruments of influence befitting a "normal" power, including expanding its own maritime security presence in Southeast Asia.[18]

Early Japanese Proposals

In November 1999, then Japanese Prime Minister Obuchi proposed that ships of the Japan Coast Guard and those of China and South Korea conduct combined patrols of the Malacca Strait and several Indonesian sea lanes with the maritime forces of Indonesia, Malaysia, and Singapore.[19] The inclusion of China and South Korea may have been an attempt to make the scheme seem more "multilateral" and to preempt Chinese opposition. Japanese interests subsequently organized two conferences on piracy and armed robbery at sea held in Tokyo in early 2000. The first, in March, brought together representatives from the government agencies of 14 Asian states, the IMO, and commercial organizations. The resulting "Tokyo Appeal" resolved to "cooperate, devise and implement all possible measures to combat piracy and armed robbery against ships."[20] In April, the second of the two conferences issued a Model Action Plan to combat piracy and sea robbery, although the practical measures for cooperation were limited to information exchange.[21]

Starting around 1996, Japan's National Institute for Defense Studies (NIDS), a research arm of the Japan Defense Agency, developed a concept termed "Ocean Peacekeeping" (OPK). In this concept, "regional maritime forces" would cooperate to form a coordinated, multilateral OPK force to prevent armed conflict at sea, protect marine resources and the marine environment, and facilitate the benign exploitation of the sea by peaceful and lawful sea users. The OPK force would thus ensure "ocean stabilization." Notably, the OPK concept represents an attempt to counter the "creeping jurisdiction" of coastal states. An OPK force would thus seek to carry out maritime-enforcement roles not only on the high seas but also in the exclusive economic zones and archipelagic waters of regional states,[22] a highly unrealistic prospect, considering national sensitivities.

The Japan Coast Guard

The Japan Coast Guard (JCG) has been used as a leading instrument of Japanese security engagement in Southeast Asia. Whereas the political leaders of many Southeast Asian states remain somewhat leery of the Japanese military, given the experience of Japanese aggression and brutality during the Pacific War, the Japan Coast Guard, as a civilian paramilitary force, has become the acceptable face of Tokyo's security cooperation with the region. However, China remains especially suspicious of Japanese maritime security initiatives and missions to Southeast Asia, and consistently opposes what it deems to be anti-China militarism — perhaps a harbinger of things to come in East Asia.[23]

Ships and aircraft of the Japan Coast Guard have been deployed to several Southeast Asian countries on a regular basis since 2000, carrying out patrols, combined exercises, and other engagement and capacity-building activities. Such activities have involved education and training, including training officers from regional coast guard agencies at the Japan Coast Guard Academy; technical and other specialist assistance; and assistance to establish coast guard organizations in states such as Indonesia and Malaysia.[24] A frequent visitor to the region is the 5,200 ton JCG cutter, *Mizuho*, which seems to be a favored vessel for conducting bilateral combined antipiracy exercises in Southeast

Asia and beyond.[25] In November 2004, the *Mizuho* conducted an antipiracy drill with the Indian Coast Guard in the Arabian Sea, the fifth in a series of bilateral exercises between the two forces. Representatives from the Malaysian Maritime Enforcement Agency and Vietnamese Coast Guard observed the exercise,[26] demonstrating the way in which the Japan Coast Guard is taking a leading role in promoting practicable maritime security cooperation in the region.

Another example of JCG activism is its leading role in developing the Asia Maritime Security Initiative 2004 (AMARSECTIVE 2004),[27] which was adopted at a meeting of the Heads of Asian Coast Guard Agencies hosted by the Japan Coast Guard in Tokyo in June 2004. AMARSECTIVE 2004 is another cooperative arrangement aimed at combating piracy and other threats to good order at sea which reportedly "sets out the commitments and responsibilities of coastguard agencies" and promotes further technical assistance and information sharing among the region's coast guards. A further proposal advanced at the June 2004 meeting was to establish a mechanism for enhanced data exchange on ship movements in the region,[28] mirroring the efforts of other groups and individual states to create improved "situational awareness" of at-sea activities in the East Asian maritime environment.

ReCAAP

The Regional Cooperation Agreement on Combating Piracy and Armed Robbery against Ships in Asia (ReCAAP) was first mooted by Japanese Prime Minister Koizumi in 2001 and is a direct descendant of the Tokyo Appeal and Model Action Plan of 2000. It is a legal arrangement adopted in November 2004 of the type mooted by ASEAN and the ARF, which sets out the basis in international law for multilateral cooperation to combat piracy and sea robbery. One of ReCAAP's most interesting features is that it creates an obligation for parties to agree to "make every effort to take effective and practical measures" to implement a request for cooperation from another party to detect and "take appropriate measures, including arrest or seizure" against people, ships, or aircraft involved in acts of piracy or sea robbery consistent with relevant national and international law.[29] ReCAAP's other main function involves the establishment of an Information Sharing Center in Singapore to collect, collate, analyze, and disseminate information on piratical attacks and threats.

ReCAAP will take effect once 10 of the 16 parties have ratified the agreement, although by mid-2005 only four states — Japan, Singapore, Cambodia, and Laos — had even signed it. There remains some doubts over how easy it will be to operationalize, given national sensitivities. Malaysia, for example, is believed to be aggrieved that the Information Sharing Center was established in Singapore and not in Kuala Lumpur, which is already the host to the International Maritime Bureau's Piracy Reporting Centre. Although the agreement currently involves only Asian nations,[30] once it comes into force any state can apply to join.

Tokyo Declaration on Securing the Oceans

The Tokyo Declaration on Securing the Oceans of December 2004 is the result of several conferences organized by the Japanese think tank, the Institute of Ocean Policy (part of the Ship and Ocean Foundation), with funding from the Nippon Foundation. It develops the concept of "Securing the Oceans" as a means of improving the peaceful management of activities at sea, and seems to be similar to the NIDS ocean-stabilization concept sans the OPK force.[31] The Declaration calls for conflict prevention, environmental protection and surveillance, and monitoring and enforcement "systems" to combat threats such as piracy. Additionally, and reflecting Japan's interests and extant contributions to regional maritime security, it also calls for burden sharing by maritime user states and improved capacity building to assist coastal states.[32] Although some national officials took part in developing the Declaration, most participants were academics or think-tank members, suggesting that it will not tangibly influence cooperative behavior by regional states.

American Maritime Security Initiatives

The United States and, in particular, the U.S. Navy-dominated U.S. Pacific Command, has a longstanding role as the guarantor of wider regional security in East Asia. Over the past decade it has had to rejuvenate and modify its role and presence to take account of its post–Cold War strategic posture and priorities, and the changing threat environment. Apart from its bilateral alliance relationships and related military exercise programs,[33] Washington has been active in building capacity and bilateral cooperation between forces of the U.S. Pacific Command and regional militaries and coast guards. The events of 11 September 2001, and the subsequent increased awareness of al-Qaeda–connected terrorist activity in the southern Philippines, including the threat of actual and potential maritime terrorism, has been a spur to American reengagement in Southeast Asia. The intensive use of the Malacca Strait by U.S. Navy and other support and supply ships to feed into Operations Enduring Freedom in Afghanistan and Iraqi Freedom in Iraq is another contributory factor in directing American attention to the area. The U.S. Navy is the traditional guarantor of SLOC security throughout the world, and the increased frequency of reported piratical attacks in Southeast Asian maritime choke points, combined with the tendency to conflate threats from piracy and maritime terrorism, has also been an important driver of American coalition and capacity-building activities in the region. Finally, like Japan, the United States is wary of China's maritime expansion and growing influence in Southeast Asia, and is retuning its Pacific force posture and regional-security cooperation to take account of its increasingly adversarial relationship with Beijing.[34]

A leading instrument of American maritime-security engagement and capacity building in Southeast Asia has been the annual series of bilateral Cooperation Afloat Readiness and Training (CARAT) exercises held since 1995. Each year the U.S. Navy, together with other arms of the U.S. military and the U.S. Coast Guard, undertake CARAT exercises in the region with the navies and other maritime forces of Singapore, Malaysia, Indonesia, the Philippines, Thailand, and Brunei.[35] CARAT focuses on exercising a range of operational contingencies and improving interoperability between American and CARAT partner forces. The growing importance of maritime security concerns has seen an increased focus in recent CARAT exercises on maritime surveillance, search and seizure and antipiracy and counterterrorism drills.[36] The problem of regional piracy and the potential for maritime terrorism thus provide the United States with a real opportunity to advance its security relationships in Southeast Asia through CARAT and to provide meaningful capacity-building assistance.

U.S. Pacific Command also hosts a range of other training, education, and exercise schemes, and forums for multilateral cooperation. Examples of such activity include the International Military Education and Training scheme, which sends officers from Southeast Asian militaries to the United States for education; the Asia-Pacific Center for Security Studies in Honolulu, which also runs courses for officers from the region; Multinational Planning Augmentation Team workshops, which involve command-post exercises to build cooperation and interoperability for various low-level military operations in the coalition or other multinational contexts (such as disaster relief); the Asia-Pacific Area Network and other web-based networks which facilitate communication and information exchange among the region's armed forces; and the annual Chiefs of Defense and Military Operations and Law conferences.[37] Another aspect of U.S. Pacific Command activity worthy of note is the Joint Interagency Task Force (JIATF) West. Although JIATF West's primary focus is to counter drug-related transnational crime in the U.S. Pacific Command's area of responsibility, it also is beginning to play a role in surveillance and other activities to counter other forms of transnational criminal activity in the region such as piracy, including "increasing international maritime security awareness in the Strait of Malacca and its approaches."[38]

RMSI

The Regional Maritime Security Initiative (RMSI) is perhaps U.S. Pacific Command's vanguard project to improve regional maritime security against piracy and other threats to good order at sea. First mooted at the 2003 Shangri-la Dialogue by then-Commander, U.S. Pacific Command, Admiral Thomas Fargo, and outlined in more detail in early 2004, it has continued to evolve into a more substantial concept.[39] Comments allegedly made by Admiral Fargo in March 2004 (and perhaps exaggerated by the media) that the United States was prepared to dispatch U.S. Marines in high-speed vessels to patrol the Malacca Strait created an almost hysterical reaction in Malaysia and Indonesia, which both take any potential threat to their respective sovereignty in the Strait very seriously indeed. The political situation was not helped by Singaporean officials publicly stating their support for cooperative American patrols in the Strait. U.S. officials were required to state explicitly that the United States had no intention of conducting such patrols, while Malaysia gave Singapore a public dressing down.[40]

The RMSI as it presently stands is a cooperative framework that seeks to "synchronize and align maritime security activities of willing nations."[41] Its four main elements are: "increased situational awareness and information sharing"; "responsive decision-making architectures"; "enhanced maritime interception capacity"; and "agency, ministerial and international cooperation."[42] What all that means is that states, on a voluntary basis, would cooperate in improving and fusing surveillance and other data for improved Maritime Domain Awareness; create standard operating procedures between national and other states' agencies for dealing with operational and legal issues arising from enforcement activities; develop the maritime security capacities of regional states to improve enforcement capabilities in their own waters; and developing cooperation between states across various levels of government to improve monitoring and enforcement of illegal activities at sea. Despite the conceptual development, the RMSI remains somewhat vague with regard to specifics and is something of a work in progress. There will also remain some suspicion in certain regional states of any American-initiated scheme, while the technology-focused goal of improved situational awareness, although sound in principle, will remain beyond the capacity of some states, even with financial and technical assistance.

Bilateral and Other Cooperative Security Activity

Perhaps some of the most effective cooperative efforts to combat piracy have involved nonmultilateral forms of cooperation; that is, exclusive arrangements on a bilateral or multinational basis to conduct specific practical measures at sea. The most common form of such cooperation has been cooperative patrolling of sea-border areas. There is a significant number of bilateral schemes or informal cooperation of this nature between many of the coastal states of Southeast Asia,[43] while India, as a local state due to its Andaman Sea possessions, also is developing such arrangements with its neighbors, Indonesia, Malaysia, and Thailand.[44]

It is important to note, however, that such cooperation represents coordinated, not combined (or "joint"), patrols. The Indonesia-Singapore Coordinated Patrols (ISCP) first established in 1992 to combat piratical attacks in the Singapore Strait is the model for this type of activity. Under such arrangements, states coordinate their patrolling activities, share information and otherwise cooperate, but enforcement forces must remain within their own zones of national maritime jurisdiction. The ISCP has had some success in the Singapore Strait, reducing the incidence of piratical attacks to a negligible level. A further agreement in May 2005 established Project SURPIC, a maritime surveillance system which allows the navies of the two states to share a common tactical picture of the Strait to enable a faster and more effective coordinated response to threats.[45] It will involve a tracking station based on the Indonesian island of Batam that will receive data from radar and satellite sources.[46]

However, securing the Singapore Strait is far easier than doing the same for the Malacca Strait, a physically much longer and more difficult proposition. Malaysia and, in particular, Indonesia do not possess the same operational, technological or financial capacity as the Singaporeans to combat piracy in an area historically prone to pirate attacks and political unrest, especially in the Aceh province of northern Sumatra. Indonesia's bilateral coordinated patrol agreements with Singapore and Malaysia were expanded into a trilateral arrangement in July 2004. However, combined patrols with Singapore were explicitly ruled out by both Kuala Lumpur and Jakarta,[47] and the resulting Malaysia-Singapore-Indonesia (Malsindo) Coordinated Patrols remain hampered by political sensitivity over protecting sovereignty and a lack of capacity.

Nevertheless, the Malsindo arrangement is striving to become more effective, and Singapore's Defense Minister, Teo Chee Hean, seems hopeful that Malsindo may eventually overcome political sensitivities and evolve into a genuinely combined operation to secure the Malacca Strait.[48] Efforts are being made to improve Malsindo's standard operating procedures, especially between Indonesia and Malaysia,[49] while the three states will invite Thailand to join the coordinated patrols to improve security in the northern entrance of the Malacca Strait. Furthermore, the arrangement will expand to include aerial patrols in addition to those on the water. It has been suggested that personnel from all four states man aircraft to improve surveillance.[50] If this plan to include personnel from the four states on a single aircraft is actually operationalized, it would represent a significant half step from coordination to combination, at least for surveillance if not actual enforcement.

Contributions from external actors and maritime user states to assist the straits states have generally been welcomed, as long as they do not, in the words of Malaysia's defense minister, "impinge on the territorial integrity and national sovereignty of the littoral states." He has specifically welcomed capacity-building contributions such as training, equipment, and surveillance and data-fusing technologies, including contributions from U.S. Pacific Command.[51] Japan and the United States have been, and are likely to remain, the main outside contributors, although other states may also play a part, including Australia and possibly even China.

One further example of practical defense cooperation to improve maritime security has been the inclusion of maritime interdiction exercises for the first time as part of the Five Power Defence Arrangements (FPDA) in 2004. The FPDA involves Australia, Britain, and New Zealand in the external defense of Malaysia and Singapore. Exercise Bersama Lima [Bahasa Indonesia/Malay for "Five Together," ed.], conducted in the South China Sea in September 2004, demonstrated the heightened concern of all FPDA members with regional maritime security.

Conclusion: To Talk or to Act?

It has been demonstrated that a lack of activity in addressing the problem of violence at sea in Southeast Asia is hardly an issue. Much of that effort, however, has gone into repetitive and redundant talk shops, and rather less upon practical, at-sea cooperation to physically enforce good order on the water. That is not to argue that cooperative security processes are entirely wasteful, only that talking about the problem will not suffice to actually improve the fight against piracy and other violent acts at sea. Ultimately, states must act rather than talk if the seas are to become tangibly safer. Moreover, the most effective cooperation to date has been the result of individual states working together, as in the coordinated patrols, rather than multilateral processes. Initiatives by individual states, especially Japan, Singapore, and the United States, have also been more successful in advancing cooperation to combat piracy and other threats than those initiated in the multilateral context. These states have contributed real capacity-enhancing cooperation, which may yet pay dividends.

Nevertheless, the political sensitivities held especially by Malaysia and Indonesia over sovereignty and sovereign rights at sea may be impossible to overcome, and Indonesia will continue to be the most difficult case to deal with in the Malacca Strait due to its underfunded and underequipped navy. The technological solutions to improved data management, fusion, and sharing, while conceptually relatively simple, will remain difficult in practical terms. And, underpinning local sensitivities in Southeast Asia, an increasingly intense competition among the major powers for influence and strategic advantage in Southeast Asia, especially centered around the rise of China, is likely to complicate any form of multilateral maritime security cooperation in the years to come, despite the shared interest in SLOC and energy security.

Notes

1. All IMO data is based on information available on its web site: www.imo.org/home.asp.
2. The most notable of which include the Convention for the Suppression of Unlawful Acts against the Safety of Maritime Navigation (SUA), 1988; and the International Convention for the Safety of Life at Sea (SOLAS), 1974, plus its amendments, including the ISPS Code. All IMO members were required to comply with the ISPS Code by 1 July 2004. Additionally, there also exists a range of other IMO Assembly resolutions and circulars dealing with aspects of piracy and armed robbery at sea.

3. The regulation applies to all ships of 300 gross tonnage and above used on international voyages, cargo ships 500 gross tonnage and above not used on international routes, and all passenger vessels.
4. The technologies and data involved include electronic charts, AIS, Global Positioning Systems, ship-to-shore communication links, Geographical Information Systems and meteorological information.
5. The participants are the governments of Indonesia, Malaysia, and Singapore, sponsored by the IMO and the Global Environment Facility/World Bank, with active involvement from, *inter alia*, the International Hydrographic Organization, the International Association of Independent Tanker Owners (INTERTANKO) and the International Chamber of Shipping.
6. All APEC data is based on information and reports available on the APEC web site: www.apec.org/apec.html.
7. The International Maritime Bureau's Piracy Reporting Centre in Kuala Lumpur is an initiative of the private sector International Chamber of Commerce.
8. The project is termed STAR BEST (Bangkok/Laem Chabang Efficient and Secure Trade). Another scheme to apply new technologies and processes to improve supply chain security, and which also supports the APEC STAR project, is the private sector Smart and Secure Trade Lanes (SST) initiative.
9. ASEAN, "Work Programme to Implement the ASEAN Plan of Action to Combat Transnational Crime," Kuala Lumpur, 17 May 2002.
10. There are currently 24 participants in the ARF process, comprising the 10 ASEAN states plus Australia, Canada, China, the European Union, India, Japan, both Koreas, Mongolia, New Zealand, Pakistan, Papua New Guinea, Russia, and the United States.
11. "ARF Statement on Cooperation Against Piracy and Other Threats to Security," 17 June 2003.
12. Ibid.
13. Ibid.
14. For details on the WPNS, see Chris Rahman, *Naval Cooperation and Coalition Building in Southeast Asia and the Southwest Pacific: Status and Prospect*, Sea Power Centre and Centre for Maritime Policy Working Paper No. 7, RAN Sea Power Centre, Canberra, October 2001, pp. 29-32. The WPNS currently comprises 22 participant nations: 18 full members and four states with observer status.
15. [Singapore] Chief of Defence Force, LG Ng Yat Chung, speech to the Opening of the 3rd Western Pacific Naval Symposium (WPNS) Multilateral Exercise, Inaugural Sea Exercise and Maritime Security Information Exchange Seminar, Singapore, 18 May 2005. Available at the Singapore Ministry of Defence web site: www.mindef.gov.sg.
16. The Philippines did not even send personnel to observe the sea exercise, although Indonesia and the Philippines both made presentations during the Maritime Security Information Exchange Seminar.
17. For a friendly critique of the ARF, see Tan See Seng et al., *A New Agenda for the ASEAN Regional Forum*, IDSS Monograph No. 4, Institute of Defence and Strategic Studies, Singapore, 2002.
18. Chris Rahman, "The Rise of China as a Regional Maritime Power: Strategic Implications for a New Century," Ph.D. dissertation, University of Wollongong, 2003, pp. 309-321.
19. See "Foot in the Water," *Far Eastern Economic Review*, 9 March 2000, pp. 28-29. For—further background on the various Japanese proposals, see also John F. Bradford, "Japanese Anti-piracy Initiatives in Southeast Asia: Policy Formulation and the Coastal State Responses," *Contemporary Southeast Asia*, Vol. 26, No. 3, December 2004, esp. pp. 488–505.
20. International Conference of All Maritime Related Concerns, Both Governmental and Private, on Combating Piracy and Armed Robbery against Ships, "Tokyo Appeal," Tokyo, 28-30 March 2000, p. 3.
21. Regional Conference on Combating Piracy and Armed Robbery against Ships, "Model Action Plan for Maritime Policy Authorities and Private Maritime Related Concerns to Combat Piracy and Armed Robbery against Ships," Tokyo, 27-29 April 2000.
22. See Susumu Takai and Kazumine Akimoto, "Ocean-Peace Keeping and New Roles for Maritime Force," *NIDS Security Studies*, No. 1, March 2000. For the latest evolution of the OPK concept, see NIDS, *East Asian Strategic Review 2004*, The Japan Times for NIDS, Tokyo, 2004, Ch. 2.

23. Rahman, "The Rise of China as a Regional Maritime Power," pp. 282–284.
24. Ibid., pp. 320–321.
25. Ibid.
26. "India, Japan Conduct Anti-piracy Exercise," *The Hindu*, 5 November 2004.
27. According to the IMO Secretary-General, the Japan Coast Guard was "instrumental" in getting AMARSECTIVE 2004 adopted. See Efthimios Mitropoulos, lecture to the Japan International Transport Institute, 21 October 2004: available at www.imo.org/Newsroom.
28. See "Coastguards Adopt Amarsective 2004," *The Star* online (Malaysia), 28 June 2004.
29. Regional Cooperation Agreement on Combating Piracy and Armed Robbery against Ships in Asia, Articles 10 and 11.
30. The parties to ReCAAP are the ASEAN 10, Japan, China, South Korea, India, Bangladesh and Sri Lanka.
31. Some of the same individuals were involved in developing the two concepts.
32. Institute of Ocean Policy, Ship and Ocean Foundation, "Tokyo Declaration on Securing the Oceans," Tokyo, 3 December 2004, Part II.
33. See, for example, Rahman, *Naval Cooperation and Coalition Building in Southeast Asia and the Southwest Pacific*, pp. 25-28 and 51-53.
34. Rahman, "The Rise of China as a Regional Maritime Power," pp. 325–330.
35. CARAT Indonesia was cancelled in 2003 and 2004 due to a diplomatic conflict between Jakarta and Washington, but recommenced in July 2005.
36. For further detail on CARAT, see the U.S. Pacific Command web site: www.pacom.mil/.
37. See Rahman, *Naval Cooperation and Coalition Building in Southeast Asia and the Southwest Pacific*.
38. Admiral William J. Fallon, USN, Commander, U.S. Pacific Command, statement before the Senate Armed Services Committee on U.S. Pacific Command Posture, 8 March 2005, p. 7.
39. For the full version, see Commander, United States Pacific Command, *Strategy for Regional Maritime Security*, November 2004.
40. See, for example, "U.S. Warns of Terror Attacks on Shipping in SE Asia," *CNSNews.com*, 23 April 2004; "Malaysia Says U.S. Intervention in Malacca Straits Could Create Problems," *channelnewsasia.com*, 11 May 2004; "Some Asean States Cool to U.S. Maritime Security Plan," *The Straits Times*, 13 May 2004; "Straits Threat: Now's Time to Act, Says DPM," *The Straits Times*, 21 May 2004; "Don't Raise Straits Security Issues through Media, Says KL," *The Straits Times*, 1 June 2004; and "Singapore Goes It Alone in Maritime Security Drill," *The Washington Post*, 2 June 2004.
41. *Strategy for Regional Maritime Security*, p. 9.
42. Ibid.
43. See, for example, Rahman, *Naval Cooperation and Coalition Building in Southeast Asia and the Southwest Pacific*, pp. 37–39.
44. See "Malacca Straits Security: Role Seen for Indian Navy," *The Hindu*, 8 September 2004; and "India for Joint Naval Patrols with Indonesia, Malaysia," *newkerala.com*, 11 August 2004. It should also be noted that, during the height of operations in Afghanistan in Operation Enduring Freedom, Indian Navy ships escorted U.S. Navy vessels through the Malacca Strait.
45. "Surveillance System Strengthens Vision on Monitoring Singapore Strait," *Jane's Defence Weekly*, 22 June 2005, p. 16.
46. Dato' Sri Mohd Najib Tun Haji Abd Razak, Deputy Prime Minister and Minister of Defence, Malaysia, "Enhancing Maritime Security Cooperation," speech to the 4th Annual Shangri-la Dialogue, Singapore, 5 June 2005.
47. "Malaysia, Indonesia Rule Out Joint Patrols in Malacca Straits," *channelnewsasia.com*, 1 July 2004.
48. "Joint Patrols of Malacca Strait 'Possible,'" *The Australian*, 6 June 2005.
49. "RI, Malaysia to Discuss SOP for Patrol in Malacca Strait," *Antara*, 2 August 2005.
50. "Thailand May Join Malacca Strait Patrols," *The Jakarta Post*, 9 August 2005.
51. Dato' Sri Mohd Najib Tun Haji Abd Razak, "Enhancing Maritime Security Cooperation."

9

Pirates, Renegades, and Fishermen: The Politics of "Sustainable" Piracy in the Strait of Malacca

J.N. MAK

Introduction

The Strait of Malacca has been regarded as one of the most pirate-infested areas of the world since the 1990s. However, the devastation caused by the December 2004 tsunami off Sumatra brought a lull in piratical activities in the waterway for two months, and users of the Strait were optimistic that the tsunami had crippled the piracy infrastructure for the long term. Instead, the pirates bounced back and carried out a spate of bold, daring hijackings of ships and maritime kidnappings in February and March 2005. The most celebrated or notorious of these was the 14 March attack on the Japanese tug *Idaten*, and the kidnapping of three of its crew. This sudden and violent revival of piracy brought international attention to bear on the Strait. The attack on the Idaten in particular resulted in Japan's launching a diplomatic offensive, together with the International Maritime Bureau (IMB), to put pressure on the littoral states to boost security in the waterway.[1]

The second major development that underlined the apparent vulnerability of the Strait was the June 2005 announcement by Lloyd's Joint War Committee (JWC) that the entire waterway is a zone at risk from "war, strikes, terrorism and related perils." This "war zone" listing resulted partly from a sudden and "massive rise" in the number of kidnap-for-ransom cases and the increasing use of firearms and violence in recent years.[2] The JWC also emphasized that the Malacca Strait would remain on the list "until it was clear that the (security) measures planned by government and other agencies in the area had been implemented and were effective."[3]

Developments such as the JWC listing of the Malacca Strait as a high-risk zone and the international publicity given to piracy in the waterway indicate that the safety of international shipping is given priority as far as Malacca Strait security is concerned. Indeed, the pressure to enhance security in the area has come mainly from the "international community led by China, South

Korea, and Japan."[4] This international perspective is also reflected in recent writings on the Malacca Strait, which invariably point out that nearly a quarter of the world's trade passes thorough the waterway; about 11 million barrels of oil are shipped through it daily and that 60,000 ships transit the Strait annually. This "internationalist" approach to the issue of piracy tends to emphasize the number of incidents taking place in the area. It inevitably focuses on the symptoms or outward manifestation of piracy, that is, the number of incidents that take place over a given period, and the degree of violence and the types of arms used. A natural consequence of such an approach is an emphasis on preventive, prophylactic measures, with the victims of piracy pressing for more maritime patrols and for the littoral states to undertake more stringent measures to suppress piracy. More significant, there have been attempts of late to conflate piracy with terrorism, with Singapore taking a leading role in underlining the dangers of terrorism-cum-piracy.[5]

However, most proponents of this internationalist approach pay little attention to the roots and dynamics of piracy, which highlight another dimension of Malacca Strait piracy that has salience for how policymakers deal with it. Piracy in the waterway is not a phenomenon that started only in the 1990s, becoming especially serious after the 1997 Asian financial crisis, which, by contributing to sharply rising poverty in countries such as Indonesia, led to an increase in piracy in Indonesian waters, as some have claimed.[6] Moreover, the tendency to see the increasing use of firearms and violence by pirates since 2000 as an indication that they are acting more and more like terrorists fails to place piracy in what I argue to be its particular historic and socioeconomic context. In fact, Malacca Strait maritime predators have been attacking local craft, such as barter boats and fishing vessels since at least the 1980s. These attacks are probably more numerous and certainly more persistent and sustained than attacks against international shipping.

This chapter traces the development of one form of this latter-type of piracy — maritime predations against a Malaysian fishing community. By undertaking an empirical analysis of the piracy-fishing nexus through a case study of the most important fishing community in Malaysia, that of Hutan Melintang situated along the Malacca Strait coast, this paper provides a richer understanding of how this form of maritime predation developed over more than three decades in response to both economic and technological changes in Malaysian trawling in the Strait. The analysis yields two main findings that have salience for how the piracy problem could be addressed.

The first, and most important, is that maritime predation is highly adaptive to changing circumstances. It is also clear that all the various groups of predators operate from and are probably based in Sumatra. Piracy or maritime predation against fishermen is very much an activity that is rooted in economics rather than ideology. As Malaysian fishermen developed their fishing techniques by investing in larger boats and fishing farther offshore, the arms used by maritime predators changed from knives and machetes to powerful firearms, while the modes of attack developed from simple robberies, to ship hijacking to kidnap-for-ransom over the years. And as the costs of Malaysian fishing trawlers and their gear escalated over the years, the pirates proportionately increased the amount of ransom, compensation, and protection money demanded. In short, the actions and reactions of both the pirates and the fishing community have created a self-sustaining transnational underground market. A second finding is that weak or poor governance in the outlying areas of Sumatra has allowed maritime predations against fishermen to become well-organized and to persist for over 30 years. Most significantly, not only are "common" criminals involved in hijacking fishing vessels and extorting ransoms from their owners, but all the fishermen, fishing traders and equipment suppliers interviewed for this study are unanimous that rogue elements from Indonesian maritime enforcement agencies are also involved in maritime predation. Indeed, they claim that maritime predations by these rogue elements in 2005 have become more persistent and serious than those committed by pirates.

This study is important because it provides new insights into the dynamics of Malacca Strait maritime predation. The paper's findings suggest that such predations have been a sustainable economic activity, deeply embedded in eastern coastal Sumatra with long historical roots. This calls for a broader set of measures to tackle the "piracy" problem beyond the current prophylactic emphasis adopted. The primary root of the maritime raiding problem in the Malacca Strait is the lack of effective government along the Sumatran coast coupled with the absence of viable, legitimate economic opportunities for coastal communities. Much like the drug eradication programs worldwide, measures to weed out piracy must include provisions for viable alternative employment or economic opportunities for coastal communities. In addition, governance reforms in Indonesia to address corruption in law enforcement and other public agencies and to provide more effective public administration in the outlying areas are equally vital. If poor governance has allowed the maritime-predation problem to persist for more than 30 years, including the participation of rogue officials, then the present emphasis on more efficient and better coordinated patrols at sea is addressing only part of the problem. The fact that there are no pirate bands based on the Malaysian side of the Strait (leaving aside ship hijacking rings which contract out the actual hijackings) suggests that economic development and effective administration and governance are key factors in addressing piracy in the Malacca Strait.[7]

Research on Malacca Strait Maritime Predations

There has been a great deal of controversy over the definition and use of the terms piracy, political piracy, sea robberies, and terrorism. While the IMB considers "piracy" to include all crimes committed at sea and in port,[8] the

1982 United Nations Convention on the Law of the Sea (UNCLOS) confines piracy only to crimes committed on the high sea by private individuals for private gain.[9] From the point of view of the fishermen of Hutan Melintang, however, such semantic squabbles are immaterial because they consider themselves to be victims of predatory acts, irrespective of how these acts are defined, committed by both private criminals and rogue elements of the Indonesian enforcement agencies. Thus this paper will use the more inclusive term "maritime predations" to cover attacks by both criminals and rogue elements of enforcement agencies.

Studies on piracy tend to be of three types. The first looks at piracy through socioeconomic, and historical lenses, while the second are historical accounts of colonial attempts to suppress and wipe out piracy in the region. The writings of James Warren best illustrate the attempts to explain the socioeconomic origins of piracy from a historical perspective,[10] while Owen Rutter's book on the sea robbers of Malaya first published in 1930, as well as Tarling's work on piracy and politics are more straightforward historical accounts.[11]

The third type, represented by most current writings on piracy in the region, tend to adopt a more policy-oriented and prescriptive stance.[12] However, I argue here that while the problem of maritime predations in the Malacca Strait has generated a slew of policy-oriented writings, the issue has so far not been studied in depth. It is only in the last few years that a handful of scholars have embarked on a number of serious primary studies. This ongoing work should generate new insights into the problem of piracy. Until these findings are made public, the understanding of piracy in Southeast Asia in general and the Strait of Malacca in particular is still somewhat superficial. For instance, most of the policy studies to date have depended mainly on secondary sources, such as reports from national enforcement agencies, and in particular, on the IMB for data on piracy incidents. In this regard, the IMB has done a commendable job of keeping a record of reported attacks, usually on commercial international ships. However, attacks on local craft, such as fishing boats, barges and small barter craft, are seldom reported to the IMB. In this sense, the IMB, through no fault of its own, has been underreporting maritime predations in the Malacca Strait. Nevertheless, numbers are not everything. In fact, a fixation on numbers can distract researchers from developing deeper insights into, and a better understanding of, the dynamics of modern piracy.

Tracing maritime predations against a particular community over a significant time period is important because it provides a historical perspective and understanding of piracy — linking the past with the present. In addition, it can provide insights into how piracy is sustained and therefore highlight how to more effectively contain it. Historically, piracy flourished in areas where state control and boundaries were disputed and state governance and administration weak or nonexistent. Second, for piracy to flourish over the long term, a distinct market economy had to be established. Successful maritime raiders required strong logistical and administrative bases, usually underpinned by a de facto political structure. The third point of note is that punitive expeditions by themselves seldom succeeded in ending maritime predations. It is therefore not enough to destroy pirates and their bases. The political and economic vacuum left behind must be supplanted by effective alternative economic systems and administrative structures that people can trust and identify with. The state, in short, must become a new and legitimate patron for the local populace, which previously had depended on the piratical market economy and owed allegiance to the piratical "administration." The persistence of predations against Malaysian trawler fishermen therefore prompts us to ask whether such acts of piracy are uncoordinated, spontaneous episodes of opportunistic predation, or whether, as with history, they reveal the existence of a sustainable, underground market economy centered on the fishing-piracy nexus.

Introducing the "Silent Victims": Background of the Hutan Melintang Fishing Community

The Hutang Melintang fishing community was chosen as the initial case study for the analysis of long-term maritime predations in the Malacca Strait for two reasons — its economic significance as the primary focus of the fishing industry in Malaysia and its historical experience as a victim of maritime predations in one of the two major piracy zones in the Malacca Strait. Of the three major fishing areas on the west coast of Peninsular Malaysia, Hutan Melintang is the most important in terms of total tonnage and value of fish landings and the number of fishing boats and trawlers based in the area.[13] Hutan Melintang has grown steadily as the most important base for Malacca Strait trawlers because of its more than 60 jetties that are accessible 24 hours a day, good loading and unloading facilities so that trawlers do not have to wait to land their catches, and an efficient infrastructure to support the fleet. Hutan Melintang has a population of 200,000 people,[14] and more than 900 fishing boats from the west coast of Peninsular Malaysia are based there, of which almost 400 fish regularly offshore in the middle and northern approaches of the Strait. When we consider that these 400 trawlers stay out for 10-day stretches, their contribution to the density of Strait traffic is considerable.[15] It is also the one fishing community that has suffered the most from maritime predations since the 1970s. Since the year 2000, maritime predations have averaged one a month.

Geographically, pirate groups operate in two general areas in the Strait. The first group is based in the Riau archipelago in the southern end of the waterway. There the narrows near Singapore force ships to slow to a few knots in the interests of safety, thereby exposing them to boarding by pirates. The second zone of operations for pirates is in the northern end of the Strait, with most of the pirates based in Aceh province in north Sumatra.[16] In this zone, transiting tankers and other large ships are able to maintain relatively high cruising speeds, making them relatively more difficult to board. Thus, it is Malaysian fishermen, or more precisely, the fishing community of Hutan Melintang that has remained the primary prey and most regular source of income for the pirates of north Sumatra.

For this case study of the Hutan Melintang fishing community, selective face-to-face interviews with members of the community who had been victims of maritime predations, or who have an overall understanding of the problem, were deemed the most feasible. Comprehensive lists of questions in English and Mandarin were sent to community leaders in order to prepare them for the interviews as well as for them to suggest other members of the community who could be interviewed. All the interviews were conducted in the local Chinese dialect as all boat owners and fishing traders were Chinese. The following information was sought in each interview:

Total number of attacks each year.
Frequency, number, date, and time of piracy attacks.
The types of attacks and weapons used.
Identity of the predators.
Whether the attackers belonged to any organized groups.
Number of attackers in each incident.
Losses incurred by the victims in each incident.
Injuries and or fatalities sustained by the victims.
Changes, if any, in the types and patterns of attacks.
When and whether the attack was reported to the Malaysian authorities.
Subsequent follow-up action if any by the authorities.
How piracy/maritime predations have affected both the community in general and particular individuals.
How the community has coped with piracy/maritime predations in the past, the present, and in the expected future.
What kinds of help the community has received from the local authorities and local enforcement officials — past and present.
What the community thinks should and can be done about piracy/maritime predations.

The year 2004 was spent primarily in laying the groundwork and identifying key players to be interviewed in Hutan Melintang and its surroundings. Altogether, more than a dozen key players in the industry were identified and comprehensively interviewed in the first 10 months of 2005. They included heads of fishery associations, fishery traders, equipment suppliers, boat builders, and taikongs (skippers of trawlers). In addition, numerous informal or incidental, unplanned interviews were also conducted. Perhaps the most important players are the more than 80 fishery traders of Hutan Melintang. They play a pivotal role in the industry, and constitute a hub around which a whole host of activities revolve. They underwrite loans given to boat owners by shipyards and equipment suppliers, and continue to finance the building of new boats. These fishing traders of the Malacca Strait have been performing this vital service since the 1960s. In return for their services, these traders not only receive all the fish caught by members of their "syndicates," but also at a predetermined price. The following account of piracy in the Northern Malacca Strait is based on these primary interviews, supplemented by interviews with scholars and policy analysts. In addition, a great number of secondary sources were consulted, such as newspaper reports, books, journals, and papers posted on the Internet, especially for information on the situation in Sumatra. However, further primary research would be needed in Sumatra to complete this particular account of Malacca Strait maritime predations, especially the socioeconomic factors that have allowed maritime predations to exist for more than three decades.

Changing With the Times: The History of Sustainable Maritime Predations

The Strait is relatively shallow for most of its 500-nautical-mile length, making it eminently suitable for bottom trawling. The primary fishing area of the Hutan Melintang fishermen is located between the middle to the northern entrance of the Strait, which contains some of the richest fishing grounds of the waterway. The trawlers also operate near Sumatra, because the Malaysian-Indonesian maritime boundary agreements of the early 1970s had, from the view of Kuala Lumpur at least, given it control over a maritime space that extended close to the Acehnese coast. It was at the end of the 1970s and early 1980s when the fishermen of Hutan Melintang area first ventured some distance out to sea and onto the Malaysia-Indonesian border. This was the result of two factors. The first was that by the mid 1970s, fish stocks along the west coast had been severely depleted by "mini-trawlers" of about 10 Gross Registered Tons (GRT) powered by 10–24 horsepower engines.[17] In addition, the Fisheries Licensing Policy was introduced in 1981 by Malaysia to restrict the larger fishing boats and their gear to the outer limits of the fishing zones in an attempt to protect inshore, traditional artisanal fisheries.[18] The fishers of Hutan Melintang were therefore increasingly attracted to the richer fishing grounds towards the middle and north of the waterway, near Sumatra, which meant investing in larger boats and more sophisticated equipment.[19] As a consequence, the average size of trawlers in Hutan Melintang grew from between 10 and 15 GRT in the 1970s to 20 to 25 GRT by the 1980s. By 1997, there were 510 trawlers of above 30 GRT licensed in Perak, out of which 305 were more than 40 GRT.[20]

These boats not only fished farther from the coast, but stayed out longer, with fishing trips lasting from a week to 10 days. Since they were now fishing near the Sumatran coast, the trawlers found themselves sharing the fishing grounds with small Indonesian "longliners" or kapal rawai — boats using long lines of baited hooks normally manned by a crew of two. Some of these longliners, with three or four pirates hidden aboard, would approach the trawlers under the pretext of asking for bait or water. Once alongside, the pirates, armed with parangs (machetes), would rush the trawler and rob the crew. After the Malaysian trawlers refused to stop for the longliners, the pirates changed tactics. They would attack at night when the trawler was anchored and its crew asleep. However, the Malaysian fishermen soon became wary of the sound of approaching Indonesian longliners whose engines apparently made a distinctive throbbing sound. They would thwart the pirates by switching on all the trawler lights. The maritime predators therefore resorted to drifting down to their prey using the prevailing currents, with their engines switched off. The late 1980s therefore saw the introduction of radars aboard Malaysian trawlers, not so much for navigation as for providing warning of approaching craft at night, especially pirate craft.[21]

Guns, Goons, and Hijackers

The 1990s saw the increasing use of firearms by Indonesian maritime predators. The increasing use of assault rifles and other powerful firearms during this period is not surprising given the revival of the Gerakan Aceh Merdeka (GAM) armed rebellion in the northern Sumatra province towards the end of the 1980s which led to an influx of weapons into Aceh. Besides the use of firearms, the late 1980s and early 1990s also saw the advent of ship hijacking. This was the result of the increasing value of trawlers, and the fact that fishermen began to carry less and less cash to deal with contingencies at sea. At one point in the 1980s, taikongs or trawler skippers used to carry several thousand ringgit to deal with contingencies such as emergency repairs. But by the 1990s, most taikongs would only have a few hundred ringgit on board.

Moreover, by the 1990s, the cost of a trawler had escalated to about RM1 million each. Whereas the mini-trawlers of the 1970s were small, converted barter boats, the modern Hutan Melintang trawlers are generally about 26 meters long. The bare, wooden hull alone costs about RM300,000. Engines, trawling gear, winches, ice making machines and electronics add another RM500,000. Thus modern, state-of-the-art Hutan Melintang trawlers cost from RM800,000 to RM1 million each [approximately US$210,000 to 275,000, ed.]. These trawlers require just a crew of four to operate.[22] The relatively huge outlay to launch a new trawler did not escape the attention of maritime predators — both pirates and renegades. They realized that a far more lucrative trade would be to hijack boats for ransom instead of merely robbing the boats of cash, fuel, catch, and equipment. The first hijacking incident occurred around the early 1990s, when a boat was hijacked near Sumatra and RM150,000 demanded for the release of the trawler. The ransom was finally reduced to RM30,000 and the boat owner told to pay the amount into a certain bank account in Medan. Two weeks after paying the money, the boat returned to Hutan Melintang. All in all, the whole incident took three weeks from the hijacking to the return of the trawler.[23]

This pattern was to repeat itself. However, instead of paying the ransom in Medan or Belawan in Sumatra, there would be various permutations, ranging from cash transfers in the Strait itself, ransoms paid in Indonesia by the business partners of trawler owners to the relevant parties, to payments into various Indonesian bank accounts. "We really don't know how the payment is made. All we are concerned about is our safety," said the taikong of a Hutan Melintang trawler.[24] By the late 1990s, the "standard" ransom for a new, well-equipped trawler was around RM100,000 [approximately US$27,500, ed.]. In fact, the "going rate" for the return of a boat would be about 10 percent of its cost.[25] Nevertheless, sometimes things do not go as planned. In the late 1990s, two Hutan Melintang fishermen were kidnapped and taken to Aceh province together with their trawler while the non-Chinese crewmen were released. Although a ransom was negotiated and paid, the trawler was found by the Indonesian military which put it under surveillance. The two hostages and their boat could not therefore be released. They spent two weeks with their captors before the two hostages escaped and were taken by the Indonesian military to the local military headquarters in Lhokseumawe. They were then flown to Medan before finally flying to Kuala Lumpur. In this instance, the pirates could not keep their part of the bargain although they did their best. Although the boat owner got his boat back after a year, he had to spend a considerable amount repairing the trawler, besides losing the ransom money.[26]

The Twenty-First Century and the Age of Maritime Kidnappings

A different and more troubling development in maritime predations in the northern end of the Strait began to emerge in the year 2000, and became especially marked after 11 September 2001. This was the trend to kidnap skippers or taikongs of the fishing vessels for ransom rather than hijacking the boat. This development resulted partly from increased maritime patrols in the Malacca Strait in the wake of 9/11. More significant, however, was the renewed Indonesian military offensive against GAM beginning in May 2003. This included a tight maritime blockade which made it especially hard for pirates to hijack ships and escape with their prize. For instance, in February 2004, an Indonesian navy ship intercepted and sank a tug purportedly hijacked by members of GAM 14 nautical miles from Pulau Berhala, southeast of Medan.[27] In the third week of February 2004, an Indonesian navy ship sank a hijacked fishing boat off Tanjung Balai Asahan in northern Sumatra. A total of 11 fishermen survived and were rescued, and three alleged GAM members captured.[28] The pirates were apparently well-armed with rocket-propelled grenade launchers and assault guns. What the brief report did not say was that the pirates had earlier hijacked two Indonesian fishing boats and a Hutan Melintang trawler.

They then placed all 11 fishermen including the four fishermen from Hutan Melintang, into one fishing boat while a few pirates made off with the trawler that was intercepted and later sunk.

Another technological development that facilitated kidnap-for-ransom was the widespread use of cell phones in the 1990s. This made negotiations between kidnappers and the families of their hostages direct and rapid. Kidnappings had occurred so regularly that the Hutan Melintang community and the pirates had a "standard operating procedure." The pirates would invariably kidnap the taikong, who is the most valuable member of the crew and usually a member of the tightly-knit Hutan Melintang Chinese community. The Thai or Myanmarese crewmen are hardly ever kidnapped. The going rate for the release of the hostage again depends on the value of the boat he was taken from. As in the case of boat hijacking, the going rate for a ransom is more or less understood to be around 10 percent of the value of the trawler. Once a sum is agreed upon, the mode and date of paying the ransom is then decided. If everything goes smoothly, the hostages would be released within five days. Negotiations rarely drag beyond two weeks.

Maritime Trojan Horses of the Strait

The heightened vigilance on the part of transiting ships in recent years has also made it more difficult for maritime predators to attack large commercial craft. Many of these ships have high freeboards and often maintain antipiracy watches in the Strait. Again, the predators showed great adaptability by first taking over Malaysian trawlers to use as maritime Trojan horses to attack larger foreign vessels. The most celebrated of these cases was the attack on the Japanese-registered tug *Idaten* on 14 March 2005 when it was towing a laden barge off Penang. The pirates, armed with assault rifles and grenade launchers, used a Hutan Melintang trawler to board and kidnap the *Idaten's* Japanese captain, chief engineer, and a Filipino engineer.[29] The fact that two Japanese were kidnapped aroused a great deal of media attention, and much play was made of the fact that a Malaysian fishing boat was involved in the piracy-kidnapping. The registration number of the boat PKFB1223 was noted, and four days after the attack, the Malaysian police detained the Malaysian taikong and his four Thai crewmen for possible complicity in the incident.[30] The crew were cleared and released by police by Saturday, 19 March 2005.[31]

According to the fishing trader responsible for PKFB1223, the trawler left Hutan Melintang on 11 March 2005. The fishing boat was hijacked the day before the Idaten attack, and the crew robbed of their valuables and 2,000 liters of fuel. However, the taikong was told by the pirate leader that the boat would be used to attack a more valuable prize. The next day, the *Idaten* was spotted and the pirate leader ordered the taikong to ram the tug three times altogether. Finally, after the pirates fired a few shots, the tug came to a stop. After kidnapping the three crewmen of the *Idaten*, the pirate leader ordered

PKFB1223 to sail for the Sumatran coast. The pirates apparently slipped through a maritime cordon because the enforcement agencies were on the lookout for a pirate ship, and not an innocuous Malaysian fishing boat.[32] The Malaysian boat and crew were apparently released by the pirates on Tuesday, 15 March. But instead of sailing home to Hutan Melintang right away to report to the authorities, the taikong decided to continue with his fishing trip. The seriousness of the situation did not strike him apparently because one of his Hutan Melintang colleagues had been involved in a similar event in December 2004. This was when another Hutan Melintang trawler was hijacked in the north of the Malacca Strait, and together with another fishing boat, was used by maritime predators to attack the Singapore-registered tug *Ena Sovereign* on 15 December, 2004. The pirates fired at the tug, forced it to a stop and ransacked it before fleeing with the captain and chief engineer. The skipper of the trawler involved in the *Ena Sovereign* attack apparently carried on fishing after the piracy incident without anyone creating a fuss.[33] The *Ena Sovereign* and *Idaten* incidents illustrate how inured to maritime muggings the fisher folk of Hutan Melintang have become, and indeed how much it has become part of the fabric of their daily lives.

Politics, Boundary Disputes and Renegades: The Chain of Corruption

The fact that the main fishing ground of the Hutan Melintang fishermen is located in the middle and northern approaches of the Malacca Strait exposes them not only to piratical attacks, but also to predations by what one author has called the "lost commands" or "renegades" of Indonesian enforcement agencies.[34] The Malaysian-Indonesian continental-shelf boundary — agreed upon in two agreements in 1969 and 1971, juts out as one side of a triangle from the Malaysian coast off Perak towards the Acehnese coast. Besides the continental-shelf agreements, Malaysia and Indonesia also concluded a territorial sea boundary agreement in 1970. However, this agreement covers only the southern end of the Malacca Strait, stopping at about two degrees north.[35] Indonesia and Malaysia, up to the present moment, have not concluded a territorial sea agreement covering the northern end of the Malacca Strait, nor have they initialed any Exclusive Economic Zone (EEZ) agreement.

The Malaysian position, embodied in the country's Peta Baru (Malay for: "New Map") published in 1979, is that both the EEZ line and the continental-shelf boundary line are identical, that is, the Peta Baru uses the concept of a single maritime boundary. Haller-Trost has expressed the view that Malaysia's position that the delimitation of extended maritime zones "should be identical where the distance does not exceed 200 nm" is entirely reasonable for the Malacca Strait and that a new single maritime boundary "will probably eventuate."[36] Nevertheless, Indonesia has been pressing since 1998 for a new maritime delimitation in the Strait, since it feels that the 1969 continental shelf boundary agreement is not "equitable" and has been quietly challenging Malaysian jurisdiction in the Strait, especially over fishing rights in the northern end of the Strait.[37] This is because Jakarta recognizes only the continental shelf boundary, which gives Malaysia the right to exploit the resources of the seabed and subsoil, but not that of the water column. In contrast, a country's EEZ would endow the country "with sovereign rights for the purpose of exploring and exploiting, conserving and managing the natural resources, whether living or non-living, of the waters superjacent to the sea-bed and of the sea-bed and its subsoil," including of course fish.[38]

Thus Malaysian fishermen have been facing a dilemma. On the one hand, they are assured by the Malaysian authorities that they are fishing in the Malaysian fishing zone which coincides with the Malaysian continental shelf area. On the other, they face constant harassment, both officially and unofficially, by Indonesian maritime enforcement agencies whenever they go beyond Malaysian territorial waters because of the current Malaysia-Indonesia maritime dispute. This boundary dispute gives rogue enforcement officials from Sumatra extra leverage to use against the fishermen.

According to the Hutan Melintang community, as long ago as the 1970s, corrupt elements of Indonesian enforcement agencies would harass Malaysian fishermen in the Strait and extort RM200 to RM300 each time. However, as the trawlers began to increasingly fish in the disputed maritime zone towards the northern end of the Strait, the extortions changed in scope and scale. Renegade officials, after detaining a boat and crew, would demand that its owner settle the issue quietly, otherwise the boat would be officially detained for illegal fishing in Indonesian waters. In the early 1990s, before the widespread introduction of mobile phones and direct negotiations, a fishery trader became the de facto chief representative and negotiator for the fishers of Hutan Melintang. Sources close to him said that in the early 1990s, he traveled at least once in two months to Medan to obtain the release of yet-to-be officially detained fishing boats. He paid money into Indonesian bank accounts on at least two occasions, but for the most part, he negotiated the amount of "ransom" and then arranged for the date and mode of "ransom" to be handed over. In this sense, there was not much difference between the "lost commands" and the pirates, even as to the amount of ransom to be handed over — usually about 10 percent of the cost of what the boat held — which ranged from RM30,000 to RM40,000. Eventually, by the turn of the century, the amount demanded had increased to RM50,000 to RM100,000 per trawler. How serious are the predations of the "lost commands"? According to one community leader in Hutan Melintang, "renegades" are responsible for about half of all maritime predations against them in number, but their demands for payoffs for trawlers seized or arrested have gone up steeply of late. He attributed the increasingly unreasonable payments demanded by the rogue elements primarily to the ongoing maritime disputes between Malaysia and Indonesia, which escalated after the International Court of Justice awarded the islands of Pulau Sipadan and Ligitan in the Celebes Sea to Malaysia in December 2002.[39]

What happens if the fishing trader or taikong cannot, or refuses to pay off the "lost commands"? The personal experience of the chief negotiator himself is telling. In early 2002, two of his trawlers, one skippered by his own son, were seized by an Indonesian enforcement agency for illegally fishing in Indonesian waters off Sumatra. For various reasons he failed to pay the sum required to "settle" the case. The result was that both his boats were officially detained in Medan, and the eight crew members arrested. He spent the next 12 months commuting between Hutan Melintang and Medan, during which time he was involved in a complex process of payoffs ranging from court officials to prison warders. His son was sentenced to an 18-month jail sentence, which he negotiated to 10, and finally 8 months. He claimed that in addition, he had to pay extra to ensure that his son was properly fed in prison, and that he was incarcerated in a cell — equipped with an electric fan — with just three other prisoners. In any event, the fishing trader estimated that the detention of his boats and crew cost him nearly RM250,000. If he had settled the case unofficially at that time, he estimated he would have had to pay RM60,000.[40]

While these allegations regarding the judiciary in Sumatra might be hard to believe, it must be noted that that more than one criticism of the corruptible nature of the Indonesian judiciary has been made. To cite a 2004 article by Indonesia Corruption Watch:

> ... court mobsters is a systematical corruption. The court mobsters include all subjects in the court of law. In criminal court, corruption involving police, clerk, lawyer, prosecutor, and judge and also officers in the jail institutions. In the citizen and commercial court, the court mobsters also involve the lawyer, clerk and judge.[41]

The essence of the article was that corruption among certain elements of the Indonesian judiciary had become systemic and entrenched, and while the post-Suharto decentralization process had enabled court institutions to be more independent, "corruption in court has also become independent and uncontrollable" at the same time.[42]

And who will guard us from the Guards?

The allegations by the Hutan Melintang fishermen that rogue elements of Indonesian enforcement agencies are also involved in maritime predations are given credence by a July 2005 incident. On 25 July 2005, the Malaysian official news agency Bernama reported that a Royal Malaysian Navy (RMN) ship had rescued three Hutan Melintang fishing boats detained by Indonesian marine police in Malaysian waters.[43] The report alleged that:

> … shortly after the boats were detained about 33 nautical miles west of Kuala Selangor at 8:20 am, the chairman of the Hutan Melintang Fishermen's Association in Perak, Kee Keo Poh reported the incident to RMN's Armada Operations Centre (AOC) at RMN's base in Lumut.[44]

The Malaysian navy vessel KD Kinabalu was dispatched to the scene, and its commanding officer managed to convince the Indonesian marine police involved that the Malaysian trawlers had not encroached into Indonesian waters. The trawlers were then released. However, Indonesia subsequently claimed that the Malaysian boats had been fishing illegally in Indonesian waters, and pressed the Malaysian government to return the Malaysian fishermen to Indonesia to "face the law."[45] In reply, the Malaysian embassy in Jakarta questioned why the Indonesian Marine Police officers found on board one of the Malaysian fishing boats were not in uniform, why these officers had "taken goods belonging to the fishermen including handphones," and why they had used the Malaysian fishing boat to tow the Indonesian Marine Police vessel.[46] Indonesia countered instead that KD Kinabalu's commanding officer had obviously violated Indonesian sovereignty, and demanded that he "be surrendered to them for further action."[47] The Malaysian navy chief replied that the RMN commanding officer had acted properly and legitimately, and moreover "the Malaysian fishermen were within Malaysian waters, that is 38 nautical miles west of Kuala Selangor, and the Indonesian marine police had no right to detain them."[48] This latest incident again illustrates how vulnerable Malaysian fishermen are in the Strait of Malacca. Besides being preyed on by pirates, they are also pawns in the great maritime boundary game played between Malaysia and Indonesia.[49]

The recent introduction of the politics of maritime sovereignty into the Malacca Strait apparently has had a very negative spillover effect for the fishermen of Hutan Melintang. Several fishery traders and taikongs claimed that Indonesian enforcement officers are invariably aggressive and violent when they arrest the trawlermen for allegedly crossing into Indonesian waters nowadays.[50] More significantly, it has also disrupted "market forces," with the price for the return of seized boats going up sharply in the last few months of 2005. From a "standard" 10 percent of the value of the boat, renegade officials now demand up to RM400,000 to "settle" the return of a trawler. The owner of two boats seized in September 2005 paid a total of RM600,000 — RM400,000 for a large trawler, and RM200,000 for a smaller boat. He had three options: pay the "ransom," write off boats and crews completely, or pay the official fine with his crews serving jail terms. Even if he paid the official fine in court, his boats would be returned months later in a state of disrepair, and all removable gear would have disappeared. "At least by paying the RM600,000 his boats and crew are back already, earning income to cover his losses," said the trader. According to him, the unofficial fines have skyrocketed because Indonesian enforcement agencies are under pressure from Jakarta to increasingly assert Indonesia's maritime sovereignty.

These recent incidents also highlight the problem of identifying the key maritime predators in the Malacca Strait. Are they the "lost commands" of the Indonesian armed forces, maritime mafia networks, common pirates, or are they the separatist guerrillas of Aceh? One analyst, Schutzer, suggests that GAM might have been both directly and indirectly involved — indirectly because the military offensive and maritime blockade in northern Sumatra against GAM which began in 2003 stretched the resources of the Indonesian navy so thin that it allowed pirates the freedom to maneuver elsewhere in the Malacca Strait.[51] But more than that, he claims that the Indonesian armed forces not only lacked the "political motivation" to stop piracy, but there was the "disturbing possibility that renegade navy and coast guard units are behind some of the attacks."[52] Malaysia's official position, however, is that the Indonesian military is not involved in piracy. "It is not, at least officially, a problem legitimised by the military's leaders," said Mr Iskander Sazlan of the Maritime Institute of Malaysia.[53] He added that while Malaysian enforcement agencies have apprehended members of the Indonesian enforcement agencies for certain illegal activities in Malaysian waters, such incidents are regarded as individual breakdowns in the Indonesian chain of command. No official protests are therefore lodged for the sake of ensuring continued cooperation between the two countries, as well as not to undermine the credibility of the Indonesian enforcement agencies.

However, the managing director of the Singapore shipping firm Eastern Navigation, owners of the *Ena Sovereign*, is convinced that GAM played a major role in maritime predations. In an outspoken interview with Singapore's Business Times, Mr. Tan Ser Giam recounted how he spent two "hellish weeks" negotiating for the release of two kidnapped crew members of the tug in 2004. He was convinced that "GAM has a big network" of informants and sympathizers in the region."[54] Similarly, the IMB claimed that the rash of maritime kidnappings after June 2003 bore all "the hallmarks of the Free Aceh Movement."[55] But for the fishermen of Hutan Melintang, the biggest threat comes from rogue elements of the Indonesian enforcement agencies. "We can at least negotiate with pirates, and they are very reasonable people," claimed a taikong. "In contrast, the renegades use a great deal of violence, and you cannot negotiate with them anymore."

Calculating the Cost of Maritime Predations

Whoever the culprits, what all the fishermen of Hutan Melintang are certain of is that they have suffered an average of one maritime predation each month over the last five years. During this period, the price for operating in the Malacca Strait has been increasing slowly but surely, to the point that pirates demand ransoms of RM30,000 to RM100,000, while rogue Indonesian officials demand up to RM300,000 for the return of seized boats. According to most sources interviewed, the monthly costs paid out by the Hutan Melintang community to predators total RM150,000 to RM200,000.

In addition, a maritime protection racket has also surfaced since 2000. The issue was highlighted by a Malaysian Fisheries Department official in May 2004 when he told the press that pirates had been issuing monthly "safe fishing certificates" to Malacca Strait fishermen at a price of between RM300 to RM400 per vessel, depending on size.[56] The Malaysian Fisheries Department's Protection of Resources branch chief, Abdullah Jaafar, also referred to "three bands of pirates from a neighbouring country" being involved in the racket, and that 80 percent of the approximately 200 boats affected were paying up.[57] Mr. Abdullah also alleged that the racketeers issued official-looking "fishing certificates" in the name of the "Aceh Sumatra National Liberation Front." He speculated that the protection racket involved the collaboration of three parties — the pirates, some corrupt Indonesian officials, and the Free Aceh Movement (GAM).[58] Mr. Iskander Sazlan of the Maritime Institute of Malaysia commented that a "mafia-like" network was most likely involved. Each boat had to pay roughly RM3,000 as the initial "entry fee" to join the protection ring.[59] According to the head of the Hutan Melintang Fishermen's Association, the protection racket is of fairly recent origins and appeared to be quite effective. Others involved in the fishing trade however, said the protection racket did not work at all because too many pirate bands were involved. Yet another observer, Sew Leong of Klang, alleged that some members of the Indonesian enforcement agencies used to impose their own toll on fishermen found trawling in Indonesian waters. Instead of impounding the boat or asking for a huge ransom, they expect the taikong to pay a toll based on the number of days he would be fishing in that particular area. The fee is about RM100 a day, again depending on the size of the boat. [60] It therefore appears that Malaysian fishermen have to pay, one way or another, unofficial "taxes" for fishing in the Strait. A rough calculation therefore indicates that maritime predations, protection rackets, and unofficial tolls must cost the Hutan Melintang fishing community about RM200,000 to RM250,000 a month (at 2004 prices).

As such, the crucial question is to what extent the Hutan Melintang fishing community has been economically crippled by these predations. And also, how did the community manage to cope with the problem for more than 30 years? To get a sense of the degree maritime predations have impacted the community, we need to be able to estimate the economic and financial size of the fishing industry. For a start, we know that there are about 400 large trawlers and purse seiners operating from Hutan Melintang. Each boat goes to sea twice a month, with each trip averaging 10 days. Each large trawler uses up to 1,000 liters of diesel fuel a day, which at 2003 prices, would mean an expenditure of RM1,000 per fishing day. Each boat has four crew members, and the skipper is usually a Malaysian. The other crew members are usually

Thais or Myanmarese who are paid a daily wage of RM30 to RM50.[61] Altogether, inclusive of food and other incidentals such as ship overhauls and maintenance, the daily operating expenditure of a large trawler would be in the region of RM1,500 a day. This translates to RM15,000 per fishing trip, or RM30,000 each month for a large trawler. Given that there are about 400 large trawlers in Hutan Melintang, the operating expenditure of this fishing fleet alone would be about RM12 million a month. The cost of maritime predations would add at most, another RM250,000 to RM300,000 to monthly fishing costs, or an extra 2 to 2.5 percent. It can be argued that while a 2.5 percent monthly "tax" is very high, it is not so high that it would cripple the fishing industry. For comparison, an increase in diesel fuel cost of 20 sen per liter (from RM1 ringgit to RM1.20) would cost the Hutan Melintang fishing fleet an extra RM1.6 million each month, based on the use of 1,000 liters of fuel per day for 20 working days for 400 vessels. This represents an increase of more than 13 percent of monthly operating costs.[62]

In this regard, while members of the Hutan Melintang community see maritime predations as a problem, they do not regard it as the greatest threat to their industry. What they are most concerned about is increasing operating costs, especially the price of diesel fuel. The problem of increasing fuel costs is compounded by the import of cheaper fish from neighboring countries including Indonesia, Thailand, and Vietnam.[63] They are convinced that if fuel prices keeps rising and the government continues to allow the import of cheap fish, the fishing industry in Hutan Melintang will be doomed. From their point of view, piracy is a threat that they have learnt to cope with. However, escalating fuel costs and cheaper (and also higher quality) fish imports are variables beyond their control. Unlike maritime kidnappings and hijacks, fuel costs and imported fish prices are not subject to negotiations by members of the Hutan Melintang community. For instance, an Ipoh-based equipment supplier said that the newer and more expensive Hutan Melintang trawlers are playing it safe by fishing in undisputed Malaysian waters. "Only the older and less valuable trawlers now risk fishing near or in Indonesian waters," he said.[64]

Indeed, all the taikongs and fishing traders have made contingencies for kidnappings and other forms of maritime predations. Most of them are members of "tontine" groups, where individuals contribute an agreed sum of money each month to a pool. If any member of the tontine is hit by pirates, he is allowed to withdraw the total monthly pool to help him pay the ransom. In addition, fishing bosses and traders are also expected to help out, even if their boats are not hijacked, or their crews kidnapped. Finally, the fish processing factories in the Hutan Melintang area also contribute or lend money, since their own viability as an industry depends on a steady supply of fish to the factories. The entire community therefore responds to any hijacking or kidnapping, and it is an entirely self-help effort.[65] Nevertheless, there is a positive note with regard to sustainable maritime predations and sustainable fisheries. It can be argued that without the presence of the maritime predators, the fishing grounds of the northern Malacca Strait would have been cleaned out long ago by Thai and Malaysian trawlers. Maritime predations have therefore indirectly contributed to fishery management. However, the question remains for the Hutan Melintang fishing community as to whether the increasingly tough stance taken by the renegades and their demands for huge ransoms will continue. If so, then maritime predations will eventually constitute a major impediment to the trawling industry. But many fishery traders believe that the renegades themselves know that their current demands cannot be sustained by the market.

Conclusion: The Politics of Sustainable Piracy

As this chapter has tried to illustrate, maritime predations with Malaysian fishermen as their primary victims have been endemic in the Malacca Strait for more than three decades. The majority of analysts also agree that the roots of the problem lie in Sumatra, and indeed that virtually all the maritime predators are either Indonesian, or based in Aceh. It is obvious that the issue is both systemic and economic in nature. Both predators and prey know the rules of long-term survival. The fishermen know the necessity of paying up, while the predators understand that unreasonable demands for ransom or protection fees would financially ruin the fishing industry on which they depend for a steady source of income. But the problem is not only that of dealing with criminals and mafia-like networks. Maritime predations, as I have tried to show, involve criminals as well as renegade officials in Sumatra. Fundamentally, it boils down to the problem of governance and widespread official corruption. It is highly telling that current Indonesian President Susilo Bambang Yudhoyono recently observed that official corruption is alive and well in Indonesia. Despite seven years of attempted reforms after the fall of Suharto:

> … the ills of corruption, collusion and nepotism are still happening and with the handing over of financial autonomy to the regions, we can also feel the tendency for irregularities in the regions.[66]

Indeed, the Indonesian decentralization process has led not only to more autonomy for agencies such as the military and the police, but also to a greater lack of accountability. "Institutions in Indonesia have assumed such a degree of autonomy that no one can question what they are doing, much less interfere," said a former senior official in the Suharto government. "Currently, there is no mechanism in place to ensure transparency and accountability." He explained that corruption would be almost impossible to stamp out because not only are Indonesian officials badly underpaid, but corruption has become deeply entrenched and systemic. With decentralization and an increasing lack of transparency, corruption has become worse.[67] In short, the "interstitial seams between the 'sinews' of state power"[68] have opened wider with decentralization, giving piracy more opportunity to become more entrenched and flourish as an alternative source of economic power to challenge state control in Sumatra. The latest move by Indonesia to decentralize policing functions, including the management of maritime security, from the central government to the provinces will diffuse power away from Jakarta to the local level even more.[69]

With specific reference to Aceh province, a 2004 report alleged that both GAM and Indonesian military officials were profiting from the then-ongoing conflict, since "illegal loggings, road taxes and weapons sales are run by both sides and easier to operate in a conflict situation than in a peaceful situation."[70] In addition, the military in Aceh has also been accused of running maritime protection and other rackets.[71] Another study of governance in Indonesia concluded that the decentralization process had turned into a disintegrative process because no legal and economic groundwork had been put in place before provincial autonomy was granted, leading to a "culture of corruption that pervades every level of government."[72] Moreover, many studies have highlighted the problem of growing poverty in Aceh. A 2005 UNDP study noted that, while poverty in Aceh had increased by 239 percent from 1980 to 2002, the level fell by 47 percent overall for the rest of Indonesia.[73] The paper also noted the need to reduce the horizontal inequalities between native Acehnese and migrant Javanese, as well as the need to end economic and social discrimination against the former. Equally significant, the number of large and medium-sized industries in Aceh declined steadily from 128 in 1996 to only 67 in 2002.[74] The problem of the existence of dual economies, with the Acehnese being left out of mainstream development, therefore, must be addressed.[75]

Thus, with corruption apparently well entrenched in the provinces including Sumatra, enhancing patrols in the Malacca Strait can control piracy — but only at enormous costs. Maritime patrols are at best, defensive measures. Moreover, the issue of making multilateral patrols more effective by allowing hot pursuit across maritime boundaries is complicated by the existing maritime border disputes between Malaysia and Indonesia. The next problem is that of controlling and disciplining the rogue elements of the Indonesian military and turning them from maritime predators into enforcers and upkeepers of law and order in the Strait. This will not be easy given the problem of decentralization and increasing autonomy for the outlying regencies and provinces. Next, the issue of wiping out the mafia networks must be tackled. Unfortunately, it is not only the common criminals that are part of these networks. It appears that the tentacles of these criminal networks have spread among certain elements of the Indonesian administration itself, and the Indonesian armed forces (Tentara Nasional Indonesia or TNI) "accustomed to a diversity of revenue streams, may even accept a portion of the proceeds as pay-off."[76] Thus, to eliminate piracy would require the reform, if not overhaul, of the Indonesian administrative and bureaucratic structure. It is not merely a question of paying administrators enough to live decently. The challenge is to introduce a complete change in mindset so that bureaucrats will not regard rent-seeking and economic exploitation as the norm for climbing up the administrative ladder, As President Yudhoyono put it succinctly, " ... the tendency for (officials to want) to be served is still felt in various state institutions and bodies, even though the duty of the state apparatus is to serve the people."[77]

This is the great challenge for Indonesia. As for the issue of piracy and terrorism, the experience of the fishing community of Hutan Melintang seems to show that piracy and maritime predations has existed as an underground, illegal economic activity for more than 30 years. It has not even crossed the minds of the victims that terrorism or religious factionalism will become part of the problem. "All the pirates want is money. Pay them, and you will be fine. They have so far, not deliberately harmed us and I am convinced they will not, provided we live and left live," said a fishery trader.[78] But what will be the consequences of the peace treaty between GAM and the Indonesian government? It seems to me that since maritime predations have been primarily an economic and not a political activity, peace will not bring an end to the predations. In fact, pardoned former members of GAM might find it necessary, if not easier, to cooperate with both renegade officials, lost commands, and criminals in mounting attacks against shipping in the Strait unless they have recourse to alternative legitimate sources of income.

Moreover, the maritime predators of Sumatra have shown that they are immensely resilient. Approximately 8,000 fishermen and 7,000 boats were lost along the northeastern coast of Sumatra during the December 2004 tsunami. In addition, 1,085 fishermen were killed and 2,600 boats destroyed on the east coast.[79] Despite this devastation, maritime predations nevertheless "bounced back" in 2005. As such, it would be a little more than hopeful to believe that the GAM-Indonesia peace accord will help to curb piracy. What is required is, as I have argued, a complete revamp of the administrative and economic structure of Indonesia so that officials will no longer directly or indirectly, participate in criminal activities in any sphere — land, sea, and air. More important, the people in Sumatra must be integrated within viable socioeconomic structures. Thus, while much publicity has been given to the initiative by the four Malacca Strait littoral states — Indonesia, Malaysia, Singapore, and Thailand — to launch the joint "eyes-in-the sky" air patrols in September 2005 to enhance security in the Strait, what is required in addition would be an "eyes on the ground" program to enhance good governance, transparency, and a viable economic system along the Strait.

This chapter has used a case study of the Hutan Melintang trawling community to provide insights into the problem of maritime predations in the Malacca Strait. As such, it has presented the point of view of only one particular segment of victims, and hence a somewhat onesided picture. The next logical step would be to embark on a survey of the coastal population and administrators of Aceh province to further extend the insights into the causes and sustainability of maritime predations. Yet this paper points to the importance of a highly adaptive group of maritime predators that have targeted a specific group of Strait users for more than a generation. The longevity of this type of predation has been most likely facilitated by a combination of circumstances in Aceh province, including a breakdown in administration, widespread poverty, and a sense of grievance by the local population for being left out of mainstream development by Jakarta. Finally, the major predators, according to the Hutan Melintang community, are renegade law enforcement officers. What has sustained the existence of these "renegades"? Is it part of an attempt to supplement official incomes, or has it developed into a sociopolitical and economic system in its own right? Will the decentralization trend in Indonesia result in weaker governance, or will it strengthen state authority in areas that had provided bases for piratical operations since the 1970s? There is thus a need to conduct research in the coastal regions of Aceh to give us new explanations and deeper insights into the roots of maritime predations involving both criminals and renegade officials.

Notes

1. "Recent Attacks Prompt International Pressure to Secure Malacca Straits," The Jewish Institute for National Security Affairs (JINSA), 15 July 2005, http://www.jinsa.org/articles/articles.html/function/view/categoryid/1701/documentid/3054/history/3,2360,655,1701,3054, accessed 5 September 2005.
2. Catherine Zara Raymond, "Malacca Straits: A High-Risk Zone?" *IDSS Commentaries* (52/2005), 4 August 2005, pp. 1–2.
3. ICS(05)28, Annex 2, JWC Briefing Malacca Straits. 016/0805.
4. "Recent Attacks Prompt International Pressure…".
5. See JN Mak, "Securitising Piracy in Southeast Asia: Malaysia, the International Maritime Bureau & Singapore," Paper submitted for the Ford Foundation Programme on Non-Traditional Security Issues, Singapore, 3-4 September 2004. See also Graham Gerard Ong, "Ships Can Be Dangerous, Too: Coupling Piracy and Terrorism in Southeast Asia's Maritime Security Framework," in Derek Johnson and Mark Valencia (eds.), *Piracy in Southeast Asia: Status, Issues, and Responses, Institute of Southeast Asian Studies*, Singapore 2005, pp. 45–76.
6. Bronson Percival, *Indonesia and the United States: Shared Interests in Maritime Security*, United States—Indonesia Society (USINDO), June 2005, p. 8.
7. The last and most notorious pirate operating from the Malaysian side of the Strait was based in the large mangrove area of the Larut-Matang district north of Hutan Melintang. Known popularly as the "sea king," this Chinese pirate of the 1960s was never caught but just faded quietly away.
8. ICC International Maritime Bureau, *Piracy Report (1 January–31 December 1992)*, pp. 2.
9. Many states are unhappy with the UNCLOS definition because the requirement under Article 101 that the "acts be motivated for private ends restricts this definition to attacks committed with the intent to rob, and also limits the ability of states to claim universal jurisdiction over politically motivated attacks." In addition, it also restricts the right of hot pursuit into territorial waters. See Erik Barrios, "Casting A Wider Net Addressing the Maritime Piracy Problem in Southeast Asia," *Boston Law College Review*, 28 January 2003, http://www.bc.edu/schools/law/lawreviews/meta-elements/journals/bciclr/28_1/03_TXT.htm, accessed 9 September 2005.

10. See for example James Francis Warren, *Iranun and Balangingi: Globalization, Maritime Raiding and the Birth of Ethnicity*, Singapore University Press, Singapore 2002.
11. Owen Rutter, *The Pirate Wind: Tales of the Sea-robbers of Malaya*, Oxford University Press, Singapore, 1986; Nicholas Tarling, *Piracy and Politics in the Malay World: A Study of British Imperialism in Nineteenth-Century South-East Asia*, Donald Moore Galleries, Singapore 1963.
12. See Derek Johnson and Mark Valencia, eds., *Piracy in Southeast Asia: Status, Issues, and Responses, Institute of Southeast Asian Studies*, Singapore 2005. Of the eight articles in the book, seven examined possible options and prospects for regional cooperation to solve the piracy problem.
13. Perak trawlers have accounted for at least 25 percent in terms of tonnage of all fish landings in Malaysia since 1995, beating even Sabah. See the Annual Fisheries Statistics, various years. http://agrolink.moa.my/dof/Statistics, accessed 5 July 2005. The three fishing zones in Peninsular Malaysia are centred on Kuala Kedah in the northern state of Kedah, Hilir Perak with Hutang Melintang as the focus in the central state of Perak, and Parit Jawa in the southern state of Johor.
14. WTW Property Market 2004: Perak, http://wtw.com.my/modules.php?name=News&file=print&sid=68, accessed 20 August 2005; *Population Census, Department of Statistics Malaysia Year 2000,* http://www.jphpk.gov.my/English/populasi.html, accessed 20 August 2005.
15. Interviews, 2005.
16. Stefen Eklof lists three piracy-prone areas in the Straits. Besides the northern and southern portions of the Strait, he considers the waters east of south Sumatra as a third area. Stefan Eklof, "Piracy in Southeast Asia: Real Menace or Red Herring?" *Japan Focus*, 2 August 2005. http://www.japanfocus.org/article.asp?id=351, accessed 2 Sept. 2005.
17. John G. Butcher, *The Closing of the Frontier: A History of the Marine Fisheries of Southeast Asia c. 1850 2000* Institute of Southeast Asian Studies, Singapore, 2004, p. 206.
18. K. Kuperan Viswanathan et al., "Technical Efficiency and Fishing Skill in Developing Country Fisheries: The Kedah, Malaysia Trawl Fishery," *IIFET 2000 Proceedings*, p. 2.
19. The correlation between trawler size, equipment and yield was confirmed by a 1993–1999 Indonesian survey of catch sustainability and Catch Per Unit Effort (CPUE) of Indonesian trawlers in the northern end of the Strait of Malacca. The study concluded that the CPUE for boats of more than 70 GRT increased by more than 200 percent, probably indicating that the increased range, more powerful gear and engines and additional electronic equipment of these larger boats gave them a decided advantage over smaller trawlers. The study also concluded that Sumatran waters were still rich in fish. The CPUEs for demersal species (bottom dwelling fish) during the survey period for each category of boat did not decrease, indicating that fish stocks were sustainable. See Kiagus Abdul Aziz, "Analysis of commercial catch per unit effort data of trawl fisheries in Indonesian exclusive economic zone of Malacca Straits," Makalah Falsafah Sains (PPs 702), Program Pasca Sarjana / S3, Institut Pertanian Bogor, January 2002, http://rudyct.250x.com/sem1_012/kiagus_a_aziz.htm.
20. Table 2, "Malaysia: Number of Licensed Fishing Vessels by State and Tonnage Class, 1997," Information on Fisheries Management in Malaysia, FAO April 2001, http://www.fao.org/fi/fcp/en/MYS/body.htm, accessed 25 April 2005.
21. Interview fishery trader, Hutan Melintang, 2 October 2005.
22. Interview with manager of marine engine firm, Ipoh, 1 September 2005. See also "Tried and True: Malaysian Fishermen Doing Fine with the Familiar," Cummins hottips 264, 27 July 2004. http://www.haig-brown.com/hottips/hotip264.htm, accessed 18 September 2004.
23. Interview with fishery trader, Hutan Melintang, 12 August 2005.
24. Interview with *taikong*, Hutan Melintang, 2 October 2005.
25. Interview with head of Hutan Melintang Fishery Association, 2 April 2005.
26. Interview with head of Hutan Melintang Fishery Association, 8 April 2005. Indonesian fishermen were apparently also kidnapped for ransom by pirates during this period. In August 2002, six Indonesian fishing boats and their 46 crew were reportedly kidnapped and US$88,000 demanded for the release of each boat. In May 2004, the North Sumatra Fishery Office estimated that 8,000 of the 12,000 fishing boats in north Sumatra were laid up because of the piracy threat. Jakarta Post, 10 May 2004. cited in Stefan Eklof, "Political

Piracy and Maritime Terrorism: A Comparison between the Southern Philippines and the Straits of Malacca," paper presented at the Workshop on Maritime Security, Maritime Terrorism and Piracy in Asia, 23 September–24, Institute of Southeast Asian Studies, Singapore.

27. "Hijacked Tug Sunk by Indonesian Navy," Associated Press, February 14, 2004.
28. "Missing Tug and Barge Feared Hijacked," Maritime Protective Services Newsletter, Week of February 25, 2004, http://www.mpsint.com/newsletter/02292004.html, accessed September 4, 2005.
29. "Attacks work of same pirates, Malaysia and Indonesia launch joint op," Star, 16 March 2005.
30. "Malaysia detains Thais and Malaysian over Japanese tugboat attack," AFP-Channel News Asia, 18 March 2005. http://www.channelnewsasia.com/stories/afp_asiapacific/view/138022/1/.html, accessed 25 March 2005.
31. "Pirates release fishing boat used in Malacca Strait attack," Asahi Shimbun, 19 March 2005. http://www.asahi.com/english/Herald-asahi/TKY200503190163.html, accessed 20 August 2005.
32. "Marine Police intensifies patrols in Malacca Straits," Bernama, 24 March 2005.
33. Interview with trawler *taikong*, 23 August 2005.
34. John S. Burnett, *Dangerous Waters: Modern Piracy and Terror on the High Seas*, Plume Book, New York, 2003, chapter 11, pp. 161–75.
35. R. Haller-Trost, *The Contested Maritime and Territorial Boundaries of Malaysia: An International Law Perspective*, Kluwer Law International Ltd, London 1998, p. 23.
36. R. Haller-Trost, op. cit., pp. 30, 32.
37. R. Haller-Trost, op. cit., p. 29. Many experts in maritime boundary issues have pointed out that the "inequitable" maritime boundary in the Straits agreed on in 1969 was the result of a trade-off between Malaysia and Indonesia. Indonesia agreed that Malaysia could use two offshore islands — Pulau Jarak and Pulau Perak — as turning points for its continental shelf line in return for Malaysian support of Indonesia's attempts to gain international recognition for its archipelagic baseline system which faced great opposition at that time from the maritime powers. See Haller-Trost, op. cit., p. 29; Dino Patti Djalal, *The Geopolitics of Indonesia's Maritime Territorial Policy*, Centre for Strategic and International Studies, Jakarta, 1996, pp. 115–124. At a meeting to discuss the origins of the Peta Baru, Malaysia's legal and policy makers of the 1960s and early 1970s attributed the shape of the Peta Baru, and its delimitations, largely to Malaysia's then decision to support Indonesia's archipelagic claims in the United Nations. See Maritime Institute of Malaysia (MIMA) Report on "Defending our Final Frontier: A History of Malaysia's Maritime Negotiations and Claims," Kuala Lumpur, 9 September 2003
38. UNCLOS Article 56 para 1(a).
39. Interview with managing director of Teluk Intan boat yard, 23 August 2005.
40. Interview with fishery trader, 23 August 2005.
41. Indonesia Corruption Watch, "Research of Lifting the Lid 'Judicial Mafia'," 15 June 2004. http://www.antikorupsi.org/eng/mod.php?mod=publisher&op=viewarticle&artid=6&PHPSESSID=9cccaf6572dc01f1f5b8a8b3105d2bcf, accessed 3 September 2005.
42. Ibid.
43. "RMN Comes To The Rescue Of M'sian Fishermen," Bernama 25 July, http://www.bernama.com/maritime/news.php?id=147047&lang=en, accessed 20 August 2005.
44. Ibid.
45. "Malaysia Says Fishing Boat Did Not Encroach Into Indon Waters," Bernama, 29 July 2005, http://www.bernama.com.my/bernama/v3/news.php?id=147653, accessed 20 August 2005.
46. Ibid.
47. "Navy Not Handing Over Officer To Indonesians," Bernama, 1 August 2005, http://www.bernama.com/maritime/news.php?id=148034&lang=en, accessed 20 August 2005.
48. Ibid.
49. The Malaysian Foreign Minister said in March 2005 that his Ministry would check on reports that 25 Malaysian fishermen had been detained by Indonesia for encroaching into Indonesian waters. He had been informed by Malaysian sources, however, that these fishermen had been fishing within Malaysian waters. "Wisma Putra probes report on fishermen's detention," Star, 26 March 2005.
50. Interviews Hutan Melintang, Oct. 02, 2005.

51. Jamie Schutzer, "Piracy in Indonesia," November 30, 2003, p. 8, http://www.sais-jhu.edu/bwelsh/JamiePolicyPaper.pdf, accessed 4 September 2005.
52. Schutzer, op. cit., p. 9.
53. Personal interview, Kuala Lumpur, 20 July 2005.
54. Business Times, Ibid.
55. "Aceh rebels blamed for piracy," BBC News Online, 8 September 2005, http://news.bbc.co.uk/2/hi/asia-pacific/3090136.stm,accessed 12 December 2003; "MALACCA STRAITS: Armed piracy increasing in Aceh - News Alert from the IMB," Statement issued by the International Chamber of Commerce, 24 June 2004.
56. "Fish only if you have Certificates," The New Paper Online, 18 May 2004, http://newpaper.asia1.com.sg/, accessed 20 May 2004.
57. "Fishermen forced to pay protection money to pirates," Utusan Malaysia, 16 May 2004, http://www.utusan.com.my/utusan/content.asp?y=2004&dt=0517&pub=Utusan_Express&sec=Home_News&pg=hn_09.htm, accessed 4 Sept 2005.
58. "Fish only if you have Certificates," op. cit.
59. Telephone interview, Kuala Lumpur, 17 August, 2005.
60. Series of personal interviews, Klang, February 2005.
61. Indonesian crewmen are *verboten* as far as the Hutan Melintang community is concerned. This is because they can take over their trawler and escape easily to Indonesia. Thai and Myanmarese crewmen, on the other hand, have a long and slow voyage ahead of them if they decide to mutiny.
62. The Malaysian government announced on 6 September 2005 that the price of diesel fuel would continue to be sold to fishermen at RM1 a litre, compared to the public price of RM1.28. "Diesel now RM1 a litre for fishermen," Star, 9 September 2005.
63. Imported fish and fish products rose from 230,000 metric tons in 1990 to 323,000 metric tons in 2000 in Malaysia. Of the total tonnage imported in 2000, Indonesia and Thailand accounted for 227,000 metric tons, or 46.7 percent of imports. Source: Annual Fisheries Statistics, various years. In 2003 "trash fish" accounted for 32 percent of all capture fisheries in Malaysia. Significantly, trawlers contribute about 80 percent of all landings of low-value trash fish on the west coast of Peninsular Malaysia between 1973 and 2003. See Che Utama Che Musa and Ahmad Adnan Nuruddin, "Trash fish production and national fish feed requirement in Malaysia," Paper presented at the "Regional Workshop on Low Value and 'Trash Fish' in the Asia-Pacific Region," Hanoi, Vietnam, 7-9 June 2005.
64. Interview with manager of marine engine firm, Ipoh, 1 September 2005.
65. Interview with trawler *taikong*, 2 October 2005.
66. "Indonesia President Says Little Progress on Reform," AFP, 23 August 2005. http://sg.news.yahoo.com/050823/1/3ufjx.html, accessed 7 September 2005.
67. Interview with former senior Indonesian official, Singapore, 24 August 2005.
68. Eric Tagliacozzo, "Kettle on a Slow Boil: Batavia's Threat Perceptions in the Indies Outer islands, 1870–1910," *Journal of Southeast Asian Studies* 31, no. 1. March 2000, p. 74, cited in Adam J. Young, "Roots of Contemporary Maritime Piracy in Southeast Asia," in Derek Johnson and Mark Valencia (eds.), op. cit., p. 15.
69. See Joshua Ho, "Managing the Peace-conflict Continuum: A Coast Guard for Singapore?" *IDSS Commentaries* (86/2005), 28 November 2005, p. 2., http://www.ntu.edu.sg/idss/publications/Perspective/IDSS862005.pdf, accessed 30 November 2005.
70. Kerry McCormack, Saori Ishida, and Nathan Hara, "Aceh: Negotiating Substantive Issues: Briefing Packet for the Indonesian Government Delegation," March 2004. www.publicinternationallaw.org/areas/peacebuilding/simulations/Aceh/FinalAcehIndonesia.pdf, accessed 30 August 2005.
71. Lesley McCulloch, "Greed: the silent force of the conflict in Aceh," University of Deakin, Melbourne, October 2003, http://www.preventconflict.org/portal/main/greed.pdf,accessed 29 September 2005, p. 17.
72. Donald E. Weatherbee, "Governance in Southeast Asia: The Good, the Bad, and the Ugly," in Yoichiro Sato (ed), *Growth and Governance in Asia*, Asia-Pacific Center for Security Studies, Honolulu, 2004, p. 185., www.apcss.org/.../GrowthGovernance_files/Pub_Growth%20Governance/Pub_Growth%20%20Governance%20ch14.pdf.
73. Graham K. Brown, "Horizontal Inequalities, Ethnic Separatism and Violent Conflict: The Case of Aceh, Indonesia," Human Development Report 2005, Occasional Paper 2005/29, UNDP Human Development Report Office 2005, p. 4.

74. Number of Establisments (sic) Large and Medium Manufacturing in Nanggroe Aceh Darussalam, 1996–2002. Source: BPS-Statistics of Nanggroe Aceh Darussalam.
75. Anthony L. Smith, "Aceh: Democratic Times, Authoritarian Solutions," New Zealand Journal of Asian Studies 4, 2 (December, 2002), p. 87.
76. Jamie Schutzer, op. cit., p. 9.
77. "Indonesia President Says Little Progress on Reform," op. cit.
78. Interview Hutan Melintang, 8 April 2005.
79. "Rebuilding boats may not equal rebuilding livelihoods," CONSRN *(Consortium to Restore Shattered Livelihoods in Tsunami-Devastated Nations)* Policy Brief No. 1, World Fish Center, 2005. http://www.worldfishcenter.org/news/CONSRN_PolicyBrief1.pdf.

10

Piracy and Maritime Terrorism: Naval Responses to Existing and Emerging Threats to the Global Seaborne Economy

ROBERT SNODDON

Much has been written in the media, and there have been many works of both fiction and nonfiction, about piracy. An equal number, if not more, have been written about terrorism. Both subjects raise interest levels when reported in the media. When both these "scourges" of modern society are linked together, the world sits up and takes notice. Piracy has been on the increase for over a decade. Acts of piracy are being reported on an almost daily basis in both regional press articles and in the maritime trade publications. Type "maritime piracy" into an Internet search engine and the scale of the problem is readily apparent. Type in "maritime terrorism" and the results are equally impressive. But there have been fewer recorded maritime terrorism events that have actually taken place. Those that have occurred have been particularly lethal, and the incidents have spurred governments into taking direct action, whereas reported acts of piracy appear to spur governments only to pontificate about who the perpetrators are. In some areas piracy is considered an annoying activity that is ignored in the hope that, sooner or later, it will go away.

In Southeast Asia, the area most affected by it, there is a considerable amount of exposure about piracy in the regional press, which occasionally makes its way into the world media. On occasion, piracy and terrorism are linked together, and not without good cause. When pirates attack a vessel using automatic weapons, take hostages, and commit murder, it is sometimes difficult to know whether to view the attack as an act of terrorism or an act of piracy.

In the maritime domain, the distinction between terrorism and piracy has become narrow and distorted. Certain terrorist groups have both the capacity and opportunity to conduct pirate attacks in order to obtain revenue. However, there are many in the maritime trade, both seafarers and policy makers, who are quick to label pirate attacks as maritime terrorism. Pirate attacks and maritime terrorism have a lot in common; both have used high speed boats, often two or three per attack, each carrying personnel armed with a sophisticated array of automatic weapons. The attack in January 2004 on an Indonesian flagged product tanker, MV *Cherry 201*, was conducted by members of the Free Aceh Movement (GAM). This group is an internationally recognized terrorist group, but the event was recorded as a pirate attack. With piracy in the Indonesian archipelago and in particular the Malacca Straits at an all time high, it is probable that much is actually maritime terrorism as opposed to piracy. It can also be considered maritime armed crime, when committed inside territorial waters.[1]

Maritime terrorism may possibly be more prevalent than is actually reported because of incidents similar to the attack on MV *Cherry 201*, being labeled as piracy. Normally when maritime terrorism is mentioned the attacks on the USS *Cole*, MV *Limburg*, and the *Superferry 14* are the ones that immediately come to mind. There are some who would prefer piracy to be labeled as maritime terrorism because it allows government funds to be channeled into funding maritime security projects that otherwise would have to be funded by a law-enforcement budget. Notwithstanding that, how would you know that pirates attacking a ship are those motivated by political ideals and are part of a group of extremists intent on causing an economic downturn in the maritime markets?

In November 2001, two months after the 9/11 attacks, the International Maritime Organization (IMO) resolved to review measures and procedures to prevent acts of terrorism which threaten the security of passengers and crews, and the safety of ships. The result was the introduction of the International Ship and Port Security (ISPS) Code, developed by the IMO's Maritime Security Committee (MSC). Within its framework, the code was also designed to help reduce acts of piracy and maritime armed crime. Although the regulation addresses all threats to ships at sea, the fight against piracy and robbery rests with the contracting governments who should ensure security for ships operating in their maritime domains. The ISPS code also identified a new timetable for the fitting of Automatic Identification Systems (AIS). AIS would be a compulsory fit on ships of 300 gross tonnage and upward involved in international trade, cargo ships of 500 gross tonnage and upwards not involved in international trade, and on all passenger ships irrespective of size.[2] Ships were required to fit AIS not later than the first safety-equipment survey after July 2004. Ships fitted with AIS will be required to have it operational at all times, except when international agreements permit it to be off. Along with AIS, safety alert systems will be fitted, which would enable vessels to instantly report attacks by terrorists and pirates, identifying where the vessel is located.

Despite these advances in maritime security, attacks by pirates have been on the increase. Reported maritime terrorist attacks are rare by comparison, although as mentioned before, they may well be contributing to the increase in piracy. A maritime attack on the Northern Arabian Gulf Oil Terminal (NAGOT) in April 2004 was thwarted because of the vigilance of U.S. naval and Coast Guard units monitoring vessel traffic in the restricted areas surrounding the facility. The new regulations introduced by IMO would have done little to prevent this attack, as the vessels in question, dhows and small boats, are not included in the IMO security measures.

As we look at maritime security now, we can see that the ISPS code, and the fitting of AIS and reporting systems to alert on piracy attacks are in place. This demonstrates that the maritime industry has been proactive in making the maritime domain safer for vessels and seafarers. But despite these efforts, piracy attacks continue unabated, and are increasing in frequency. So where do the navies of the world and other law-enforcement agencies stand, and what have they done to prevent both piracy and maritime terrorism? But before we deal with these questions, a definition of both piracy and (maritime) terrorism is in order.

Piracy

Statistics from the Piracy Reporting Centre of the International Maritime Bureau (IMB) in Kuala Lumpur, Malaysia, show that acts of piracy are increasing in certain geographical areas. Since 1990, there was a marked increase in reported cases of piracy. This figure rose steadily until 1995 when the figure suddenly increased dramatically and continued to rise unabated until 2001.[3] The figures continue to rise even now, though the rate is somewhat slower. This could be put down to some key factors. The Piracy Reporting Centre in Kuala Lumpur, Malaysia, is using more advanced reporting procedures, allowing an easier reporting method, including reports by e-mail. Also, vessel operators and crew are more aware of the situation and are reporting even minor acts of theft directly to the IMB center. By doing this, crews are freed from the burden of bureaucracy that accompanied a piracy report to a local authority. But are all the reported incidents piracy?

For the reader it depends on which definition of piracy one uses, because depending on which definition is used, it can be seen that the majority of incidents reported are not piracy, but maritime armed crime and petty theft. The IMO and IMB statistics also show that certain regions are becoming more susceptible to piracy than others. Currently, West Africa, the Horn of Africa, the Malacca Straits, South China Sea, Bangladesh, and the Indonesian Archipelago are considered to be those areas where attacks are most likely to occur. These regions have also seen significant internal conflicts, which may have resulted in some acts of piracy being branded as terrorism.

But what is piracy? Acts of piracy tend to be generalized, and include maritime armed crime. The majority of maritime armed crime takes place in territorial waters, and is not, in the true definition of the word, piracy. For statistical purposes, the IMB defines piracy and armed robbery as:

> An act of boarding or attempting to board any ship with the apparent intent to commit theft or any other crime and with the apparent

intent or capability to use force in the furtherance of that act. This definition thus covers actual or attempted attacks whether the ship is berthed, at anchor or underway. Petty thefts are excluded, unless the thieves are armed.

The following definition of piracy is contained in article 101 of the United Nations Convention on the Law of the Sea (UNCLOS). "Piracy consists of any of the following acts":

- Any illegal acts of violence or detention, or any act of depredation, committed for private ends by the crew or the passengers of a private ship or a private aircraft, and directed: on the high seas, against another ship or aircraft, or against persons or property on board such ship or aircraft; against a ship, aircraft, persons or property in a place outside the jurisdiction of any State
- Any act of voluntary participation in the operation of a ship or of an aircraft with knowledge of facts making it a pirate ship or aircraft
- Any act inciting or of intentionally facilitating an act described in sub paragraph (a) or (b)

It is believed that the IMB definition is more favorable for those involved in the frontline of maritime security as it is deemed to be more relevant because it does not exclude acts committed within national waters. In theory, acts of terrorism could be included in this definition as criminal acts. The UNCLOS definition in paragraph (a) includes acts of violence, but only for private ends, rather than ideological, political, or religious purposes.

At the center of any definition of piracy is its association with the sea. A British criminologist, J Vagg, wrote in a paper that piracy is the maritime equivalent of banditry.[4] Most of the acts of piracy that are reported to the IMB are in fact armed robbery using violence or the threat of violence in remote areas, particularly in developing countries, where authorities are unable or unwilling to intervene. This is evident from the fact that piracy is particularly endemic in the areas previously mentioned.

(Maritime) Terrorism

Terrorism on the other hand is relatively easy and simple to define. In the context of this article, terrorism can be defined as:

> [the] unlawful use or threatened use of force or violence against people or property to coerce or intimidate governments or societies, often to achieve political, religious, or ideological objectives.

Reports from intelligence agencies throughout the Western world stated that certain Islamic terrorist groups have declared that they are intent on bringing down the economies of the West in order to further their own religious aims. These statements infer that these terrorist groups could see piracy as a means to damage the Western economy. The reason for the attack on the *NAGOT* was possibly to inflict economic damage. The result is that it is easy to see the indirect benefit piracy can have to terrorist groups. Terrorist groups could commit an act such as sinking a vessel in a maritime chokepoint, such as the Suez, Strait of Hormuz, or the Malacca Strait, and although terrorist groups would undoubtedly claim responsibility, their method of attack would probably be similar to that of a pirate attack. That said, there is still no evidence to suggest that terrorists are actively pursuing piracy as a deliberate method of conflict. The attack on the *NAGOT* was not an act of piracy, and the attacks on the USS *Cole* and MV *Limburg* also had nothing to do with piracy. These were specific terrorist attacks aimed at specific targets, both military and economic.

A notable example of this was the Palestine Liberation Front's (PLF) seizure, in 1985, of the passenger ship *Achille Lauro*, and the taking of its crew (331), and passengers (120 of 754), as hostages.[5] The initial aim of the hijacking was to seize the vessel and use it to conduct a terrorist attack on an Israeli oil terminal in the port of Ashdod, but when that attack was thwarted the hijackers, pirates, or terrorists (using whichever terminology you wish) opted to demand the release of Palestinian prisoners. The aftermath of the *Achille Lauro* incident saw a significant downturn in the cruise liner industry, with a resulting economic effect on the countries frequented by cruise ships. That the incident has not been repeated, owes much to luck rather than increased security. The PLF did not intend for any economic downturn to occur, but as previously said, certain terrorist groups could actively seek to put pressure on some fragile Western economies. An attack now, some twenty years after this event, could not only have an adverse effect on the cruise industry, but could also contribute to any downturn in the global economy.[6] It could be argued that the attack on the *Achille Lauro* was not an act of piracy, and was purely an act of terrorism, and the perpetrators had a political motive, rather than a private agenda.

A Nexus Between Piracy and Terrorism?

Terrorist groups could see their aims furthered by pirate activity, and some have used methodologies similar to those that have been used by pirates during attacks. However, the previously mentioned terrorist attacks have been quite specific in their targets, whereas pirate attacks appear to be random and uncoordinated. It is extremely doubtful that terrorist groups would form an alliance with any external group, and that includes pirates. Terrorist groups are very closely knit, suspicious of outsiders or those who are unknown to them, especially if they do not share the same ideology. It is probable that terrorists would conduct their own piracy campaign rather than using any criminal group. The Abu Sayyaf Group (ASG), which is based in the Southern

Philippines, has been linked to hijacking and kidnapping for ransom, including raids from the sea on holiday resorts.[7] International reporting has indicated that the line between piracy and terrorism is narrow and that the group is believed to have moved from being an Islamic separatist group to a criminal enterprise.[8] If that is the case, then the group is moving from political ends to private ends in its criminal enterprises. This does not suggest that the ASG has moved away from terrorism. ASG claimed responsibility for the attack on the *Superferry 14* in early 2004. This suggests that the group will continue to engage in acts of terrorism, while engaging in piracy to raise funds to continue to conduct a campaign of terror.

Another Southeast Asian group that has been linked to piracy is the Free Aceh Movement (Gerakan Aceh Merdeka; GAM). GAM seeks the removal of Indonesian government structures and forces from the Aceh region of Sumatra. The Indonesian and Malaysian authorities have linked this group to acts of piracy in order to raise funds.[9] The main maritime operating area for this group is within the confines of the Malacca Straits, and it is probable that they are involved in a vast number of the incidents that are reported in the region. It has not been possible to assess the full extent of this activity, as GAM has denied some of the attacks attributed to it. It has been reported that pirate groups in the region have copied GAM's uniforms and tactics, leading to an inflated number of attacks being attributed to GAM. This is supported by reports that GAM funding has mainly come from other sources.[10]

In another piracy hotspot, the Horn of Africa, the indigenous terrorist organization Al Ittihad Al Islamiya (AIAI) may be involved in piracy. AIAI is a very loose arrangement of individuals, whose tribal loyalties, and shifting external alliances, produce a wide spectrum of terrorist and criminal acts, from banditry to piracy and sea-jacking. AIAI seeks to establish an Islamic nation in the Horn of Africa (HOA). There have been reports that suggest that they have engaged in acts of piracy in order to raise funds. The majority of reported incidents in the HOA, however, have been conducted by armed gangs, whose loyalty is clan based rather than linked specifically to AIAI. These gangs are heavily armed and, in the true sense of the word, pirates, not terrorists. In recent months, piracy in the HOA has escalated: ships attempting to bring food aid into the region have been taken, along with their crews, and have been held hostage by armed militia — sometimes for several weeks, even months. In order to reduce the likelihood of an attack, and under the instructions from the IMO, ships not bound for HOA destinations have been navigating further and further from the coast. Though this may prevent attacks in coastal waters, it may subsequently drive the pirates farther out to sea as well.

In West Africa the Ijaw militias are conducting a civil war and are also involved in intertribal conflicts in the Niger Delta region of Nigeria. Over the last two years, there have been increasing reports of piracy in the region, including attacks against oil-support vessels and offshore installations. This has helped turning the region into one of the most reported in terms of piracy, second only to the Malacca Straits. The attacks have been accompanied by theft and kidnapping for ransom, and those involved have become more violent in their methods. Because of the level of corruption in the region, the amount of money that the oil industry is making has enabled criminal gangs to move into what was hitherto thought to be a political conflict against the government. Those attacks attributable to the Ijaw militia are possibly being committed in order to raise funds in order to support their continued attacks on the Nigerian government and the country's oil industry. However, it is likely that many of the attacks reported are criminal, and motivated much by political corruption. The remainder of the incidents are acts of petty theft and have little to do with piracy in its general description.

There has been much speculation about the role that Al Qaeda have had in the incidents of piracy and terrorism. In the immediate post-9/11 analysis of the maritime domain, government agencies reporting, coupled with a plethora of press reports, identified Al Qaeda (AQ) as having a fleet of ships that were ready to attack ships and ports throughout the world. The organization undoubtedly has links to the maritime industry, but that is through ship owners and operators who are sympathetic to Islamic rather than terrorist aims. There is little evidence to suggest that a fleet of hundreds of vessels and phantom ships is anything more than speculative. Evidence in the trial of Wadi Al Hage, who was convicted of involvement in the embassy bombings in East Africa, identified that a vessel had been used for logistics purposes, MV *Sky 1*. Intelligence agencies targeted the holding companies and vessels linked to them, which provided a framework of suspect vessels considered to be linked to terrorism. In the years that followed, none of these suspect vessels have been linked to terrorist acts, and just a few have been linked to illicit activity such as human trafficking and contraband smuggling. Al Qaeda operators have obviously been linked to the bombings of the USS *Cole* and MV *Limburg*, but they have to date, never been linked to any act of piracy.

There are two terrorist organizations who have known maritime links, and those are the Liberation Tigers of Tamil Elam (LTTE) and the Lebanese group Hezbollah. LTTE has an established maritime arm, the "Sea Tigers," which has been linked to acts of piracy against foreign-owned commercial vessels.[11] It has recently been reported that LTTE no longer requires funding from illegal activities such as piracy, but there remains a determination to conduct maritime terrorist acts.[12] Hezbollah are known to operate in the Eastern Mediterranean, but they are not linked to piracy and they have not been involved in any terrorist attacks on Western shipping interests in the region. There is no doubt that they have the capacity and the expertise to conduct such terrorist attacks and may well be predisposed to do so.

Attacks in South East Asia are almost always attributed to terrorism, rather than piracy. In March 2003, the MV *Dewi Madrim*, a chemical tanker was boarded by pirates while underway, and it has been speculated by many that these pirates were in fact terrorists. Reports were circulated that suggested that they had not been after "booty," but had boarded the vessel to gain experience in ship handling, prior to conducting an attack using a similar vessel against U.S. naval vessels in port. There were also reports that suggested that certain members of the crew were taken as hostages in order to teach the terrorists ship-handling techniques. In the aftermath there has been much speculation by alleged maritime-security experts that this was a terrorist attack, but there is little evidence to support this view. It was probable that the pirates had sufficient skill to steer the ship anyway, and had reduced speed to a minimum in order to maintain steerage way, and to enable the pirates' own vessel to stay alongside. The pirates had left the vessel after approximately one hour taking cash, personal property, and ship's equipment with them, when they absconded.

So Where Do the Navies of the World Stand When It Comes to Piracy and Maritime Terrorism?

Maritime terrorism is most certainly the top priority for all navies throughout the world. Piracy, on the other hand, is certainly a priority for regional navies surrounding those areas where piracy activity is high. There is no doubt that navies such as the Royal Navy and the U.S. Navy would assist in apprehending pirates, providing that it happened on the high seas and not in territorial waters. If the incident is one of maritime armed crime, and taking place in littoral waters, then there is no legal precedent or authority for these navies to get involved. The Royal Navy is committed to providing support to any vessel who may be subjected to pirate attack. However, this commitment does not allow for hot pursuit into the territorial waters of any nation. And of course there is the question of powers of detention and arrest, which the RN does not have, and neither does the USN. The RN's policy is to provide support and surveillance, and assistance, when asked, to regional law-enforcement agencies. Regional navies have a more responsive role in fighting piracy, and those in the "front line" need to take action. The problem for major navies is that piracy almost always involves merchant vessels. Despite the plethora of equipment for analyzing everything from acoustic signatures to the communications and radar emissions of ships and aircraft, most major warships are poorly equipped to target and track merchant vessels. In the past, merchant ships were just there and had to be avoided when carrying out operations and exercises, so much so that they were benignly referred to as "White Shipping." During the last four years this has changed dramatically. Naval units now regularly report on merchant ships encountered while at sea and in harbor. Teams of specialists are examining the operations of merchant ships, to assist in identifying anomalies that could indicate a possible terrorist attack. All of these efforts are enabling the military intelligence analysts to better understand the commercial maritime business. Strong ties with commercial maritime security companies assist in the military's understanding of what merchant ships are doing.

Both the RN and the USN compile monthly reports on piracy and issue the reports on the internet. In the UK the Ministry of Defence issues a World Wide Threat to Shipping report monthly through the Defence Intelligence Staff in London. The report is a compilation of "open source reports" and analysis which is available to the UK maritime industry. A similar report is issued by the Office of Naval Intelligence in the United States, and covers the same incidents. These reports show that piracy is being given attention by the major navies of the world. The RN recently used helicopters from the aircraft carrier HMS *Invincible* to shadow a yacht that was threatened by pirates in the Gulf of Oman. The sight of military assets, whether they be ships or aircraft, is an obvious deterrent to piracy, but incredibly expensive. The RN and the USN cannot afford to allocate money and resources to patrol piracy hot spots, particularly when the incidents that occur are predominately within the territorial limits of a country. It will be necessary for governments in the main piracy regions to police the waters, with vessels that are built specifically for the task. However, many of the navies of these countries are poorly equipped and manned and often lack the desire to engage in combat with an adversary who may well be better armed than they are.

The navies of Indonesia, Malaysia, and Singapore have the task of patrolling the worlds busiest shipping lane, the Malacca Straits. To a lesser extent the Indian Navy has some responsibility, but this is limited to the Northern extremities of the waterway, in the vicinity of the Andaman and Nicobar Islands. The Malacca Straits sees two thirds of all the oil produced that moves by sea, passing through its narrow waterways. Security experts believe that should terrorists wish to make a significant impact on the global economy, then it is here that they are most likely to attack. The Straits could be closed or severely hampered by a large merchant vessel sunk in its narrow sea-lanes. This would mean that vessels would have to move to the south of Indonesia, increasing sailing times by as much as three days. Insurers would increase their costs, shippers would increase their costs, and the South East Asian Markets could conceivably crash. The Western markets could also suffer, and the impact would be felt throughout the world. It is because of this that Western governments should be increasingly concerned about the security of this narrow stretch of water.

In mid-2004, the governments of Indonesia, Malaya, and Singapore signed an accord linking three naval command centers and each contributing a significant naval capability, so as to best patrol the region and keep it safe from maritime attack. The three governments are extremely protective of their sovereignty in the Malacca Straits and this recent accord marks a major step in joint policing of the waters surrounding their countries. Both Indonesia and Malaya were dismissive of offers from both Japan and the United

States to provide maritime patrols in the region, as it could be seen as a damning indictment of their lack of ability to face the threat of both terrorism and piracy. Also concerned about the safety of the waterway is China. Though yet to offer maritime assistance the Chinese government could be forced to get involved if oil supplies for their growing economy are hampered. Beijing may also wish to be involved if the three nations change their mind and agree to U.S. involvement in the security of the region, as distrust over the U.S. naval activities in the region abounds.

Of the three nations, Indonesia is currently engaged in a massive naval upgrade, in order to replace its aging fleet of second hand vessels. There are currently plans to spend some US$2 billion to upgrade their existing fleet. Reporting on a variety of Internet web sites suggests that this upgrade will consist of submarines and frigates that have been decommissioned from European navies, as well as up to sixty modern patrol vessels. Indonesia has the largest navy in South East Asia, but currently lacks the technology of its regional counterparts such as Singapore. The Indonesian navy requires a significant patrol boat capability in order to patrol the world's largest archipelagic nation. Should the Indonesian navy decide to purchase surplus warships from the West, this may prove counterproductive to their efforts to conduct antipiracy and counterterrorism patrols in the region. The Indonesian navy has acquired 13 new patrol vessels since 2003 and has budgeted to buy five to six vessels each year, for the next three years. This should significantly upgrade the Indonesian capability in the region and also strengthen their political standing. The vessels have significant armament for a vessel of their size, and they have the speed and maneuverability to conduct a successful engagement against a pirate vessel. Where they may be lacking is in having the will to openly engage in a skirmish with an adversary who may well be better trained and armed than they are. Once Indonesia's navy completes its modernization, they will be better able to patrol its vast archipelago with unparalleled efficiency. The Indonesian, Malaysian, and other regional governments must ensure that they do not purchase obsolete Western naval vessels that are not compatible with that navy's emerging role. Though these countries may aspire to having a blue water navy, this aspiration is pointless if they cannot protect vessels within their own territorial waters.

Malaysia has a significant interest in the security of the Straits. The country's major ports and tourist centers along with its equally important fishing grounds border the Malacca Straits. Its naval forces are significant, but there are shortcomings. The navy recently transferred its aging Vosper class patrol boats to the coast guard but these vessels are not suitable for operations against pirates or terrorists. Backed by a sound economy, the Malaysian government has an ambitious modernization plan that includes addressing the security of shipping in the Straits. Their plans should include the introduction of new patrol boats for its new coast guard. Again, the government needs to make sure that suitable equipment is bought for the role. Like Indonesia, the navy and coast guard require small, fast and well armed vessels to provide a visible deterrent, and to be able to engage and pursue pirates or terrorists.

Singapore has a restricted maritime zone, compared to that of the Malaysians and Indonesians. However, extensive radar coverage, maritime patrol aircraft, and an extensive fleet of capable patrol boats give Singapore the edge in maritime security in the region. But the vessels are not necessarily suited for patrolling the less confined waters of the Straits.

For all three countries, piracy is a major consideration. But equally if not more so is the threat from drug trafficking, illegal immigration, and terrorism. In trying to combat all maritime threats these navies are spread thinly on the ground. Their previous lack of action in combating piracy has resulted in security firms offering armed escorts to vessels transiting the region. This can include companies such as "Background Asia Risk Solutions" (BARS), who are offering an armor-plated vessel, with an ex-military crew, to provide escort to ships operating in the region's most dangerous waters.

The IMO's position against armed escorts is in common with that of the International Maritime Bureau (IMB), a leading authority in countering piracy. They share an antipiracy philosophy that places primacy on the safety and welfare of commercial seafarers. Consequently, they fear that radical measures might spark a backlash from piracy syndicates. The use of armed escorts — whether private or from state militaries — contravenes their prudential approach. First, they consider the use of arms on board a vessel an aggressive move that can instigate an "arms race," compelling pirates to counter this by employing heavier weapons. Second, an on-board shoot-out between the ship's defenders and pirates may risk incurring high casualties among the ship's crew. For these reasons, bodies like the IMO and the IMB have attempted to focus the private sector on more benign means of protection instead, such as using new technology. The IMB, for instance, has supported the use of a Dutch-designed electrified fence system covering the perimeter of a ship's deck to deter pirates from boarding.

In contrast, most regional states concerned with the threat of maritime piracy (as well as terrorism) do not in principle object to the role of armed escorts. Singapore and Malaysia's recent decision to provide armed escort services indicates that regional governments are willing to take some risks in using such personnel. The real issue for countries such as Malaysia is the use of private armed guards. This hinges on the prevailing paradigm of international law relating to the innocent passage of vessels through a state's territorial waters. As the convention on state sovereignty dictates, the legitimate monopoly over the use of force in matters of security lies with the state and not with vessels seeking passage.

While state-sponsored armed escorts are in line with a country's legal hold over the use of force, the supply of such services by private companies can be viewed as prejudicial to innocent passage. This helps explain the Malaysian authorities' response in the form of a directive to its marine police. Vessels providing armed escort services to merchant shipping could be considered a terrorist threat and their crew could be arrested if they encroached on Malaysian waters.[13]

Apart from Southeast Asia as the region most affected by acts of piracy, there are several other hot spots along the world's busiest sea lines of communication. As previously stated, acts of piracy in the Horn of Africa are increasing in frequency. It is widely reported that the terrorist group AIAI are involved, but this is a financial crime and not ideological. Besides, AIAI tends to operate more to the south and inland. In the Gulf of Oman, and off the coast of the breakaway regions of Somaliland and Puntland, the perpetrators are criminals acting on behalf, or with the complicity of, the ruling government. Also many of the events surrounding the region are conducted on an opportunistic basis. Vessels moving slowly in coastal waters are considered fair game. The vessels and crew are held to ransom and the cargo is stolen. With the whole of Somalia, a country embroiled in civil and inter clan warfare and with no apparent government and absolutely no rule of law, the region is prime for groups to involve themselves in maritime armed crime, piracy and if the opportunity exists, terrorism. Attacks in the region have continued despite the patrolling in the region by coalition vessels, as part of the multinational maritime force engaged in the Global War on Terrorism (GWOT). There must be at least six vessels ranging from frigates and destroyers to larger capital ships operating in the region, supported by maritime patrol aircraft, yet still piracy flourishes. It is easy to see why pirates continue to operate in the region despite the presence of Western navies. Naval vessels that are currently deployed to the region are not suitable to interdict pirates, a lesson that should be heeded by developing nations in Asia and Africa. Yes, most of the frigates and destroyers are capable of launching a helicopter to deploy at short notice, and they can quickly prepare a boarding team. But, they once again lack the authority to engage in hot pursuit of perpetrators into territorial waters.

Somalia, with its lack of a credible government, is considered the regional haven for pirates and terrorists. Yemen, on the other hand, is being supported by both the United States and other Western governments in their battle against terrorism and piracy. Yet Yemen was the country where the USS *Cole* and MV *Limburg* were both attacked, in similar fashion, by a waterborne improvized explosive device (WBIED). To prevent similar attacks, the U.S. government is assisting the Yemeni coast guard with equipment and training. Australia is providing ten patrol boats to the Yemeni government to enable them to effectively patrol their coastline. These vessels will mainly be used to provide security against maritime terrorism especially in the Bab-el-Mandeb Straits. The United States has provided, in addition to training, eight refitted motor boats which will be used for port security duties. It will be interesting to note whether Yemen considers piracy to be a priority, alongside terrorism, or whether they will quietly ignore the activity while searching for terrorists.

Another country in the HOA region is Djibouti, which has been host for many years to coalition forces in the region. They too have a navy which is a small and relatively junior force. They are predominately a harbor police force and do not have the ability to operate outside of the Gulf of Tadjoura. The Djibouti naval force has established links with its Yemeni neighbors, in order to collaborate on illegal fishing practices in their territorial waters.

The Gulf of Guinea and the coastal waters of Nigeria have seen one of the largest rises in piracy in recent years.[14] The initial response of the Nigerian government was minimal, and although harbor patrols were stepped up, the majority of the incidents were occurring outside of the main patrol areas. These reported incidents are more to do with maritime armed crime than piracy, but statistically they are reported by the IMB as the same. The incidents are predominately opportunistic, and the nature of the theft, such as items from upper-deck lockers is typical. However, in the southern regions of the Niger Delta, the maritime community is being targeted by both pirates, armed criminals, and Ijaw separatists. The oil industry has been severely affected by these activities, with oil vessels and oil workers being targeted. Despite oil workers having armed escorts, the rebels and pirates often outgun them, and casualties on both sides have been high. Though kidnapping has been rare, such acts seem to happen more frequently now, thus adding a new dimension to the conflict in the region.

The Nigerian government has also seen a rise in illegal bunkering, which is being perpetrated by criminals and rebels for financial gain. The typical operation is for smaller vessels to move oil products to either larger vessels or to other countries. Recent assessments suggest that Nigeria is losing around 100,000 barrels per day to this activity. With around 20 percent of U.S. oil coming from the region, the Nigerian government has asked the United States for assistance in the form of equipment. The Nigerian government is taking a positive step towards combating the problem, but has been hampered by lack of naval units, training, and the endemic corruption of government, law-enforcement, and naval personnel. In October 2003, the Nigerian navy seized a Russian-flagged tanker, the MT *African Pride*, and arrested the 13 Russian sailors who made up the crew. The vessel was attempting to smuggle over 11,000 tons of crude oil. Three very senior Nigerian naval officers were tried on corruption charges, and two were found guilty. The vessel though, while under arrest by the Nigerian Navy, actually disappeared and is the subject of much embarrassment for both the navy and the government.[15]

The Nigerian government has taken delivery of former U.S. navy vessels in order to upgrade their fleet. However, the vessels may be unsuitable to engage in conflict with separatists in the coastal waters and rivers of the Niger Delta. The country, like Indonesia, requires a maritime force of fast capable and well armed vessels, capable of operations in the coastal waters, as well as patrolling the deeper waters out to their economic exclusion zone.

The Involvement of Larger Navies in Counterpiracy

The main region where the larger navies of the world would like to consider joint patrols is the Strait of Malacca. The United States has been keen to establish patrols in this region. During the run-up to Operation Enduring Freedom, the war in Afghanistan, United States and Indian vessels patrolled the Malacca Straits jointly. When the U.S. vessels deployed to the military operation, Indian vessels relieved them. However, when the United States voiced concern over the security of the Malacca Straits, regional countries, in particular Indonesia, declined to include the U.S. forces in any maritime patrol. One of the reasons behind this refusal probably was a wave of anti-United States feeling throughout the civilian population.[16] When Japan, after a series of pirate attacks against its vessels in early 2005, offered to assist in patrolling the region, this was again refused by both Indonesia and Malaysia.

With the rising demand in the Far East for fuel, particularly from China, Japan, and Korea, the movement of oil through the Straits accounts for 60 percent of the world's total. Should either pirates or terrorists restrict this flow, the consequences to the economy of East Asia would be dramatic. But so far China seems willing to play a waiting game and leave policing the Straits to the three littoral countries. This may change should the United States involve itself in the security of the Straits.

India is another major naval power with an interest in the region. Indian naval forces have operated with U. S., British, and littoral navies in exercises and patrols in the region. Should a major naval power have "first dibs" on patrolling the region, it would probably be India. The Indians already operate joint patrols with Indonesia, and so this should not be surprising to anyone. The latest edition of the Indian Maritime Doctrine lays down multilateral naval cooperation as one of the guiding principles for naval forces to address common security concerns like protection of sea-lines, terrorism, piracy, drug trafficking, and transportation of WMDs by sea. The security of the Straits is vital for India due to the economic importance of energy and trade flow. Additionally the maritime traffic transiting the Malacca Straits passes through India's maritime zone and any contingency in the Straits has security and environmental implications for India, as well as China and Japan. Piracy and armed robbery of vessels is steadily spilling over into the Bay of Bengal. On the basis of IMB statistics, Bangladesh, and India are becoming regions of concern with regard to piracy.

So Is It Piracy or Maritime Terrorism That Is the Main Threat?

Maritime terrorism is without doubt a major problem, and reporting suggests that an attack by terrorists in the Malacca Straits, Nigeria or the Horn of Africa is inevitable. But before jumping to conclusions, is the increase in piracy linked to terrorism? There are some who would say that there is no link between the two. However, a former colleague, Frank Guitterez, formerly a U.S. Navy intelligence officer, once said to me, "You don't know what you don't know."[17]

I would like to leave the reader with the following conclusion. Piracy is not known to be linked to terrorism and vice-versa. I am certain that it is not, but there is no evidence to support this; conversely, there is no evidence to refute it either. The major Western navies are spending large sums of money in combating maritime terrorism, while piracy goes unchecked and thrives. We equip our law-enforcement agencies to combat organized crime in our cities, but do little to combat organized crime on the high seas. The sea, and the waterways that the merchant fleet use, are largely unregulated in developing countries, while in the North European maritime domain, they are relatively well administered, and the maritime industry does much of its own policing.

Yes, the world's navies could do more, but emerging and developing nations need to do more for themselves. They need to be advised carefully and logically as to what they need to do, rather than be sold or given obsolete Western warships that cost more to run than the country can afford. How often have these countries taken delivery of a vessel that within months is incapable of leaving the harbor wall because it is not seaworthy and mechanically neglected?

All the major navies need to have a specific policy on dealing with, and taking action against, pirates. Rules of Engagement should allow for vessels to take strong and decisive action. The regional navies should be equipped for what they need to do, and advised accordingly.

Notes

1. *Jane's Intelligence Review*, volume 16, number 9 — Sept. 2004, p. 30.
2. IMO: "Regulations for Carriage of AIS," at http://www.imo.org/Safety/mainframe.asp?topic_id=754 (accessed 24 May 2006).
3. See for example the statistics compiled by Mark Bruyneel at his website "Modern Day Piracy Statistics," http://home.wanadoo.nl/m.bruyneel/archive/modern/figures.htm (accessed 24 January 2006).
4. Vagg, J: "Rough Seas? Contemporary piracy in South East Asia." *British Journal of Criminology* (1995).
5. *Jane's Trends in Maritime Violence* 1996.
6. However, the (unsuccessful) pirate attack on the cruise liner Seabourn Spirit off the coast of Somalia in early November 2005 did not result in any measurable downturns for the cruise industry, probably because nobody was killed and because the attack was thwarted by the crew's determined counter action.
7. Abu Sayyaf eyed in abduction of six workers in Borneo — *Philippine Daily Inquirer*, 7 October 2003.
8. *Jane's World Insurgency and Terrorism* 19 — 8 January 2004.
9. "New Piracy" by Charles Glass, *London Review of Books*, December 2003.
10. *Jane's Sentinel Security Assessment* — SE Asia, December 2003.
11. *Jane's World Insurgency and Terrorism*, February 2004.

12. Ibid.
13. The Strait's Times Interactive — 26 May 2005.
14. IMB Statistics.
15. Vanguard Nigeria; by Bolade Omonijo, deputy political editor, Friday, 27 May 2005.
16. *The Chinese Youth Newspaper* Z — 15 June 2004.
17. Cdr Frank Guitterez USN Retd.

11
Outlook: The New Threat of Maritime Terrorism

SAM BATEMAN

Introduction

About 90 percent of the world's trade by volume moves by sea and this volume may double over the next fifteen years. Seaborne trade is potentially vulnerable to terrorist attack due to the quantity of cargo involved, its diverse and large international labor force, difficulties of enforcement both in port and at sea, and the poor regulatory environment of international shipping with low levels of accountability, complicated chains of ownership, and a high incidence of fraudulent documentation. Terrorists could potentially exploit these weaknesses to use sea transport for evil purposes, or to launch an attack on shipping and port infrastructure that could cause massive economic disruption.

The need to counter the threat of maritime terrorism has led to fundamental changes in the international maritime security environment. The new countermeasures have imposed large additional costs on the transport system and have required significant effort from both government and industry. However at this stage, the maritime terrorist threat has had no significant impact on the volume or pattern of international trade. We have had stronger than expected economic growth in Asia, and this situation would not have been any different without the terrorist attacks on the World Trade Center in New York on 11 September 2001 (9/11). While the maritime terrorist attacks that have occurred in recent years have been relatively minor in terms of their overall impact, the 9/11 attacks are usually regarded as examples of the extreme events that might be possible, including on maritime targets, and for which countermeasures are required.

This chapter makes a critical assessment of the new threat of maritime terrorism and the outlook into the near future. This includes consideration of the threat and net impact of piracy worldwide, including the possibility that a high incidence of piracy in a particular area might increase the risk of a maritime terrorist attack. The chapter also considers the effectiveness of the new international security measures that have been introduced in recent years. Appreciations of the risks of maritime terrorist attacks, or of international shipping being used for terrorist purposes, have led to major developments in global maritime security, especially the introduction of the International Ship and Port Facility Security (ISPS) Code, and a range of initiatives from the United States, particularly the Container Security Initiative (CSI) and the Proliferation Security Initiative (PSI).

Based on a proposition that there may have been rather too much emphasis on highly remote and speculative "doomsday" scenarios in assessing the risks of maritime terrorism, this chapter seeks to provide something of a reality check. It attempts to introduce some balance into consideration of the risks and likelihood of a serious maritime terrorist attack occurring somewhere in the world in the near future. The economic impact of the countermeasures to the threat of maritime terrorism may well have been much larger than that of the 9/11 attacks themselves, although undoubtedly the attribution of costs and benefits from the countermeasures have varied significantly between different countries and industry sectors.

The chapter concludes with a plea for both balance and equity in managing the threat of terrorism. Any one interest group, be it a particular country, group of countries, or a particular industry sector, such as the ship owners, marine insurers, or providers of security equipment or services, should not be in a position from which they can "beat up" a threat and exploit the current situation to their own advantage. Unfortunately, developments in maritime security in recent years provide some examples of this occurring. Horrific scenarios of maritime terrorist attacks that would previously have been dismissed as fantasy have been presented as real and present dangers.[1]

Assessing the Threat

Fiction and Reality

Several bestsellers have been written around the threat of maritime terrorism. These usually describe the seizure of an oil tanker or other ship by terrorists who threaten to cause massive nuclear or oil pollution by sinking the vessel unless their demands are met. In 1980 Frederick Forsyth published his novel, *The Devil's Alternative,* in which terrorists hijack an ultralarge crude carrier (ULCC), the *Freya,* a gigantic vessel of fictitious proportions (515 meters long and 90 meters wide), carrying one million tons of crude oil.[2] They threaten to blow the ship up, causing massive pollution of the North Sea, unless colleagues held in a German jail are released.

It may only be a coincidence, but Frederick Forsyth is a shareholder of Aegis Defence Services (ADS), the U.K. company that has made some of the more extreme assessments of the risks of maritime terrorism in recent years.[3] A study published by ADS in October 2003 identified what it said were several new and disturbing developments in maritime terrorism in Southeast Asia, including the assessment that an attack on the chemical tanker *Dewi Madrim* in March 2003 had been a case of terrorists learning to drive a ship. However, the International Maritime Bureau (IMB) stated that its Piracy Reporting Centre (PRC) in Kuala Lumpur had received confirmation from the owners of the ship that the attack was not as described by Aegis.[4] In another somewhat extreme prediction, the intelligence director of ADS claimed in December 2004 that al-Qaeda was likely to launch a spectacular maritime attack during the year 2005.[5]

Despite fictional accounts of maritime terrorism, reality is somewhat different and there have been relatively few confirmed acts of maritime terrorism. Passenger ships and ferries have been preferred targets. The sinking of *Superferry 14* in February 2004 near Manila in the Philippines has been the most serious act of maritime terrorism so far in terms of loss of life with 116 people killed.[6] However, the attacks on the USS *Cole* in Aden in October 2000 and on the French tanker *Limburg* off Yemen in October 2002 usually attract the most attention in writings on maritime terrorism because they were initiated by al-Qaeda and occurred in the context of 9/11. The numerous maritime terrorist attacks by the "Sea Tigers" of the Liberation Tigers of Tamil Eelam (LTTE) on both merchant ships and Sri Lankan warships are also often cited as examples of what might be possible, including the assessment that al-Qaeda has benefited from the technologies and techniques of the LTTE.[7]

It is not too difficult to conjure up "doomsday" scenarios for a maritime terrorist attack. A ship carrying a highly dangerous cargo could be hijacked and used as a floating bomb to destroy a port and cause large loss of human life, or a shipping container or a ship itself could be used to import a nuclear bomb or other weapons of mass destruction (WMD).[8] These are very low-probability, high-consequence scenarios that can lead to some lack of balance in decision making both by governments and the business sector. Assessments of the threat of maritime terrorism must be rational and represent a reasonable balance between the likelihood of an attack occurring and the costs of providing adequate security against such an attack. The assessments depend on a multitude of factors, especially the capabilities and intentions of prospective maritime terrorists, the vulnerability of particular targets, and the consequences of an attack, should one occur.

Terrorist Capabilities

The main maritime terrorist threat is usually seen as coming from al-Qaeda and its associated groups in Southeast Asia, particularly Jemaah Islamiyah (JI), and the Abu Sayyaf Group (ASG). These groups have training camps in the southern Philippines where they train together and share expertise.[9] Members of these groups routinely move between Sabah (Indonesian Borneo) and these camps by speedboat, local craft, and ferries. The ASG in the Philippines has already shown that it can attack ships, having claimed responsibility for the *Superferry 14* attack, and more recently has been blamed for the bomb attack on the ferry *Dona Ramona* in August 2005 as the ship was about to depart from the port of Zamboanga.[10] These attacks show that ferries, and potentially cruise liners, are vulnerable to attack. With passenger ships and ferries, it is not so much the bomb that does the damage but rather the fire and panic that might follow an explosion with so many people in a relatively confined area. Threats have been made on ships passing through the Strait of Gibraltar,[11] as well as U.S. Naval ships and facilities in Singapore. In March 2004, Philippine military sources were quoted as saying that the ASG was training with JI to prepare for possible seaborne and underwater attacks outside the Philippines.[12]

Terrorism is not just about killing people. An attack that caused maximum disruption to a country's economy or transportation system might be as attractive as an attack that led to major loss of life but did not directly cause disruption. Al-Qaeda has stated that it might attack vital economic centers and strategic enterprises of the "Jewish-Christian alliance," including operations on land, at sea, and in the air.[13] In August 2005, a French terrorism expert warned that Singapore, Tokyo, and Sydney could be targets of an al-Qaeda strike at a major financial center.[14]

In relative terms, maritime targets may be less attractive than land or air targets. Ships at sea are difficult targets, and an attack on port infrastructure may have rather less impact than an attack on a major building or facility (such as a mass transportation system) that has both high economic and iconic value. Unless a ship itself was used as a bomb or as a means of introducing a WMD, a maritime terrorist attack may not cause large loss of life. The destruction of a port facility would have significant economic impact but might not figure prominently in the public consciousness. The potential list of targets for a terrorist is limitless but maritime targets may not figure prominently on it. The preferred targets for terrorists are likely to remain on land where, as shown by the attacks on mass urban transport in London and Madrid, success is more readily assured.

Piracy and Terrorism

The incidence of piracy and armed robbery against ships in some parts of the world has led to perceptions of higher risks of terrorist attack in those waters.[15] The number of acts of piracy and armed robbery against ships (actual and attempted) worldwide reported by the IMB in 2004 was 325, a decrease of 120 (27.0 percent) over 2003.[16] By far the greatest concentration of these incidents was in Southeast Asia (156 incidents; 48.0 percent of total attacks worldwide), with 93 of these occurring in Indonesian waters, 9 in Malaysian waters, and 37 in the Malacca Straits. Other concentrations of attacks were in Indian and Bangladeshi waters with 32 reported attacks (9.8 percent), and West Africa with 52 attacks (16.0 percent) mostly off the coast of Nigeria. The annual report of the IMB for 2004 also drew attention to the trend towards greater violence in the attacks, and to an increase in the number of crew killed in attacks from 21 in 2003 to 30 in 2004.[17] Hijacking of small vessels, such as tugs and fishing boats, with their crews held for ransom was also a new and developing phenomenon in some areas around the world.[18]

Some reservations should be noted about the IMB statistics. On the one hand, there could be some underreporting of piratical acts. Both the IMB and the IMO have noted the reluctance by some ship masters and ship owners to report incidents due to concern that any investigation will disrupt the ship's schedule, the adverse publicity possibly involved, and the possibility that insurance premiums may increase.[19] But on the other hand, over reporting of the number of incidents is also possible. Many of the incidents are really just petty theft (of small items such as paint, mooring ropes, or outboard motors), or occur when a ship is alongside in port or at anchor.

It seems likely that prior to 1992, when the PRC was established, many incidents, particularly the relatively minor ones and the attacks in port, may have gone unreported. In 1994, Beckman, Grundy-Warr, and Forbes completed a comprehensive study of acts of piracy in the Malacca and Singapore Straits, and this provides a benchmark for assessing more recent trends.[20] In contrast with current data, virtually all reported piratical acts in the Straits were on vessels underway, and raids on vessels in port and at anchor were not common.[21] Attempted attacks were not apparently recorded.

The IMB attack statistics often vary widely from one year to the next both in aggregate terms and in particular features of the attacks. Short-term trends are often quoted as support for assessments of increasing violence or incidence of attacks, whereas longer-term trends may give a different picture. For example, the maximum number of total attacks worldwide has generally tended downwards from the total number of attacks worldwide of 469 in 2000. Similarly, while the number of seafarers killed in 2004 (32) was higher than in 2003 (21), greater numbers were in fact killed in earlier years for which data is available: 1998 (78 killed), 2000 (72) and 1997 (51).[22]

Aggregate figures also obscure trends with different types of ship. The current categorization of attacks by vessel type used by the IMB is unsatisfactory for making proper assessments of the risks of piracy to different types of ship. The IMB currently uses 37 different ship types in its database, but most of these do not lend themselves to valid threat assessments (e.g. cable layer, storage ship, and dredger), as very few attacks have occurred in each of these categories over the last decade. On the other hand, some major categories (e.g. container ship, bulk carrier, and tanker) conflate many ships of vastly different size and purpose. These categories record many attacks but the large figures can distort the picture. For example, smaller, feeder container ships and product tankers on local voyages are much more vulnerable than larger vessels. This can give the impression that "mainline" container vessels and large tankers on international voyages through the Malacca and Singapore

Straits between Europe or the Middle East and East Asia are being attacked when in fact, they are not.

The potential for cooperation between pirates and terrorists has probably been overstated.[23] Piracy and maritime terrorism are closely related activities involving "armed violence at sea which is not a lawful act of war."[24] But a distinction exists between the two acts: piracy is conducted for private ends while terrorism has political motives. In assessments of the risk of maritime terrorism, pirates have been seen as having skills and expertise that might be attractive to a terrorist group, but these are not so specialized that they are not readily available. Former naval personnel and fishermen, as well as the multitude of people throughout Asia that have some experience as commercial seafarers, all offer a basis of knowledge that could be of use to a terrorist group. The many terrorist attacks by the Sri Lankan Tamil Tigers on merchant ships and Sri Lankan warships were largely possible because many Tamil Tigers were formerly fishermen.

In June 2005, the London insurance market's Joint War Committee (JWC) declared the Malacca and Singapore Straits a "war risk zone."[25] This was on the basis of assessments by ADS that the levels of piracy in the Straits were increasing and the pirates were making greater use of small arms and light weapons. ADS also suggested that there were potential links between the incidence of piracy and the risk of terrorism due to the increasing sophistication of weaponry and techniques being used by pirates that made them largely indistinguishable from those of terrorists. This latter assessment has been criticized as there is little or no real evidence to suggest that pirates are forming links with international or regional groups in order to carry out a devastating maritime attack.[26] The increasing use of small arms and light weapons by the pirates is symptomatic of the more general problem associated with the ready availability of these weapons around the world.

For the reasons outlined above, the key assessments by ADS are questionable. Rather than the situation deteriorating in recent years, it could well have improved due to the greater effort by the littoral States to ensure the security of shipping in the Straits. Despite this, the JWC declaration has justified insurers raising premiums for ships transiting the Straits. Both international ship-owning associations and the littoral States concerned have protested the declaration,[27] but the JWC has stuck by its decision, declaring that the Malacca Straits would remain on the "war risk zone" list until "it was clear that the measures planned by governments and other agencies in the area had been implemented and were effective."[28]

Threats to Ships

Ships are more vulnerable in port, or in the approaches to a port, than when they are at sea where they might gain considerable protection from their size and speed. Most large, modern merchant ships travel at speeds in excess of fourteen knots and it is both difficult and dangerous for small craft to attempt to approach them at this speed. Smaller ships and vessels alongside or at anchor figure prominently in the statistics on acts of piracy and armed attacks on ships collected by the IMB. In port ships face threats from the landside, small boats, and underwater swimmers. The attack on USS *Cole* demonstrated this vulnerability. This has led to the U.S. Navy and other Western navies devoting much greater attention to the force protection of their ships during port calls.[29]

The ships that are most vulnerable to terrorist attack are those carrying hazardous or dangerous cargoes that could turn the ship into a bomb, passenger ferries, and cruise liners, as well as naval vessels. Tankers with cargoes of lighter, more volatile crude oils, as well as refined products such as gasoline, kerosene, and diesoline, are potentially a greater risk than large ships carrying heavy crude oil which is difficult to ignite. While most attention has focused on the larger tankers and LNG carriers, smaller vessels such as product tankers, LPG carriers, and chemical tankers are more prominent in the piracy statistics and may be more vulnerable to terrorist attack. These vessels are generally slower than larger vessels, and have smaller crews and lower freeboards. But generally, it remains the case that gas carriers and tankers are more vulnerable when loading or unloading than at sea. Thus the problem is more one of terminal security rather than of ship security and of providing security for ships entering port.[30]

The security of a merchant ship in port is more the responsibility of the port rather than of the ship. Most modern commercial vessels have small crews, typically about twenty or even fewer personnel manning a large container ship or oil tanker. This is an obvious consideration in ship security that becomes more critical at higher threat levels. Maintaining an adequate gangway watch is a major problem when the ship's crew is also heavily involved in other activities, including working cargo. A tanker, loading or discharging at an oil terminal where there are strict security controls ashore, may be less vulnerable than a vessel working general cargo with possibly large numbers of port employees coming and going. It might be impractical for a gangway watchman to leave his post to patrol or attend to other ship's business.

Apart from problems of physical security, assessments of the threat to ships are complicated by difficulties associated with identifying the owners of a particular ship and being confident in the identity of individual seafarers. The OECD in a July 2003 report had the following to say about international shipping:

> Here is a sector characterised by an extremely diverse international labour force, transporting a vast range of goods whose provenance, description and ownership are often left remarkably vague. This is a system where international transport chains involve thousands

> of intermediaries, on vessels registered in dozens of countries that sometimes choose not to uphold their international responsibilities and where some vessel owners can and do easily hide their true identities using a complex web of international corporate registration practices.[31]

Following 9/11, there were frequent reports of al-Qaeda either owning or being involved in the ownership of merchant ships, and there have been instances of ships flying particular flags of convenience being used to carry WMD or related materials. Clearly, the risks of this occurring are much higher if a ship is not owned by a readily identifiable and reputable owner. Despite efforts by the IMO, including the introduction of a ship identification number (SIN), marked either on the ship's hull or superstructure, and the requirement for flag state administrations to issue each ship with a Continuous Synopsis Record (CSR) providing information on the ship's name, SIN, flag state, date of registration, port of registry and classification society, problems still remain in determining ship ownership and who has effective control of a ship for the purposes of ensuring both that the vessel is not used for terrorist purposes, and that it has effective security arrangements in place.

Threats to Ports

There are at least 1,600 ports around the world used by ships trading internationally. Port security, and maritime security more generally, is very different from aviation security. The public generally understands and accepts the need for aviation security, but this may not be so with maritime security. The security of ports and ships must consider all environments: land, air, sea surface, and subsurface. Airports have defined perimeters and usually some form of "buffer zone" between an airport and other activities. Access to an airport is more easily controlled than to a port. Airline passengers expect to be screened with their baggage, and airline and airport workers can be closely monitored. In comparison, ports may not have a clearly defined perimeter, even on the land side where they might be located in or adjacent to heavily populated urban areas.

Ports vary greatly with regard to their physical attributes while airports are all basically similar. Each port is different by virtue of its geography, topography, surroundings, and population.[32] Ports by their very nature are vulnerable. They are busy areas with access by land and sea. While separate facilities may not be large in area, the geographical extent of a port may be very wide. The public in many countries expects to be able to visit ports to watch ships or to fish. On the waterside, ports are practically impossible to secure physically.

The security regime of a port facility depends on the trade that uses it. It might range from heavily secured oil terminal and refinery complexes, which already have tight security primarily for safety reasons, to small general-cargo or bulk-cargo loading ports that traditionally might have had unmonitored public access to the wharves. Control of access to a port facility is fundamental. The security risk at ports varies widely depending on their location, size, and nature of activities. Similarly, appropriate security responses will vary depending on the assessed level of risk. Waterside security will generally be more difficult and costly than land side security. It is difficult to assess just what would be the impact of closing a port. Much would depend on how easy it was to shift trade to another port.

Containers and Supply Chain Security

Most nonbulk sea cargo is carried in marine shipping containers, with about 232 million containers moved through container ports around the world in 2001.[33] Container fraud has been of concern for many years, but the risk that terrorists might exploit the vulnerability of the container system has focused greater attention on container security. There are many ways that containers may be used for illegal purposes, including:

- substituting legal cargo with illicit materials
- mixing bogus shipments in a container of multiple shipments
- packing legitimate cargo at the front of a container with illicit material behind
- shipping empty containers with hidden compartments
- shipping a container through one or more transit ports to mask its origins

The problem with ensuring the security of the container-transportation chain is that it is a system characterized by complex interactions among multiple actors representing different government agencies and transport modes.[34] Ports are just one node in the supply chain, and a ship is but a link between nodes. Security cannot begin and end at the regulated security zone of a port or onboard ship, but must be integrated into the entire logistics of the supply chain. The vulnerability of a container may well be highest in rail yards and road stops rather than in the port terminal or onboard ship. The security implications of the transport, packing, and reporting of dangerous goods through the supply chain are assuming greater priority. This is where the real challenges will be in the future.

The best approach is one that looks at the supply chain in its totality. The security issues go across the supply chain for each consignment, from point of origin to point of destination. Many security concerns in the container transport chain are related to inland carriers and freight integrators — the first and last few links of the chain. Vulnerabilities in the container environment are highest in rail yards, road stops and shipping/loading terminals. Supply-chain security requires the active participation of the logistics and transport industry to ensure that all parts of the container transport chain are included in a comprehensive security framework. The problem is compounded at a national level by the demands of introducing an effective system that crosses transport nodes, licensing agencies, and regulatory regimes.

Assessing the Response

International Measures

The global solutions to problems of maritime security have been pitched at four levels: the security of ships and ports, the tracking of vessels, the integrity of container cargo, and verifying seafarer identity. They include the new measures by the IMO, particularly the International Ship and Port Security (ISPS) Code, other amendments to the 1974 Safety of Life at Sea (SOLAS) Convention, such as the mandatory fitting of ship-borne Automatic Identification Systems (AIS), and planned amendments to the 1988 Convention for the Suppression of Unlawful Acts against the Safety of Maritime Navigation (SUA Convention) and its Protocol covering offshore facilities.[35]

Then there are the range of global initiatives by the United States to enhance maritime cargo security, especially the Container Security Initiative (CSI),[36] Customs-Trade Partnership against Terrorism (C-TPAT),[37] and enhanced information management, particularly the 24-hour Manifest Rule.[38] The Regional Maritime Security Initiative (RMSI)[39] and related aspects of the Proliferation Security Initiative (PSI)[40] are other US efforts to build maritime security cooperation at the global and regional levels. In a recent development, the United States is now taking a more active role in ensuring maritime security in the oil-rich Gulf of Guinea which is believed vulnerable to piracy, political instability, and terrorism, and from which the United States receives a significant proportion of its oil imports.[41]

ISPS Code

The main contribution by the IMO to international maritime security, the ISPS Code, entered into force on 1 July 2004. According to the latest figures from the IMO Secretariat, 97 percent of over 9,600 declared port facilities now have their Port Facility Security Plans (PFSPs) approved, and the compliance rate for ships issued with their International Ship Security Certificates (ISSCs) is well beyond the 90 percent mark.[42] This compares favorably with the 86 percent of approved ship security plans reported on 1 July 2004.

Despite the overall optimism with implementation of the ISPS Code, there are residual problems with its effectiveness as a maritime security measure. First, the Code applies only to the so-called SOLAS ships, that is, commercial ships over 500 gross tonnage employed on international voyages. Unless extended by national legislation,[43] it does not apply to fishing vessels, ships under 500 gross tonnage, or to ships employed only in the domestic trade. The number of vessels to which the ISPS Code does not apply is particularly large in the Asia-Pacific region where there are large fishing fleets, many smaller trading vessels, and big domestic commercial fleets, particularly in China, Japan, Indonesia, and the Philippines.[44]

Secondly, ISPS is basically a U.S. code that gives many difficulties to other contracting parties.[45] The debates over the Code in the IMO were "complex and heated,"[46] and it is understood that the United States had to provide significant special funding to the IMO to secure acceptance of the Code. Developing countries do not accord quite the same priority to measures that are primarily about countering the terrorist threat and in the final analysis, securing the interests of major Western countries rather than their own. Developing countries would accord higher priority to programs of economic development and poverty alleviation rather than investing in the capacity to implement the provisions of the ISPS Code. Threats by the United States to deny entry to noncompliant ships and thus make compliance a condition of trading with the United States are seen as just another example of the American abuse of power.

Thirdly, the ISPS Code imposes significant additional costs on ship owners, including possibly having to employ extra crew.[47] The OECD estimated that the initial burden on ship operators to be at least US$1,279 million and US$730 million per year thereafter, primarily for additional management staff and security-related equipment.[48] There may be some irony here in that the international shipping market is buoyant at present, and the market may be absorbing the costs of the new maritime security measures. A "crunch" may well come with the next slump in global shipping.

The ultimate objective of enhancing maritime security is a worthy one, as indeed are the objectives of all the other safety and environmental protection conventions that have been introduced by the IMO. The IMO can point to the "runs on the board" with reduced numbers of oil spills and maritime accidents, but there has been a price with the increased concentration of ownership of international shipping. Smaller ship owners in developing countries, including national shipping fleets, have largely been priced out of the market by the high costs of complying with international shipping regulations. The reality is that the owners of substandard "flag of convenience" ships are generally not in the Third World but in the traditional ship-owning capitals such as London, Tokyo, Athens, or New York, whose resident ship owners gain comparative advantage from increased regulation.

Lastly, and despite some rhetoric to the contrary, the ISPS Code, like other instruments of international law, cannot be enforced effectively. The IMO can monitor compliance but ultimately it depends on individual countries effectively implementing the Code. Flag states have to ensure compliance of ships flying their flag, port states have to manage implementation of the Code in their ports and port facilities, and seafarer supplying countries, such as Bangladesh, Indonesia, and the Philippines, have to have the bureaucracy in place to implement the new seafarer ID documentation.

Tracking Ships

In an ideal security-conscious world, ships would move around the world like civil aircraft, being passed from one national system of traffic control to another. With initiatives promoted by the United States and now under consideration by the IMO for the Long Range Identification and Tracking (LRIT) of vessels, a system may eventually emerge for commercial ships above a certain size and making use of AIS data. The United States intends to develop a system that will integrate current and future surveillance and tracking resources to identify and track the world's 121,000 merchant ships of more than 300 tons.[49] It will use a database similar to that used for tracking Soviet submarines during the Cold War. However, many other vessels using the world's oceans will remain outside its scope. This inability to monitor the movement of fishing vessels, as well as cruising yachts and other private vessels, will remain a major gap in international arrangements for maritime security.

Even with current LRIT plans, there are still unresolved issues. It is by no means certain, for example, that a coastal state has a right to identify and track ships exercising the freedom of navigation either through its Exclusive Economic Zone (EEZ) or on the high seas, and not intending to proceed to a port or an anchorage located within the territory of that coastal state.[50] As well as tracking at sea, an effective international system should also include standardized reporting of shipping arrivals and departures, but this might arouse both security and commercial sensitivities.

Container Security

The measures used to improve container security include higher computer-scanning targets, ensuring the security of the container itself with better sealing devices,[51] tracking containers, and assessing container risk with trade-related data.[52] Customs administrations have enthusiastically embraced enhanced container security not so much because it reduces the risks of terrorism, but because it reduces the opportunities for containers to be used for illegal imports generally, or for avoiding the payment of import duties.

Since 9/11, the United States has attached considerable importance to securing its national transportation system from terrorist attack. A major concern has been to prevent the system from being used to introduce terrorists or their materials into the United States (a WMD in the worst case scenario). The major initiatives regarding ships and their cargoes have been the CSI and C-TPAT. Core elements of CSI include the establishment of new security criteria to identify high-risk containers and the introduction of new technology to screen containers and make containers more secure. Other requirements of the United States include requiring that a foreign vessel must have a valid ISSC to enter a U.S. port and that a ship's last port of call must have valid antiterrorism measures in place that are open to audit by U.S. inspectors.

These U.S. maritime cargo initiatives have encountered some reservations. At a national level in the United States, major gaps have been found in both the CSI and the C-TPAT with key targets not being met.[53] At the international level, countries that do not implement required CSI procedures will be disadvantaged because their shipments will be subject to more complex examinations and will be cleared more slowly. Yet even the United States is showing that it lacks the capacity itself to ensure a watertight supply chain. The playing field is not level with the new measures; countries which can afford them will gain significant comparative advantage. Or to put it bluntly, unless adequate programs of technical cooperation and financial assistance are available, "the rich will get richer and the poor poorer." U.S. rhetoric that CSI and C-TPAT "push out the borders" also sends the wrong message, with the implication that these measures only serve to export the terrorist threat away from North America.

Seafarer Identity Issues

Other vulnerabilities exist in international shipping, not least of all being the difficulty of establishing the identity of individual seafarers. There are about 1.3 million international seafarers, and many come from countries where terrorist cells are known to exist.[54] Research conducted by the Seafarers International Research Centre at Cardiff for the IMO found that many international seafarers have fraudulent documentation.[55] It would not be difficult for a terrorist to assume the identity of a seafarer to gain the skills required to operate a ship, or to move around the world.

The IMO and the International Labour Organization have developed the Seafarers' Identity Documents Convention (revised 2003) to deal with the issues of seafarer identity and fraudulent documentation, but this Convention is not without problems. Each State party to the Convention has to permit the entry into its territory of a seafarer holding the identity document, but Australia, for example, is unlikely to ratify the Convention due to this concession of visa-free entry. Other concerns with the Convention include the feasibility of its requirements for the physical security of the document itself, and for the basic infrastructure for issuance and verification, including the maintenance of a national database. Even with a biometric, the system depends on the person supplying the biometric actually being the person he or she claims to be.[56]

As well as issues with seafarer identity, there are gaps in education, training, and certification for both seafarers and port workers. While there are mandatory requirements for designated personnel such as ship security officers and port facility security officers, there are no mandatory requirements for industry workers generally. With a view to fostering the creation of a security conscious culture, the requirement for mandatory security-related education, training, and certification of seafarers and port workers might be considered, irrespective of rank or discipline.[57]

Seafarers and port workers should be treated as partners in the fight against terrorism. Seafarers, in particular, should not feel persecuted by security measures that inhibit their access to shore leave and the opportunity for rest and recreation before returning to sea. However, there is anecdotal evidence of Muslim crew members of ships trading to the United States being replaced by non-Muslims due to concerns of ship owners that their vessels might be delayed in U.S. ports, or ship crews may not be allowed ashore. This development obviously works against the interests of major Islamic countries, particularly Bangladesh and Indonesia, which are leading providers of personnel for the international shipping industry.

Conclusions

The maritime transportation industry has been greatly affected by the threat of maritime terrorism. It now has a vastly different regulatory environment from the one that prevailed prior to 9/11. However, for the reasons discussed in this chapter, there must be some reservations about the credibility of the threat and the cost benefits of the new countermeasures. We have had a plethora of assertions about the risks and outcomes of a catastrophic maritime terrorist attack, including assessments of a nexus between piracy and maritime terrorism. To some extent, these have distorted perspectives of the probability of a major attack in the future. The maritime terrorist incidents that have occurred have had miniscule impact on the free movement of shipping and seaborne trade in comparison with the massive costs of implementing the new countermeasures.

It is yet to be seen how effective the new measures will be, or indeed how enduring they might be in an international industry that has been characterized by double standards and regulation avoidance. It is essential that a proper balance is maintained between security on the one hand, and the free movement of trade on the other. The basic question is one of "how much security is enough?" All the new measures for maritime security imply extra costs for ship owners, port operators, and shippers, including potential delays in the handling of cargo. Additional barriers to competition are involved and some ports, especially ones in developing countries, face difficulties due to their lack of capacity to introduce such measures. There is a real concern over whether all the measures being introduced are appropriate to the threat, as well as a perception that many of the measures only serve the national interests of the United States and other major Western countries.

So far, the approach to countering the threat of maritime terrorism has been a generalized one, with all ships and ports being required to meet new international standards. In the United States for example, the Department of Homeland Security has been criticized for spending millions of dollars on port security without sufficiently focusing on those that are most vulnerable.[58] There would appear to be a need now to modify this approach somewhat by concentrating on key vulnerabilities, including the security of the full supply chain and the identification of ships, port facilities, and cargoes that pose a greater risk. For example, a petrochemical port facility located in a built-up area is clearly much more vulnerable than a bulk ore or grain loading facility in a remote area. Probably too much emphasis has been given to "worst case" scenarios. Despite the huge costs of such a scenario happening, the costs of ensuring against such scenarios are proving to be equally massive. In the interests of responsible public expenditure and avoidance of unreasonable burdens on the private sector, new security measures should be subject to rigorous analysis and testing against realistic and commonsense risk assessments.

The main challenge is how to enhance transportation security without compromising on efficiency and adding to costs. But others include building the capacity of individual countries to manage the risks, achieving some form of standardization across individual ports, ensuring the security of data, achieving a fair distribution of the relevant costs, and sustaining just-in-time (JIT) business practices. As the Secretary General of the International Chamber of Shipping has noted, "It is not far fetched to say that trade … is now under threat, not just from terrorism itself but also from the measures that might be taken to combat it."[59]

The countermeasures to the threat of maritime terrorism have imposed major additional costs on ship owners, ports, and shippers.[60] They are also imposing delays on port operations and slowing down the process of international trade.[61] Ports are imposing significant extra charges to cover the costs of additional security, insurance companies have increased security premiums, and providers of security services and equipment are doing good business. Furthermore, the new focus on maritime security has led to an environment of increased naval and military spending generally. When developing countries should be pursuing programs that will drive down poverty and social unrest and thus remove root causes of piracy and terrorism, they are being pressed to improve their capacity to protect their domestic supply chain and to provide maritime security in their adjacent waters.

It is time now for a reality check and to consider the broader maritime strategic and security environment rather than remaining fixated on the threat of maritime terrorism. Problems such as the root causes of piracy and terrorism and the ready availability of small arms around the world must be addressed. There must also be some limit to the current booming levels of naval arms spending in parts of the world.[62] This spending has significant opportunity costs, particularly with regard to the provision of resources to address poverty and injustice. Meanwhile, the international community seems to be giving lower priority and fewer resources to measures to protect and preserve the marine environment and to conserve its biodiversity, despite the established importance of the health of the oceans to the future of the world.[63]

Notes

1. Marcus Hand, "Maritime Threats 'Could Be Overplayed'," *Lloyd's List*, Friday 2 July 2004.
2. Frederick Forsyth, *The Devil's Alternative* (London: Corgi Books, 1980).
3. The Chairman and CEO of Aegis Defence Services is Lt.Col. Tim Spicer, whose previous companies include Executive Outcomes and the Sandline Corporation, which have achieved some notoriety for their mercenary activities in developing countries. http://sourcewatch.org/index.php?title=Aegis_Defence_Services.
4. Michael Richardson, *A Time Bomb for Global Trade — Maritime-related Terrorism in an Age of Weapons of Mass Destruction*, Singapore, Institute of Southeast Asian Studies, 2004, pp. 32–33.
5. "Sea attack by Al-Qaeda is likely: analysts," *The Straits Times*, 11 December 2004.
6. Other attacks on ferries in Southeast Asia include the February 2000 bombing of the Philippine ferry *Our Lady Mediatrix*, which killed 40 people; and the December 2001 bombing of the Indonesian ferry *Kailifornia*, which killed 10. John F. Bradford, "The Growing Prospects for Maritime Security Cooperation in Southeast Asia," *Naval War College Review*, Summer 2005, vol. 58, no. 3, p. 67.
7. Rohan Gunaratna "Terrorist Threat to Shipping Is 'Imminent and Growing'" *Lloyd's List*, Wednesday 29 September 2004.
8. Richardson, *A Time Bomb for Global Trade*, pp. 112–133.
9. Rommel Banlaoi, "Romulo: RP won't be frontline of terror attack," *Philippine Daily Inquirer*, 13 August 2005, p.A1.
10. "Ferry Blast Injures 30 in Southern Philippines, *The New York Times* online, 28 August 2005.
11. Brian Reyes, "Spain uncovers Strait of Gibraltar terror plot," *Lloyd's List*, Tuesday 29 March 2005
12. "Terrorists train for Seaborne Attacks," *JoyoNews*, Joyo@aol.com, Friday 18 March 2005.
13. Anthony Bergin and Sam Bateman (with Aldo Borgu), *Future unknown: The terrorist threat to Australian maritime security*, Australian Strategic Policy Institute, Canberra, April 2005, p. 14.
14. Shefali Rekhi, "French expert warns on terror strike in Asia," *The Straits Times*, 27 August 2005.
15. See for example, Gal Luft and Anne Korin, "Terrorism Goes to Sea," *Foreign Affairs*, vol. 83, no.6, September/October 2004, pp. 61–71. This paper, however, was later roundly criticized in a letter from an established expert on piracy to the Editor of *Foreign Affairs* because of its "uncritically repeating myths, half truths and unsupportable assertions of an alleged nexus of piracy and terrorism." Charles Dragonette, "Lost at Sea," *Foreign Affairs*, March/April 2005.
16. The data in this paragraph is from the ICC International Maritime Bureau (IMB), *Piracy and Armed Robbery Against Ships — Annual Report for the Period 1 January- 31 December 2004*, 7 February 2005.
17. Ibid., Table 7, p. 9.
18. For example in August 2005, a commercial fishing trawler or small freighter was hijacked off the coast of Somalia. This was the latest of a series of similar incidents in Somali waters. "Somalia piracy warning as new ship is hijacked," *Mail & Guardian* online, 18 August 2005.
19. IMO, "Piracy and armed robbery at sea," *Focus on IMO*, January 2000, p. 2.
20. Robert C. Beckman, Carl Grudy-Warr, and Vivian L. Forbes, "Acts of Piracy in the Malacca and Singapore Straits," *Maritime Briefing*, vol. 1, no. 4, International Boundaries Unit, University of Durham, 1994.
21. Ibid., p.11.
22. IMB, *Annual Report for 2004*, Table 7, p. 9.
23. Adam Young and Mark J. Valencia, "Conflation of Piracy and Terrorism in Southeast Asia: Rectitude and Utility," *Contemporary Southeast Asia*, vol. 25, no. 2, August 2003, pp. 269–283.
24. This is the shorter definition of *piracy* found in the classic case of *In re Piracy Jure Gentium*. Gerhard von Glahn, *Law Among Nations*, 6th ed., New York, Macmillan, 1992, p. 326.
25. Bobby Thomas, "Malacca Straits a 'war risk zone'? Lloyds should review its assessment," *IDSS Commentaries*, 57/2005, 19 August 2005.

26. Catherine Zara Raymond, "Perils in the Straits of Malacca," *The Standard,* August 25, 2005.
27. "Malacca Straits safe for vessels," *The Star* online, 31 August 2005; and Mike Grinter, "Joint War Committee urged to review Malacca terror risk status," *Lloyd's List,* Wednesday August 3, 2005.
28. James Brewer, "Joint War Committee stands by Strait ruling," *Lloyd's List International,* August 17, 2005, p. 1.
29. For example, each USN ship has an integrated tactical team (SITT) that protects the ship against a variety of threats while in port. Paul Mullen and Jon Bartee, "Put a SWAT Team on Every Ship," U.S. Naval Institute Proceedings, December 2002, pp. 30–33,
30. Singapore has recognised this vulnerability with the introduction of ASSET teams and Harbour Craft Transponder System (HARTS). Brewer, "Small vessels, big security risk."
31. *Security in Maritime Transport: Risk Factors and Economic Impact,* OECD, July 2003, p. 5
32. Chris Mayer, "Access and Identity Are Key Points," *Lloyd's List,* Thursday September 30, 2005.
33. OECD Maritime Transport Committee, *Security in Maritime Transport: Risk Factors and Economic Impact,* Directorate for Science, Technology and Industry, Organisation for Economic Co-operation and Development (OECD), Paris, July 2003, p.6.
34. OECD, *Report on Container Security across Modes*, OECD, Paris, 27 May 2004, p.1
35. A new Protocol to the SUA Convention is under consideration by the IMO. It will include new offences and expanded provisions on ship-boarding. New provisions would allow flag states to request assistance with ship-boarding and law enforcement, or another party to seek the approval of a flag state to board and search a suspect ship claiming the nationality of the flag state. A Diplomatic Conference to adopt amendments to the SUA Convention and its Protocol will be held by the IMO in October 2005.
36. The CSI involves basing U.S. customs inspectors in foreign ports to oversee the targeting and pre-screening of high-risk containers bound for U.S. ports. Almost two-thirds of all containers that arrive in the United States by sea are shipped from 20 top ports, including Hong Kong, Shanghai, Singapore, Kaohsiung, Pusan, Tokyo, Yantian, Nagoya, Kobe, Yokohama, and Laem Chabang in the Asia Pacific. About 44 percent of all containers entering the United States originate from Asian ports.
37. C-TPAT focuses on the security of the supply chain and builds a linked security model within each segment of the supply chain (i.e. production, transportation, importation, and distribution). It includes U.S. Customs guidelines for industries and firms and comprehensive security self-assessment.
38. Information Management requires the presentation of a Vessel Cargo Declaration to U.S. Customs before cargo is loaded onboard at a foreign port for shipment to the United States (the 24 hour Manifest Rule). Generic descriptions of cargo are not acceptable. The Rule does not apply to bulk cargo or empty containers.
39. The U.S. promoted the Regional Maritime Security Initiative (RMSI) to improve international cooperation, specifically in the Malacca Straits, against the transnational threats of terrorism, piracy and trafficking. Major elements of RMSI include increased situational awareness ("maritime domain awareness"), information sharing, a decision-making architecture and interagency cooperation. Malaysia and Indonesia were both initially opposed to the implementation of RMSI, but this opposition may have been based on a misunderstanding of what the U.S. was proposing.
40. The Proliferation Security Initiative (PSI) seeks to establish a coalition of willing partners to respond to challenges posed by the proliferation of weapons of mass destruction (WMD). It involves a set of principles identifying practical steps to interdict shipments of WMD and associated materials flowing to and from state or non-state actors.
41. Todd Pitman, "U.S. Strategic Interests in West Africa's Oil-Rich Gulf of Guinea," Associated Press, 7 August 2005, SignOnSan Diego.com.
42. The information and statistics in this and the following paragraph are drawn from the IMO website at: http://www.imo.org/home.asp (accessed 9 November 2004).
43. The Maritime Transport Security Act (Commonwealth) 2003 in Australia, for example, extends ISPS provisions to all ships employed on interstate voyages but not to ones employed on intrastate voyages.
44. James Brewer, "Small Vessels, Big Security Risk," *Lloyd's List,* Tuesday 7 June 2005.
45. Tamara Renee Shie, "The Nexus Between Counterterrorism, Counterproliferation, and Maritime Security in Southeast Asia," *Issues and Insights 04-04,* Pacific Forum CSIS, Executive Summary, p. 2.

46. Eric Jackson, "Maritime lawyers vs. Mireyistas on ISPS certification process," *The Panama,* http://www.the panamanews.com/pn/v_10/issue_o5/business_01.html (accessed 8/11/2004).
47. Katrin Berkenkopf, "ISPS Benefits Doubtful, Says German Tramp Owner," *Lloyd's List* online, 28 October 2004
48. OECD, *Security in Maritime Transport*, p. 2.
49. David Munns, "121,000 Tracks," *Seapower,* July 2005, pp. 10–13.
50. Hartmut Hesse and Nicolaos L. Charalambous, "New Security Measures for the International Shipping Community," *WMU Journal of Maritime Affairs*, 2004, Vol. 3, No. 2, p. 138.
51. Currently containers are mainly sealed with passive, indicator seals. This does not physically prevent entry but merely indicates that the container has at one point been opened.
52. OECD, *Report on Container Transport Security across Modes*, p. 2.
53. John McLaughlin, "US security system has 'crippling flaw'," *Lloyd's List,* Friday 27 May 2005.
54. About one-fifth of all international seafarers come from the Philippines and a further one-sixth from Indonesia and Turkey combined. International Commission on Shipping (ICONS), *Ships, Slaves and Competition,* Charlestown NSW, 2000 (available on website at: www.icons.org.au), p. 41.
55. Ibid., p. 48.
56. David Oster, "Why Biometric Card Solution Is Not at Hand," *Lloyd's List,* Friday 3 June 2005.
57. Hesse and Charalambous, "New Security Measures," p. 138.
58. Eric Lipton, "Audit Faults U.S. for Its Spending on Port Defence," *The New York Times*, 20 February 2005.
59. Chris Horrocks, "Greater transparency," *Lloyd's Ship Manager,* November 2002, p. 24.
60. A study conducted by the Maritime Institute of Malaysia (MIMA) concluded that Malaysia's efforts to comply with the ISPS Code cost her ports US$21.5 million and shipping companies US$2.8 million. Noor Apandi Osman, "Financial Implications of the ISPS Code in Malaysia," *Maritime Studies 141*, March-April 2005, pp. 16–23.
61. Alexander Da Silva, "Harbor rules hit small shops," *Honolulu Star-Bulletin,* Thursday 18 August 2005.
62. By 2009, Asia-Pacific countries may be spending a combined US$14 billion on new naval ships or almost double the figure for 2003. "Naval ship spending to increase in Asia Pacific, defense experts say," *The China Post* online, 11 November 2003.
63. Independent World Commission on the Oceans, *The Ocean Our Future,* Cambridge, Cambridge University Press, 1998.

Contributors

Dr. Rommel C. Banlaoi is a professor of Political Science at the National Defense College of the Philippines where he previously served as Vice President for Administrative Affairs and Assistant Vice President for Research and Special Studies. He is the author and coauthor of five books to date, which include *War on Terrorism in Southeast Asia* published by Rex Book Store International in October 2004. His articles and book reviews have appeared in various books and internationally refereed journals such as *Contemporary Southeast Asia, Parameters, Naval War College Review, Asian Affairs, Indian Ocean Survey, Studies in Conflict and Terrorism, and Intelligence and National Security.* He finished his BA and MA in Political Science at the University of the Philippines where he is currently finishing his Ph.D. in Political Science.

Dr. Sam Bateman is a Professorial Research Fellow at the Centre for Maritime Policy, University of Wollongong, Australia (email address: sbateman@uow.edu.au), and currently also a Senior Fellow and Adviser to the Maritime Security Programme at the Institute of Defence and Strategic Studies (IDSS) in Singapore (email address: issambateman@ntu.edu.sg).

Jeffrey Chen is currently an Adjunct Fellow, Centre for Maritime Policy, University of Wollongong, Australia, researching on the issues of maritime security and cooperative regimes in the Straits of Malacca. He has participated in the prestigious SLOC conference in Hawaii in 2004 and several other international conferences on maritime security. Chen has written a seminal piece on the Trilateral Cooperation between Singapore, Malaysia and Indonesia: "Prospects and Limits of Co-operation" and written on the need to evaluate the likelihood of terrorism at sea in leading shipping newspapers (Lloyds List). He has also written a commentary on "Six Months After the Joint War Committee's Decision Regarding Malacca Straits: An Interim Review" for the Singapore Institute of International Affairs (SIIA). Chen, along with a United States Navy Lieutenant, John Bradford, has been instrumental in creating an international maritime security community and forum on the web where interested individuals in maritime security issues from around the world can learn from each other, participate in exchanging views and networking. Members of this forum include security analysts, leading academics, captains of industry, government officials in the foreign and defence ministry and senior retired navy officials. He is also the administrator and moderator of this forum.

Rupert Herbert-Burns is the senior maritime security consultant with Lloyd's Marine Intelligence Unit (LMIU), specializing in security concerns within the commercial shipping environment, and asymmetrical and criminal threats emanating from within, and directed at, the maritime realm, specifically ports and sea lanes of communication. Since joining LMIU in late 2002, he has worked on projects for branches of the U.S. government, New York Police Department, Project SeaHawk at the Port of Charleston, UK Metropolitan Police, Transport Canada, and NATO. He has also briefed international media on various aspects of maritime security, authored several articles on issues pertaining to maritime security threat and risk analysis, and addressed international conferences. Prior to joining LMIU, Herbert-Burns served at sea as a warfare officer in the Royal Navy in operational theatres worldwide. Ensuing military service included appointments as an infantry platoon commander and a military intelligence officer within the British Army's Brigade of Gurkhas, with tours in Brunei, Hong Kong, Nepal, and the United Kingdom. Herbert-Burns has a BSc in International Relations and Politics, and a Masters degree in International Security Studies from the University of St. Andrews. Mr Herbert-Burns is a third-year Ph.D candidate at the University of St Andrews, writing a treatise on securitised energy geopolitics — analysing the security of maritime and terrestrial modes of crude oil, product, and gas/liquefied gas conveyance within Eurasia and the Indo-Pacific region.

Hendrick Lehmann, M.A., is assistant editor at a German publishing house specialized in civil law. He is also a Ph.D. candidate at the South Asia Institute, University of Heidelberg, writing a thesis on Indian's foreign policy towards the United States. Since 1995, he also works for the HIIK (Heidelberg Institute on International Conflict Research), covering the Middle East conflict between Israel and the Palestinians for the annual *Conflict Barometer.*

Dr. Peter Lehr is Informa Group research fellow at the Centre for the Study of Terrorism and Political Violence (CSTPV), University of St. Andrews, Scotland/United Kingdom. Prior to his appointment at St. Andrews in September 2004, he was lecturer at the Department of Political Science, South Asia Institute, University of Heidelberg/Germany, and visiting fellow at the Institute for Strategic and International Studies (ISIS), Chulalongkorn University, Bangkok/Thailand. Being a regional specialist on the Indian Ocean, he currently works on security issues such as piracy, organized crime, and (maritime) terrorism with a strong focus on South and Southeast Asia. He is also involved in the development of the Informa Group/CSTPV e-learning course on terrorism, for which he designed the module on maritime terrorism.

J.N. Mak is a Visiting Research Fellow at the Singaporean Institute for Southeast Asian Studies (ISEAS), working on ASEAN Maritime Cooperation. Prior to that, he was Director of Research at the Malaysian Institute of Maritime Affairs (MIMA). Being a maritime defense analyst, his publications focus on Asian maritime and naval security issues, among them piracy and maritime terrorism. Mak holds an MA (hons) from the University of Malaya and an MSC Econs of the University of Wales in Aberystwith, Wales/United Kingdom.

Martin Murphy is Senior Strategic Analyst at the University of Reading (UK) and a recognised expert on naval irregular warfare and maritime security. He is the author of the forthcoming Adelphi Paper on modern piracy and maritime terrorism to be published by IISS in autumn 2006. He has recently completed a study of the marine insurance industry's response to piracy and terrorism. He is a regular contributor to *Jane's Intelligence Review*. He lives in London with his wife and daughter.

Graham Gerard Ong-Webb is an Associate Research Fellow under the Transportation Security Programme at the Centre for Excellence in National Security, based at the Institute of Defence and Strategic Studies (IDSS), the Nanyang Technological University, Singapore. Previously, he was a Research Associate under the Regional Strategic and Political Studies Programme at the Institute of Southeast Asian Studies (ISEAS). He is the editor of *Piracy, Maritime Terrorism and Securing the Malacca Straits* (Singapore: Institute of Southeast Asian Studies; International Institute of Asian Studies, Leiden University, 2006) [Forthcoming].

Chris Rahman is a Research Fellow at the Centre for Maritime Policy, University of Wollongong, Australia. He currently researches issues in maritime strategy and security, with a focus on the Asia-Pacific region, and his publications have focused on the implications of Chinese maritime power and ambitions for Asian security.

Dr. Vijay Sakhuja is a Research Fellow at the Observer Research Foundation, New Delhi, India. He is a former Indian Navy officer and has held several appointments, including Commanding Officer. He received his MPhil and doctorate from the Jawaharlal Nehru University, New Delhi. He was Research Fellow at the Institute for Defence Studies and Analyses, New Delhi, and at the United Service Institution of India, New Delhi. He has authored a book titled *Confidence Building From The Sea: An Indian Initiative* and is the recipient of the Vice Admiral S L Sethi National Maritime Media Award of 2002.

Robert Snoddon is a former Lieutenant Commander in the Royal Navy. He joined the navy as a boy seaman in 1972 at the age of 15 and was commissioned as a Special Duties Officer in 1989. A specialist in Electronic Warfare, he has also held several naval intelligence posts, most notably within the Defence

Intelligence Staff of the MOD, and also as the United Kingdom Exchange Officer at the Office of Naval Intelligence, Washington D.C. He left the navy in early 2005 and currently works as a maritime security consultant for a variety of companies, including Lloyds Maritime Intelligence Unit.

Index

B

C

D

E

F

G

H

I

R

S

T